The Mediterranean Debt Crescent

The Mediterranean Debt Crescent

Money and Power in Algeria, Egypt, Morocco, Tunisia, and Turkey

Clement M. Henry

University Press of Florida
Gainesville / Tallahassee / Tampa / Boca Raton
Pensacola / Orlando / Miami / Jacksonville

Printed in the United States of America on acid-free paper

01 00 99 98 97 96 6 5 4 3 2 1

Library of Congress Cataloging-in-Publication Data

Henry, Clement M., 1937–
The Mediterranean debt crescent: money and power in Algeria, Egypt, Morocco, Tunisia, and Turkey / Clement M. Henry.
p. cm.
Includes bibliographical references and index.
ISBN 0-8130-1380-1 (alk. paper)
1. Banks and banking—Africa, North. 2. Banks and banking—Turkey. 3. Money—Africa, North. 4. Money—Turkey. 5. Structural adjustment (Economic policy)—Africa, North. 6. Structural adjustment (Economic policy)—Turkey. 7. Debts, External—Africa, North. 8. Debts, External—Turkey. 9. Banks and banking—Religious aspects—Islam. I. Title.
HG3381.A6H46 1996 95-23644
332.1'0961—dc20 CIP

The University Press of Florida is the scholarly publishing agency for the State University System of Florida, comprised of Florida A & M University, Florida Atlantic University, Florida International University, Florida State University, University of Central Florida, University of Florida, University of North Florida, University of South Florida, and University of West Florida.

University Press of Florida
15 Northwest 15th Street
Gainesville, FL 32611

In memory of my father,
Clement S. Henry, Jr.

Contents

Figures

Tables

Preface

This book analyzes the structural power of commercial banking systems emerging in five Mediterranean countries. The arc of countries stretching from Morocco in the west to Turkey in the northeast constitutes a "debt crescent" of predominantly Muslim peoples whose economies, heavily indebted to the outside world, are undergoing major structural adjustment programs in the financial sector. The focus on the emerging power of commercial banking's finance capital is intended to shed further light on possible relationships between democracy and capitalist development. This study is designed for students of comparative politics and political economy as well as Middle Eastern studies and international business programs. It also responds to the international financial community's growing interest in political development and may stimulate the curiosity of professional bankers and economists without overwhelming the general reader in detailed financial analysis.

Political scientists do not normally focus on money and banking even though many assume that there are economic "correlates" or "preconditions" of democracy. Unless there is a major scandal, commercial banking systems are of only marginal interest to political scientists and most economists. Personal experience and the encouragement of several colleagues at the American University of Beirut led me to wonder whether banks under certain conditions might be hidden hands of political development and whether a study of them might lead to a better understanding of relationships between political and economic structures. While directing AUB's business school in the early 1980s, I was sheltered from most of Lebanon's agony but could appreciate the resiliency of its banking system. It appeared to be a functional substitute for political order, which had shattered. I thought that banking systems deserved further attention in other countries where political order had not broken down. After leaving Beirut in 1984, I began to reexamine some of the other southern Mediterranean countries, currently undergoing structural adjustment, that I had previously studied from other perspectives. Unlike Lebanon, they had strong states and their banking systems were not politically salient. If a commercial banking system could substitute for political order in Lebanon, however, it surely wielded some power in other, less troubled settings. And the structural adjustment being applied to the financial sector might alter political parameters as well. In the course of my research I tried to relate the emerging power of finance capital to political changes in the region. Evidence for these relationships is necessarily circumstantial, but bankers in some of the countries displayed a considerable capacity for collective action. This book tries to spell out the relationships.

The research involved extensive fieldwork in all five countries. Over the course of numerous visits from 1987 to 1992, I spent a total of six weeks to two months in each country. Most of the time was devoted to interviews with leading politicians, bankers, businesspeople, and academics, but I also had to collect the financial statements of over 150 commercial banks in the region for as many years as possible, in order to supplement the qualitative insights of bankers with quantitative data. Fortunately, bankers' associations in Tunisia and Turkey published these data, but it was necessary to collect the documentation from each bank in Algeria, Egypt, and Morocco. I could not have accomplished this task in Egypt without help from the Banks' Association of Egypt and the research departments of the National Bank of Egypt and the Export Development Bank of Egypt, and I am especially grateful to Mohammed Noureddine of Arab Bank for his generous assistance. I also wish to thank Professor Ali E. Hillal Dessouki of Cairo University and the late Bill Harrison for helping me gather some initial data.

I cannot begin to do justice to the many friends and acquaintances as well as officials and commercial bank managers in the region who have helped my research. The fieldwork let me renew friendships which in some cases, at least in the Maghrib, have extended over more than three decades. If I single out some, I do not mean to exclude others, who may prefer to guard their anonymity in these troubled times. In particular I wish to thank Hédi Baccouche and Mohammed Sayah, retired ministers, for their gracious hospitality and wise insights. Dr. Moncef Cheikhrouhou and Brad LaLonde, who had moved from Turkey, were helpful on the Tunisian banking front. Jeanne Jeffers Mrad, director of the Centre des Études Maghrébines à Tunis (CEMAT), offered much-appreciated logistic support. While serving as Algeria's ambassador to Tunisia, Messaoud Ait Chalaal introduced me to the Algerian bankers, and Jelloul Baghli, another old friend from student days, introduced me to Algeria's new system of state holding companies. I also wish to thank Dr. Mohammed Abdulwahab Bekhechi, a member of Algeria's Constitutional Council, for his help and support. In Morocco, Nadia Salah and Abdelmounaim Dilami, respectively the editor-in-chief and publisher of *L'Economiste,* introduced me to the intricacies of Morocco's business world. I am also grateful to an old friend, Professor Mohammed Guessous, and a new one, Professor M. Said Saâdi, for sharing their insights about business groups with me.

In Egypt, despite lip service to the new age of information, research is restricted for nationals and foreigners alike. Friendships, however, are not. Tahsin Bechir gave me much encouragement and excellent advice. Ragaa A. Khalil, a managing director of Egypt's Central Bank, helped me unofficially as much as her responsibilities permitted and then efficiently shepherded me through the bureaucracy once I was officially cleared. I also wish to thank Ali Negm, former governor of the Central Bank, for many insights, and Mahmud Abdel Aziz, chairman of the National Bank of Egypt and president of the Banks' Association, for his unstinting support. I owe a special debt of thanks to Jean-Claude Vatin, an old friend as well as director until 1992 of France's Centre d'Études et de Documentation Économique, Juridique et Sociale, for his personal and professional hospitality and a dynamic research environment. Finally, Turkey was the country I had least explored, and I wish to thank another dear friend, Professor Barbara Kellner-Heinkele, director of the Institute of Turkology at the Free University of Berlin, for helping me to navigate. I am also grateful to Dr. Hassan Ersel, who served as research director of the Central Bank before becoming senior executive vice president of Yapi ve Kredi Bankası. He shared with me his insights into Turkey's financial reform process and offered prodigious documentation. I also benefited greatly from discussions with Professors Ilter Turan and Birol Yeşılada.

I owe a special debt to former colleagues at the American University of Beirut. The late Peter Franck, an economist, challenged me to develop a new interdisciplinary subfield of banking and politics, and Michael Penniman, who was teaching part-time at our business school while managing one of Beirut's leading banks on behalf of Morgan Guaranty, taught me how to analyze a commercial bank's financial statements.

In the course of my travels collecting data from bankers, I was often asked whether the World Bank or some other official agency or business enterprise was supporting the research. The truth was that I relied on a variety of small grants and a couple of speaking tours funded by the United States Information Agency to do the fieldwork. I gratefully acknowledge support from the Social Science Research Council, the American Institute of Maghrib Studies, the Egyptian-American Fulbright Commission, the Earhart Foundation, the Institute of Turkish Studies, the Policy Research Institute of the LBJ School at the University of Texas, and the University Research Institute of the University of Texas, which granted me one semester's leave to do much of the writing and provided some funds for research assistance. I would like to thank Caroline Attié for her painstaking help in building up my data base of commercial banks. I am also grateful to Roger Owen, Brian Roberts, Robert Vitalis, and anonymous reviewers for their critical comments on an earlier draft of this manuscript and to Suzanne Colwell and Elaine David for cheerfully processing and reprocessing it.

List of Abbreviations in Tables and Figures

APBT	Association Professionnelle de Banques de Tunisie
ATB (Tunisia)	Arab-Tunisian Bank
BADR (Algeria)	Banque Algérienne de Développement Rural
BCCM (Egypt)	Bank of Credit and Commerce (Misr)
BCM (Morocco)	Banque du Crédit Marocain
BCP (Morocco)	Banque du Crédit Populaire
BDL (Algeria)	Banque de Développement Local
BEA (Algeria)	Banque Extérieure d'Algérie
BFT (Tunisia)	Banque Franco-Tunisienne
BIAT (Tunisia)	Banque Internationale Arabe de Tunisie
BMAO	Banque Marocaine pour a'Afrique et l'Orient
BMCE (Morocco)	Banque Marocaine du Commerce Extérieur
BMCI (Morocco)	Banque Marocaine pour le Commerce et l'Industrie
BNA (Algeria)	Banque Nationale d'Algérie
BNA (Tunisia)	Banque Nationale Agricole
BS (Tunisia)	Banque du Sud
BT (Tunisia)	Banque de Tunisie
CDM (Morocco)	Crédit du Maroc
CFCT (Tunisia)	Crédit Foncier et Commercial de Tunisie
CIB (Egypt)	Commerce International Bank
CPA (Algeria)	Crédit Populaire Algérien
ESFB	Egyptian Saudi Finance Bank
FIBE (Egypt)	Faisal Islamic Bank of Egypt
IIBID (Egypt)	Islamic International Bank for Investment and Development
NBD (Egypt)	National Bank for Development
SAIB (Egypt)	Société Arabe Internationale de Banque
SBC	Société de Banque et de Crédit
SGMB (Morocco)	Société Générale Marocaine de Banque
STB (Tunisia)	Société Tunisienne de Banque

UBCI (Tunisia)	Union Bancaire pour le Commerce et l'Industrie
UIB (Tunisia)	Union Internationale des Banques
UNIBAN	Union Bancaria Hispano Marroqui
Wafa (Morocco)	Wafabank

Chapter 1

Financial Reform and Political Change

> The "black box"—containing all aspects of power and influence that cannot readily be explained—needs to be replaced with a box far less opaque. If the money trail is followed, or the cash-nexus, most of the secrets of the box will soon be exposed.
>
> (Henry Bretton 1980: 330)

The international debt crises of the 1980s are provoking major restructurings of the internal financial orders of most developing countries. The question to be addressed here is whether these reforms promoted by the IMF and the World Bank in turn encourage domestic political regime changes. The debt crises in the nineteenth century led to direct political and military interventions, often resulting in colonial rule, but in the late twentieth century such political outcomes are ruled out. The independent political orders established in the 1950s and 1960s are all threatened, to varying degrees, by the burdens of economic adjustment programs, but they are likely to retain their nominal sovereignty. The question is whether their regimes will change and, if so, in which direction—toward more democracy or toward tougher patterns of authoritarian rule?

Intuitively it seems plausible to suppose that altering financial flows will alter power relationships. The present focus on money and power differs, however, from most studies of political economy. The earlier literature on finance and development focused on financial, not political "repression" (Cameron 1967, 1972; Goldsmith 1969, 1975; McKinnon 1973; Shaw 1973; Drake 1980), and most contemporary studies of "adjustment" seem more concerned with the conditions under which financial and economic reforms succeed or falter than with their impact upon domestic institutions and constellations of political power (Nelson 1990; Haggard and Kaufman 1992; Haggard et al. 1993). Political regimes, while viewed as important independent or intervening variables, are only exceptionally viewed as dependent variables (Frieden 1991; Haggard and Kaufman 1992: 319–50). In this book they will be viewed not only as active agents affecting processes of financial liberalization but also as potential victims in their own right of these very processes. Also, this study is more micro-oriented than the collective works on adjustment or Sylvia Maxfield's pioneering study of the "bankers' alliance" in Mexico (Maxfield 1990). The major intervening variable studied here is finance capital's "structural power" (Przeworski and Wallerstein 1988; Winters 1994) rather than government policies or international capital inflows, and this sort of power is concretely embedded in local banking industry structures and reflected in the financial strategies of individual commercial banks. Consequently this book draws extensively upon the financial statements of individual banks as well as historical materials and interviews with financial and political elites.

The countries to be reviewed are an arc of Muslim debtor states extending from Turkey on the eastern shores of the Mediterranean south to Egypt and westward to include Tunisia, Algeria, and Morocco. The Mediterranean Debt Crescent is related to Europe much as Mexico is related to the United States. Like Mexico, these Muslim countries are heavily indebted to various northern financial institutions and governments. They also share physical proximity to big northern neighbors, substantial invisible earnings from their migrant workers, and relatively strong state administrations built on distinctive national identities. Like Mexico, too, Algeria, Egypt, and Tunisia are modest oil producers, and the entire region depends in part upon capital transfers from wealthier petroleum-exporting neighbors. Like Mexico and other big Third World debtors, each country is also under a variety of internal and external pressures to deregulate its economy and to encourage private enterprise. Indeed, each crescent country is so dependent upon Europe for vital goods and services and the means of financing them that it cannot reverse the prevailing international tides toward ever greater economic interdependence.

While hardly a microcosm of the Third World, the crescent illustrates in exaggerated form some of the dilemmas of financial and political transitions affecting much of Africa, Asia, and the former Communist states of Eastern Europe and the Soviet Union. The crescent is among the world's most heavily indebted regions, relative to gross domestic product (GDP), and it also displays among the highest ratios of domestic credit to GDP. New forms of credit expanded much more rapidly in the 1970s and 1980s throughout the world than either trade or productive capacity (Bryant 1987: 20), and the crescent amplified them. Financial flows, derived from oil and from expatriate workers' remittances, are also among the highest in the world. Moreover, the region has a rich history of debt crises and external intervention. Contemporary pressures from the IMF are hardly new.

Gunboats of various European states used to patrol the shores of the crescent in the nineteenth century in the interests of their creditors. External interventions were arguably more ubiquitous and politically destabilizing in the crescent than in other parts of the Third World because they were fueled by great power rivalries (Brown 1984). No European power ever entertained the idea of a Monroe Doctrine for the Mediterranean (cf. Fieldhouse 1973: 105).

The region's debt crises offer a common theme for controlled comparisons. The five debt crescent countries offer enough underlying similarities to highlight subtle political and financial differences. All of them have predominantly Muslim populations and share Islamic cultural traditions. Except for Morocco, they were integrated in varying degrees into the Ottoman Empire. Each in some measure also succumbed to European control in the course of the nineteenth century, and one of the causes or pretexts was invariably financial, although it was the French debtor that seized the Algerian creditor in 1830. From 1869 the other crescent countries lost control over their state finances to foreign creditors and became colonies or semi-colonies of creditor states. A century later, beginning with Egypt and Turkey, each state underwent official negotiations with the International Monetary Fund in the face of new foreign debts which had created balance of payments crises. In 1980, Turkey embarked upon a substantial stabilization and adjustment program, while Egypt signed up for various programs but did not move decisively on the path of reform until 1991. Morocco and Tunisia launched their respective stabilization programs in 1983 and 1986, and then Algeria finally joined the club in 1989 by writing a letter of intent to the IMF promising a series of internal reforms in exchange for supplementary drawing rights.

As in the nineteenth century, each country has been obliged to open its economy to international markets, to stabilize government spending, to raise more revenues for heavy debt servicing, and in general to allocate its economic resources with greater regard for market forces (McKinnon and Mathieson 1981; Roe et al. 1989). The new fiscal and monetary discipline is not associated with triumphant imperialism, colonial occupation, or any apparent losses of political autonomy. However, the American-led intervention in Iraq was viewed by many Arabs and other Muslims as yet another manifestation of Western imperialism. The regimes of the crescent states were fragile even before the war, and the subsequent political fallout contributed to their weakening, to the rise of nationalism expressed in Islamist discourses, and to increasing political polarization.

Dilemmas of Patrimonial Regimes

Of greatest interest, from the standpoint of political change, is the fragile nature of these regimes. Each regime runs a strong state administration inherited from the Ottomans and, in the Algerian, Moroccan, and Tunisian cases, from the French. The crescent states are strong in the sense that they habitually extract taxes more than commensurate with the size and structure of their economies.[1] Using Lewis Snider's data, figure 1–1 documents their respective extractive capabilities over time, from 1950 to the mid-1980s. Most of them consistently extracted more taxes than fiscal economists would have predicted and thus achieved scores greater than 1. In fact the average of all the crescent observations should be 1.21, substantially above the norm—if not quite up to Israel's 1.55. These states were certainly not rentier states like the petroleum producers of the Gulf Cooperation Council, unwilling or incapable of taxing their citizenry. The ability to tax, however, "does not tell us much about social control," much less about the legitimacy of existing regimes (Migdal 1988: 283). At best a time series may reveal significant increases or decreases in capacity which are associated with other policy changes. Whether they are also associated with enhanced or diminished legitimacy is moot. Visible in figure 1–1, for instance, Turkey's decline in the 1980s was associated with an economic reform program, not necessarily with losses of legitimacy. Algeria's decline in 1979–82 was accompanied by changes of economic policy after Houari Boumédienne's death, but it may also have reflected higher oil prices following the Iranian revolution. The regime's extractive capability returned to higher levels in the five years preceding the 1988 riots, while its legitimacy was dissipating.

With the exception of Turkey, each regime exemplified a weak patrimonial form of authoritarianism rather than the bureaucratic authoritarianism characteristic of a number of Latin American regimes in the 1960s and 1970s. Despite impressive administrations backed by strong tax bases, the four North African regimes were riddled with patronage networks and classes of crony capitalists (Haggard 1990: 216–17) that marginalized their respective technocrats. Despite some variations, each regime should be vulnerable and heavily dependent on patronage by the late 1980s for its very survival. Each should be and remains in a state of transition from somewhat different starting points achieved with formal independence—a reinforced monarchy in Morocco and populist single-party systems in the other countries. Turkey, in transition ever since the formal breakup of its single-party system in 1950, has also made the most progress toward the exercise of formal democracy in which individuals and interests are free to compete for

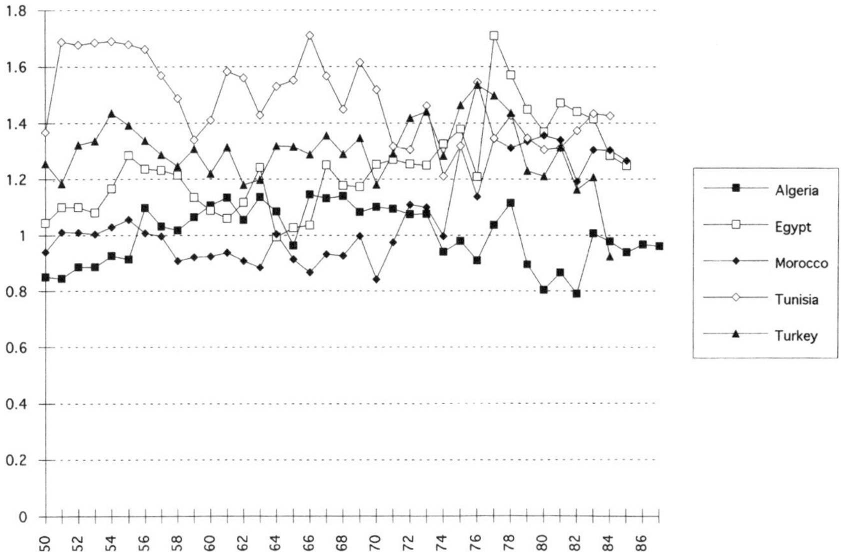

Fig. 1.1. Relative extractive capabilities, 1950–87. *Source:* Lewis Snider.

power and influence, but these freedoms, currently circumscribed, were periodically violated by military coups.

From the late 1960s, Egypt, Tunisia, and eventually Algeria underwent a series of political crises. In Egypt, Gamal Abdul Nasser's personal popularity withstood a crushing defeat at the hands of Israel in 1967—indeed the defeat should be the occasion for a "spontaneous" national plebescite to dissuade him from resigning—but his regime was already in trouble in 1965, when Egyptian troops were bogged down in Yemen and the bureaucrats at home were unable to meet the five-year plan or even to draft a new one. In Tunisia, Habib Bourguiba survived the dismantling of his economic plan in 1969, but his Destour Socialist regime gradually lost legitimacy associated with its ideology of modernization from above. The considerable personal legitimacy Bourguiba had attained as the Mujahid al-Akbar (Supreme Warrior) for national emancipation also evaporated in the early 1970s, though rising oil prices temporarily boosted the state's capacity to control the economy. Made president for life in 1974, Bourguiba in effect legalized his new status as a traditional patrimonial ruler. Algeria's greater oil wealth enabled Boumédienne to pursue more ambitious economic plans over a longer period of time, but he, too, trimmed the plans in 1977 while striving unsuccessfully before his death in 1978 to institutionalize a single-party regime. While his memory continued to evoke respect and even nostalgia, the Algerian masses trashed the FLN regime in extensive rioting in October 1988. Of the southern Mediterranean economic dreams and visions of the state—the "monument without cracks," in Bourguiba's words—only "Nasserism" survived into the 1990s, the hero having conveniently offered the opportunity of yet another national plebescite at his funeral in 1970. Bourguiba lived on, surviving riots in 1984 which were a foretaste of Algeria's, to suffer deposition and enforced retirement in 1987.

Each regime somehow had to "project a capability to 'deliver the goods'" (Dawisha 1986: 41) even as its legitimating ideologies eroded. Legitimacy and capacity interact in various ways. For Jean Leca (1990: 155) any economic retreat may bring about a loss of legitimacy resulting from more transparent inequalities. But in whose eyes? Certainly for any authoritarian regime "what matters most is always the support or acquiescence not of the popular majority of society but of the politically powerful and mobilized groups, invariably including the regime's own cadres" (Skocpol 1979: 32). In the language of microeconomic theory (North 1981), losses in legitimacy will in turn increase agency costs (that is, the expenses incurred by political principals in monitoring their economic agents, the regime's cadres) and hence reduce a regime's ability to regulate its economy, leading to further reductions of legitimacy and increased costs. The interaction seemed to be a vicious circle, raising the specter of a disorderly rout rather than a strategic disengagement of a regime from micromanaging its economy.

The very weakness of their regimes, however, offered the rulers possible strategies of transition. Few of the cadres whose support was critical were convinced socialists, not even in Algeria. Each of the statist regimes even at the peak of their power in the 1960s—had veiled intense factionalism within their ruling circles. Instead of striving to meet impossible ideological promises, it became more practical to let the demoralized cadres become dependent crony "capitalists." Circles of friends could compete for resources to solidify the loyalties of their fickle followings. Nasser in the late 1960s, Sadat and Bourguiba in the 1970s, and Chadly and Ben Ali in the 1980s would each experiment in restructuring their respective networks of political support. They would each tolerate some privatization of patronage, enabling their political subordinates to develop slightly more independent bases of power in return for the support of their clients, and so on, down the line. Instead of the direct divide-and-rule tactics exercised by Nasser, Bourguiba, and Boumédienne at their peaks, the orchestrators of the transitions would resort to more indirect tactics of balancing associated with greater degrees of political pluralism. Ironically they were engaging in the very artifices that King Hassan had pioneered in Morocco.

The monarchy, however, had mobilized its patronage resources by privatizing—or "personalizing" (Diouri 1992: 122)—much of Morocco's colonial legacy, whereas the single-party regimes had tried to socialize theirs. These regimes had discouraged the concentrations of private property that supported durable vertical networks of patrons, clients, and clients of clients. Egalitarian Algeria and modernizing Egypt and Tunisia had rejected such asymetrical relationships even if they tolerated or could not eliminate shallow, fragile combines of politicians, administrators, and their cousins in the private sector. Deep and durable networks buttressed multipartism, whereas shallow and fragile ones had kept one-party systems unitary.

The crescent regimes with shallow networks seemed on the verge of breaking down. Algeria's military rulers were waging a civil war against their Islamist opposition after 1991, and its neighbor, too, faced a severe crisis. In Tunisia, President Ben Ali multiplied the police and turned Bourguiba's presidential palace in Carthage into a bunker. The only Arab republic, besides Lebanon, that had never depended upon a military base was then incarcerating thousands of Islamist opponents amid Amnesty International's allegations of torture and rape at least as widespread as in the neighboring countries (*Middle East International,* 11 June 1993, 9–10). Egypt was assaulting its Islamist opposition almost as vigorously as Tunisia. Like the Tunisians, the Mubarak regime consistently violated the human rights of various oppositions while claiming progress toward greater democracy. After surviving crises in the 1960s and 1970s, the Moroccan monarchy had camouflaged its bunkers more successfully, but *Notre Ami le Roi,* a book describing the horrors of Moroccan torture chambers, created a diplomatic incident between Morocco and France, where it was a bestseller (Perrault 1990). Smuggled copies could no longer shock the knowledgeable, chastened citizenry. Sadly, the book could equally well have been about Algeria, Egypt, or Tunisia. Even Turkey was waging a low-intensity war with the Kurds and experiencing renewed urban terrorism for the second time in barely more than a decade.

From their bunkers the respective political leaderships were ever in need of new schemes for staying in power. They were all heavily in debt and undergoing financial adjustment programs, but the struggle for political survival conditioned any efforts of financial reform far more than any technical advice from the World Bank or the IMF. Financial systems were an integral part of their respective "black boxes" of power and patronage. Despite their impressive fiscal development and "extractive capability," the keys to propping up these patrimonial regimes were patronage and fear.

Briefly the argument here is that real financial liberalization, defined as "the process of reducing government control over the allocation of credit" (Haggard et al. 1993: 314), enhances the structural power of commercial bankers. Structural power is a form of leverage that depends "more on signaling [their] demands and objections, and then backing up their stance with capital flight and sluggish investment rates in the event that policymakers had not already anticipated the reaction of business or ignored the signals . . . [than] political pressure through 'voice'" (Winters 1994: 431–32) Structural power endangers any patrimonial regime by breaking into its black box of patronage. To defend itself, the regime may try to develop alternative patronage networks in the business community, sabotage the reform, or reinforce its bunkers with new ideological justifications for repressing political oppositions. Each of the three responses is fraught with political risk. Building up patronage networks in the business community may enhance the autonomy of the private sector. As Paul D. Hutchcroft argues, "A patrimonial administrative state may contain the seeds of its own destruction, because the process of economic growth can create a new social force—an autonomous business class—that is likely to begin to challenge the patrimonial basis of power" (1993: 167n.4). Indeed, irrespective of growth, greater business autonomy unleashed by financial deregulation may pressure regimes for greater accountability. Financial reform thus no longer augurs colonial occupation as in the nineteenth century, but it threatens patrimonial rulers and their crony capitalists and may reinforce tendencies toward greater political pluralism and democracy.

Yet the second response of sidestepping reform is also risky for patrimonial rulers. Defecting from adjustment programs may carry unacceptable political costs. An internationally indebted regime will lose its credit ratings if it loses the confidence of international financial institutions. The available evidence suggests that the financial liberalization of the Mediterranean Debt Crescent is inescapable. The region is too close to Europe and too dependent on its markets—and European export credits and debt relief—for any regime definitively to reverse the reforms presently under way. Deprived of credit, most of the crescent countries would be unable to feed their populations, much less finance imports for their privileged sectors.

In the early 1990s the former single-party regimes of North Africa appeared to be responding in the third way, by reinforcing their bunkers. By 1992 they were coordinating their efforts to combat a new common enemy, political Islam, and rallying support from their Westernized elites, including much of their respective business communities, without allowing them any significant degree of autonomy. But the political strategies of the hard-liners were also fraught with considerable risk because they could not count upon the unconditional loyalty of their respective military and security services. Ultimately, political deals would have to be struck between the regimes and their Islamist oppositions. Meanwhile financial reform might gradually be strengthening autonomous tendencies within the business communities, encouraging demands for greater government accountability.

While a basic assumption underlying this study is that financial reform is irreversible, the current confrontations between regimes and Islamist oppositions do not bode well for any easy political transitions. If indeed financial reform, breaking into the black box of a patrimonial regime, sets a stage for transition, the change could go as equally in an authoritarian as in a democratic direction. Islamist political movements enjoy strong popular support, among middle and upper-middle as well as popular strata of North African populations, and they inspire fear among incumbent elites. Like their Latin American counterparts of the 1960s (O'Donnell 1979b), the incumbents may build anti-Islamist political ideologies and bureaucratic-authoritarian structures upon these fears. Muslim "fascism," in fact, is more likely to come from this quarter of threatened, ostensibly "secular" political and economic elites than from any of the organized Islamist political movements. Islamism seems instead to be yet another version of Muslim populism, replacing various other forms of populism expressed earlier in terms of local and Arab nationalisms and socialism. The Muslim variant of fascism, by contrast, has shallow roots in the crescent's Western ideological enclaves. On the heuristic assumption that anti-Islamist regimes cannot be consolidated, this book examines the alternative possibility, namely, that financial liberalization may indirectly encourage greater business autonomy and political pluralism.

Patronage, Commercial Banks, and Political Power

The critical hypothesis is that financial liberalization can make business communities sufficiently organized and autonomous to promote political pluralism. It is not immediately obvious, however, why commercial banks may be expected to play the pivotal role. In patrimonial regimes bankers by definition are no more autonomous than the other elements of their respective business communities, all of which are part of the ruler's personal domain (Weber 1978: 998). Though they may mediate the interests of rulers and businesses, their discretion in allocating credit is minimal in any patrimonial regime unless the bankers also happen to be the rulers. The reason that they may be midwives of political change is that they also mediate between their local rulers and the international financial system. Adjustment programs promote greater autonomy for commercial banking systems.

In indebted economies, moreover, banks mirror the rest of the business community: the more leveraged the other businesses, the more their liabilities appear as "assets" in the form of loans on commercial banks' balance sheets. In most Third World countries, including the Mediterranean Debt Crescent, the commercial banks are virtually the only source of funds for businesses. Other capital markets, such as stock exchanges, are thin or nonexistent, and most businesses have no alternative to commercial banks except self-financing or informal markets. Banks control most of the crescent businesses' working capital. In these patrimonial contexts, the banks are a vital yet largely unresearched link between the rulers and the businesses (Maxfield 1990; Winters 1994).

There are powerful theoretical grounds for suspecting that bankers and financiers may have a hidden hand in political development. They are principal intermediaries between economic interests and power in any political system because credit is such a convenient cover for distributing political patronage. Contemporary mainstream political science is almost as discreet as the bankers themselves about these matters (Bretton 1980: 331–32), but in any political system bankers can do wholesale what others can do only retail. In contemporary America, for instance, an eminent political economist of the Chicago School conjectures that so many politicians are lawyers "because everyone employs lawyers, so the congressman's firm is a suitable avenue of compensation, whereas a physician would have to be given bribes rather than patronage" (Stigler 1984: 75). "Everyone" also borrows money, and, witting or not, bankers are the intermediaries in such transactions because they allocate the credit. Unlike Stigler's lawyers, they need not be politicians in their own right. Nor are they necessarily corrupt, however much they service shadowy patronage networks. The Bank of Credit and Commerce International (BCCI), the so-called bank of crooks and criminals finally closed down in July 1991, merely exaggerated practices of political lending and creative bookkeeping exercised by many banks throughout the world. The United States is hardly immune to these practices: bailing out reckless savings and loan institutions has cost the American taxpayer far more than the $18 billion that vanished with BCCI (Beaty and Gwynne 1993: 98).

In patrimonial systems the bankers invariably perform political as well as economic services when they match up savers with borrowers. While they may appear to be allocating credit on apolitical, economic grounds, the pretense is transparent because political and economic elites are so highly interrelated, their political and economic strategies so tightly interwoven. In the Middle East, banking had a history of "dangerous but lucrative employment" (Slade, cited by Issawi 1980: 69). Even in Lebanon, where banking achieved a relatively high degree of professionalism and banking families enjoyed a distinctive status and sense of identity, "the hell of the old politics resurgent" could not really be separated from "the benign utopia of finance" (Ajami 1981: 2). Lebanese bankers benignly kept the militias shooting; and utopia's "great Saudi financier," Adnan Khashoggi, was an arms dealer who eventually fell out of royal favor. Whether or not they enjoy a distinctive social status, bankers occupy a unique position in patrimonial polities. One famous historical example may serve to illustrate their potential role as power brokers.

Fifteenth-Century Florence: The Medici Bank

In his *Florentine History,* Machiavelli praises Giovanni di Bicci de Medici (1360–1429) for "his many excellences" but apparently misses the essential contribution of this prototypical godfather. Giovanni founded the Medici Bank and died "very rich in treasure, but far richer in fame and goodwill." It may also be true that "he never sought the honors of government; yet enjoyed them all; and never went to the palace unless by request" and that on his deathbed he advised his son Cosimo to "take just such a share [of state offices] as the laws and your countrymen think proper to bestow" (Machiavelli, *History* IV:4, 174–75). Doubtless, too, Giovanni should be "first of all a business man who stayed aloof from politics" (Roover 1966: 57), in appearance at least. But if J. R. Hale is correct, his most innovative (though "undercover") activity should be "building up a political party to safeguard his fortune and to bring the Medici clan for the first time into the mainstream of civic politics" (Hale 1977: 13). Here indeed should be the model of a prince for Machiavelli, from the viewpoint of modern machine politics.

Under Giovanni's son Cosimo, in fact, Florence became a virtual one-party system. Helped by "indiscriminate" lending ("not to private persons only, but to the public; and not to Florentines only, but to the *condottiere,* the soldiers of fortune" IV:6, 191), Cosimo became, as Hale puts it, the "concealed puppet-master of Florentine politics" (1977: 40) until his death in 1464. From 1434 until France intervened in 1494, Florence's informal one-party system supported three more Medici successions in the context of the city's republican institutions. The first Medici dynasty fell apart in 1494 when Cosimo's great-grandson was exiled from the city for having made an alliance with the French without sufficient consultation. It was hardly coincidental that the Medici Bank promptly collapsed.

The bank was the basic source of patronage that had sustained the Medici machine. Hale describes how it worked:

> The party was built up and kept together by an assiduous correspondence with members who were temporarily absent on business or in exile as well as through day to day contact with the city. The means adopted to advance the party's power were unspectacular but cumulatively effective. Its members solicited votes, which was illegal. They advocated enlarging the numbers of names in the electoral bags in order to dilute the ranks of their opponents. They helped one another to administrative posts as far as personal influence and the electoral laws permitted. The richer members of the family offered loans to members of the party who were in arrears with their taxes and thus ineligible for office; they also offered advice on business and legal matters. The style of party management was canny and avuncular. The enterprise was in itself corrupt, but it involved neither outright bribery nor coercion. The aim was to plait together an increasing number of influential men who would vote on Medici lines when chosen for the leading offices and commissions, of lesser men who would create a pro-Medicean atmosphere within the guilds, and a solid bloc of all classes within the district where most members of the family lived, in the parish of San Lorenzo. (Hale 1977: 21)

The bank performed two key functions. It cemented patron-client networks within the city, and its branch directors across Italy and northern Europe "had access to inside information and served the Medici not only as business managers but also as informants and diplomatic agents" (Roover 1966: 96). At its zenith in 1460 it was "the largest banking house of its time" with a total of 57 employees, a giant among the 33 moneychanging banks registered in the city of Florence (Roover 1966: 5, 16, 31, 95). The Medici machine originated as a defense against arbitrary power in a city riddled by political factions and banking competitors. Bankers were obliged to organize politically in fifteenth-century Florence; indeed, the principal threats to the Medicis came from competitive banking interests. The Pazzi conspiracy against Lorenzo the Magnificent, for instance, was as much a plot by the Pazzi Bank to destroy its chief competitor as it was an attempted political coup (Roover 1966: 366). Though Machiavelli's Florence—a world financial center in decline—displayed a remarkable, almost pathological identification of banking with politics, its patterns of patronage and power would be replicated in other established polities.

While Florence was a city, not a nation-state, its political and moneyed strata of several thousand families seem comparable in size and structure to the elites of most contemporary Third and Fourth World states, which exclude most of the masses and members of so-called new middle classes from substantial credit or political influence. Certainly in the Mediterranean polities under discussion, indebted business and political elites commingle. In Tunisia, for instance, the entire banking system provided only 1,017 loans of half a million dinars ($600,000) or more per loan to public and private enterprises in 1986 (Banque Centrale de Tunisie, personal letter from the governor). As in Florence, the differentiation between political (or administrative) and economic elites was minimal. In Bourguiba's name, palace retainers had extorted loans from banks, but after 1987 the Tunisian Republic slipped into an era of veiled oligarchy and ill-defined pluralism. Bankers and politicians would have to develop more careful cooperation under increasingly competitive pressures generated by financial adjustment programs.

Bankers do not usually become political actors in their own right; even the Medici had initially preferred to veil their political roles. But in patrimonial regimes, bankers serve the active politicians through strategic lending that firms up critical patron-client networks. Their command and allocation of credit necessarily involve them in politics wherever elites are relatively small and undifferentiated, whether in fifteenth-century Florence or contemporary Tunis or Cairo. Whatever the lender's intention, bank loans are political resources, selective incentives that bind the borrowers to their political patrons. The banker is then serving not only as a financial intermediary, relating investors to borrowers, but also as a political broker, relating patrons to clients.

Bankers, Classes, and Business Groups

Assuming that a commercial banking system undergoes structural adjustment to meet the requirements of the international financial community, under what conditions might it foster sufficient business autonomy and organization, intentionally or unintentionally, to transform a patrimonial regime? One general condition is that the economy be sufficiently developed to have generated a potentially powerful array of business enterprises. Samuel P. Huntington (1991: 62–63) has suggested a possible proxy for measuring their power potential: an annual per capita income of about $2,000 ($1,000 in 1976 dollars) may be a threshold above which democratization is more likely to occur in the 1990s. But even poorer economies, including those of the debt crescent, may support powerful enterprises. Second, the enterprises must be substantially indebted to the commercial banking system. Third, the finance capital must be concentrated in the hands of a small number of commercial banks capable of engaging in collective action. An oligopolistic structure is a major source of structural power. It is the commercial banking system's defense against predatory regimes and their business enterprises. Fourth, a critical nucleus of financial oligopolists must wield enough market power to discipline their weaker sisters and induce them to be "good" oligopolists. The nucleus is more likely to consist predominantly of private sector banks than those of the public sector. These conditions, coupled with continuing "advice" and prodding by international financial institutions for more financial liberalization and privatization, favor the rise of business conglomerates. These groups, while competing with each other, are also capable of collective action, providing real influence and backbone to formal business organizations. Their emergence will mark the end of a patrimonial regime unless the ruler also owns the principal conglomerate.

Coincidentally, these four conditions describe the banking legacy of Imperial Germany at the turn of century, which should be bequeathed to some of the Mediterranean Debt Crescent countries. The Austrian-born Social Democrat Rudolf Hilferding,[2] writing in 1910, discovered the virtues of universal German banks. Controlled, organized, based on trust and direct human relationships with creditors, these banks appeared to be the antithesis of unstable capitalism; indeed, they practiced "a fraudulent kind of socialism" (Hilferding 1981 [1910]: 180). Beneath their innocuous exterior, the German cartel, originally a defensive response to industrial cartels, had concentrated industrial capital and transformed it into finance capital. Then, in competing for foreign contracts (such as Serbian arms deals), "political power becomes decisive" and "finance capital acquires a direct profit interest in the power position of the state" (330).

Lenin placed six Berlin banks at the "commanding heights of the economy"—with help from Hilferding. "A steadily increasing proportion of capital in industry," Hilferding writes, "does not belong to the industrialists who employ it. They obtain the use of it only through the medium of the banks, which, in relation to them, represent the owners of the capital. On the other hand, the bank is forced to keep an increasing share of its funds engaged in industry. Thus, to an increasing degree the bank is being transformed into an industrial capitalist. This bank capital, i.e., capital in money form which is thus readily transformed into industrial capital, I call 'finance capital.' . . . Finance capital is controlled by banks and employed by industrialists" (Lenin 1939 [1917]: 47, citing Hilferding 1912: 283; cf. Hilferding 1981 [1910]: 225). The German model best exemplified "the highest stage of capitalism" by concentrating the control of industrial cartels in a small number of universal banks. These banks had evolved since Marx's time from "modest intermediary enterprises into the monopolists of finance capital" (Lenin 1939 [1917]: 123–34). Karl Marx had already noted that credit and competition were the "two most powerful levers of centralization" (Marx 1977 [1867]: 779) whereby capital could be horizontally as well as vertically integrated. But Marx completed his definitive volume 1 of *Das Kapital* in 1866, before the integrative mechanisms of advanced capitalism were fully visible. Owners and controllers of most capital-intensive means of production, the bankers fused economic with political power, driving imperialism forward and fulfilling Hilferding's prophecy (1981 [1910]: 331) of a world war.

Lenin carried Hilferding's analysis a step further, in fact, by dissociating finance capital from industry. Both writers agreed that the German "monopolists of financial capital" represented a more advanced stage of capitalist development than Britain's competitive financial markets. In *Imperialism the Highest Stage of Capitalism,* however, Lenin goes on to place the concentrated French banking system on a par with the German system, despite its declining share of French industrial capital. What matters most is no longer the industrial substance of the imperialist power but rather the surplus capital deployed by concentrated financial intermediaries. "The characteristic feature of imperialism is *not* industrial capital, *but* finance capital. It is not an accident that in France it should be precisely the extraordinarily rapid development of *finance* capital, and the weakening of industrial capital, that, from 1880 onwards, gave rise to the extreme extension of annexationist (colonial) policy" (Lenin 1939 [1917]: 91; cf. Bouvier et al. 1982: 28). The big northern banks thus acquired a peculiar degree of autonomy from relationships of production in Lenin's variant of the Marxist tradition. Their tight financial oligarchies were reputed to concentrate more power ranging over wider spaces than that of any standard dictator.

Colonial Legacies

After most colonies disappeared in the wake of World War II, the old imperial mechanisms acquired new institutional forms. However much influence international bankers actually wielded—either in the latter third of the nineteenth century, the heyday of Western imperialism, or a century later—they clearly helped to shape the traditions of banking in their "host" countries. No longer were the indigenous bankers of the Islamic Mediterranean left alone to be exploited by ravenous princes or khedives; if they stayed in business, they would enjoy the protection of the City of London, Paris, or Berlin, whether they wanted it or not. The northern systems exercised their financial hegemony—Paris over Algeria, Tunisia, and Morocco; London and Paris over Egypt; and all three European centers over Ottoman Turkey. The northern practices in turn reshaped the structure and practices of the local banks, whether or not they were directly owned by the northern banks. Despite formal emancipation and the experiences of state-run economies, these legacies are still visible today. There were major differences, however, in the exposures of the rest of the Islamic Mediterranean to the new engines of European capitalism. The new financial institutions underwent considerable transformation in their home countries in the course of the nineteenth century. Consequently the institutional components projected across the sea depended not only upon respective spheres of great power influence but also upon the timing of the colonial takeovers.

The respective European legacies to the southern shores of the Mediterranean depended above all on how long the target countries remained open to European capital. Hilferding would surely agree that "Algeria is of almost no value for a study of the working of economic forces of nineteenth-century imperialism" (Fieldhouse 1973: 106). The country became a French provincial backwater, ignored by British capital and only marginally touched even by the new French, much less upstart German, finance machines reflecting later stages of capitalist concentration. Neighboring Tunisia would be closed down too soon, in 1881, to become much better financially endowed than Algeria. By contrast, Morocco, open until 1912, would absorb the same industrial model of banking that should be being imposed upon Turkey. Egypt, despite a British military occupation from 1882 to 1954, would remain relatively open until 1956 and would reflect a mosaic of models, but above all the competition among them, a British legacy of sorts to muddle through. The different legacies would in turn be assimilated by victorious nationalists to varying degrees, depending upon the timing of independence. In the 1920s and 1930s Mustafa Kemal Atatürk was bound to be less destructive of European legacies than Bourguiba, Nasser, or Ben Bella and Boumédienne in the 1960s. Moroccan monarchs, however, went against the dominant trend of this later period. They protected their French legacy against the nationalists in return for efficient service to the royal household.

Two features of these legacies seem especially significant: the relative autonomy of the respective banking systems and the degree of competition among banks and other financial intermediaries within a given system. Autonomy with respect to state administration should be the critical assumption underlying both the Hilferding model and the more competitive British model. It enabled the followers of Karl Marx to specify how the state could serve as the executive committee of the bourgeoisie: it was Imperial Germany's peculiarly concentrated system of universal banks that allocated the credit to the industrial bourgeoisie and enabled "monopoly capitalism" to reach its full development. In the less concentrated British model, featuring relatively unregulated equity markets on stock exchanges, the financial system should be at least as autonomous, but it did not formally concentrate power in the boardrooms of a small number of banks. The British model tended also to graft greater competition upon a peripheral financial system. The respective imperial legacies, rejected in varying degrees by independent nationalist regimes, would reemerge in the 1980s with the restructuring of their respective finances.

Hilferding should be wrong to dismiss "the English system" as "an outmoded one and . . . everywhere on the decline" (Hilferding 1981 [1910]: 293) simply because the German stock exchange seemed to be losing out to the bankers' inside control of capital markets. He propounded a bizarre theory of "promoter's profit," or the gains of banks from underwriting stock market issues, as evidence that banks liberated "the industrial capitalist from the function of industrial entrepreneur" (107). But presumably these profits took second place to straightforward lending because the stock markets, controlled in any event by the major banks, were in his view becoming obsolete: "The stock exchange has lost its faithful and kept only its priests, who make their money from the faith of others. Since faith has become a business, the business of faith has declined. The seductive and lucrative craze has spent itself, the tulips have long since faded, and the coffee bush, though it still yields a commercial profit, no longer produces true speculative gains. Prose has vanquished the poetry of gain" (294).

Stock markets certainly did not decline as Hilferding had so poetically predicted. But although his model no longer fits advanced capitalist economies, it still applies to industrializing societies in which stock markets are weak or nonexistent, enterprises remain secretive, and commercial banks carry the major burden of mediating between savers and borrowers. Indeed, bankers are more likely to command the heights of indebted, dependent economies, even in the absence of much industry, than to tower over advanced industrial economies. In much of the Middle East and North Africa, international and domestic debt, relative to GDP, takes on Latin American dimensions and pushes bankers into major political roles. Although they do not finance much manufacturing, their credit allocations will largely condition the articulation of any bourgeois class interests.

Democratic Virtues of Oligopoly?

With the German experience clearly in mind, Max Weber offered tantalizing insight into possible relationships between banking and political systems. Although he sharply distinguished between "domination by virtue of constellation of interests" and "domination by authority," Weber recognized that the former could

> be transformed gradually into the latter, . . . particularly [in the case of] monopoly. . . . A bank, for instance, in order to control more effectively a debtor corporation, may demand as a condition for credit that some member of its board be made a member of the board of the debtor corporation. That board, in turn, can give decisive orders to the management by virtue of the latter's obligation to obey. . . . This kind of domination might become quite like the authoritative domination of a bureaucratic state agency. The same observation can be made with respect to the domination by the breweries over the tavern owners whom they supply with their equipment, or the domination to which book dealers would have to submit if there should some day be a German publishers' cartel with power to issue and withhold retailers' licenses, or the domination of the gasoline dealers by the Standard Oil Company" (Weber 1978: 943–44).

Although Max Weber clearly differentiated between such forms of "domination by authority" and the legitimate forms of authority characteristic of modern states, it is possible to push his "abstract and sometimes also somewhat indefinite" propositions relating "forms of economic organization and of domination" (942) a step further. The patrimonial crescent states have extensive administrations and fiscal capabilities. They are akin to Weber's debtor corporation and will tend to prevent any external tampering with their respective black boxes of patronage. Yet these states illustrate not "domination by authority" but rather "domination by virtue of a constellation of interests" insofar as they rely on patronage to survive. This form of domination is market power: the more concentrated the interests, the more power they will generate. The threat to the patrimonial ruler is that his networks of patronage become decentralized, escaping his personal control. The threat increases along with increasing concentration of the external constellation of interests, such as the banking system. The black box of a patrimonial regime will be heavily defended, and a financial oligopoly, reflecting a concentration of finance capital, is more likely to pressure it toward greater accountability than would a more competitive commercial banking system.

But it does not necessarily follow that a patrimonial regime, under pressure, will move in a democratic rather than a more authoritarian direction. Intuitively, in fact, it would seem that oligopolists might prefer a tougher bureaucratic-authoritarian regime to a more pluralistic one. Why might their business communities offer an environment more conducive to democracy than to oligarchy? Why might their relative autonomy encourage progress along any of the three dimensions that, following Philippe Schmitter and Terry Karl, offer a useful working definition of democracy: "(1) *contestation* over policy and political competition for office; (2) *participation* of the citizenry through partisan, associational, and other forms of collective action; (3) *accountability* of rulers to the ruled through mechanisms of representation and the rule of law" (which presumably protect the rights "essential to meaningful contestation, participation, and accountability")? (See Collier and Mahon 1993: 851; cf. Rueschemeyer et al. 1992: 43–44.)

There is no need to assume that bankers and other business leaders have any special elective affinities with democracy or any other form of government, as long as their property rights are respected. As one of Bismarck's contemporaries observed, "High finance shakes its knees whenever any kind of political complication comes up" (Kindleberger 1970: 75). Bankers' interest in political stability will surely outweigh any abstract concerns about government accountability, much less contestation or participation. It is rather the environment introduced by an autonomous business community that is crucial for democratic transitions. Secure property rights offer resources for a more democratic politics.

The crescent's bankers and other business leaders cannot be expected to engage in the rough-and-tumble of practical politics, much less deliberately to plot for changes of regime. But at least three of the incumbent regimes, those of Algeria, Egypt, and Tunisia, are already in a state of crisis. In times of crisis the oligopolists of a relatively autonomous business community can be expected to hedge their bets, to have allies in as many of the contending political camps as possible so as to ensure their property rights, whatever the outcome of the crisis. Business may also support electoral competition and multiparty politics to keep the government weak. As Çağlar Keyder (1987: 142) explains the Turkish transition following World War II, "A faction of the bourgeoisie had . . . achieved a status from which they could forcefully express their wishes and preferences for a parliamentary regime at the political level. One reason for this preference was that in a competing party system attentive to electoral politics which were open to monetary influence, state agencies were much more accessible than in the case of a bureaucratic polity." In a crisis, then, big business may nudge an authoritarian regime toward more political pluralism and greater accountability, two of democracy's three dimensions. And although big business may have no particular interest outside its marketing departments for the more widespread participation characteristic of democracy, it is ready to cope with an existing state of affairs. Along the crescent the masses are already mobilized, and "Islam is the solution" for many.

However consonant with greater accountability and political contestation, capital concentration in strong private sector groups may appear to be incompatible with the widespread participation that democratization also entails. How can business constituencies relate to, much less encourage, a mobilization of masses consonant with electoral participation and other forms of democratic participation? Business may favor political contestation in order to make any incumbent government more responsive to its interests, but how may it reach the mass constituencies that have already been mobilized by national liberation struggles, populist appeals, and now Islamism? Among crescent and other Muslim countries, Islam's new financial intermediaries offered a possible answer.

Political Islam and Islamic Banking

"Islamic" banking is a distinctively modern phenomenon—an international effort to make contemporary economic practice in Muslim countries conform to Islamic norms. By legitimating certain forms of modern business, Islam may strengthen civil society and reinforce constraints on the arbitrary exercise of power (Richards 1993: 225). Islamic banking, to be sure, is only one of many forms that modern business enterprise assumes in the region. Western models still predominate, in banking as in other sectors of economic activity. But Islamic banks, situated in a confluence of financial and political forces, have steadily increased their market share in some of the crescent countries as well as other Muslim countries.

These banks, privately owned for the most part, learned to coexist with the conventional Western-style banking systems in their respective countries and occasionally cooperated with them to promote further financial liberalization. Their presence also reflected a selective integration of Islamist elements into a competitive political process, for the banks had ideological affinities, sometimes reinforced by personal connections, with certain "Islamist" political factions and parties. If financial liberalization were to increase their structural power, Islamic banks would be likely to foster liberal trends within the Islamist movements. And any successful transitions in the Arab world to a more genuinely competitive politics will depend upon liberals gaining the upper hand within the Islamist mainstream opposition movements of their respective countries. Hence Islamic banking deserves close scrutiny.

These new banking institutions are one of the very few distinctively Islamic economic innovations advocated by Islamist movements. They seem central to any Islamist vision of society that contains an economic dimension. "In Pakistan, for instance, a politician who fails to endorse Islamic banking may find his aspirations thwarted. Siginificantly, Islamic banking is on the platform of every major political party" (Kuran 1993: 307). "Islam is the solution," Islamists insist, and the slogan implies that Islam is a complete system of commands and norms that should govern all aspects of human existence. "Islamic economics" is one aspect of this total social vision, and it has generated an immense multidisciplinary literature (Kuran 1986, 1989, 1993). Much of it is written by scholars specializing in Quranic studies, in the *hadith,* or sayings of the Prophet, and in Islamic ethics and jurisprudence, but Western-trained Muslim economists, too, have contributed in recent years to the growing body of literature. In fact "Islamic economics" incorporates most of the econometric techniques of mainstream economics, but there seems to be little that is distinctively Islamic in its principles of equality and fairness. Samir Amin, an Egyptian Marxist critic, once observed that "Islamic economy, in the real sense of the word, outside of a number of fundamental slogans and measures, can hardly be regarded as Islamic" (Amin 1982: 56). The postulate which stands out as the most distinctively Islamic, shared by the most Islamists in the contemporary world, is the equation of usury, which Christian doctrine also condemns, with any form of lending that obligates the borrower to pay a fixed rate of interest. Islam's prohibition of interest is "the most celebrated" of the homilies and injunctions that constitute Islamic economic theory (Kuran 1989: 174). Its practical application, Islamic banking, has also generated the most attention among Muslims and non-Muslims alike.

Political Islamists naturally tend to vary in their emphases, depending on the national context in which they operate and the constituencies they attempt to mobilize. Not all practitioners of interest-free banking are radical Islamists (despite Shepard 1987: 317–18), nor do all radicals make common cause with the bankers who currently practice it. Indeed, there is an obvious tension between the total vision of social change projected by Islamist radicals and the incremental change fostered by Islamic banking practices in contemporary Muslim societies. While Islamic bankers do not necessarily share any commitment to Western-style liberalism or democracy, their drive for markets and profits may indirectly contribute to a more competitive politics. Their economic success sets the stage for greater democracy by encouraging popular participation in financial activities, by shifting the political weight within popular Islamist movements in favor of "responsible" business elements ready to coexist with the capitalist order, and by accumulating finance capital, helping to consolidate the structural power of the commercial banking system and the autonomy of the private business sector. Political pluralism also contributes to Islamic business success. Political systems that tolerate Islamist oppositions enhance the banks' distinctive competitive advantages and help them offset some of their distinctive limitations.

Like other financial intermediaries, Islamic banks make profits from putting the savings of investors at the service of borrowers. Instead of charging fixed rates, or interest, to borrowers, however, they are expected to share in the profits—and risks of losses—of the latter's business transactions and to divide up their share of the profits, in turn, with investors who deposited funds in the bank. Rates of return, calculated ex post facto, are variable, a function of the complex of business transactions, rather than a predetermined, fixed rate, which would be tantamount to interest. The logic of Islamic banking in any competitive profit-seeking climate requires especially close relations between bankers, depositors, and borrowers. Since the depositors are in theory to share in the bank's profits rather than receiving interest, they also share the business risks of the borrowers. Most Islamic bank deposits, apart from a small percentage parked in unremunerated current accounts, take the form of investment accounts. In any medium- or long-term lending, moreover, the bank and the borrower are engaged in an unusually close and trusting relationship. The distinctively Islamic financial instruments for term lending, *mudaraba* and *musharaka,* are akin to equity financing. Musharaka is a flexible form of equity financing: the bank holds shares in the borrowing firm's equity and participates in its management but may be bought out by the other partners' shares of subsequent profits. In mudaraba the bank supplies the capital and receives a prearranged share of the borrower's eventual profits. In these arrnagements it is too easy for the borrower to manipulate financial statements to minimize the profits to be shared. If the borrower is honest and has a good project, conversely, there may be a preference not to share the risk with an Islamic bank (Nienhaus 1983). Given a choice, a borrower may prefer conventional, interest-based banking. Assuming efficient markets, conventional banks should offer cheaper money than Islamic banks because they do not share as many risks. With their hands-off approach, they may also better protect business secrets (Campbell 1979).

The Islamic requirement to share business risk with borrowers in practice encourages Islamic banks to devote most of their activity to short-term trade financing (*murabaha,* whereby the bank sells a good to the borrower for the deferred payment of a marked-up price) and leasing (*ijara*), which carries less risk but presumably generated less revenue than medium- and long-term lending. Even the Islamic Development Bank, owned by 44 governments rather than private entrepreneurs, altered its strategy in the 1980s toward more short-term lending (Kuran 1993: 311). The private sector banks, obliged to make sufficient profits to compete with conventional banks, have always minimized their exposure to risky mudaraba and musharaka contracts with private borrowers. The combined balance sheet of the 22 members of the International Association of Islamic Banks shows that only 5.6 percent of their funds were invested in medium- and long-term operations in 1989 (Metwally 1991: 13). From 4.4 percent in 1983, they had reached a peak of 7.5 percent in 1986, when many banks throughout the region were squeezed directly or indirectly by declining oil revenues (Metwally 1986, 1988).

Information costs—monitoring the borrower's business as well as checking credit and financial ratings—were high, understandably deterring Islamic bankers from jumping into their most distinctively Islamic lines of long-term financing; but market segmentation is increasing with the rise of Islamic social and political forces. Islamic-minded publics constitute distinctive market segments, courted by governments, political oppositions, and businesses alike. Wherever Islamic banks compete with conventional ones, competitive politics are likely to deepen the segmentation, enhancing the cohesion of the Islamic banking constituencies and presumably diminishing their information costs. In the eyes of their respective publics the banks are often identified with Islamist political tendencies. So far as these perceptions are valid, the politicians associated with the banks, in turn, have an ideological as well as a material interest in offering reliable information about prospective borrowers rather than simply milking the banks. A bank failure would not only eliminate an important source of patronage—a consideration equally applicable to conventional banks—but would also discredit the politician's Islamist message. In theory, at least, the Islamic bank may compensate for higher-risk credit policies by obtaining better information about its borrowers than conventional banks can. In the long run, a pattern of successful competitive coexistence between the two sectors may reinforce political pluralism by generating more Islamic businesses committed to free markets and peaceful political coexistence. Conversely, however, Islamic banking has better prospects for expansion and development in countries that tolerate competitive politics than it has under more restrictive regimes.

Comparative Perspectives

To summarize the argument of this book, financial liberalization is expected to favor democratic transitions in patrimonial authoritarian regimes. Progress along democratic lines in a given Muslim country will depend upon the structural power of finance capital, the emergence of business conglomerates, and the inclusion of Islamic financial institutions in the commercial banking system. The structural power of finance capital depends, in turn, upon the autonomy and degree of concentration of the banking system. The systems under study, which differ with respect to their degree of private ownership and concentration, will illustrate these relationships between money and power. A key variable in explaining the structural differences is each country's colonial banking legacy. Capital concentration in business conglomerates will have a head start in countries that experienced a "German" tradition of universal banking, notably Turkey and Morocco.

As yet, to be sure, the experiences of the crescent countries offer little direct evidence that financial liberalization sets the stage for democratic transitions. The reforms have barely taken root in North Africa, much less laid the ground for autonomous business communities. Despite significant variations in their commercial banking and business structures, however, the crescent countries all share a major stimulus to reform, namely their debt situations and "advice" on their debts from international financial institutions. Unless the international climate drastically changes, they are likely to pursue their respective financial reforms, with consequences Montesquieu had predicted to accompany the rise of commerce between nations in the early eighteenth century. It should be no longer rational for patrimonial rulers to extort gold from the moneylenders once *lettres de change* facilitated the free flow of capital (Hirschman 1977; Montesquieu 1964). Then, as now, "gentle commerce" could be expected to soften political manners so as to attract capital rather than scare it away. The specter of capital flight drives financial reform, which in turn increases the "structural" power of a commercial banking system (Winters 1994: 431–32, 447).

The following chapter will discuss the international impetus for financial reform and the divergent responses of the crescent regimes. It will become evident that economic factors alone, such as the size and structure of their respective debts, do not explain their distinctive paths of financial reform. The subsequent chapter will present explanations derived from their respective political strategies of survival. Chapters 4–8 will then examine each commercial banking system in greater detail, comparing their colonial legacies, degrees of private bank ownership and capital concentration, and their emerging structural power, coupled with government responses, including strategies for containing the challenges of Islamic finance capital. To anticipate, Turkey has progressed furthest along the parallel roads of democratization and financial liberalization and best illustrates the synergies that could work elsewhere along the crescent. Laboring under the most adverse colonial heritage, Algeria has made the least progress. A careful look at its recent reform efforts, however, will illustrate not only the opposition of a patrimonial regime to financial reform but also potential support for reform from an unlikely quarter, the Islamist opposition. Tunisia, in appearance a much more promising candidate for both financial and political reform, also underlines the obstacles and demonstrates their connections. It reinforces the view that a tough financial oligopoly may be needed to break the hold of a patrimonial administration and suggests the need for Islamic as well as conventional intermediaries to pursue the reform process. Despite greater economic difficulties, Egypt came closer to the Turkish model of accumulating finance capital until the government cracked down on the Islamic money management companies. Egypt also enjoyed a colonial legacy more favorable to financial reform than either Algeria or Tunisia. Morocco has preserved a colonial legacy of business conglomerates that most closely resembles the Turkish model—except that the monarchy still controls them. Ironically the preemptive royal strategy offers the best confirmation that financial liberalization enhances the structural power of a commercial banking system and lays the groundwork in a patrimonial system for transition to democracy.

Chapter 2

External Debts and Economies of Adjustment

> The only part of the so-called national wealth that actually enters into the collective possession of a modern nation is—the national debt.
>
> (Marx 1977 [1867]: 919)

For the Mediterranean Debt Crescent, as for much of the rest of the Third World, the balance-of-payments and debt crises of the 1970s and 1980s stimulated extensive reforms in consultation with the IMF and the World Bank. Moves toward more autonomous and more competitive financial systems were included in the reform packages, but they were constrained by the more immediate priorities of cutting fiscal and trade deficits and controlling the money supply. More efficient, market-driven credit allocation presupposed a measure of macroeconomic stability. While the crescent countries did not experience as much inflation as some of the Latin American countries, they shared a special problem with other Arab, Mediterranean, and East European countries near the industrial heartlands of Western Europe. They were drowning in domestic as well as foreign debt.

Karl Marx's dictum on the national debt is especially relevant to these countries. Whether the debt is interpreted narrowly to mean outstanding credits to government and state enterprises or more broadly to include loans to private enterprises and individuals as well, the debt crescent was awash in credit by the 1980s. Whatever their colonial legacies, the respective banking systems amplified the Third World phenomenon of indebted development. Indeed, their respective ratios of total domestic credit to gross domestic product were significantly above Third World norms.[1] Egypt's and Algeria's ratios (respectively, 116 and 106 percent in 1988) were among the highest in the world, outdone only by the little countries in the vortex of the Arab-Israeli conflict: Israel, Jordan, and Lebanon.

These hefty domestic debt ratios, shown in figure 2–1, signified neither financial "deepening" nor development. Much of the credit distributed in the 1970s and 1980s took the form of short-term commercial bank loans rolled over year after year on the balance sheets of state enterprises. It reflected per-

Fig. 2.1. Total domestic credit to GDP, 1975–89. *Source:* IMF, International Financial Statistics.

missive accounting practices but also deeper maladies characteristic of the region. Each of the Mediterranean states had lived off a rentier economy, directly or indirectly depending upon oil revenues, workers' remittances, and strategic rents from Europe, the United States, or the Soviet Union. With the exception of Algeria, they ran chronic balance-of-payments and budgetary deficits, covered by ever greater international borrowing in the 1970s. Eventually the rents failed to sustain the debt servicing requirements, and each country, like other Third World debtors, then faced major problems of adjustment. Algeria became squeezed like its neighbors when, with the fall in oil prices and consequent decline of its export revenues, its debt service ratio increased to 56 percent in 1986 and topped 100 percent (including short-term debt repayments) in 1988. Each country would have to undergo substantial economic reform.

Dimensions of External Debt

This chapter analyzes the dimensions of the respective external debts, the consequent pressures for adjustment, and macroeconomic constraints on financial reform in the five countries. The reforms actually undertaken up to 1992 will then be discussed, and it will become apparent that economic variables and external pressures do not adequately explain the respective strategies. (Political explanations will be left to the following chapter.) The economies were so heavily indebted that any adjustment was bound to put the banks as well as many of their clients at risk. Restructuring, in turn, would have major economic and political reverberations if the banking systems actually acquired greater autonomy in allocating credit.

By 1988 Europe's "Mexico" had accumulated a total external debt (including short- as well as long-term loans) of almost $140 billion. Europe's southern debtors were rather worse off, in fact, than Mexico, which owed about $102 billion. Their collective external debt was 75 percent of gross national product (GNP), compared with Mexico's 58 percent. Morocco and Egypt had become addicted to foreign credit, with fixes (including short-term debt) approaching 150 percent of GNP in the mid-1980s. Figure 2–2 summarizes the evolution of the crescent's long-term external indebtedness between 1970 and 1988.[2] Coincidentally, Tunisia had the highest ratio of external long-term debt (LTD) to gross national product in 1970, just as it had been the first to fall into the hands of European receivers a century earlier. This time, however, it backed away from the abyss; in 1969 it halted its comprehensive programs of state socialism, and its debt service ratio (of principal and interest payments to export revenues; see fig. 2–3) would remain below the critical 20 percent mark until 1983. But Egypt would blunder on, followed by Morocco, as if reliving their nineteenth-century debt odysseys and compressing them into the decade of the 1970s.

What counted, more than the stocks of debt, were the debt service ratios. These varied considerably from country to country, independent of the accumulation of debt. For instance, in 1988 Egypt earmarked only $1.8 billion (21 percent of its export revenues) to service a debt of $48 billion, whereas Algeria disbursed $8.5 billion (100.3 percent of its export revenues) against half as much external, including short-term, debt. Not only was Egypt chronically in arrears in paying interest, not to speak of repaying principal, but the lending terms were much more generous than those accorded Algeria. Almost half of Egypt's loans were made on soft "concessional" terms, compared with about 3 percent of Algeria's. International bankers and financiers shunned Egypt, known for its wayward finances, whereas they provided steadfast Algeria with two-thirds of its long-term debt. Algeria paid heavily for its good financial reputation.

Figure 2–3 provides the critical debt service ratios. Though not as heavily indebted in 1973 as Algeria or Tunisia, Egypt had bare coffers that year. It could not bear a debt service ratio of 53 percent on top of increased import requirements. Sadat launched the October War against Israel to re-

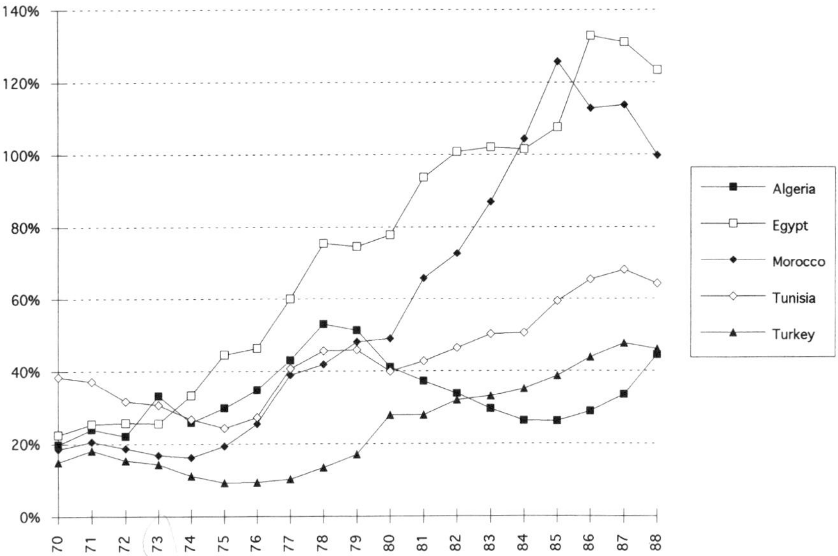

Fig. 2.2. Long-term external debt to GNP, 1970–88. *Source:* World Bank, World Debt Tables.

shuffle his economic as well as his political cards (cf. Waterbury 1983: 127–28). Turkey faced its moment of truth in 1977,[3] as did Morocco in 1982, Tunisia in 1986, and Algeria, finally, in 1988. The countries varied in the amounts of debt servicing, relative to exports, that they could sustain, but each seemed to have certain limits. In the 1980s Algeria and Turkey seemed able to disburse up to 35 percent, whereas Egypt, Morocco, and Tunisia could not pay out more than 20 percent to 25 percent without taking on more debt. Egypt built up arrears equaling the year's debt service by 1986. Despite some long-term debt rescheduling in 1987 and 1988, the arrears grew to over $10 billion by 1991 (*Middle East Economic Digest* [*MEED*], 31 May 1991: 18). Morocco, the other country with a big debt proportional to GNP, preserved better appearances. It sustained a larger debt service, despite numerous reschedulings after 1982, but did not fall into arrears on its interest payments. Both Morocco and Egypt were virtually bankrupt and locked into protracted negotiations with the IMF and other creditors, whereas the other countries only intermittently faced the prospects of insolvency.

In some ways Egypt was more fortunate than Morocco. While accumulating more long-term debt, it practiced a self-determination of sorts by lagging its payments; after 1978 its debt service ratio was consistently lower than Morocco's, and reimbursements hovered around 5 percent of

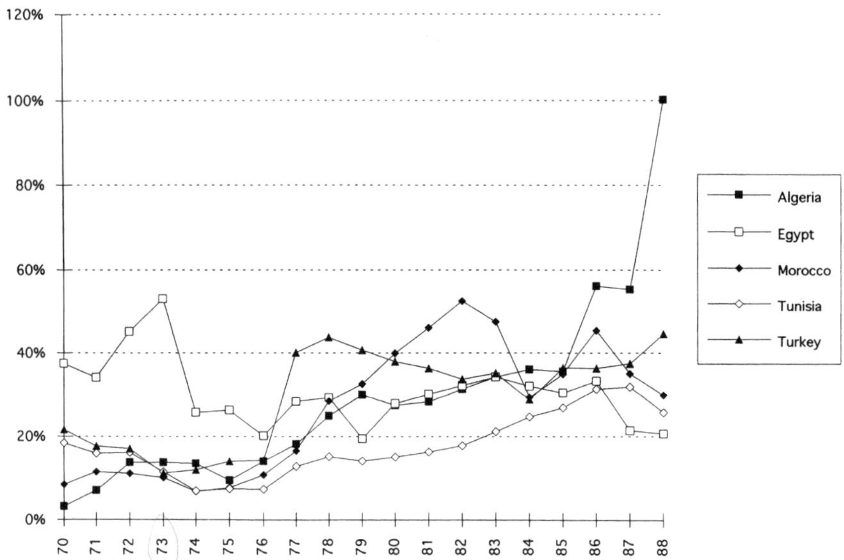

Fig. 2.3. Debt service to exports, 1970–88. *Source:* World Bank, World Debt Tables.

Egyptian GNP whereas Morocco was paying out closer to 10 percent in the late 1980s. Morocco could not get away with Egyptian tactics, had it so desired. Its debt profile more closely resembled Tunisia's in that roughly one-fifth of it remained in the hands of international bankers, whereas less than 3 percent of the Egyptian long-term debt was in private hands in 1988. Figure 2–4 traces the crescent countries' respective shares of debt financed over the years 1970–88 by private financial institutions, bonds, or other private creditors. "Socialist" Algeria relied the most on private financing, followed by Turkey in the mid-1980s. Conversely, Algeria hardly benefited at all from concessional lending, and Turkey fared only half as well as the others.

Morocco was almost as heavily indebted as Egypt, relative to GNP, but its debt profile resembled Tunisia's and Turkey's more than Egypt's. In the 1970s international bankers had liberally sprayed the region, like the rest of the world, with their petrodollars. They clearly displayed less appetite for Moroccan risk after 1983, when they stopped contributing new money to Morocco's long-term debt, but their portfolios kept expanding more or less in step with Morocco's GNP. Privately held long-term debt amounted to almost $5 billion in 1989, close to one-quarter of the GNP. Morocco received modest debt relief in 1990 under the Brady Plan but still faced periodic

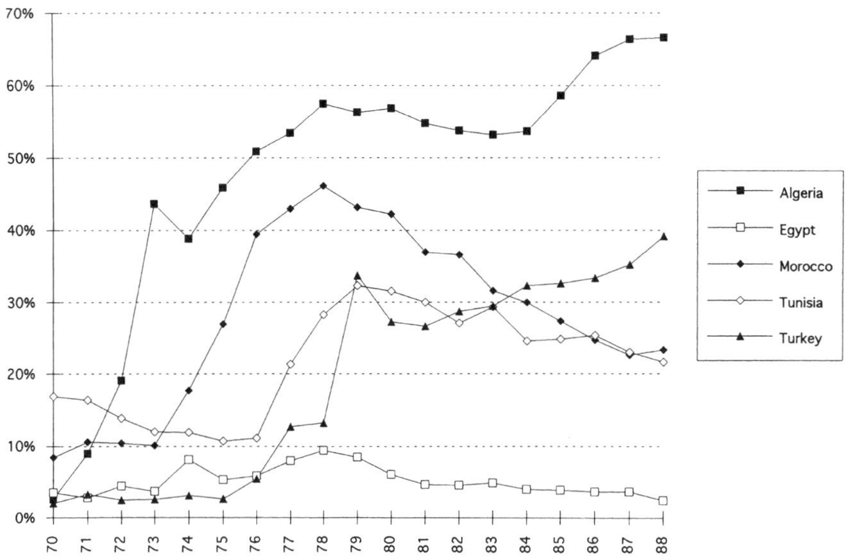

Fig. 2.4. Private sector lending as a percentage of total external loans, 1970–88. *Source:* World Bank, World Debt Tables.

London Club, as well as Paris Club, meetings to reschedule with the banks as well as official creditors.

Tunisia, more prudent than Morocco, had limited its exposure to the international banks. No more than one-third of its external long-term debt ever fell into their hands, even in the late 1970s when borrowing was easy and government deficits (mostly financed by external borrowing) were expanding in efforts to smother social unrest. When Tunisia embarked on its adjustment program in 1986, it avoided rescheduling. Unlike Morocco or Turkey, Tunisia never had to meet up with the London Club. Its privately held debt peaked in 1979 at 32 percent of GNP, and its debt service ratio remained lower than that of Morocco or Turkey. Prudent management was also rewarded in other ways. By 1988 Tunisia's share of concessional ("soft") loans, relative to long-term debt, was almost as great as Egypt's. It exceeded Morocco's, even though Morocco was poorer and more favored by soft loans from OPEC countries.

Turkey, too, kept the international bankers at arm's length until the late 1970s. But by extending its occupation to 40 percent of Cyprus, Turkey lost access in 1975 to official sources of long-term debt and therefore had to resort to commercial short-term debt to meet the foreign exchange shortfalls caused by oil price increases and declines in workers' remittances from Europe (Arıcanlı 1990: 241). Turkey then quickly fell into trouble, long before the shocks of the second oil price increase and high interest rates propelled many other countries, including Morocco, into similar crises (Belassa and McCarthy 1984: 3). Between 1978 and 1980 Turkey rescheduled over $9 billion of debt, mostly from official creditors (World Bank, *World Development Report* 1985: 67). The private sector international bankers showed little appetite for Turkish risk. In 1979 they grudgingly converted some $3 billion of arrears into long-term debt. Only in 1983 could Turkey return to the Euromarkets (Hewin et al. 1988: 43). The international bankers and financiers then accumulated ever greater shares of Turkey's long-term debt, pushing up its debt service ratio even as exports, too, took spectacular leaps forward, attracting more bankers to the Turkish debt feast. Were the growth in exports to diminish, Turkey could face a new debt crisis. In the summer of 1991 the IMF was already warning the government to reduce its deficits, and by 1994 the crisis was at hand.

By the late 1980s Turkey's debt profile resembled Algeria's: few soft loans and substantial amounts placed in international financial markets, driving a high debt service ratio. Despite relatively low stocks of external debt to GNP compared with the others, both countries teetered on the brink of a serious debt crisis. But Turkey's integration with international markets reflected a certain level of financial maturity, whereas Algeria's was the product of an oil economy gone awry. Virtually all of Algeria's exports depended upon the price of oil, which collapsed in 1986. Official GNP was grossly overvalued until 1990–91. By then, Algeria was undertaking an informal "reprofiling," lengthening the terms of its external debt so as to reduce debt servicing requirements. While avoiding the embarrassments of an official rescheduling, it had written a letter of intent to the IMF in April 1989 and had embarked upon a draconian program of adjustment.

Pressures for Adjustment

Like the Turkish economist who compared the Hobart-Foster Mission of 1860 to contemporary IMF missions to her country (Kiray 1990), many of the region's intellectuals and politicians viewed external pressures for adjustment in light of their respective nineteenth-century encounters with imperialism. An Egyptian book jacket depicted the IMF as Superman and replaced the "S" on Clark Kent's uniform with a big red "IMF" in Arabic (Hilāl 1987). The United States had replaced Britain and was perceived as part of the problem. The center of world capitalism was perceived as endangering the sovereignty of the peripheral states that had struggled so long for formal independence and real autonomy. Yet even as Hilāl was writing, a consensus was emerging among economists and policy-makers, including some of the Egyptians he interviewed (World Bank, *World Development Report* 1991: 1–11; "Sisters in the Wood" 1991: 41; Lofgren 1993), favoring a "market-friendly" approach and "rethinking the state" whose sovereignty and bargaining power were so highly valued by the dependency theorists. External pressures or promptings for structural reform and adjustment could not really be dissociated from internal ones in either school of thought. Willy-nilly, markets or social classes, depending on one's perspective, were being integrated into a new world order.

For analytic purposes, however, it is possible to isolate and compare external pressures, just as colonial situations once offered a suitable terrain for comparative inquiry. Superman hovered incessantly over Egypt, Morocco, and Turkey but stayed pretty much out of Algeria's and Tunisia's air space. After 1971, when Algeria joined the IMF, it received periodic visitations like other member countries but did not ask for credits until 1989. One way of assessing the IMF's influence is to compare the amounts of credit it released and the agreements reached in standbys and other arrangements with the respective countries. If money were the sole criterion, the IMF had the most clout over Morocco and Turkey, as figure 2–5 illustrates. It also concluded the most agreements with these two countries, conditioning the credits to various "performance criteria" determined by their respective governments and central banks (see notes to fig. 2–5). These credits really amounted to high-powered money because agreements with the IMF in turn influenced the credit decisions of commercial banks and official creditors, as well as possibilities of loan reschedulings. Morocco and Turkey were more concerned than Egypt about their credit ratings and their access to international financial markets.

Indeed Egypt, falling into arrears, seemed almost beyond the pale of IMF influence during much of the 1980s. Until conditionally relieved of half its debt in 1991, it had little incentive to get good marks from the international financial community. It benefited from a strategic relationship with the United States. To be sure, Turkey enjoyed similar benefits in 1979–80, once Khomeini seized power in Iran and the Soviets invaded Afghanistan. But U.S. support for Turkey took a different form: the IMF committed a record 870 percent of its quota in the standby arrangement of June 1980, and "many executive directors of the Fund felt uneasy about the special flexibility shown to Turkey" (Celâsun and Rodrik, cited by Arıcanlı 1990: 245). Similarly, when Egypt finally signed a standby with the IMF in 1987, one of

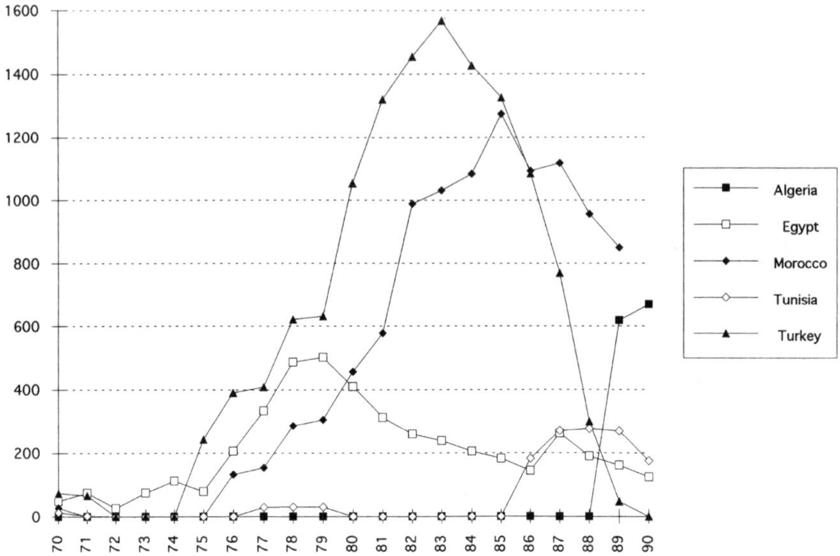

Fig. 2.5. IMF credits, 1970–90 (in $U.S. millions). *Sources:* World Bank, World Debt Tables; de Vries 1987; IMF Annual Reports; IMF Survey; Horton 1990.

IMF Agreements 1976–91

Algeria	SB 5/31-5/30/90 SDR 155.7m
	SB 6/91-3/92 SDR 300m
Egypt	SB 4/20/77 - 4/19/78 SDR 125m (105 drawn)
	EFF 7/78-7/81 SDR 600m (75 drawn)
	SB 5/87 - 11/88 SDR 250m (116 drawn)
	SB 5/91-11/92 SDR 278m
Morocco	CFF 4/76 SDR 57m
	Oil 5/76 SDR 18m
	EEF 10/80-10/83 SDR 147m (canceled 3/81)
	EEF 3/81-10/83 SDR 817m (canceled 4/82)
	SB 4/82-7/83 SDR 281m (canceled 12/85, 10m drawn)
	CFF 4/82 SDR 236m
	SB 8/83-3/85 SDR 300m (246 drawn)
	SB 8/85-2/87 SDR 225m
	CFF 9/85 SDR 115m
	SB 12/86-2/88 SDR 230m (148 drawn)
	SB 8/88-12/89 SDR 210m (140 drawn)
Tunisia	SB 11/4/86 - 11/3/88 SDR 103.65m (91m drawn)
	EEF 7/88-7/91 SDR 207m (70 drawn)
	EEF extended 1 year; credit line raised from SDR 138 to 207m
Turkey	SB 4/78-4/80 SDR 300m (90 drawn), canceled 7/18/79
	SB 7/79-7/80 SDR 250m (230 drawn), canceled 6/17/80
	SB 6/80-6/83 SDR 1250m
	SB 6/83-6/84 SDR 225m (56 drawn)
	SB 4/84-4/85 SDR 225m (169 drawn)

CFF=compensatory financing facility
EFF=extended fund facility
Oil=oil facility
SB=standby arrangement

the Fund's directors, shocked by the easy terms, took the occasion to announce his retirement. Turkey, however, met its obligations.

Strategic rents probably mitigated but certainly did not eliminate IMF pressures on the five countries' economic policies. The "rents" were also quite variable. Until its invasion of Cyprus in 1974, Turkey regularly enjoyed generous access to concessional credits, and workers' remittances, too, helped its current account balances. After 1980, despite periodic standby agreements with the IMF ending only in 1985, Turkey was held on a "long leash" once the military seized power and decisively supported Özal's export-oriented policies: "conditionality should be loose . . . as compared to other places," one connoisseur of IMF programs asserts (Serge Taylor, in Arıcanlı and Rodrik 1990: 269). Was the length of the leash another sign of strategic rents, political pressure placed on the IMF by Turkey's NATO allies? The Turkish leadership still had to retain the confidence of the international financial community and keep increasing its exports to service the debt. In fact new Middle Eastern markets and modest amounts of Arab capital helped as much as any Western "rents" or goodwill to keep Turkey financially afloat in the early 1980s.

Each of the countries enjoyed a variety of strategic rents and alliances by virtue of their common geography. Algeria, though nonaligned, was specially favored by Italy and France. Special relationships mattered the most, however, to the two poorest, most indebted countries, Egypt and Morocco, for they were the most subjected to IMF prescriptions, reform packages, and negotiations for standby agreements. Like Turkey, they enjoyed special relationships with the United States as well as the European Community. Fears of more migrant workers perhaps offered Morocco more leverage than Egypt over Europe. The United States, however, was considerably more committed to Egypt after 1975, once a peace process with Israel could be sustained. Not only did the troop disengagement in the Sinai, Camp David, and the Egyptian-Israeli peace agreement elicit tens of billions of dollars of U.S. commitments to both Egypt and Israel. The United States also took on a strategic commitment to preserving political stability in Egypt far in excess of any commitments to the Moroccan monarchy despite the latter's help in balancing radical forces in the region and in protecting residual American military installations in Morocco. In the 1980s U.S. leverage probably preserved for Egypt a margin of maneuvering with the IMF that Morocco lacked. On occasion King Hassan tried to position himself as another valuable interlocutor between Arabs and Israelis. Morocco also received soft OPEC loans of almost $3 billion to meet the external shocks of 1979–82, but they did not suffice to stave off major crisis and the need for adjustment in 1983.

By the mid-1980s Morocco seemed gradually to be reversing the economic decolonization pursued in the 1960s and the early 1970s. In 1984 Rémy Leveau reported that it had become "one of those countries which has to rely on the aid of international financial organizations to make ends meet each month" and feed the cities (Leveau 1985: 267). "Perhaps after twenty years the insoluble and repetitive nature of Moroccan social and economic problems has made the sovereign react with lassitude, desiring the bureaucracy to fulfill its responsibilities" (266). In 1987 he concluded that the king had "conceded the co-direction of the country's modernization to the IMF and the World Bank" (Leveau 1987: 14), so dependent had Morocco become on their loans and advice and so pervasive their consultations with the various technical ministries. Leveau's observations carry weight because he served in the mid-1960s as a French technical assistant in the Ministry of Interior while preparing an authoritative study on Moroccan politics. Living hand to mouth, the monarchy seemed as dependent on these international bodies as it had been on France in the early days of its independence.

As figure 2–5 illustrates, Morocco continually borrowed from the IMF after 1975. As the accompanying notes indicate, it failed to meet the conditions attached to Extended Fund Facilities negotiated in 1980 and 1981 and consequently received less than one-third of the promised credits. After 1980 the World Bank, too, shifted from project lending to structural adjustment loans, but negotiations for $500 million broke down in 1981. Morocco was then tightly leashed to a succession of standby agreements with the IMF, supplemented by sectoral adjustment loans from the World Bank. In 1985 it was unable to meet the conditions of the September standby, and the agreement was canceled in December after Morocco had received only SDR 10 million. Standbys required Morocco to limit the public budget deficit, the money supply, credit to the central government, and total domestic credit, not to mention external nonconcessional borrowing by the government, including short-term debt. By 1987 the IMF had also clamped down on the government's practice of meeting performance criteria by lagging its payments to domestic suppliers (Horton 1990: 39–47). After five years of belt tightening, the central government's deficit in 1988 was still about 5.5 percent of GDP, at the outer edge of the required performance, but surges in exports had temporarily eliminated the current account deficit (Havrylyshyn et al. 1990: 1.7, 1.14).

Egypt could afford to be less responsive than Morocco to IMF advice despite greater external and domestic indebtedness. In 1975 Egypt's dialogue with the IMF entered its first critical phase since the negotiation of a stabilization program in 1962. With the help of the United States and the Gulf countries, Egypt survived a huge current account deficit in 1975, then finally, after much hesitation, signed a letter of intent to the IMF on 9 May 1976.[4] Efforts to implement it led to the food riots of 17–18 January 1977, protesting price increases. Since some of the Gulf funds hinged on agreement with the IMF, an informal agreement was reached in March 1977, and a letter of intent finally signed in June. It facilitated rescheduling of various official credits of other donor states, while Egypt sidestepped official Paris Club meetings in favor of a Consultative Group of Donor States. A year later a formal agreement was reached with the IMF for an Extended Fund Facility lasting three years, but it did not give rise to any further reschedulings, just an additional $650 million from the Gulf Organization for the Development of Egypt. This consortium of donor Gulf states had provided Egypt with a total of $1,725 million, together with a guarantee of a $250 million syndicated bank loan, since its founding in 1976 (van den Boogaerde 1991: 21). Within four months, between July and November 1978, the agreement with the IMF became a dead letter though it was never officially canceled. Egypt found other ways to meet its pressing needs for imports.

As a result of the Camp David accords of September 1978, the Gulf states stopped their concessional lending, but Western donors took up the slack. As their grants and loans were supplemented by increasing oil revenues, Suez canal tolls, tourist expenditures, and workers' remittances, Egypt was able to dispense with IMF conditions. It began to lag interest payments on some foreign debts in 1980, yet managed to convene its principal non-Arab creditors in Aswan rather than Paris in January 1981 and to collect additional commitments for $3 billion of soft loans and grants. As exports and invisible revenues diminished, relative to imports, the IMF insisted that Egypt reduce the balance-of-payments gap and the government deficit. Instead, Egypt survived the oil price collapse of 1986 by doubling its accumulated arrears to $2 billion and then, as noted earlier, by obtaining an IMF standby and official debt rescheduling in 1987 on relatively easy terms supported by the United States and other Western partners. Finally, in 1991, its participation in the Second Gulf War reduced the external debt by half and eliminated the troublesome military debt to the United States. Failure to service that debt of $7 billion would have required the United States to cut off an annual $2 billion of military and economic assistance.

Its strategic position at the center of the Arab world and in the vortex of the Arab-Israeli conflict gave Egypt greater room than Morocco for maneuvering with Superman. For years it had stalled on economic reforms, implementing IMF "advice" selectively at its own pace, excused by the specter of further food riots. Ultimately, however, Egypt, too, came to terms with the IMF and reached a standby agreement in May 1991, calling for further price rises, particularly for energy; a unified foreign exchange rate; trade liberalization; a major cut in the budget deficit (down from about 20 percent to 9.5 percent of GDP); and curbs on domestic credit and interest rate increases. It unified its foreign exchange rates ahead of schedule and finally seemed committed to the entire package of reforms (*MEED,* 17 and 25 May 1991, 20 September 1991; Lofgren 1993: 408). The write-off of half its debt depended on its commitment, and arrears on existing debt service would no longer be tolerated. The Paris Club even obliged Egypt to put over $3 billion into an escrow account with the Bank of France (*MEED,* 14 June 1991: 19).

Egypt, unlike Morocco, had often managed to skip class in collusion with more permissive parents. Turkey, learning its lessons early, had been released from class in the 1980s. Tunisia never needed much schooling, and Algeria, too, had anticipated IMF reforms in its own austere way, consistently cutting back on imports after 1981. Whether Superman attacked or stayed in the background, the outcomes were broadly similar, once oil prices collapsed and Algeria voluntarily enrolled in 1989 in the IMF's school of macroeconomic discipline. On balance, Superman seems to have exerted the most leverage on Morocco, the least on Algeria and Tunisia, but IMF pressures do not seem to have significantly affected the timing of the respective adjustment programs.

Macroeconomic Constraints on Financial Reform

These programs came in standard packages, known as the Washington consensus (Williamson 1994: 17, 26–28), which facilitate cross-national comparison. The IMF promoted a standard stabilization package to debtor states, coupled with longer-term structural adjustment programs. An Egyptian minister once compared its prescriptions to those doled out by the public hospitals in his country—"iron and arsenic to all, whatever the illness" (Hilāl 1987: 171). The IMF's immediate concern should be to curtail the deficits in the patient country's international balance-of-payments and its domestic government budget. In addition to advocating "realistic" foreign exchange rates to curb balance-of-payments deficits, it tackled budgetary deficits by imposing limits on domestic credit and money creation. Clamping down on the money supply had the virtue not only of controlling inflation but also of discouraging government expenditure, since governments were the biggest beneficiaries of easy money. If they were unable to borrow, they could not spend more unless they taxed more. The IMF therefore encouraged countries to "liberalize" their banking systems by increasing interest rates to realistic levels above prevailing rates of inflation, so as to reduce the demand for credit while encouraging more savings. Usually the IMF also imposed administrative ceilings, monitored every three months during standby agreements, on the amounts of credit to be generated by the entire banking system and the amounts to be borrowed by the respective governments. At times Egypt, Morocco, Turkey, and Tunisia had experienced such surveillance, and Algeria faced similar controls under the new standby agreement signed in June 1991, once credit from the IMF surpassed the country's first tranche (25 percent of its IMF quota). Rigorous credit control seemed an essential first step for curbing the "terrible twin" deficits in government budgets and in balances of payments.

The crescent countries, so heavily indebted domestically as well as internationally, were prime candidates for the IMF workout. A sample of 47 lower-middle-income countries displayed little relationship in 1987 between external debt and domestic credit; instead, a factor analysis revealed four distinct clusters of economic variables on which countries could be scored. First came the basket cases, characterized by heavy burdens of external debt, much of it on concessional terms or at least sheltered from international financial markets. The second factor captured the statism so characteristic of Mediterranean Crescent and other Middle Eastern and European debtors. Not only total domestic credit but also credit to the central government and two measures of the money supply loaded heavily on this factor, but it was only weakly and negatively related to heavy external debt burdens. Third came the export-oriented debtors, loading heavily on exports and debt service burdens and moderately on the foreign long-term debt financed in part by international markets. Fourth, only moderately correlated with the first factor, was a dimension loading heavily upon OPEC concessional lending.

IMF credit curbs are designed by definition to bring the second dimension of indebtedness under control—to limit total domestic credit, credit to the government, and the money supply. Analysis of the cross-section of 1987 debtors suggests that the IMF is right on target. Of the four dimensions of indebtedness, factor 2 was the only one to be significantly correlated with both of the terrible twins.[5] In this single slice of time across countries, the trade and fiscal deficits were unrelated, however much they fed upon one another in individual countries over time, but their independent effects were captured in factor 2. Whatever the actual paths of causality, the twins explained 28 percent of the variation of this factor across countries. Restricting credit could help kill two birds with one stone.

On factor 2, all of the crescent countries ranked among the top 15 in the sample. Even after simultaneously controlling for the twin deficits and per capita income associated with this factor, further analysis pointed to an irreducible crescent effect.[6] Apparently the domestic indebtedness of countries in this part of the world outruns not only economic development but also Third World patterns of deficit financing. State enterprises became addicted to easy credit, especially in Algeria and Egypt—and in Israel, too, for that matter.

There were, however, important variations between the crescent countries. Algeria and Egypt, which had experienced the most state intervention in their respective economies, had accumulated roughly twice as much domestic debt, relative to GDP, as their neighbors. Total domestic credit regularly exceeded Egypt's GDP after 1980 (fig. 2–1), and the central government was borrowing almost half of it, while the state enterprises consumed an additional 20 percent. In Algeria, too, total domestic credit surpassed GDP in 1988. When public sectors are also included as government borrowers, Algeria surpassed not only Egypt but even Communist countries that provided sufficient data to the IMF in 1987. Richards and Waterbury (1990: 192) noted that state-owned enterprises in Algeria and Egypt, like Syria's, accounted for substantially higher proportions of GDP and value-added in manufacturing than Turkey's. Algerian banks allocated virtually all their credit to the central government and public enterprises, and they exceeded Egypt's equivalent lending to hungry public borrowers after 1983. For reasons discussed earlier, each country avoided any binding commitments to the IMF concerning domestic credit ceilings until 1991. They consequently enjoyed more latitude than their neighbors in expanding domestic credit to cover government deficits. On balance, however, the Algerians displayed much greater fiscal discipline than the Egyptians. Algeria's overall government deficit rarely exceeded 10 percent of GDP, whereas Egypt's consistently hovered around 20 percent. Algeria's foreign trade deficit was also kept under control—by the simple expedient of cutting imports when oil revenues declined. Egypt's trade deficit, by contrast, rarely dipped below 20 percent of GNP. Inflation, too, was higher in Egypt until 1990, averaging about 18 percent during the 1980s, compared to Algeria's 9 percent.

The other debtors along the crescent kept tighter control over their domestic credit. The standby agreements with the IMF presumably contributed to hemming it in. Turkey, Morocco, and Tunisia, embarked on sustained programs with the IMF in 1978, 1980, and 1986, respectively. Turkey immediately put on the brakes in 1978, as did Tunisia in 1986. After several false starts, Morocco systematically curbed domestic credit expansion after 1983. Morocco's twin deficits, however, remained relatively high. In the 1980s the trade deficit averaged about 15 percent, compared to 10 percent for Tunisia and 6 for Turkey. The government deficit averaged about 8 percent, compared to 4 percent for each of the other two countries. External pressures to limit domestic credit, reflected also by the number of standby agreements with the IMF, weighed more heavily on Morocco than on Tunisia or Turkey.

Macroeconomic constraints weighed most heavily on Egypt and Morocco until the mid-1980s; subsequently Algeria, too, experienced major shocks. Less constrained, Tunisia and Turkey seemed to be more likely candidates for real financial liberalization. Even so, Turkey had experienced the highest rates of inflation, averaging 52 percent in the 1980s, about triple Egypt's and more than five times as much as the others' rates. From a macroeconomic standpoint, Tunisia seemed best equipped to undergo a structural adjustment of its financial sector, but a balance-of-payments crisis was first needed to push its government onto the path of reform.

Adjustment Packages and Financial Reforms

For the medium and long run, once stabilization is achieved, the IMF and the World Bank promote structural adjustment designed to integrate local financial markets with international ones and to alleviate the need for direct controls on credit, interest rates, and foreign exchange rates. Local commercial banking systems are the prime targets of financial reform, pending the emergence or reactivation of stock exchanges. Structural adjustment is designed to render a banking system more efficient and—here is the political rub—more autonomous with respect to its government. Greater autonomy entails not only an enhanced independent status for central banks but also efforts on their part to deregulate credit allocation by replacing direct administrative controls over commercial banks with impersonal market forces. Structural adjustment also supports closer technical supervision of the banks, requiring them to observe various prudential ratios and to undergo external audits. In the long run each commercial bank is expected to be financially solvent and to allocate credit by standard business criteria. The banking system and its constituent commercial banks must enjoy sufficient autonomy to determine their own credit policies within professional norms. Political interventions in the allocation of credit are ubiquitous, but in the last analysis the individual bank is expected to become autonomous—free to make its own decisions regarding its loan portfolio.

Depending on the severity of macroeconomic disequilibria, however, encouraging commercial banking autonomy could conflict with the goal of keeping interest rates above inflation. To attract savings, interest rates had to be adjusted upward from the negative real rates prevailing throughout the crescent in the 1960s and 1970s. Foreign exchange rates, pegged at artificial levels, also had to be revised so as to stimulate exports and workers' remittances and to discourage unrealistically priced imports. The IMF encouraged these changes in interest and foreign exchange rates, just as it imposed restrictions on domestic credit. Together with measures to liberalize foreign trade, they constituted the core of the IMF's short-term adjustment packages. Usually the short-term objectives could be harmonized. For instance, domestic interest rates might climb so steeply as to endanger exports by overvaluing local currency, but then local authorities could respond by buying up foreign exchange, in effect speculating against their own currency.

However, such measures usually worked against structural reform designed to make the financial system more efficient in the long run. They tended to impede efforts toward greater autonomy and more competition among banks. Greater autonomy entailed not only an enhanced independent status for central banks but also efforts on their part to deregulate credit allocation by replacing direct administrative controls with impersonal market forces. Markets were unlikely to guarantee the "right" interest rates, however, if the banks were truly competitive. Greater competition for clients could easily drive them to exceed the credit ceilings imposed by the IMF. Obviously it made more economic sense to straighten out interest rates and foreign exchange rates before tackling the structural problems—unless the banks remained under government control in some other way.

Defying macroeconomic constraints, Egypt was the first in the crescent to engage in extensive financial reform, under the name Infitah, meaning a general opening of the economy, although in practice the banks and financial institutions were the largest beneficiaries of the famous Investment Law 43 of 1974. Turkey cautiously followed suit after 1980, opening up its domestic banking system to foreign competition in certain sectors. Tunisia encouraged offshore banking and joint venture development banks in the early 1980s but did not embark on major domestic reform until 1986, the same year that Algeria, too, took its first theoretical steps toward reform. Morocco lagged behind the others. In textbook sequencing, it substantially reduced its twin deficits before finally, in 1991, removing the restrictions on credit allocation that had prevented any meaningful competition between commercial banks. Each country's "financial structural adjustment" was supposed to lead to a more autonomous and more competitive banking system, but greater autonomy and competition usually were in conflict, at least in the short run, with restrictions on credit needed to combat the twin deficits and inflation.

Egypt

Egypt put the cart before the horse. Instead of sequencing its reforms in orderly technocratic fashion like Morocco, it immediately opened the doors to foreign and domestic competition. The first entrant, which may have helped to legitimate the idea of opening up Egyptian finance to foreigners, was the Arab International Bank, an offshore consortium that Egypt, Libya, and Oman established by treaty in July 1974. Chase Manhattan entered a year later into a joint venture with the National Bank of Egypt, and First Chicago helped found Misr International Bank. In all, four new banks opened in Egypt in 1975, two in 1976, and four in 1977, including Misr Romanian and the Misr Iran Development Bank as well as joint ventures with mainstream American, British, and French banks. In addition, 13 branches of foreign banks were licensed for dealing in foreign exchange but not Egyptian pounds. Infitah then really picked up in 1978, when Egyptians received permission to set up their own private banks, enjoying the same privileges as the joint ventures. In the following five years, 33 new joint ventures and private commercial banks were founded, together with six investment and business banks and nine additional branches of foreign banks. Cairo in these oil boom years again became a "Klondike on the Nile" reminiscent of the cotton boom in the 1860s (Landes 1958: 69–101).

By 1982 the new commercial banks had captured more than one-quarter of the Big Four public sector commercial banks' deposits. If the new investment banks are also included, the private and joint venture enterprises then held over one-third of the market. The Central Bank of Egypt was clearly overwhelmed by the invasion. Its Banks Inspection Department had stagnated during the Nasser years under the misguided assumption that public sector banks do not need supervision. The new banks raided the public sector for experienced staff, and new Central Bank inspectors tended to be picked up as soon as they were trained, either by the private sector or by petrodollar banks in the Gulf. Consequently the new banks enjoyed wide latitude, whatever the formal regulations. Their free-wheeling activities further complicated Egyptian government efforts to negotiate foreign exchange rates and interest rates with the IMF. Ironically they helped undermine a major government initiative to attract Egyptian remittances into the official banking system of which they were a part.

Foreign exchange rates had been one of the IMF's perennial bugbears. Efforts in 1976 to establish a unified rate of exchange had foundered over Egyptian complaints that the IMF's proposed stabilization fund was inadequate (Hilāl 1987: 142–45). As a temporary measure the government then permitted importers to pay directly for goods with their own foreign exchange rather than hand it over to the Central Bank and later queue for it. In this way importers could directly tap remittances from the Gulf, and the Egyptian workers and professionals paid in hard currencies could circumvent official rates of exchange that undervalued their earnings.

Many of the new joint venture banks and foreign bank branches became intermediaries, working for the importers in lucrative and expanding businesses. A study of the balance sheets of the infitah banks in 1981 showed that they were also draining dollars out of Egypt rather than attracting foreign capital. For every dollar of a foreigner's account placed in Egypt, the investment banks placed $5.65 with their main offices or correspondent banks abroad, while the new commercial banks exported even more, $22.42 for every dollar in a foreigner's account. Over half of Egyptian residents' accounts in foreign exchange hemorrhaged out of the country to the foreign banks (Moore 1986: 642; Al-Bawab 1985: 59). But neither Citibank nor the various joint ventures with Egyptian public sector banks developed much presence among the Egyptians scattered in the Gulf.

Instead, a new breed of young and mobile Egyptian money-changers came into being, led by Sami Ali Hassan. By 1983 he had cornered much of the $4 billion market. The money-changers in turn provided the importers with the necessary cash for their bankers' letters of credit. As differences grew between the official "incentive" rate and the parallel or black market rate for the dollar, some elements in the Egyptian government perceived the market power of the money-changers to be at the root of Egypt's macroeconomic problems. Dr. Mustafa Said, the Minister of the Economy, first tried to coopt Sami Ali Hassan into the system by promising him the same rate of exchange that public sector banks would negotiate with large foreign exchange dealers in the Gulf. When these efforts failed (as the minister knew they would, because Sami needed a premium to survive in the business), he prosecuted him and other black marketeers and, in January 1985, introduced a new system of foreign exchange auctions and allocations. Importers were required to work through the official banking system, but within weeks, as imports became blocked, a combination of pressures ended the government's efforts to control foreign exchange. Much of the pressure came from the infitah banks, in league with the money-changers. The prime minister eventually became the chairman of one of the joint venture banks that was most actively involved with the money-changers.

With and without IMF standbys, however, Egypt moved steadily toward market rates in the 1980s. Awash with foreign exchange in the wake of the Gulf War, in 1991 it finally achieved the unified market rate that the IMF had been urging for 15 years. Indeed, the steady erosion in the value of the Egyptian pound was temporarily reversed, with an influx of foreign exchange seeking attractive interest rates on Egyptian pounds. Some observers in early 1992 thought that the Central Bank of Egypt might even be intervening to keep the pound from appreciating in value. A more expensive pound would make Egyptian exports and tourism less attractive.

Egypt and the IMF had also disagreed over domestic interest rates. A temporary accommodation was reached in 1987, but the ceiling of 11 percent on deposits failed that year to keep up with inflation. It was increased to 11.7 percent in 1989 and finally to 12 percent in 1990, but the IMF still held out for more. Finally, in January 1991, the government liberated most interest rates and the Central Bank of Egypt introduced auctions on treasury bills to define market rates (*MEED*, 11 January 1991: 9). An accord was reached with the IMF in May, once a number of reforms, including those concerning interest rates and foreign exchange, had already been implemented. Interest rates continued to be controversial in Egypt, however. How could industrial and commercial enterprises, public or private, survive in a world of real positive interest rates? Some observers raised specters of massive bankruptcies and unemployment (Shafe'i 1991: 30–32). Nevertheless the Central Bank's discount rate rose above 20 percent in 1992, endangering many enterprises and some banks. By official calculations the discount rate then exceeded the annual rate of inflation.

Egypt was poised after the Gulf War to undertake a second infitah. An entire set of new laws was being enacted, including a new banking law. Ironically one major issue at stake, delaying passage of the law, concerned the fate of the multitude of banks launched under the first infitah. Many of them, to be discussed in chapter 7, were bankrupt, but should the Central Bank have the right to oblige them to merge or be dissolved? Also at issue were the powers of the Central Bank and the authority of its governor. Relative autonomy for the banking system entailed an independent governor, appointed for a fixed term, but recent governors had rarely served lengthy terms, tending instead to be reshuffled with other cabinet ministers. Could a Central Bank governor be more independent than a prime minister in Mubarak's presidential regime? As to the bank's powers, how much control could it legitimately exercise over Egypt's banking personnel? Ought it, as one draft of the law stipulated, vet the appointments of all senior personnel—the hundreds employed at the general manager level throughout

Egypt's 99 banks? The scandal of the Bank of Commerce and Credit International (BCCI), which left its Egyptian joint venture in limbo after July 1991, had perhaps inspired this provision against crooks and criminals, but some of the bankers questioned the Central Bank's ability to make the necessary judgments.

The deliberations reflected Egypt's remarkable progress since 1975 toward a more competitive banking system. But the rise of interest rates to real levels, coupled with more effective supervision of the banking system, augured a radical shakedown of the system. The first infitah had made little economic sense. Few of the new banks would be viable once Egypt had made the necessary macroeconomic adjustments. They had meanwhile compounded the difficulties of macro-level management and sabotaged government reforms.

Turkey

Like Egypt after 1974, Turkey deliberately opened up its economy to international market forces after suffering a series of balance-of-payments crises in the late 1970s. But Turkey already enjoyed an impressive array of public and private sector banks, tightly controlled by the Central Bank. All but four of them were exclusively Turkish. The Imperial Ottoman Bank, founded in 1863 as the principal outpost of Western finance capital, discreetly survived, no longer "Imperial," under joint French and Turkish management, but most of the other Western banks vanished in the depths of the Great Depression. The Germans were finally packed off in 1945, while the Soviets departed in 1951. By the 1960s it seems that the only foreign banks to survive Turkey's rudely statist economic environment, apart from the Osmanli Bankası, were the branches of Banco di Roma, founded in 1911, and of Holantse Bank, founded in 1921. In 1964 the Turkish authorities admitted the Bank of America's entry into Turkey in the form of a joint venture with İş Bankası in which the foreign interests contributed 24 percent of the capital. But the Bank of America subsequently sold out, and Dişbank became one of many Turkish private sector commercial banks.

As in Sadat's Egypt, a joint venture with Libya finally broke the ice, in 1977. The Arap-Türk Bankası became the first bank in modern Turkish history to be established with a majority of foreign capital.[7] Led by Citibank in 1981, a number of branches of foreign banks—including the infamous BCCI—were then permitted to join the Dutch and the Italians, and other joint ventures with foreign banks also obtained licenses. But the effects were not the same as in Egypt because the Turkish authorities were used to supervising private banks. The major impact, as the authorities had sought, was to transfer new financial technology to the Turkish sectors. Foreign trade finance, initially a gold mine for Citibank and other foreign banks that enjoyed easy access to foreign exchange, was a case in point. Foreign exchange shortages diminished as Turkey's exports dramatically increased, encouraged by devaluations of the Turkish lire, and Turkish banks hired away bankers trained in the new technologies (mainly by Citibank). As foreign trade expanded, only Turkish banks had the capital base sufficient to finance large loans. Consequently the foreigners lost market share to a number of established Turkish private sector banks (including Diş) which had acquired the Citibank techniques.

Crafted by Turgut Özal, Turkey's reforms were hailed by the World Bank as an exemplary effort to overcome the twin traps of external indebtedness and internal budgetary deficits in which much of the Third World is caught. Financial reform was built on a successful switch from an industrial policy of import substitution to one of export-oriented growth. Though Turkey never completed its escape, it seemed much more successful than Egypt in the 1980s in repaying its debts and envisaging a viable strategy of debt management. Indeed, one group of World Bank experts observed at the end of the decade that "Turkey is one of a half dozen countries, at most, that are on the path to achieving this" (World Bank 1990: xv).

Nevertheless, in Turkey's inflationary environment the reforms initially led to financial chaos. When in July 1981 the Central Bank of the Republic of Turkey liberated interest rates on time deposits in an effort to mobilize savings, the large commercial banks acted like a cartel to limit their rise. Since real interest rates remained negative as inflation soared in 1981, informal intermediaries—the brokerage houses—devised new financial instruments promising more competitive rates. In June 1982 the largest of them collapsed. The military government stopped the financial reforms, and Turgut Özal, the architect of Turkey's economic reforms, resigned along with the finance minister. A year later, however, Özal would attain political power, backed by an unlikely Center-Right coalition of big business, secular liberal politicians, and Islamists detached from Erbaken's extreme right-wing National Salvation Party.

Turkey's efforts to foster a more competitive climate, to regulate the financial sector by market forces rather than direct administrative controls of the Treasury and the Central Bank, had floundered on oligopolistic structures inherited from previous regimes. Since 1950, when Turkey moved from a one-party regime to competitive politics and an ostensibly liberal economy, massive private sector combines—Koç and Sabancı, to mention the two largest holdings—had emerged in the shadows of Atatürk's old public sector enterprises. The Çukarova and Sabancı groups commanded two of largest commercial deposit banks and could easily manipulate any deregulated markets with the acquiescence of Ziraat Bankası, Turkey's giant public sector bank, and İş Bankası, technically a private sector bank. The Big Four virtually guaranteed that deposits would remain cheap, reimbursed at levels well below inflation. Their market power—commanding two-thirds of the funds deposited in Turkey's commercial banking system—also ensured that companies in their respective groups would have access to cheap funds. Commercial bank deposits, in fact, were virtually the sole source of finance for the Turkish economy apart from direct Central Bank financing.

In the wake of the June 1982 crisis, the Turkish authorities reinstituted direct controls over interest rates, and the Central Bank engaged in even more direct regulative activity than in the period prior to 1980. With Özal's return to power at the end of 1983, however, the stage was set for further reform of the financial system. Since the commercial banks were, and are—in the words of the Central Bank's research director—"in the core of the Turkish financial system" (Ersel and Sak 1988: 2), they were the object of a new banking law passed on 25 April 1985. The banks would be subjected to more rigorous monitoring by the government, the Central Bank, and various public auditors, and they were expected to improve their capital structure and to diversify their ownership and loan portfolios, so as to be more independent of the various family holdings. A young generation of American-trained "princes" (recruited through the Özal family) was mandated—with mixed results—to restructure various public sector banks.

Credit allocation was somewhat liberalized. From 1983 to 1986 the Central Bank reduced its direct financing of total credits to the economy from 49 percent to 15 percent, before ceasing virtually all intervention in 1989 (Central Bank of the Republic of Turkey, *Annual Report* 1989: 36). Instead of receiving discounted funds directly from the Central Bank, the commercial banks were encouraged to lend and borrow on the interbank market, established in 1986. Selective credits decreased from 42 percent of the total in 1983 to 23 percent in 1987, and the share of credits to public sector companies accorded by the entire banking system dramatically diminished (Coşan and Ersel 1987: 44, table IV.3). Yet by 1987 the private sector was also experiencing a credit squeeze, caused in part by the government's continued need to finance its budget deficit and its greater use of new financial instruments, especially treasury bills and public sector securities (Ersel and Sak 1988: 7). Though interest rates were deregulated, the Central Bank again acted to reduce them in late 1988, when the banks bid up rates on deposits to precarious heights well above the rate of inflation. They then sank back to negative real rates in 1989 and 1990. Turkey did not labor under the huge cloud of domestic debt that threatened to bankrupt firms in Egypt and Algeria, but high inflation rates posed special problems. At a meeting of financial policy-makers held by the World Bank in Istanbul, "participants generally acknowledged that it is extremely difficult for a financial system to function efficiently when inflation rates move significantly beyond 20 percent per annum and stay there for a considerable period of time" (Roe et al. 1989: 10). Interest rates and tax incentives rarely kept up with the "inflation tax" that discouraged savers and depositors away from domestic financial institutions. As the private sector was crowded out, other sources of funding, such as foreign direct investment, became all the more important.

Like Egypt, Turkey offered incentives to foreign investors, including Turkish workers in Europe. Through the Dresdener scheme the Turkish banking system mopped up remittances far more effectively than the Egyptian banks, though informal Egyptian markets attracted higher overall totals, reflecting a larger overseas labor force. The Turks had attracted $5 billion in foreign direct investment by 1990 (TÜSİAD 1990: 79), exceeding Egypt's $3.8 billion total of law 43 investments at prevailing exchange rates (Misr Development Bank 1990). The Turks also moved more quickly to develop alternative capital markets to supplement the banking system's finance capital.

Turkey became the first crescent country to reorganize its stock exchange. Legally established in 1981, the Capital Markets Board took shape under the leadership of a Wharton School (University of Pennsylvania) professor to promote privatization. Reopened in 1986, the Istanbul Stock Exchange surged in 1990, the index of shares increasing from 701.4 to 5384.5 during the year ending July 31, 1990, as the daily volume of shares traded soared from 2.3 billion to over 50 billion Turkish lire; better still, the market survived a technical "correction" precipitated by Iraq's invasion of Kuwait on 2 August. Inflation, dysfunctional for most financial development, may have helped the market along, for people had few alternatives for keeping up with inflation.

The stock market, however, remained a marginal source of finance capital. The private sector still had to rely largely on the commercial banking system, plagued by continuing inflation in the early 1990s. Under the stoic leadership of Governor Rüşdü Saracoğlu, the Central Bank struggled to bring inflation under control by controlling its own balance sheet, but its nominal autonomy, supported by Özal, was under pressure as the president's authority waned, his Motherland Party suffering defeat in the 1991 elections.

Tunisia

Of the countries under review, Tunisia was in the strongest position to embark on structural reform. For many years it had kept inflation and the twin deficits under control. Before its balance-of-payments crisis, when hard currency reserves covered less than three weeks of imports (Khelil, 17 January 1989: 5), it had been gradually increasing interest rates, though not quite enough to offset inflation. It had also allowed the Tunisian dinar to slide in value against hard currencies so as to make Tunisian exports more competitive and to attract remittances from Tunisian workers in Europe. Several months before concluding its standby agreement of 4 November 1986 with the IMF, the Tunisian government had devalued the dinar by almost 10 percent. When it undertook adjustment, it was able simultaneously to control its deficits and undertake a major reform of the financial system. Its banking system, however, was more like Egypt's than like Turkey's. Whether public or private sector, the banks had been transformed into virtual loan disbursement agencies of the Central Bank, whereas Turkey's had preserved a semblance of autonomy. Tunisia determined, too, to avoid the excesses of Egyptian-style infitah. While as interested as Egypt in attracting foreign investment, especially from the Arab Gulf states, it kept new banks under tight surveillance.

Prior to the crisis of 1986 Tunisia had begun to liberalize its banking system. For instance, in 1981 the limits for lending without prior Central Bank approval were increased for most types of loans from TD 150,000 to 600,000, and some were further raised to TD 1 million in 1985, rendering the banks responsible for most of their credit decisions. Tunisia had also tried to attract foreign finance capital. The civil war in Lebanon raised hopes in some Tunisian policy circles that the country might open its economy and turn Tunis into another Beirut. Offshore banking was encouraged in the late 1970s, but it labored under too many restrictions to flourish. In the early 1980s joint venture development banks were established with Saudi Arabia, Kuwait, the United Arab Emirates, and Qatar. Commercial banking, however, remained exclusively in Tunisian hands until an amendment to the legislation on offshore banks in 1985 enabled them to take up to 1.5 percent of the deposits denominated in Tunisian dinars. Until 1990, when Citibank received a license to operate onshore as well as offshore, no newcomers were permitted to enter the system. Structural reform involved existing actors, not, as in Egypt, an invasion of new ones.

Within weeks of receiving the IMF standby, the government pushed ahead with financial reform. The Central Bank proceeded to lift the ceilings on interest rates for time deposits. In other words, banks were now encouraged to compete for deposits. This initial effort at partial liberalization, however, had the same effect as a similar Turkish experiment seven years earlier. The banks simply colluded and kept interest rates below the inflation rate. Despite a change of regime from Bourguiba to Ben Ali, however, the Banque Centrale de Tunisie persevered with liberalization. By the end of 1988 most of the reforms were in place.

Insisting that the "dynamization" of Tunisian financial markets occupied a "choice position" in the country's strategy of structural adjustment of the economy, the Central Bank governor, Ismail Khelil, spelled out the "four essential pillars" on which it rested:

> (1) improving the system of monetary regulation by reducing restrictions to the normal functioning of the market;
> (2) reinforcement of integration within the financial market by attenuating the segmentation and compartmentalization demarcating the domains of activity of its institutions;
> (3) developing the role of the stock exchange as the favored framework for mobilizing savings and financing investments;
> (4) progressive consolidation of the liberalization of foreign exchange and capital controls to facilitate the emergence of Tunis as a regional financial center. (Khelil 1988: 3)

The first pillar was really the foundation of the edifice. Removing "restrictions to the normal functioning of the market" meant not only removing or altering specific banking regulations but also trying to revive the players, the banks themselves, and inciting them to be more competitive and more capable of making their own credit decisions. "Surprising some by the ambition and rapidity" (Khelil 1988: 3) of his moves, the governor implemented the core of his strategy in 1987. After partially deregulating interest rates in January, he lifted all requirements for prior Central Bank approval of loans by the end of the year (just six weeks after Ben Ali assumed the presidency). Banks instead were required to respect certain limits on lending to individual clients. They were ordered to diversify their portfolios, raising the possibility that inefficient enterprises, whether private or public, might be caught in a credit squeeze. Credit allocation was to become more efficient, driven by bankers competing for safer, more diversified, and more profitable loan portfolios. In the words of the Central Bank governor, the reforms "incitera les agents économoqies et notamment les banques à faire le meilleur choix des opportunités de financement et surtout à s'abstenir de s'engager dans des opérations à risques démesurés" [will give economic actors, notably the banks, incentives to make the best financial choices and above all to abstain from excessively risky operations] (Khelil, 1988, p. 5). In theory, markets, not administrators, would now allocate and ration most credit to local businesses; in practice, interest rates were kept at 2 percent to 4 percent above inflation. Various banking ratios continued to be enforced, such as the requirement that 25 percent of a bank's deposits be invested in government bonds of various sorts, but all regulation became a posteriori after December 23, 1987.

Central Bank discounting facilities were discontinued—as had been promised the IMF—except for lending to certain priority sectors (agriculture and export finance), and banks in need of liquidity were dispatched instead, starting January 1, 1988, to a reorganized money market. The Central Bank continued to set the market's interest rate, but the governor announced in May 1989 that variable rates based on supply and demand would soon be introduced. "However, in a first stage, considering the indebted situation of the banks, we will try to satisfy liquidity needs by combining fixed rates with those determined by a Dutch auction" (Khelil 1989: 6). Though some of the banks were having difficulty keeping up with the governor's pace of reform, Tunisia's new money market was replacing the Central Bank's direct controls. Short-term treasury bills with attractive yields were introduced to the public.

Some progress was also made on Khelil's second pillar: breaking down artificial and legal distinctions between commercial, development, and offshore banks. Ideally "every financial institution will have three windows, one for commercial activity, a second for development and a third for offshore activities. It may choose voluntarily to specialize in one of these activities just as it can opt for a harmonious evolution of operations in all banking domains" (Khelil 1989: 13). In practice, however, integration was unlikely to have a major impact upon the principal players, the commercial banks. One commercial banker observed that his (major private sector) bank would be less inclined to increase its loans to enterprises to enable them to pay off their investment bankers if the latter were also commercial competitors. Ironically, though integration was supposed to increase competition, one result was a merger between a large commercial bank and an agricultural development bank to form the Banque Nationale Agricole, enjoying a virtual monopoly in the agricultural sector.

Plans were also underway to modernize Tunis's small stock exchange. This third pillar, however, was also of limited significance because enterprises were generally unwilling to disclose adequate financial information about themselves even if they were willing to raise capital from the general public. In societies like Tunisia, where public accounting standards lacked credibility, stock markets could not replace banks and governments as the principal sources of capital. Even in financially more open and sophisticated economies, bankers retain their function of financial intermediation to the extent that borrowers insist on confidentiality. In Tunisia financial reporting conveyed little information despite much talk about *transparance.* So great was the atmosphere of suspicion that one prominent accountant promptly expelled me from his office, with advice to see a colleague in Paris, when innocently queried about local accounting conventions.

The reform process continued at a more relaxed pace after Khelil's departure from the Central Bank in late 1989. A secondary market for treasury bills developed, and there were plans in 1991 to retire various kinds of government bonds that the banks had been required to purchase at below-market yields. After the reverberations of the Gulf War subsided in Tunisia, the World Bank concluded an agreement for a structural adjustment loan to accelerate Tunisia's economic and financial reforms. Requirements that the banks subsidize loans for agriculture, exporters, and small enterprises were to be phased out. A real foreign exchange market, eliminating a commercial bank's obligation to go through the Central Bank, was under discussion. Finally, in late 1992, the pace of reform quickened. Convertibility of the Tunisian dinar was again under discussion, signifying that the domestic reform package was being successfully implemented. President Ben Ali announced the decision on December 27, 1992, to accelerate Tunisia's timetable toward full convertibility. "The convertibility of the dinar has not been dictated by the IMF, it's the result of Tunisia's success," IMF managing director Paul Camdessus explained (*MEED,* 15 January 1993: 30). Tunisia's fourth pillar was apparently being erected in record time. As a World Bank consultant explained, "The first principle of reform sequencing . . . is that international capital controls should only be lifted after the domestic financial market has been reformed and domestic interest rates have been raised" (Edwards 1987: 10). Capital controls would not have prevented capital flight from an economy depending largely on tourism and workers' remittances from Europe (Karm 1989), but keeping capital in Tunisia depended on competitive interest rates and a relatively stable dinar propped up by export-led growth.

By the early 1990s Tunisia, spurred by the specter of capital flight, seemed to be catching up with Turkey, which had initiated its cleanup of the commercial banking system in 1986 with a structural adjustment loan from the World Bank. Tunisia received its first adjustment loan for the financial sector in 1991. With less inflation, and without Turkey's entrenched private oligopolies, Tunisia perhaps stood better chances of fostering a more competitive banking system. But uncompetitive public sector banks and enterprises posed major limitations. As in Egypt and Turkey, credit ceilings (still imposed in 1992 under the IMF's extended credit facility) threatened many undercapitalized enterprises. The Turkish palliative of a more active stock exchange, also under study in Tunisia, seemed even less promising because there were few companies to trade on the tiny exchange. Public trading of shares also presupposed a certain transparency of economic information that seemed less congenial to the Tunisian business establishment than to its larger and more mature Turkish or Egyptian counterparts.

Algeria

Financial reform in Algeria had a surrealistic tone, so far removed were its "banks" from any commercial realities pertaining to banking. The radical transformation of economic structures that Algeria undertook between 1986 and 1990 appeared to be mainly a legal exercise. The first piece of legislation, the Banking Law of July 1986, was probably decided upon because the banks seemed the least significant actors on the Algerian economic stage, hence the least controversial target for reform. The law was not implemented because the banks could not be encouraged to play a role in credit allocation as long as the rest of the rigid system of state enterprises remained intact. Algeria could not act like Tunisia in 1986, giving priority to financial reform to stimulate other changes, in response to a balance-of-payments crisis.

Reflecting its nineteenth-century legacy, followed by years of state socialism, the Algerian banking system was far less developed than those of the other crescent countries. A huge, largely informal cash economy escaped the banks. It exceeded Egypt's during the oil boom and then spiraled upward after 1985 as supplies of real goods diminished. Figure 2–6 compares the volumes of Algerian currency as a percentage of GDP with those of the other crescent countries. By this measure Algeria's supply was double Egypt's by the end of the 1980s. Egypt's supply was shrinking to the levels of the more closely managed Moroccan and Tunisian banking systems, while they were still perhaps a generation behind Turkey's.

Distortions were so great in Algeria that any reform of interest rates in the absence of other reforms was virtually meaningless. Until they were restructured in 1990, the public enterprises and their banks were engaged in paper transactions, rolling over loans and arrears in interest payments. In

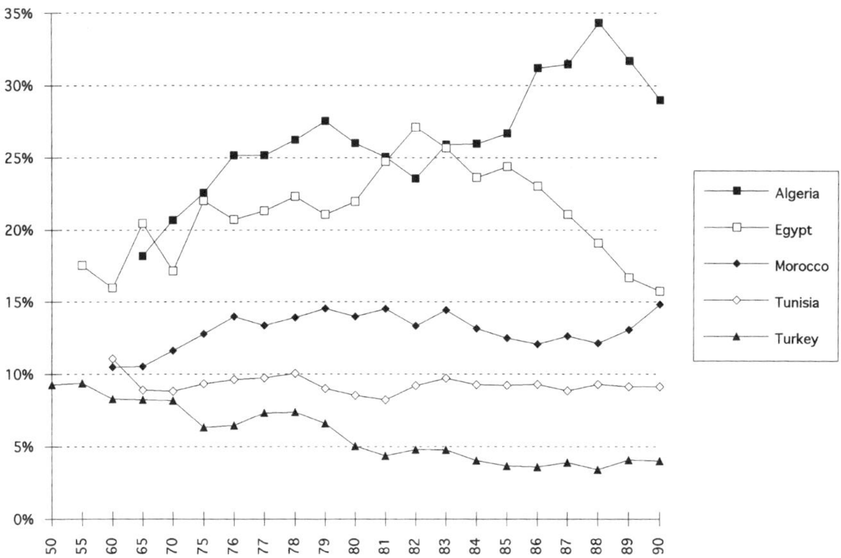

Fig. 2.6 Cash as a percentage of GDP, 1950–90. *Source:* IMF, International Financial Statistics.

1989 the Central Bank raised the discount rate from 5 to 7 percent, but inflation was running at least 12 percent and doubled the following year, when the discount rate was raised from 10.5 to 11.5 percent. As a series of beleaguered governments tried to cope with the debt crisis, it seemed improbable that Algeria could, as planned, bring its interest rates up to real levels by the end of 1992.

Similarly, Algeria confronted the greatest distortions in its foreign exchange rate. By the late 1980s unofficial parallel markets were selling foreign currency for Algerian dinars at up to six times their official value. Steady devaluations reduced the differential to less than two by the end of 1991, risking ever greater inflation rates yet without encouraging nontraditional exports, official remittances, or foreign investment. The other crescent countries had adjusted their exchange rates more readily in the 1980s. Once they shifted to policies of export-led growth, they had pegged their respective currencies to baskets of foreign currencies aligned with those of their competitors for European markets.

Enmired in political as well as economic crises after 1988, Algeria attempted to restructure the banks and the public enterprises simultaneously. "Participation funds" were established in the summer of 1988 as state holding companies. Each of the eight funds was concentrated on a particular set of economic sectors, but each enterprise of a given sector was also to be partly "owned" by two other funds so as to diversify their respective portfolios. In 1989 and 1990 most of the enterprises were set loose from their mother ministries and rendered "autonomous," that is, handed over to their respective funds. With government ministers playing the role of shareholders, the participation funds supervised annual meetings of the boards of directors of the enterprises. The funds in turn held their annual assemblies of shareholders, represented by an assemblage of government ministers.

The idea behind the reform was to encourage each enterprise to act like an autonomous, profit-seeking business. The banks, also liberated in theory from the Ministry of Finance, were then to take responsibility for allocating credit to enterprises as they saw fit, rather than carry out orders, as in the past, to serve their designated clients. To strengthen their hand, a Law of Money and Credit was passed in 1990 that freed the central bank from the control of the Ministry of Finance and the Treasury. On paper the Banque d'Algérie became one of the world's most powerful central banks, responsible for the money supply and for maintaining credit ceilings. In this way the IMF had some assurance in 1991, when a new standby was signed, that Algeria's performance criteria could be respected.

The reforms augured radical change from a rigidly managed state economy to a more liberal and competitive one. But, in the words of an astute Algerian commentator, "It is striking to observe that the so-called economic reforms are carried out with the same formalism and dogmatism which inspired the *gestion socialiste des entreprises* and the Agrarian Revolution of yesteryear" (Addi 1991: 120). The freeing of the public enterprises repeated the 1982 attempt to financially restructure them and encourage them to be independent profit centers, although only 172 out of 480 had become profitable as a result of the earlier reform (Brahimi 1991: 291). The new participation funds had little staff or expertise, and investment decisions, so far as any funds were available, were still the responsibility of the financial experts in the planning ministry (now relegated to the prime minister's office as a national commission but not downsized). "The year 1989 marked the beginning of implementing a new system of economic planning," the annual report of one of the funds asserted.

Algeria's five commercial banks in theory could now choose their clients and base their credit decisions on economic criteria, subject to the Banque d'Algérie's credit ceilings. But in practice they each insisted on keeping their good clients from running off to other banks while refusing each other's less solvent ones. Any competition simply augmented the informal cash economy, which had expanded from 40 percent in 1988 to more than 50 percent of the M1 money supply in 1990, with no signs of diminishing in early 1992. An enterprise seeking a loan from a second bank would have to pay it off in cash lest the first bank get wind of the deal and insist on its loans being paid off. Free in theory to manage their banks, directors were reshuffled much as before with changing political currents. The directors general of two of the major banks lost their jobs for trying to exercise their legal right to stand up to the Treasury. The major bulwark of autonomy, the governor of the Banque d'Algérie, risked losing his job long before completing his six-year term, once the military made his patron, President Chadly Benjedid, resign on 12 January 1992. The governor finally "resigned" on 20 July, one day after Prime Minister Belaid Abdesselam constituted his new government, in which he concentrated "complete power in the economic sphere" (*MEED,* 31 July 1992: 8). He, in turn, was replaced in 1994 by Algeria's new president, retired General Lamine Zeroual, and Algeria then embarked on another round of negotiations with the IMF, leading finally to a substantial devaluation of the Algerian dinar and a formal rescheduling of international debt in the Paris Club. Algeria persisted in its strategy of informal debt "reprofiling" in bilateral negotiations with various creditors until May 1995, when it finally consented to a formal rescheduling of private commercial bank debts through the London Club. (*MEED,* 26 May 1995: 16).

The banks were meanwhile paralyzed by their nonperforming portfolios, estimated at 138 billion dinars by the end of 1990 and still increasing a year later. By one central bank estimate, inflation was then running at an annual 60 percent, raising the specter of hyperinflation. Algeria invited international banks to establish local presences, but political events disrupted plans for establishing European and American joint venture commercial banks. In late 1991, however, an Islamic bank supported by the Saudi Al Baraka Group opened its doors for business and was planning new branches in some of the major cities. Other joint banking ventures and private banks were being planned in 1992, and the First International Bank of Algeria, Algeria's first fully privately owned bank, announced that it would offer Islamic banking services (*MEED,* 9 July 1993).

Morocco

Though engaged in continual negotiations with the IMF over credit ceilings, Morocco finally went ahead in 1991, despite the Gulf crisis, with a series of measures to "liberalize" the banking system. In his Throne Speech of 3 March 1991, commemorating the thirtieth anniversary of his reign, King

Hassan II explained that "some may consider that this reform experienced delays incompatible with the driver's role to be assumed by the private sector in the economic and social development of our country . . . but it was necessary first to establish the basic [macroeconomic] equilibria" (*Le Matin du Sahara,* 21 March 1991). In careful sequencing, Morocco had brought its twin deficits under control before launching its reform of financial structures. Graced, like Egypt, by IMF and Arab windfalls from the Gulf War, Morocco was then able in 1991 simultaneously to control its credit ceilings and deregulate interest rates, up to a point.

Unlike Tunisia, which was less heavily encumbered by central government debt, Morocco could not altogether replace direct controls on credit allocation by indirect control through a money market. IMF suggestions for controlling credit by liberating interest rates were rejected in favor of a complex formula that determined interest rate ceilings while removing restrictions on the quantities of credit each bank could allocate. The decision on 1 January 1991 to remove these restrictions was nevertheless a major step toward a more efficient and competitive banking system. A new banking law was also in the works.

Since independence in 1956, the system had enjoyed relative autonomy, like Turkey's, and had been even less burdened by the debt of deadbeat state enterprises. Autonomy was assured for years by a central bank governor who was a member of the royal family. But credit restrictions imposed in 1976 as a result of a boom in phosphate prices had foreclosed any meaningful competition among banks for new clients. Faced with IMF demands in 1983 for higher interest rates, the Bank al-Maghrib (Morocco's central bank) had raised the interest rate ceiling on deposits from 6.5 percent in 1984 to 8 percent in 1985 and a steady 8.5 percent thereafter, to stay comfortably above the rate of inflation. It also protected the banks' margins but carefully restricted their new loans to existing market shares. Over the years the eight large public and private sector banks had steadily enlarged their market shares, not against each other but at the expense of six smaller ones. Because of the rigid credit rationing, as well as better insulation by the Bank al-Maghrib from political pressures to grant loans, they seemed in better shape than most other major banks of the crescent countries in 1991 to survive the rigors of competition.

When credit restrictions were lifted, however, the banks raced after new clients and collectively expanded their credits by 32 percent, far surpassing the 10 percent increase planned by the monetary authorities. Indirect controls were not working. Competition among the banks for deposits heated up in anticipation of the lifting of credit restrictions, but a gentleman's agreement brokered by the Groupement Professionnel des Banques du Maroc (GPBM) limited their rise. Informal caps on deposits in turn limited the rise of interest rates on loans; moreover, borrowers seemed less concerned with interest rates than with getting loans, whatever the price.

Higher interest rates did not keep the aggregate money supply under control as the IMF had wanted. Originally interest rates were to have been indexed on the price of treasury bills fixed by weekly auctions (as in Egypt). The government changed the index, however, once it became apparent that interest rates would have increased too much to be acceptable to the business community. The index was instead based on the average of various short-term deposit rates that the GPBM informally negotiated. The Bank al-Maghrib, however, retained an arsenal of instruments to enforce the credit ceilings imposed by the 1992 standby agreement with the IMF. It could increase the banks' reserve requirements, toughen the various ratios of financial performance required of each bank, and further reduce its rediscounting facilities. It also supervised reserve requirements and other regulations on tighter timetables. As an important sign of confidence, the World Bank granted Morocco a structural adjustment loan in June 1991, similar to those accorded Turkey in 1986 and Tunisia in 1991.

Success depended on how tightly the government could rein in its budget deficit, reduced in 1992 to little more than 1 percent. Financial liberalization could proceed if the commercial banks could be relieved of some of their heavy burden of government debt. In 1991 banks were still required to hold 32 percent of their sight deposits in treasury bonds, which yielded only 4.5 percent, and they were saddled with other forms of subsidized lending for an additional 13 percent of their deposits, as well as reserve requirements of 20 percent. If the government deficit remained under control, the burden of the bonds and other credit subsidies could be eased and the Treasury could raise funds on a money market without crowding out the private sector. But until Morocco instituted a money market, including a secondary market for government securities, the banks and the Treasury remained in a tug of war—the Treasury auctioning off treasury bills while the banks, offering slightly lower rates on time deposits, insisted on compensating balances for aspiring borrowers.

While the tug-of-war continued, competition between the banks had an unreal quality. They were free to lend only about one-third of their sight deposits at market rates but these were interest-free and outnumbered time deposits by more than 2 to 1. The system guaranteed them comfortable margins. Lending rates could be up to one-third above a weighted average cost of time deposits, but there was not much incentive for banks to compete publicly and advertise their interest rates as long as sight deposits were so much more profitable. Bidding wars over interest rates perhaps reflected personal rivalries between two leading Moroccan bankers more than any real competition for new markets. Banking remained a closely guarded cartel.

Comparative Perspectives

Under the pressures of adjustment, the states of the debt crescent all embarked upon the reform of their banking systems, promising them greater autonomy and giving lip service, at least, to greater competition for the sake of greater financial efficiency. One crude but readily available measure of intermediation, if not overall efficiency, was the banks' ability to attract time deposits, savings deposits, and foreign currency accounts. Despite a lower savings rate, Egypt seemed well ahead of the other countries. Under the infitah, time deposits as a percentage of GDP dramatically increased. To be sure, half of the increase was foreign exchange channeled out of the country by the foreign banks, but even so, time deposits in Egyptian pounds had increased substantially, as figure 2–7 illustrates for the years 1984 through 1989. In Turkey, with similar proportions of foreign currencies, banks attracted fewer local time deposits, despite higher domestic savings rates, because of higher rates of inflation. In the early 1980s, however, they improved their performance. Within the Maghreb, the Tunisians clearly outperformed their neighbors. Reforms were bringing Tunisian time deposits up to Egyptian levels.

Each country had embarked upon reform from a different starting point. Evidently Algeria and Egypt, the countries that had earlier practiced the greatest degree of state socialism, were the most difficult to reform. Their financial systems were the least autonomous and least competitive in the 1960s, and any long-term structural changes involved reestablishing the authority of the central bank as well as developing new markets and more commercially minded enterprises. Tunisia, too, had a longer road to travel than Morocco or Turkey, where banking oligopolies had preserved a greater measure of autonomy after independence.

Figures 2–8 and 2–9 offer crude indicators of the roads the countries have traveled toward greater autonomy and competitiveness. Figure 2–8 presents the percentages of commercial bank deposits acquired over the years by private sector and joint venture banks. The percentages convey a partial picture of each country's progress toward greater autonomy, although the private sector may be as tightly controlled by government directives

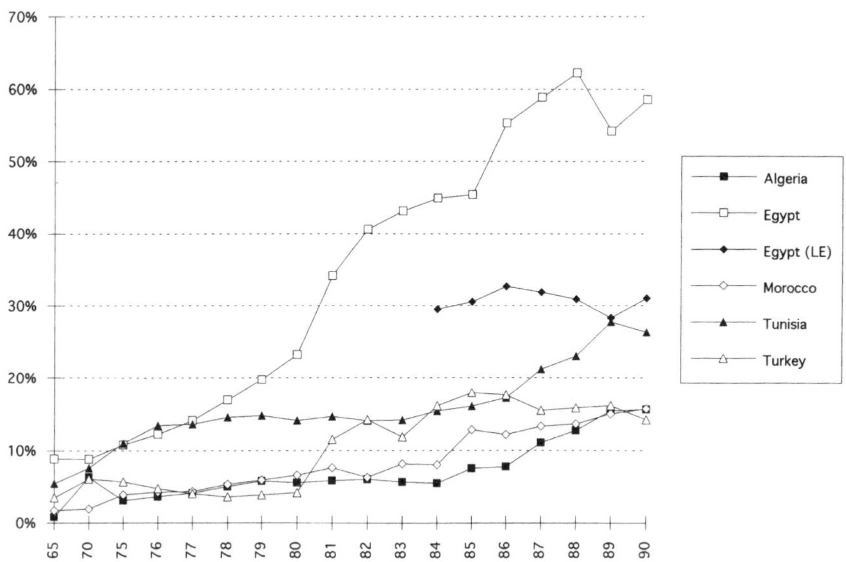

Fig. 2.7. Time, savings, and foreign currency deposits as a percentage of GDP, 1965–90. *Source:* IMF, International Financial Statistics.

as are public sector banks. Turkey and Morocco support the largest private sectors. Egypt's private sector share was catching up with Tunisia's in the early 1980s but then stagnated, while Tunisia's steadily advanced.

Assuming relatively homogeneous national markets, the concentration of commercial bank deposits within each system illustrates trends toward greater or lesser competition (fig. 2–9).[8] Egypt started in the mid-seventies with concentration ratios of over 30 percent, reflecting the monopoly of a few public sector banks. In the late 1970s and 1980s, however, the Egyptian system became highly competitive. Indeed, the commercial banking systems of Egypt and Tunisia appeared to be almost as competitive as Turkey's in the eighties: they displayed relatively low levels of industrial concentration. Morocco's system became more concentrated, however, and Algeria's remained almost as highly concentrated in 1990 as Egypt's in the mid-seventies, before the door was opened to joint ventures with foreign banks and private investors.

To become more autonomous, the respective banking systems had to be insulated from direct political intervention. Independent authorities such as a strong central bank were a step in this direction, but the autonomy of a financial system ultimately entailed replacing direct administrative controls

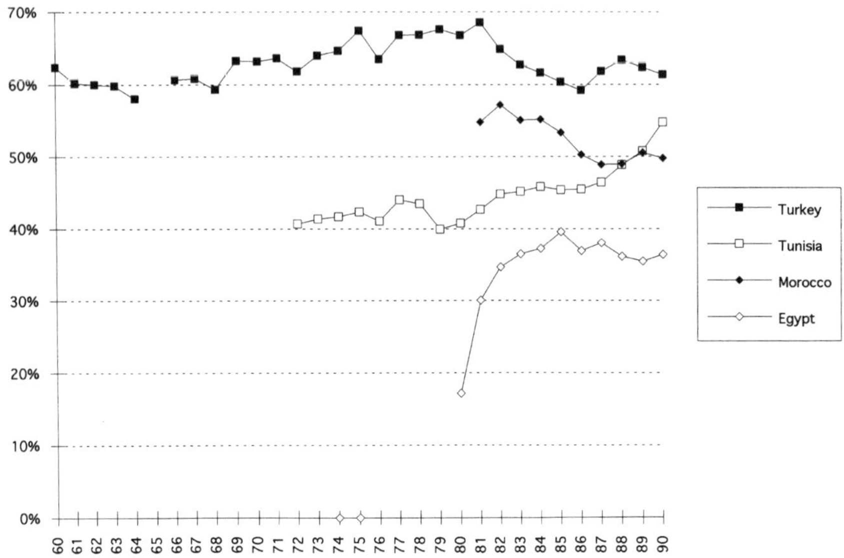

Fig. 2.8. Deposits of private and joint venture commercial banks as a percentage of total commercial bank deposits by country, 1960–90. *Sources:* Association Professionnelle des Banques de Tunisie; Banks' Association of Turkey; author's database of commercial banks.

over credit allocation with indirect signals and market forces. Indirect controls in turn presupposed responsible banks capable of exercising prudent management (defined by various norms and financial ratios) and reaching their own decisions concerning investments and loans. Any meaningful competition among them already presupposed relatively autonomous credit allocation. But since IMF guidelines constrained credit expansion along much of the crescent, financial reform was usually incremental, progressively deregulating certain kinds of credit and attempting to stimulate competition among banks within the liberated sectors.

Reflecting their different starting points as well as differing degrees of international pressure, each country adopted a distinctive strategy of reform. As noted earlier, Morocco was under the greatest pressure in the 1980s. Its strategy also constituted the most logical reading of the IMF and World Bank recipe books for reform: bring the twin deficits under control before liberating interest rates and driving toward greater autonomy and competition. Even so, macroeconomics and international pressures do not fully explain the strategy. Why did Morocco not open its doors, like Egypt and Turkey, to foreign banks or joint ventures? Delaying structural financial

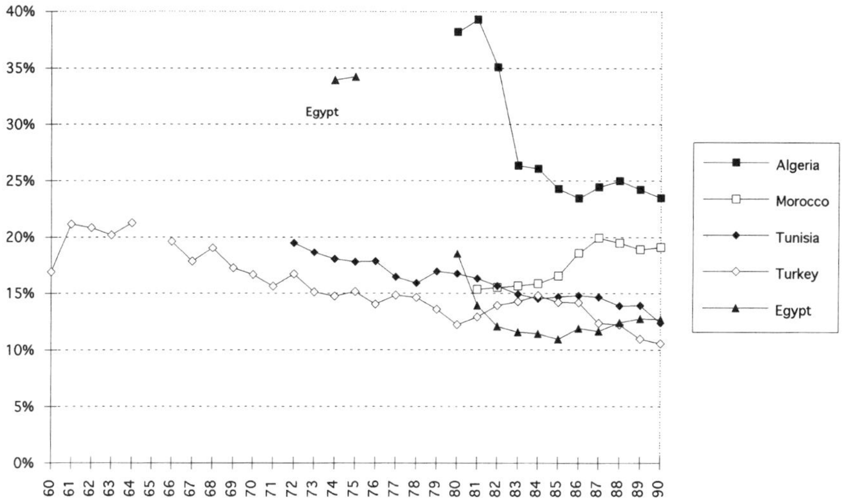

Fig. 2.9. Market concentration of commercial banks' deposits, 1960–90. *Sources:* APBT; Banks' Association of Turkey; author's database of commercial banks.

reform in good textbook fashion appeared to reinforce the existing banking oligopoly, and interest rates seemed in the last analysis to depend more upon the oligopoly than upon any new markets being fashioned by the Bank al Maghrib. Why was financial oligopoly reinforced in the name of financial liberalization?

The other country subjected to the greatest pressures, Egypt, defied any textbook logic for fifteen years. Though inheriting a banking system almost as bureaucratic as Algeria's, its doors were immediately opened to foreign competition—before the twin deficits and foreign exchange rates could be brought under control. The infitah banks then became part of the problem and reinforced parallel markets that facilitated capital flight as well as "foreign," mainly Egyptian, investment. A possible interpretation of the banks' activity is that they reflected Superman's pervasive power. But Egypt, enjoying greater strategic rents than Morocco after Camp David, had surely not been pressured into policies Morocco had so studiously avoided. Financial infitah seems incomprehensible without further analysis of internal Egyptian politics.

The Turkish opening was more skillfully crafted and controlled to fit the needs of a less politicized, somewhat more autonomous banking system. Turkey had regained access to Euromarkets before embarking in the mid-1980s on the structural reform of its banking system. The prior opening to foreign banks had been carefully tailored to the new economic strategy of promoting export-oriented growth. But Turkey, like Egypt, deviated from any textbook sequencing in these reforms. Inflation remained out of control, and government deficits increased rather than decreased when financial reform was resumed in the mid-1980s. More loosely supervised by international financial institutions than any of the other crescent countries in the late 1980s, Turkey deviated for domestic political reasons that deserve further scrutiny.

It took a major balance-of-payments crisis in 1986 to set Tunisia on the path of financial reform. But once it was jolted out of complacency, the administrative elite took decisive measures to transform the banking system. It effected a transition from state control to the indirect control of credit through money market mechanisms in barely three years—well ahead of Morocco. But the drive to autonomy outran the commercial banks' capacities to adapt to a more competitive environment. Market mechanisms were in place before the actors, numb from years of administrative directives and political interventions, could use them. Years of socialism and statism had corroded some of Tunisia's banks almost beyond repair, yet they were expected to compete with one another. Perhaps the official rhetoric of free markets in Tunisia veiled entrenched administrative interests. In Morocco, by contrast, the banks were in better shape to compete but remained protected by rigged markets.

Algeria was the least likely candidate for reform, but in some ways its economic system was more open for inspection and could shed greater light on those of its former socialist sisters, Egypt and Tunisia. Just as it had been the most radical of the state socialist regimes, so its reform program, too, spelled out most graphically the steps needed for a transition to a market economy. The Algerian reformers readily exposed the sorry financial state of their commercial banks, whereas the others veiled them under pretenses of confidentiality. Algeria sheds light on the politics of financial reform precisely because the problems were so exaggerated by its banking legacy and Boumédienne's administrative dictatorship. No serious reform efforts were undertaken upon Boumédienne's death in 1978, nor in 1982 when public enterprises were theoretically restructured and broken down into more manageable companies, nor yet again in 1986 when banking was juridically reformed without any followup. The collapse in the price of oil could not seriously rock the state planners; they just cut imports. It took the widespread riots of October 1988, laying bare the illegitimacy of a corrupt regime and unsustainable policies, for the reform process really to begin. Algeria clearly revealed some of the political obstacles to reform that also affected other regimes.

Chapter 3

Political Strategies of Reform

> C'est surtout dans le domaine financier que les mécanismes de décision dans le Tiers monde sont les plus autocratiques et que les choix de société qu'ils impliquent sont les moins élucidées. [It is above all in the financial domain that decision-making in the Third World is most autocratic and its social implications the least elucidated].
>
> (Georges Corm 1982: 36)

The timing and sequencing of financial reforms depended primarily upon each regime's political strategies. Each regime, in effect, was experimenting with new forms of patronage. Turkey's and Morocco's leaders enjoyed the greatest latitude. Their rule rested on diversified patronage networks that were partially institutionalized, for their regimes had already effected formal transitions to multiparty politics. Relatively autonomous banking systems could enhance their rulers' power rather than diminish it. They could keep control of their business communities, sources of much of the patronage, as long as the banking remained highly concentrated in a few friendly hands. At the peak of his power, Prime Minister Özal enjoyed as much economic leverage as King Hassan. He could make or break almost any business group by pulling the credit plugs.

By contrast, the one-party regimes of Egypt, Tunisia, and Algeria had originally relied less on any forms of financial patronage. The personal power that underlay these regimes also derived support from a multitude of countervailing power centers, but they were based on administrative resources rather than private property. The leaders could not altogether abolish politics or informal alliances among their respective staffs, but patronage networks tended to be less durable, more dependent upon transient constellations of power, than networks based on business and private capital. As these regimes weakened, however, new networks came into being in the interstices of the public and private sectors. The regimes tried to keep their new entrepreneurs under control, and one of the easiest ways was to keep direct control of credit allocation. Financial reform consequently posed more political problems in Egypt, Tunisia, and Algeria than in

Morocco or Turkey. It threatened their rulers' patronage monopolies, which were still needed to sustain or supplement their obsolete party machines. Patronage became all the more necessary to keep up the cadres' morale as the regimes lost legitimacy. Each of the former one-party systems, however, underwent simultaneous political and financial reforms. To what extent were they interrelated? Could financial reform serve a political strategy of transition to a multiparty system? Egypt, Tunisia, and Algeria offer fascinating illustrations of efforts simultaneously to effect political and economic transitions.

Egyptian Infitah

Anwar Sadat, one of the few Free Officers with a political past, was a strategic visionary with no particular interest in the details of economic policy. In retrospect, however, it is difficult to imagine how his financial reforms could have been better tailored to his domestic as well as foreign political strategies. In the early years of his rule, his most dangerous adversaries were some of the "centers of power" that had achieved notoriety (with help from the regime's chief publicist, Muhammad Hassenein Heikal) in Nasser's final years (Beattie 1994: 209–30). Sadat adopted the rhetoric but excluded the publicist.

The October Working Paper, submitted to a referendum in May 1974, articulated Sadat's strategic vision, once he had consolidated power and achieved some legitimacy for launching the October War. Before alluding to the policy of infitah, which Prime Minister Hegazy had proclaimed before the war, the paper lashed out at "power centers" within the army, the bureaucracy, and the Arab Socialist Union, many of whose leaders Sadat had arrested in his "rectification movement" of May 1971. "We must honestly concede that political freedom has not run the course the people wanted. Centers of power and other bodies rather imposed their custody on the masses . . . diverting measures of social conversion from their original humanitarian target and exploiting them to fulfill personal rancours and satisfy the interests of certain groups" (Sadat 1974: 38).

Infitah, the opening up of Egypt's economy to foreign technology and investment, was introduced in the paper only as a tactic for reinforcing the valued legacy of public sector industry. If Egypt was at a crossroads, Sadat continued to tell his chauffeurs to signal left while moving right, as Cairenes used to joke. Sadat still had to placate Nasser's old economic establishment and respect his social contract with labor and with new middle classes of university graduates while reorienting the country away from state socialism toward the Western world, reflecting his new international alliances.

Law 43, propelled through parliament in June 1974 on the momentum of the referendum for the working paper, not only infringed on the state's banking monopoly by allowing joint ventures but also allowed any joint venture to operate in local as well as in foreign currency provided that 51 percent of the ownership should be Egyptian, whether of the private or public sector. In one quick thrust Sadat accomplished two objectives. He created new power centers and a dynamic that would sap Nasser's establishment. Whether Sadat ever really "institutionalized his course in a political establishment whose interests were compatible, indeed served, by the main lines of his policies" (Hinnebusch 1985: 77), he certainly made banking the cutting edge of a new regime as well as an economic policy. The new banks resulting from Law 43 and its various amendments served as incentives for Sadat's clients, retirement homes for technocrats, and a system of collective action for further opening the economy. The emerging system would be consonant with Sadat's shift in style from Nasser's hands-on management of the Egyptian polity and economy.

As Raymond Hinnebusch so concisely summarized the two "presidential monarchies," Nasser "wanted to transform Egypt even if it meant running roughshod over vested elite interests; and much of his interventionism and reluctance to share power was a response of the tendency of elites to evade his demands. Sadat's goals, peace through negotiation and economic prosperity through private enterprise, required far less application of political power in society, and, far from threatening elite interests, advanced them. . . . [His] enormous personal power was tolerated precisely because its 'scope' had been considerably narrowed" (Hinnebusch 1985: 85, 90). The infitah banks indeed complicated the state's efforts to control foreign exchange, as noted in chapter 3. But these complications may also be viewed as part of Sadat's political strategy.

The banks provided focal points for new centers of power that the presidential monarchy might then balance. The "foreign" investment sought out by Law 43 came mainly from Egyptians, not Gulf Arabs or Europeans and Americans. They were either repatriating capital that had fled Nasser's regime, laundering public moneys that had slipped into private hands, or remitting their earnings from the Arab Gulf states (Imām 1986). Over half the total investment attracted from 1974 until the early 1980s went into banking and investment companies (Moore 1986: 639). The investment in Egypt's commercial and business banks, some $650 million, amounted to almost twice the capital of the four big government banks. Though the new finance capital was predominantly foreign and Egyptian public sector rather than privately owned, its capacities for political patronage should not be underestimated. Banks lent out 10 to 20 times their capital. The infitah banks lent almost exclusively to the private sector, including their own directors and managers. If joint ventures with big Western banks did not have much economic rationale (Ali al-Gritli, cited by Waterbury 1983: 148), the salaries and perks they brought to Egypt served useful political purposes. If the American manager received $100,000, the nominal Egyptian superior could not be limited to a statutory public sector maximum annual salary of $10,000 (Waterbury 1978: 226). Salaries soared—not only for former ministers. Public sector bank chairmen received many times their public salaries as the chairmen of their joint ventures and sometimes preferred to forgo their public sector salary altogether while wearing two hats, as if to resolve any conflict of interest.

The scores of new banks sheltered parts of Nasser's old establishment that Sadat wished to placate. A number of former ministers and other high officials under Nasser found new outlets in financial and related services. The new networks of banks and private sector businesses also offered some of Nasser's more dynamic power centers ways of hardening and deepening their patronage networks. Joint ventures enabled them to privatize their profits and socialize losses in their public sector enterprises without resorting to as many corrupt practices as in the Nasser years. It was also possible to get access to easy credit by investing negligible amounts of capital in the new banks.

Sadat's favorite, Osman Ahmed Osman, was a major beneficiary. Under Nasser this public contractor had been encouraged to set up an extensive patronage network to offset some of the other, more dangerous "centers of power" in the army and the Arab Socialist Union. His services also won Sadat over, and the marriage of their children consecrated the royal alliance in 1975. Osman had his Arab Contractors, a public sector firm, invest in a number of banks, which in turn financed many of his projects. His greatest triumph was the National Bank of Development, promoted by Sadat and his top ministers to bring modern capitalism to the countryside. It also provided over half the capital of Dar Mayo, Sadat's private publishing agency (Imām 1986: 142). The NBD was an assemblage of 17 banks corresponding to Egypt's governorates, each of which in turn had a number of branches. Osman cleverly encouraged each bank to keep its autonomy and a separate capital structure. In return for his support the local notables got their banks to finance projects using Osman's machinery and construction materials.

The NBD was a microcosm of infitah: free-wheeling banks escaping any central control.

The multiple centers of financial power served many of Sadat's ministers and leading public sector bankers well. Of the core political elite identified by Hinnebusch (1985: 94–95), roughly one out of six retired into bank chairmanships, including Prime Ministers Abd al-Aziz Higazy, Mustafa Khalil, and (under Mubarak) Kamal Hassan Ali. Sadat's teams of economic ministers and central bank governors found their rewards, too; ten of them still headed banks in 1992. Virtually all of the public sector bank chairmen also chaired joint ventures and held on to them even after being reassigned from the public parent to one of its competitors. The infitah banks offered financial incentives to most of Sadat's key economic decision-makers. As a system of collective action, they also pressured for policies that furthered Sadat's political design.

A fragmented system of many banks not only offered more patronage than a more concentrated system. It also more easily escaped the control of the Central Bank. Although the Big Four public sector banks still controlled two-thirds of the deposits in 1982 and serviced the public sector, the private sector was now receiving a majority of the credits, and the system of credit allocation was no longer centralized. Much of the foreign exchange, moreover, escaped any control. The exchange system Sadat had personally pushed against some of his leading advisers in 1974 could not be stopped. As noted in chapter 2, the banks themselves played a leading role in sabotaging a final effort in 1985 to regain government control. Sadat's legacy was to have set the financial machinery in motion that effectively disengaged the state from substantial areas of economic decision-making—reducing the scope of presidential power as he had intended.

He failed, to be sure, to set institutional limits on the exercise of power. Perhaps he never intended to, preferring to play the role of village elder or "father of the national family" (Hinnebusch 1985: 218). Experiments with multiple tendencies within the ruling party, followed by recognition of opposition parties, including a revived New Wafd from the pre-Nasser era, did not lead to a decisive transition, like Turkey's in 1950, to multiparty politics. Sadat's successor, however, inherited a political economy that would lend itself to further institutionalization.

If Sadat's infitah made little economic sense, its political logic was compelling. The banks were the principal beneficiaries of infitah, and they in turn set a dynamic in motion that would gradually unravel the public sector from within. They offered an elegant way for some public sector officials to deepen their patronage networks without resorting to illegal activities. They offered incentives to decision-makers for backing private over state interests. They supported projects and businesses that were often unproductive—the "parasitic" capitalism so often criticized in the Egyptian press. They attracted foreign exchange, siphoning much of it out of the country, but without parallel markets the workers' remittances would not have entered the system in the first place. For all their alleged sins the banks effected a fundamental change in the way Egypt allocated credit. Their collective pressures seemed to be propelling Egyptian banking back to the commanding heights of the economy from which state planners had dislodged it in 1961. Perhaps their collective anarchy offered a tidier, more gradual economic and political transition, in the last analysis, than "correctly" sequenced financial reform. More than any formal institutions or political associations they guaranteed Sadat's policies continuity, if not quite institutionalization. The structural power of Egyptian finance capital will be more closely examined in chapters 7 and 8.

Tunisia's Middle Way

In Tunisia financial reform took a more orderly path designed to avert the excesses of the Egyptian infitah. The gradualist strategy of political and economic change introduced in 1986 and 1987 was curiously reminiscent of Bourguibism—determined as to the eventual goals, flexible on timing and tactics. Though he approved of the stabilization program and subsequent measures of financial liberalization, however, Bourguiba was scarcely capable in the final year of his reign of incubating a political strategy. He had, after all, already responded in a more authoritarian way to the excesses of state socialism that Sadat addressed. Bourguiba had reinforced the state's control of banking while orienting the credit to a private sector spawned and protected by the single-party system. While there was an evident need for both political and economic transitions in the late 1980s, Tunisia's politicians continued to be cautious.

Financial reform lay at the center of the reformers' efforts to make Tunisian enterprise more viable and more competitive, in keeping with an export-oriented strategy reinforced by the IMF program. But reform had to be gradual. Bourguiba had understood financial power (see chapter 6), and his lessons of political organization did not escape other Tunisians. In good Bourguibian fashion, Habib Achour, Tunisia's trade union leader, had founded the Banque du Peuple in 1964 with capital subscriptions from the mass membership of the Union Générale Tunisienne du Travail (UGTT).

The bank was central to his drive for trade union autonomy vis-à-vis the party-state. After suppressing the autonomists, the government had the Banque du Sud buy out the little bank's shareholders in 1968. There would be no other free-wheeling sources of patronage, for the Central Bank would keep strict surveillance over private sector as well as government bankers. Tunisian reformers, like their Algerian cousins, could tackle bank reform in 1987 in part because it seemed so uncontroversial and technical that it would not stretch the government's limited political capacities. Once under way, they were not interrupted because Ben Ali's new regime was occupied with more pressing political matters. Incremental and almost clandestine, the reforms were nonetheless designed to have a major economic impact.

Privatization and the disengagement of the state from managing the public sector and regulating everything from prices to markets for the private sector would be controversial, but financial reform was a way of skirting some of them for a time. Before Ben Ali's coup, Ismail Khelil, the governor of the Central Bank and one of the reform's chief architects,[1] tipped the government's hand at a privatization seminar when he prudently observed, "It is better to speak of 'restructuration' than of 'privatization.' For it is necessary in a first stage to pass by an intermediary phase, a necessary relay, banking for example, to achieve the disengagement of the state from public enterprises. It is only in a second phase that the real intervention of the private sector can be envisaged" (*La Presse*, 29 April 1987: 11). The banks, in short, could become a useful instrument, helping the state to disengage from or "restructure" public enterprises by cutting their credits. As long as the Central Bank directly allocated credit, cutting back was politically difficult. Banks therefore had to be made responsible for their own credit decisions. But there was never any question of diminishing the regime's scope of power over banking or other activities. "The Central Bank must relax its grip on the banking sector in order above all to permit the banks to become responsible" (Khelil, 24 May 1988: 9). But "one should not think that deregulation means weakening the role belonging to the Institute of Emission. In reality it is only the form of managing liquidity and overseeing banking activity that will be modified" (23 May 1988:5).

Debates about broader transitions took place in other arenas and focused upon the future of Tunisia's party system rather than its economy. Ben Ali's declaration of 7 November 1987 promised a steady and orderly political transition: "Our people has attained a level of responsibility and maturity that enables all of its elements to contribute constructively to managing its affairs in conformity with the Republican idea, which confers full authority to institutions and guarantees the conditions for a responsible democracy. . . . Our people is worthy of an advanced and institutionalized political life, based on multipartism and a plurality of mass organizations." Ben Ali called for constitutional reform and new laws for political parties and the press "susceptible of assuring broader participation for constructing Tunisia and consolidating its independence in the framework of order and discipline." Shortly thereafter, he released and amnestied more than 2,000 prisoners, many of whom were Islamists incarcerated by the Bourguiba regime. Though most of the opposition parties, including the Mouvement des Démocrates Socialistes (MDS), boycotted partial elections held in early 1988, they supported the new president and awaited reforms that would ensure proper guarantees for future partisan competition. Bourguiba's old parliament passed a law on political parties in April that guaranteed a multiparty system and met most of the specifications of the MDS. It did not altogether satisfy the opposition, however, because the provision interdicting parties based on "religion, language, race, or region" apparently excluded the Mouvement de la Tendance Islamique (MTI) from any hopes of official recognition. MTI leaders remained in contact with President Ben Ali, however, and one of its representatives was included in the consultations leading, on the first anniversary of Ben Ali's presidency, to his promulgation of a national pact. On this date Ben Ali stole the opposition's thunder by announcing general elections for April 1989, in which a total of seven recognized parties would compete. Eventually reconstituted as the Nahda, the Islamists were not recognized as a party, but they were allowed to compete in the elections on lists of independents. The major problem facing Tunisia's new leaders, however, was not the relatively docile opposition but rather what to do with what had once been the ruling Destour Socialist Party, or Parti Socialiste Destourian (PSD). Housed since the early 1980s in a huge central headquarters that symbolically overlooked the government's headquarters in the Kasbah, would the party retain its trappings of power?

To signify rupture with past practices, the Central Committee changed the name of the venerable party to the Rassemblement Constitutionnel Démocratique (RCD). As if to minimize its role in decision-making, Ben Ali reshuffled his government before rather than after the extraordinary congress held in July 1988. During the transition, however, the party remained as top-heavy as in Bourguiba's vintage years of personal power. The extraordinary congress did not materially affect the president's power to name the Central Committee, an innovation Bourguiba had established in 1986 to subdue clans and potential factions. Ben Ali appointed 122 of its 200 members, and the remaining 78 were elected by regional instances, not the congress. One delegate claimed that "they should have allotted at least twenty places to delegates to raise interest in the debates" (Mezoughi 1988b: 6). The "difficult acrobatics" of incorporating new blood into the party's leadership had required tactics hardly in keeping with internal party democracy. Preparations for the party congress, including free elections throughout the party's vast apparatus, resulted in more than a 60 percent turnover at the local level and 70 percent to 80 percent at higher levels. The local cells, in turn, elected some new blood to serve as their delegates to the party congress, but Ben Ali also designated "an important number" of delegates (*Réalités* 29 July 1988: 17). Balancing the new with the old on the Central Committee still could not be left to the party congress.

If press reports were correct, this already massive apparatus—1,025,084 strong at the end of 1986 (Moore 1988: 17)—had increased its membership by 50 percent to total 1,502,291 "militants" by July 1988 (Mezoughi 1988a: 4). In other words, half the adult population, and in all likelihood a majority of adult males, belonged. Professionals and intellectuals, university professors, and even students had flocked to the RCD after years of political apathy and isolation outside the tradition-bound PSD. The number of party cells, however, did not keep up with the flood of new members. Totaling 5,248 across the country and overseas in 1988, the number of cells had increased by only 19 percent since 1986. Rapid growth obviously compounded the party's problem of defining itself. By including everybody, the party represented nothing in particular—even the name Destour, connoting its historical memories, only barely survived (as an Arabic adjective meaning "constitutional").

The parliamentary elections of 2 April 1989 underlined both the strengths and weaknesses of the refurbished party. Under a controversial electoral law,[2] the RCD demonstrated its strength by taking all the seats, although the party rank and file had occasionally displayed divided loyalties. When Ahmed Mestiri, leader of the opposition MDS, toured the region of Nabeul in early 1989, for instance, many party cell leaders cheered him on. Like Tunis, Nabeul's party apparatus had shown relative weakness before 1987. Not only Mestiri but virtually all of the opposition party leaders had once been members of the PSD, and the new members of the RCD could gravitate at least as easily to those politicians who had broken with Bourguiba's cult as to those who had stayed on, often compromising themselves. Opposition parties and independent Islamist candidates collectively gained from 25 to 41 percent of the vote in most of Tunisia's coastal urban and southern constituencies (see fig. 6–15). Although the ruling party obtained absolute majorities in all of the governorates, voting participation, the percentage of valid votes to the eligible electorate, sank to a nationwide average of 51 percent. Analysis of the results, moreover, confirmed the allegations of Mestiri and others that the administration's selective registration of voters and the occurrence of ballot stuffing had contributed to the RCD victory (Moore 1993: 53–59). The strongest of the opposition parties, Ahmed Mestiri's MDS, received little more than 3 percent of the vote—after having possibly received as much as 30 percent in 1981 elections, before the results were doctored (Zartman 1991: 23). Mestiri complained, "People like us didn't have the means to make our voices heard" (Markham 1989). In fact the MDS had suffered over the years from a lack of funds. It could not support some of its press because the business community dared not openly support the party. In the mid-1980s some were too intimidated even to place ads in surviving MDS newspapers. By contrast, the ruling party was soliciting businesses for contributions—some businessmen spoke of "extortion"—so as to lessen the party's dependence on the state budget. In 1986 the party is alleged to have received TD 3 million, or almost $4 million, from the presidency's budget; an opposition leader estimated that parliamentary by-elections for five seats in early 1988 had cost the party half a million dinars (*Réalités,* 4 November 1988). Freer credit allocation in the financial sector might have helped to alleviate some of the imbalances between governing and opposition parties, simply by promoting a stronger, more autonomous private sector, capable of making contributions to political parties. The Islamists gained far more votes than the combined totals of all the other opposition groups.

Relations between the Nahda and the authorities deteriorated after the elections. In early 1991 the director of Nahda's newspaper, *Al Fajr,* claimed to the writer that 400 to 500 party members were in jail (interview with Hamadi Jabali, 11 January 1991). In March some Islamists raided a regional headquarters of the ruling party in downtown Tunis, and a night watchman died under particularly gruesome circumstances. Whether or not the security forces manufactured some of the circumstances (making it appear that the assailants had torched a victim whom they had not intended to harm, some neutral observers believe), they took advantage of the incident to crack down on moderates and extremists alike in a tense political climate aggravated by the Gulf War. In May and again in September 1991, the authorities claimed to have discovered plots to overthrow the government and to assassinate senior officials, including the president (although the evidence did not convince the international press). The authorities arrested thousands of Nahda activists in the course of the year, and "there were increased numbers of credible reports of torture and brutal treatment of detainees, particularly of Islamists" (U.S. Department of State 1992: 1616). The Islamist party remained illegal, and the military and police support of Ben Ali's regime became more visible, tarnishing the image of the Arab world's last civilian republic. The crackdown on Islamists intensified, and by 1992 thousands had been in and out of jail—between 3,000 and 8,000 imprisoned at any given time, well-informed Tunisians suggested. Amnesty International conservatively estimated in a report released on January 12, 1994, that at least 1,020 political prisoners were in jail, and arrests were continuing on a regular if less frequent basis. Amnesty International also inferred from documented instances of torture that the practice was widespread and systematic (Fischer and Henry 1994: 12–13). Others reported that brothers and sons of Islamist opponents were subject to various forms of administrative harassment including arbitrary arrest and loss of employment.

In the long run, however, Tunisia's direction of political change might still depend as much upon the government's economic policies and strategies as on its electoral tactics and its treatment of the various opposition groups. Policies favoring the development of the private sector could eventually give opposition parties new roots. Financial reform could slowly be inducing greater autonomy and competition in the banking system that might facilitate the emergence of powerful business interests. As chapter 6 will show, the authorities have been experiencing increasing difficulties in reconciling structural adjustment in the financial sector with Ben Ali's patrimonial rule.

Algeria's Crack-up

Financial reform seems to have been an integral part of the regime's response to a major political as well economic crisis in 1988. Since assuming power nine years earlier, President Chadly Benjedid had occasionally taken initiatives to "restructure" the public enterprises, but his principal concern had been to prevent the big state holdings, such as Sonatrach, from becoming autonomous centers of power. The widespread riots of October 1988 finally provided Benjedid with the opportunity to reinforce the powers of the presidency, curtail those of the discredited ruling party, the Front of National Liberation (FLN), and push a major set of reforms through the FLN-dominated parliament. Although he ultimately failed, like Gorbachev, to engineer political reform from above, Benjedid tried between 1988 and 1992 simultaneously to build a multiparty system and a market-oriented economy. From a much less auspicious starting point, Algeria raced ahead of Tunisia toward genuinely free and competitive elections until his fellow military officers intervened and dismissed him from office in the veiled coup of

11 January 1992. Unlike Gorbachev, Benjedid had systematically integrated economic reform into his political strategy.

Benjedid, however, had never concentrated and consolidated the presidential power of his predecessor. When Boumédienne suddenly died in late 1978, Benjedid was selected by his fellow military commanders chiefly on the basis of seniority. Though he carefully neutralized principal rivals, he was not free to take major initiatives until the single-party regime virtually collapsed with the riots of 1988. In the early 1980s there had been some truth to the observation that "Algeria today is governed by a complex network of interactive structures that provide institutional stability, direction, and predictability to the political system" (Entelis 1986: 168). Power in the governorates as well as at the national level was then shared among a so-called iron triangle of top military officers, officials of the ruling Front of National Liberation, and the Ministry of the Interior, but the real power had rested with the military since independence.

Unlike the inclusive Tunisian Destour, the FLN had consisted of some 200,000 "militants," no more than 1 percent of the population. To become a member, one had to be "competent," a person of "integrity," and "committed" to the party's ideology, but since the ideology of Algerian socialism admitted of a variety of Islamic, Marxian, and other interpretations, the principal condition for membership was sponsorship by other members. Sociologically, the FLN resembled a political club more than a Leninist party; politically, however, it was supposed to exercise a Leninist hegemony over state and society. Boumédienne had reinforced its authority between 1976 and 1978 in efforts to institutionalize his power base. The party was made to play the central role in formal politics.

Ernest Gellner (1981: 149–73) once compared the party bureaucrats to medieval religious scholars, the ulama, whose political task had been to legitimate the janissaries, or military and administrative elites, in precolonial times. The FLN bureaucracy nominated candidates for elections to communal, state (*wilayat*), and national legislative bodies with impressive regularity after 1967. It also elected a president in 1976, 1979, and 1984. It even tried to spice up parliamentary elections. In 1977 the FLN nominated three candidates for each position in the Popular National Assembly. The Tunisians in fact emulated the Algerians by offering two candidates for each seat in their parliamentary elections of 1979. In 1982 the Algerians went a step further, permitting some independent candidates to run for office; but since the FLN elected only 197 out of 281 deputies, the experience was not repeated in the 1987 elections.

In his efforts to consolidate power, Benjedid instead attempted to neutralize the party apparatus by depriving it of any real power while permitting it symbolically in 1984 to occupy the government "palace" dominating downtown Algiers. This huge modern structure had once housed the top French colonial authorities and had then sheltered independent Algeria's central government. Vanguard or rear guard, however, the Algerian party still commanded a certain political edge by virtue of its exclusive character. It was not ideologically homogeneous; indeed, ideology was displaced in Algeria by concrete achievements like iron and steel works (El Kenz 1987: 28, 53) and other "industrializing industries," the failures of which would signify a legitimacy crisis. The FLN nevertheless articulated vested interests more explicitly than its more broadly based Tunisian counterpart dared to. Confronted with Chadly's reforms, the FLN fought back, whereas the Tunisian party had opened up as if to envelope Ben Ali.

Until the mid-1980s the one-party system circumvented opposition by doling out jobs and services—special development programs to disinherited regions and the like—because the "État Providence" enjoyed reasonable oil revenues and good international credit ratings. Algeria would therefore be politically as well as economically more vulnerable than its neighbors to the oil recession of the mid-1980s, yet it preferred to cut food and other consumer imports rather than to reschedule crushing debt reservicing payments. The party militants distrusted foreign private investment, and their delegates to the Popular National Assembly waged rear guard campaigns against government efforts to encourage it. Influence was also exercised through informal personal alliances with high state officials, including military officers, whose prebends were being threatened by efforts to restructure the public sector (Soudan 1988a: 38). After years of state socialism, the party was perceived as little more than an umbrella for covering the mistakes of government officials (Soudan 1988b: 30), and membership as no more than carrying a party card (El Kenz 1987: 358)—despite the fact that rank-and-file membership carried few privileges (Leca and Vatin 1979: 77). Former militants of a semiofficial opposition party, the Parti de l'Avant Garde Socialiste (PAGS), an offshoot of the Algerian Communist Party that had been offically dissolved in 1966, also allied with others in the FLN and the UGTA to oppose Chadly's restructuring of the public sector. Other potential political oppositions were not permitted to organize and consequently had turned to violence, emulating the patriots who had launched Algeria's War of Independence. Radical Islamic reformers were the most recent example. Though weaker and less articulate than their Tunisian counterparts, some of them had been incorporated into the FLN, but others were pushed almost by accident, victims of their fragmentation, into armed struggle that ended with the gunning down of their leader in 1987 (Burgat 1988a). Some "Berberists" had earlier met a similar fate for aspiring to cultural (not political) autonomy.

Apparently elements of the FLN, encouraged by PAGS, had prepared in 1988 to withdraw support for Chadly in the coming presidential elections. When the president lashed back in his speech of 17 September 1988, the party counterattacked, but mass rioting on 4 October preempted the general strike called by its trade union ally for 5 October. Ironically, the resulting slaughter of hundreds of people enabled Chadly to purge the party and keep the support of an embarrassed army. Supplemented by unusually large army reinforcements—one-third rather than the usual one-fifth of the delegates—an emergency FLN congress ratified Chadly's leadership but wavered on some of the proposed reforms. But the riots and killings had further eroded the party's narrow base. Finally, on 23 February 1989, the Algerian constitution was decisively amended: references to socialism and to the traditional principle of single-party hegemony were eliminated, and a law permitting alternative political parties was duly promulgated on 5 July (Djeghloul 1990: 200–205). The FLN was even removed from its palatial headquarters, to which some of the central government returned.

Chadly took advantage of the FLN's disarray to accelerate economic reform. He had his finance minister, Ahmed Ghozali, sign a letter of intent to the IMF in April 1989, which led to Algeria's first standby agreement in July. He promoted his chief economic adviser, Ghazi Hidoussi, to be Minister of the Economy in September 1989 and to work with Hadj Nasser, another technocrat, on creating a strong central bank. These reforms appeared to be imposed in a political vacuum, but they were not inconsistent with the economic program, dated 7 March 1989, of the Front of Islamic Salvation (FIS), Algeria's principal Islamist opposition party. The fact, too, that legislation was also promulgated at this time to permit the establishment of political parties suggests that there may have been an unofficial trade-off between economic and political reform. It is hard, in fact, to understand how the presidency could have accelerated Algeria's reform process in 1989 and 1990 without tacit support from the FIS.

The FIS program marked a sharp break with mainstream thinking about economic policy within the governing Front of National Liberation. In addition to supporting Algeria's new multiparty system and denouncing the "egoism, corruption, and individualism" of the old regime, the program called for a basic reorientation in economic policy. It bitterly attacked the old system of economic planning which had favored large-scale industrial "parasites" and urged that priority be given to agriculture. Without explicitly calling for the return of agricultural lands to their former Algerian owners (implemented in 1990–91), the FIS insisted on an end to "abusive expropriation," citing an appropriate hadith (reported citation of the Prophet Muhammad). While favoring "industrializing industry" to complement agriculture, the FIS also called for "precise limits to state intervention in industrial property to protect the private sector while seeing to it that the latter not be transformed into monopoly against the public interest and open the door to social, political and economic parasitism" (Al-Ahnaf et al. 1991: 182–83). State monopolies on commerce were also to be abolished "except to safeguard major political or economic interests." Free trade was to be encouraged "gradually, so as to prevent a disequilibrium between imports and exports." Subsidies were also to be gradually eliminated. The Algerian dinar, then selling in Paris for less than one-fifth of the official exchange rate, was to be "revalued in the sense of equalizing monetary value at home and abroad in light of financial conditions and those relative to imports and exports which are the real stimulation to production" (185–86)—in other words, devalued. Finally, "it is imperative to review relations with the IMF and other financial and commercial organizations responsible for the current world crisis. The question of [Algeria's foreign] debt must be raised in light of the new political, economic, and social policies proposed by the FIS" (185).

Indeed Algeria's first letter of intent to the IMF was written in April 1989, just one month following the elaboration of the FIS program. It promised a progressive devaluation of the dinar, which Benjedid pressed a succession of governments to implement in 1990 and 1991 in the face of an FLN-dominated parliament. Another sign of a tacit understanding between the FIS and the reformers was an agreement between the Al Baraka group and BADR to establish a joint venture Islamic bank. Al Baraka had invested 700 million sterling in revolving credits for trade with Algeria by 1990, the group's London manager claimed (*The Banker*, December 1990: 10), and the overtures served President Chadly Benjedid's economic and political purposes. The FIS program had urged the creation of Islamic banks, although it is unlikely that Al Baraka had any direct links with Algeria's Islamist parties. While Al-Baraka was the first foreign financial group allowed to set up a joint venture bank in Algeria, the reformers were more determined to break the hitherto sacrosanct state monopoly on banking than to promote Islamic banking in the country. The managers of Algeria's new Islamic bank were experienced civil servants and state bankers who did not appear to be connected with any political movement.

Coincidentally or not, one of the first parties to be recognized in 1989 was the FIS—despite a secret accord against tolerating Islamic parties, reached earlier in the year by the heads of state of the Maghrib countries (Leveau 1993: 41–42). Within a few months more than 20 "parties" materialized, but before most of them could organize nationally, they were faced on 12 June 1990 with provincial and municipal elections. The FIS astonished most Algerians as well as the rest of the world by capturing 54.2 percent of the vote and 856 (55.5 percent) of Algeria's 1,541 townships. The bigger the township, the more overwhelming was the FIS victory: the Islamists took 59 of Algeria's most populated centers (Kapil 1991: 47). The FLN ran a lackluster campaign and came in a poor second, with 28.1 percent of the vote and 31.6 percent of the townships, and, like the Tunisian government party, it did best in the more peripheral parts of the country and in the smaller townships. The other principal victor in the elections was the aggregate of various lists of independents; other parties fared poorly. Only the Kabyle-based RCD received sufficient support to gain a significant number of townships—87, with 2.1 percent of the vote—but it benefited from the decision of Hocine Ait Ahmed, the leader of another, more venerable Kabyle-based party, to boycott these elections until his FFS could get organized.

FIS had been quick to benefit from the genuinely neutral administration of the elections; from the other parties' greater degree of disorganization; from a relatively low voter turnout of 65 percent, including proxy votes, which usually went to the FIS (Kapil 1990: 31–32); and from widespread resentment against FLN corruption. Public opinion took at face value a former prime minister's speculation that government officials had pocketed $26 billion—the entire foreign debt—in commissions from foreign contractors over the previous decade (*MEED,* 13 April 1990: 19). When the issue of corruption became public, the government responded by cracking down on *trabendo* (contraband) imports, but the ensuing economic dislocations were probably another factor in FIS's favor at the elections. But FIS was not well organized. Only two years earlier, France's closest academic observer of Islamist movements in North Africa had quite correctly written that the Algerian version was "one of the least developed and structured [and hence among] the least known" (Burgat 1988b: 143). His book barely mentioned the new FIS leader, Abassi Madani, an obscure Algiers University lecturer who had spent over a decade in London to obtain a Ph.D. degree in education. Madani emerged in 1982 as the coauthor of a petition calling for more Arabization, the banning of alcohol, and a conservative personal status law in response to student rioting and police repression. A jail sentence increased his status, and he was swept into the political leadership vacuum in October 1988. Together with a younger, more radical high school teacher and imam, Ali Belhadj, he founded FIS on 21 February 1989 (Burgat 1993: 273). FIS then benefited from access to most of Algeria's mosques, and it had financial support from small merchants as well as from Saudi Arabia. No other party could command such resources, but FIS's advantages were modest: there had not been sufficient time to develop as strong an organization as the Tunisian Nahda's, even if the Algerian Islamists had appeared stronger at elections. Benjedid probably expected that the legislative elections of 1991 would elicit stronger competition. The electoral law was initially rigged so as to put the FIS at a disadvantage.

In protest against the electoral law, the Front's call for a general strike failed in late May 1991, but it offered the army a chance to flex its muscles. A state of siege was announced on 5 June, and the army not only cracked down on the FIS but also forced the resignation of the reformist government. The new government of Sid Ahmed Ghozali "was now, in effect, dominated by the army and the old-guard elites" (Entelis and Arone 1992: 32). Though a new IMF standby negotiated by the previous government was approved in June, the financial reforms were then in jeopardy. The central bank governor retained his position for another year, but two key allies in the banking sector were removed from office. President Benjedid's strategy of recognizing the FIS in exchange for its tacit support for economic reform was unraveling, for "the General staff of the army . . . decided not to let the 'error of Chadly' (i.e., the legalization of the FIS) lead to an irreversible assault on its interests" (Burgat 1993: 298).

When the legislative elections, postponed in June, were finally held, on 26 December, under a more equitable electoral law, FIS won 188 seats outright and threatened on the second round of the elections to win a two-thirds majority in the 430-seat Assemblée Nationale Populaire—enough to impose constitutional amendments. Benjedid's tactic of dividing the opposition had obviously failed, but he seemed prepared to allow the FIS to come to power in exchange for keeping him in office. In the elections the FIS had won twice as many votes as the next most powerful party, the FLN, and more than six times as many as Ait Ahmed's FFS, which was in third place (*Algérie Actualité,* 9 January 1992: 7).[3] FIS had clearly outmaneuvered the other parties. Its suppression further discredited the FLN, so that it indeed seemed "only a matter of time before the FLN dissolves or breaks up into smaller parties" (Kapil 1990: 35). Fearing the specter of an Islamic Republic of Algeria, however, the army moved on Algiers and induced President Benjedid to resign on 11 January 1992, before the second round could be held.

The senior officers then called Mohammed Boudiaf out of exile to head a five-man Higher Council of State. They hoped that Boudiaf, who had founded the FLN in 1954, could legitimate the new regime. A state of emergency was proclaimed, and the Ministry of Interior admitted to arresting 6,786 people in January and February (*MEED,* 10 April 1992: 10). Algeria's strongest party was now banned. Ait Ahmed strongly protested against interrupting Algeria's electoral processes and subsequently refused to join the new regime's Consultative Council. Algeria's emerging multiparty system was in a state of shock.

While cracking down on the Islamists, however, Boudiaf tried also to combat corruption within the existing power structure. A remarkable political figure, he had refused Boumédienne's offer, subsequently tendered to Ben Bella, to join forces and seize power at independence. In 1963, unable to continue opposition politics in Algeria, Boudiaf went into exile in Morocco and refused calls in 1979 and 1988 to return to political life in Algeria. When he finally acceded to the janissaries' call in 1992, he retained the same uncompromising qualities that had kept him in Morocco for almost three decades. At the age of 73 he refused to be a mere figurehead, and his outspoken style was slowly beginning to win him a following among a skeptical Algerian population, for whom historical revolutionary legitimacy meant little. He was gunned down, probably by state security forces, on 29 June 1992, before he could consolidate sufficient power to overcome their vested interests. His successor, Ali Kafi, then appointed Belaid Abdesselam, the architect of Boumédienne's state industry, to be prime minister. The governor of the Central Bank, the kingpin of Benjedid's reforms and the critical link with the IMF and the World Bank, was finally sacked, and Algeria briefly appeared to be returning to the "orthodox" command economy that Benjedid had tried to disassemble. But by 1994 Algeria had again switched leadership and was renegotiating with the IMF.

The Moroccan Facade of Party Competition

Like Turkey from 1945 to 1950, Morocco underwent a transition to multiparty politics during the early years of independence, while remaining an authoritarian regime. Initially the role of the French-controlled banking system was much less important than in Turkey. Patronage emanated directly from the royal family's *makhzan,* literally a "magazine" for storing grain (i.e., a "black box"). By reestablishing the French Protectorate's ties with rural notables (Leveau 1985), the monarchy gained counterweights to their urban Istiqlal Party rivals. In 1958 the Popular Movement was already undermining the Istiqlal's claim to single-party hegemony, and the split the following year within the party effectively confirmed a multiparty system. For the following two decades, however, the makhzan and the National Bloc (*al-kutla al-watani*), consisting of the Istiqlal and its derivative parties, articulated conflicting definitions of legitimate authority. Once his military support turned against him in 1971 and again in 1972, King Hassan, beholden to the parties he had dismissed in 1965, finally weaned the Istiqlal away from the kutla into power on his terms in 1977. He consummated his victory in 1979 by obliging the legal parliamentary opposition—the most significant remnants of the kutla—to wear the traditional djalaba (Claisse 1987: 44), in other words, to join the political arena on his terms. It was then just another little step in 1984 for the Union Socialiste des Forces Populaires (USFP) to become a party like the others at election time, partaking of a ritual quota system (Sehimi 1985: 27, 39).

Over the years, beginning in 1958, the monarchy had decimated the parties by playing one off against the other and by coopting individuals in key parties, enticing them to break with party discipline. Patronage networks usually cut across and blunted distinctions between government and opposition parties. Thus defection from a party could also be viewed as the party's promoting of its leaders, individually, to power. The major casualties of the system were principled leaders like Mehdi Ben Barka and Omar Benjelloun, who had rejected royal patronage, and some of the hundreds of repressed opposition party, trade union, or student militants who did not survive to reap the benefits of royal amnesties and return to the royal stables in the late 1970s. But note that political imprisonment was also a form of empowerment: it rendered tame, "complementary" oppositions (Zartman 1988) credible to their constituents—for a time (Moore 1970: 190).

By 1984 the regime was deliberately supporting the parties by barring independent candidates, thereby reversing its classic strategy of encouraging independent local notables to compete with parties. The king insisted that it would henceforth be "anti-constitutional" (on a creative reading of article 3 of the constitution of 1972) for a candidate without a party label to run for parliament (Sehimi 1986: 63). The new constitutional interpretation seemed designed to "prevent Islamist candidates, to avoid the camouflaging of 'progressive' candidates behind 'neutral' labels, to prevent a scission in the Popular Movement, and, finally, to oblige tens of cadres . . . to rejoin the Constitutional Union," the principal government party (Sehimi 1985: 33). It enabled royal clients better to control the selection of government party candidates, perhaps thereby reinforcing the cohesion of the parliamentary majority.

Majority voting in single-member constituencies—often gerrymandered so as to inject supervised rural populaces into urban districts—ensured comfortable majorities for the government parties in the 1977 and 1984 elections. As further insurance, one-third of parliament was indirectly elected. In 1984 the results of these elections, coming three weeks after the direct ones, "modulated" the outcomes not so much to favor the government parties as to restore a sort of balance between the Istiqlal and the USFP. Excluded from the informal cartel that had organized the direct elections, the Istiqlal had fared poorly, winning only 11.6 percent of the seats on 14.4 percent of the vote, compared with the USFP's 17 percent of the seats on only 12.5 percent of the vote (Sehimi 1986: 80). But "in a manner unhoped for," the Istiqlal gained 19 seats to the USFP's four in the indirect elections (116). Morocco's advanced electoral technology—offered for export to Iran before the shah's downfall (Eickelman 1987: 93)—elicited so much cynicism and apathy among Moroccan political elites and the masses alike that it is not so clear in the long run that King Hassan really was, as Paul Balta put it, the principal victor in 1984 (Sehimi 1985: 47). If even the opposition candidates were "mal élu," did not the election simply discredit the democratic process that the king was trying to use (Leveau 1985: 253)? Elections had become virtually meaningless once "the number of seats allotted to each party is established confidentially in accordance with a 'quota' system" (Claisse 1987: 45) or an "implicit political pact" (Leveau 1985: 252) rigged with alternating opposition parties—the Istiqlal in 1977, the USFP in 1984. Even a semblance of competition occurred in only 51 of Morocco's 199 constituencies in 1984 (Sehimi 1985: 39).

The opposition parties were aging, perhaps more than the government (Zartman 1982: 25), in their thinking as well as their leadership. Behind the scenes, however, significant economic changes were rearranging the patronage networks. The problem was not so much the multiplicity of new generations of potential actors whom clients of clients could not quite absorb (Leveau 1985: 266–67) as it was the diminishing resources needed to fuel the networks (Leveau 1987). Deep and durable networks require alienable riches as well as intimidation to keep clients in line. Patronage was indeed perfected: a veritable treasure of crown jewels, it ran deepest and was most centralized in Morocco, where the monarchy had shepherded the resources left by departing colonists more strategically than had the Algerians or Tunisians. Two-thirds of the colonial lands, for instance, were distributed surreptitiously to the king and his followers rather than being politically wasted in state farms or in sales on the open market (Leveau 1985: 247). French commerce and industry were barely touched until 1973, when Moroccanization could serve a useful political purpose. Senior administrators could then be shuffled off to the private sector, opening the way to government promotions for a new generation of king's men (Leveau 1985: 255). But once production was in native hands, there was little left to redistribute. Dramatic rises in world phosphate prices kept the makhzan's coffer supplied a while longer, but then they collapsed and budget deficits had to be brought under control.

Either cheaper forms of patronage had to be discovered or the system had to be changed. The IMF straitjacket diminished the government's margin for maneuver. After 1983, freezes on government employment, tariff reductions and freer trade, the elimination of most price controls and some state trading monopolies, and various other measures of economic liberalization required by either the IMF or the World Bank tended to undercut the traditional sources of patronage, which relied on selective implementations of government regulations. The international agencies were in effect devaluing the treasure of crown jewels. Yet the king, an astute political actor, acted as if he wished to give some of his jewels away. His official application to join the European Community, for instance, had the response been favorable, would have further opened Moroccan economic decision-making up to European as well as international pressures for deregulation (Leveau 1987).

King Hassan was able, in fact, to adapt his patronage system to the new international rules. Tactically, for instance, support for small and medium-sized enterprises satisfied foreign lenders insisting upon export-oriented growth while rebuilding clienteles to offset "legitimacy deficits" (Doumou 1987: 212). Strategically, Morocco's largest party, the UC, favored both economic liberalism and political restructuring—to consolidate "democracy." The makhzan seems to have devised a scheme to control political and economic reform simultaneously while sticking to Morocco's international commitments.

On this reading, the makhzan's purchase in 1980 of Omnium Nord-Africain (ONA) was the key to a new political strategy. This holding company is Morocco's most powerful conglomerate and the one best positioned to compete in liberated internal markets. Since gross revenues amounted to 5.5 percent of Morocco's GDP, new potentials for patronage seemed enormous. In 1987 ONA added Morocco's top performing bank to the portfolio of banks under its direct control or influence, which then totaled some 15 percent of the commercial banks' total assets, including at least a third of the private sector's. Significantly, too, the first thrust of "privatization" was the sale of a government sugar refinery to ONA. The makhzan then seemed in position to repeat the political achievements of the 1973 Moroccanization campaign alluded to earlier. To avoid unseemly appearances, however, the king's son-in-law, who headed the ONA, disclaimed further interest in acquiring state enterprises. When procedures for privatization were accelerated in 1991, the owners of two other major conglomerates, Kettani and Lamrani, also excluded themselves from acquisitions by agreeing to join the Privatization Council, which was to evaluate enterprises up for sale. These three king's men, however, already controlled much of Morocco's banking system, and their direct control of business enterprises could be veiled in banking secrecy. In Morocco these matters were so confidential that, on the king's request, France expelled Abdelmounen Diori to Gabon to pressure him to delay publication of his book, *A qui appartient le Maroc?* by L'Harmattan. The book was scheduled to be published in September, then delayed until November 1991, when the writer received death threats (*MEED*, 5 July 1991: 22; 25 October 1991: 16).

As privatization picked up momentum in 1993, the makhzan seemed elegantly to have adapted to the new international pressures placed on the Moroccan economy. By waiting until 1991 to proceed with financial reform, the government not only followed good financial advice but also gave the makhzan time to consolidate its command over the heights of a liberated economy. After acquiring a one-quarter stake in Morocco's best-performing private bank, the Banque du Commerce Marocain (BCM), the ONA proceeded in 1991 to buy 15 percent of the Banque Marocaine du Commerce et de l'Industrie (BMCI) and rejuvenate its management. Subsequently the ONA took over half the shares of Morocco's eighth largest bank, the Société Marocaine de Dépôt et de Crédit (SMDC). Kittani's Wafabank was especially well positioned to benefit from the lifting of credit restrictions, and it increased its loan portfolio by more than 40 percent in 1991, well above the average rate.

By disengaging the state from the economy, King Hassan not only developed new clienteles but also lightened his political responsibilities. Financial reform was obviously critical—and it was brilliantly timed. A more systematic, "Turkish" approach to constitutionalism would now be in keeping with the new strategy. Royal patronage supported an efficient multiparty system. The electoral law, majority voting in single-member constituencies, theoretically promotes bipartism under normal conditions (Charlot 1985: 501, 511). Under pressures to reform the constitution, the king could, if he chose, orchestrate alternating Constitutional Union and USFP/Istiqlal governments. In the first round of the 1993 elections the USFP and Istiqlal appeared to have won a mandate, but subsequent indirect elections under the existing constitution for one-third of the seats resulted in a parliament with no clear majority.

Turkey's Electoral Economics

For Turkey, too, financial reform was an integral part of a political strategy. But just as rampant inflation complicated the economics of the reform, so, too, did the country's more institutionalized political system. Republican Turkey had become so committed to competitive elections at regular intervals that the military junta, after seizing power in September 1980, meticulously reshaped the party system even while banning its politicians from political life. Electoral politics had to go on, however distorted and manipulated the routines might be. In the elections of November 1983, Turgut Özal benefited from these distortions. Having assembled the party least stained by military boots, he rode to a comfortable parliamentary majority with 41 percent of the popular vote. Once democracy was restored, however, he had to service the patronage networks needed for electoral purposes. He could not in the end escape the cycle of economic stabilization, electoral economics, renewed inflation, and change of government that had plagued Turkey since 1950 (Turan 1992; Onis and Riedel 1993: 91–104). Financial reform helped him for a time to preserve the center-right coalition pioneered by Bayar's Democrat Party and subsequently consolidated by Demirel's Justice Party. But the inflation fueled by electoral economics, while returning the Motherland Party with a reduced popular plurality of 36 percent (but a greater parliamentary majority) in 1987, seriously eroded Özal's power base. He successfully pressured his deputies to elect him president of the republic in 1989, but then his Motherland Party won only one-quarter of the seats in parliament (and 22 percent of the vote). Demirel returned to power in 1991 at the head of a coalition government that excluded the Motherland Party, while permitting Özal to remain president. He died in office in April 1993.

Özal's distinctive political base had been big business. Genuinely committed to market reform after directing Turkey's State Planning Organization in the early 1970s, he gained the support of many of Turkey's huge business conglomerates in the 1980s. Groups such as Koç, Sabancı, and Çukarova had achieved prominence in Turkey's mixed economy, and the Motherland Party would finally reflect their impact upon the classic Center-Right coalition initially forged by Bayar and Menderes in the 1940s and

1950s. As early as the 1970s, an association had been established to represent the interests of big business as distinct from those of the smaller businesses represented in the chambers of commerce. Founded in 1971, shortly after a military "coup by memorandum" had installed a nonpartisan cabinet to restore macroeconomic as well as other forms of order, TÜSİAD had been designed to articulate the interests of the businessmen who could afford to join this exclusive club. It would be an important, if not exactly monolithic, source of Özal's support until the late 1980s.

TÜSİAD wielded considerable political clout in the 1970s. Occasionally it went public. For instance, in 1979, after many private meetings with Turkey's leading politicans, TÜSİAD finally blitzed the media with paid advertisements against the prevarications of the Eçevit coalition government. When Eçevit resigned and Demirel took over, big business was delighted with his decision to appoint Özal, who had once worked for the Sabancı Group, as his top economic adviser. Özal then persuaded both Demirel and the military to enact the 24 January 1980 stablization program. When the military seized power in September, the officers promoted Özal to deputy prime minister for economic affairs. They, too, enjoyed many special relationships, including family intermarriages as well as board memberships, with the big-business groups.

Much of big business could afford to support Özal's major shift in economic policy from import substitution to export-oriented growth. More readily than little businesses, conglomerates could readjust their portfolios from the protected industries to export activities. In Latin America protected industries with large fixed assets tended to reject such reforms unless, as in Chile, the fear of class warfare impelled them to support the government (Frieden 1991: 166–69). But the possibilities of diversification may also have dampened sectoral solidarity and mitigated the opposition of the big Chilean conglomerates to market-oriented reforms. Özal's success, seen against the failure in the late 1960s to make such a transition, could be viewed as testimony to the growing strength of big business in Turkish political life. It usually delivered enough small business, too, to keep the ruling party's political machines rolling. The trick of the successful reformer was to cajole and threaten big business, to keep it in line behind the market-oriented reforms even when they caused short-run pain.

Özal used financial reform to good effect. The freeing of interest rates in July 1981 was implemented so as not to alienate big business. The initial response of the big banks was to blunt competition by rigging the interest rates. They went up just enough in 1981 to stem the hemorrhage of foreign exchange and keep Özal's other reforms on track. The biggest and strongest groups, Koç and Sabancı, could adapt relatively easily. Koç Holdings had the most capital tied to fixed assets, but it was relatively well capitalized, supported by joint ventures that helped to diversify the risks. The Sabancı Group preferred 100 percent ownership with a smaller surface, but it tended to concentrate in less capital-intensive industries. The profits of Akbank, owned by Sabancı, were adversely affected by banking competition, but the group was not heavily dependent upon the bank for working capital. Other important groups, such as Çukarova, were more adversely affected. Çukarova owned three banks, including one of the Big Four, Yapı ve Kredi Bankası, and had relied on their cheap funds to finance an overextended business empire founded on import substitution.

Turkey's banking oligopoly came under new pressure, however, as it tried to protect the fat margins between the interest it paid depositors and the interest it charged borrowers. Since interest rates remained well under the prevailing rate of inflation, new *bankers* (brokers) offered higher rates to the public by selling securities at a discount and then lending out the money at higher rates either to customers or to some of the banks that were losing deposits. The Central Bank properly stepped in at the end of 1981 to regulate the brokers, and a couple of the smaller brokerage houses folded, provoking a minor disruption of financial markets and further intervention by the authorities. Some banks had meanwhile come to depend upon the brokers, however, and they continued to perform their financial intermediation in a regulated setting. Kastelli, the largest of them, was eventually, in June 1982, caught in a squeeze when a large textile company was unable to meet its payments, in turn causing the brokerage firm to default on its debts to commercial banks. Some bankers interpret the Kastelli crisis as the revenge of the commercial banking establishment against unwanted competition. Özal and his handpicked finance minister, Kaya Erdem, were content to let the financial markets discipline depositors, small and large alike, who had risked their money with Kastelli for premium rates of return. The banking oligopoly was their preferred instrument of reform.

Unfortunately for the reformers, small-businessmen, pensioners, and depositors, including army officers and bureaucrats as well as many others, did not appreciate the market discipline when they lost their savings. The Kastelli crisis temporarily ended the reform process. Pressured by the Union of Chambers of Commerce (but not TÜSİAD), the generals fired the minister of finance, and Özal resigned. His setback of course turned out to be a blessing in disguise for him, for the engineer-technocrat could then turn his hand to politics, take advantage of the window of opportunity afforded by the generals' peculiar elections, and return to power in November 1983. Özal's friends in TÜSİAD could soothe any minor military embarrassments.

As prime minister, Özal waited a couple of years before pursuing financial reform and did not again liberalize interest rates until 1987, once he had established his control over the commercial banking system. Advised by his American-educated son, Ahmet, he appointed young technocrats, the "princes," to head the Central Bank, Ziraat Bankası, and another large public sector bank. His youngest brother, Yusuf, whom he had appointed earlier to head the State Planning Organization, returned from the World Bank in 1987 to be minister of state for economic coordination. With a relatively small number of appointments, the prime minister could control Turkey's rambling state bureaucracy sufficiently to allow market-oriented reforms to work. The Central Bank and the large public commercial banks had to be modernized if any reform was to take place. While reminiscent, perhaps, of Weber's "sultanic" form of patrimonial rule, Özal's choices do not seem to have been dictated by patronage considerations. Under the system prevailing since the time of Menderes, the state banks had always served the patronage needs of the party in power. Özal continued these practices but also tried to induce a structural reform of the system.

The banking law of 1985, coupled with a structural adjustment loan from the World Bank in 1986, paved the way for a process of financial liberalization that Özal could control. On the one hand, the "princes" could restructure the public sector banks and prepare them for harsher financial markets. On the other hand, the prime minister could also indirectly control two of the big private sector banks, İş Bankası and Akbank. İş was only nominally private, and Akbank was owned by Özal's closest TÜSİAD ally. The Sabancı Group publicly supported his government as late as 1989 (*Ekonomik Bülten,* 17–23 July 1989), although the need for a public statement at that time cast some doubt on its depth. Since the fourth of the big retail banks, belonging to the Çukaroka Group, was in chronic difficulties after 1980, it had to follow the others. Consequently the freeing of interest rates on 1 July 1987 put pressure on big business to support Özal in the November elections.

By then, he in effect controlled the entire banking system and could make or break any conglomerate except the very biggest, Koç and Sabancı. Akbank flourished with renewed financial liberalization, for, being one of the very few sound commercial banks, it was well positioned to benefit from the misfortunes of others. Koç did not own a big retail bank; Sabancı had discouraged Koç from imitating its business strategy by stubbornly keeping a minority share in a big retail bank that Koç had attempted to acquire in the

1970s. Özal sustained the Koç Group's enthusiasm for liberalization, however, by nationalizing its major albatross, a losing steel mill that he had earlier helped design as a young engineer in the State Planning Office. He also offered Çukarova some consolation: in 1986 its leader, who had fled to Switzerland and had been expunged from TÜSİAD's rolls, was exonerated from charges of having smuggled gold or possibly more incriminating exports. Özal further stimulated big business by cutting the credits of big Demirel supporters. After the elections of 1987 three medium-sized conglomerates would be in visible financial difficulties. Insiders close to the Motherland Party, on the other hand, enjoyed generous credits despite a general squeezing of the private sector. One of them, a Harvard Business School graduate, even acquired for his personal account a bank that the Çukarova Group had mandated him to purchase on its behalf.

Selective credit allocation whipped followers into line. Özal also timed the elections of 1987 shrewdly; once the electorate by a narrow margin had ruled in favor of reinstatement for the politicians whom the generals had banned from political life, Özal rushed the opposition parties into early general elections without giving them time to organize. Time was not on the side of the Motherland Party, once Turkey's traditional political formations resumed activity. But however necessary for Özal's political survival, the flurry of political activity in 1987 unfortunately dulled his instrument of financial reform and alienated much of the business community.

Just as inflation finally seemed to be settling down to a controllable 30 percent, electoral economics kicked it back up. Not only were interest rates liberalized before the elections but at the same time the Central Bank and Ziraat Bankası were obliged to pay off the rural notables in command of provincial patronage. The money supply visibly increased in the month prior to the elections, fueled by Central Bank discounting, and the effects at the end of the year were painfully visible on Ziraat Bankası's balance sheet. Loans as a percentage of total assets increased from 47.7 percent at the end of 1986 to 55.1 percent at the end of 1987. Renewed banking competition was also eroding Ziraat's deposit base, so that its loan-to-deposit ratio jumped from 84.8 percent to 121.4 percent.

In its annual summary of the Turkish economy, TÜSİAD bitterly complained of the "election economics" (TÜSİAD 1988: 49):

> It is . . . the policy makers' duty to ensure that public sector accounts are so balanced as to prevent conflicts between the various goals and instruments of macroeconomic policy.
>
> Whilst it cannot be denied that great economic progress has been made, it is

> unfortunately the case that these principles have not been strictly followed by Turkey's policy makers . . . due to numerous elections held in 1987.
>
> As a result, numerous legitimate economic objectives, and particularly private sector's industrial objectives, have deliberately been sacrificed in order to meet the public sector's short-term financial demands. In a word, there has been excessive public sector spending on infrastructure projects and services such as transportation, power, telecommunications, highways which had a special significance for the country's voters. (TÜSİAD 1988: iii).

Such outspoken criticism reflected a growing discontent in the business community. TÜSİAD was especially concerned about the rising costs and increased scarcity of credit, and it complained of the private sector being "crowded out" of the money market. Government and public sector borrowing requirements were increasing, not decreasing, with chronic and growing public deficits. Strains between Özal and TÜSİAD grew so great that the latter's chairman resigned in January 1989, ostensibly to devote more time to his business. His colorful successor did not complete his two-year term either. When accused by Özal of becoming too political by suggesting new elections in 1990, he responded that TÜSİAD was a business lobby, not a canary lovers' association; earlier he had become the subject of a judicial inquiry after accusing state functionaries of "kleptocracy" (*Çumhüriyet,* weekly European edition, 7–13 December 1990). Both business leaders were exporters theoretically favored by Özal's policies.

Persisting deficits and concomitant inflation and credit squeezes were unraveling the ruling coalition. On 4 February 1988, the government announced a new stabilization program to narrow once more the difference between the official foreign exchange rate and the parallel market. Interest rates on Turkish lire deposits were increased to keep up with inflation. As in 1981, the banking oligopoly had driven interest rates down once they were deregulated. This time the authorities had to stop Sabancı's bank from converting cheap Turkish lire deposits into foreign exchange and investing it in Euromarkets through its London subsidiary—a procedure very familiar to Egyptian infitah banks but unacceptable to Turkey's monetary authorities. In October domestic interest rates were again deregulated, for the third time since 1981, in the hope that market forces might make local currency deposits sufficiently attractive to offset inflation. The government was again attempting to use financial reform as a tool, this time to shift any blame for excessive inflation to impersonal market forces.

TÜSİAD still quite rightly insisted, however, that "the Turkish Commercial Banking System displays the features of an oligopolistic market structure. . . . Interest rates are likely to be determined institutionally, be it by the central monetary authority or by the joint action of a few large banks, but not by the free play of market forces" (1989: 59–60). Ziraat in fact bid up interest rates so high that the Central Bank had to put an end to the experiment within weeks. The image of Turkey's ruling family and some of the "princes" suffered. Their impersonal markets received another jolt a few weeks later, in January 1989.

One of the princes, Bülent Şemiler, resigned his position as chairman and general manager of Konutbank, Turkey's second largest public sector bank. He denied that he had leaked a story implicating Deputy Prime Minister Kaya Erdem with a bank fraud, though Konutbank had been stuck with a loss of $80 million as a result of the fraud. Erdem, one of Özal's closest allies in the Motherland Party, resigned because of the publicity and the prime minister's apparent support for Şemiler. Yavuz Canevi, a former governor of the Central Bank, also resigned his position as undersecretary of the Treasury. The brash young prince was a black sheep among the government bankers. Though he was respected by some for restructuring and turning around the two ailing banks he had merged into Konutbank, others criticized him for creative accounting on some of its real estate deals. In an interview with *The Banker* that was publicized in Turkey, Şemiler condemned the state banking system in no uncertain terms: "The 11 state banks are continuously manipulated by the politicians. They are mostly outdated and old-fashioned. They must change many things." He urged that they be privatized and effectively freed from the politicans' influence (*The Banker,* March 1989: 50; *Ekonomik Panorama,* March 1989). Özal made him his chief adviser on banking affairs, but the government then failed to get the necessary legislation through parliament to qualify for the release by the World Bank of the second tranche of its second financial sector adjustment loan. The restructuring of the big public sector banks was also behind schedule.

Özal tried to offset losses of support—within government as well as in the business community—by incorporating new conglomerates in his entourage. Asil Nader, a Turkish Cypriot, expanded his operations in Turkey after turning Polly Peck into a Fortune 500 company and one of the hottest stocks traded in the mid-1980s on the London Stock Exchange. With Özal's blessings he invested in the strategic popular press and private television as well as in white goods and electronics. But all the Turkish credit in the world could not have put Polly Peck together again once the bubble burst on the London Stock Exchange. Faced with shortfalls of over $2 billion, Nader flew to Turkey to try to raise money, but Turkey's bankers could not be budged.

Özal also experimented with another controversial financial and political strategy: encouraging the formation of "special finance houses," Islamic banks. When they first applied for permission to establish themselves in Turkey, Özal was still a technocrat serving Turkey's military government as deputy prime minister in charge of the economy. One of his first actions as prime minister was to get "Decree Dated 16/12/1983, No. 83/7506 Regarding the Foundation of Special Finance Houses" signed and published in the *Official Gazette* of 19 December. The signing was especially significant in view of the general freeze on new bank licenses at this time. As a technocrat who, like his younger brother Korkut, had been associated with the Islamist-oriented National Salvation Party (NSP), Özal had known where critical threats and opportunities lay in the early 1980s. The only potential challenge—and possible source of support—was the Islamists. In 1983 Özal's Center-Right Anavatan Partisi (ANAP), the Motherland Party, picked up votes not only from the supporters of Demirel's outlawed party but also from supporters of the National Salvation Party. In the 1987 elections, too, Islamist elements of the NSP remained loyal to the Motherland Party. As military control diminished over the civilian political elite, ANAP faced greater competition, and the "holy alliance" of up to a hundred of ANAP's 289 deputies became a major source of support.

It can be assumed that business patronage was a critical instrument of party cohesion. Despite growing discontent in the business community in 1988 and 1989, as well as diminishing pluralities in referenda and municipal elections, Özal survived as prime minister with the help of big business, notably Sabancı. As his popular support crumbled, however, he relied more heavily on the support of the Islamic networks. After the "Holy Alliance" helped elect him president in 1989, a number of its members became ministers. In November 1990, some 18 to 20 of the 28 ANAP ministers were identified as Islamist, although by then the liberal secularists were regaining leadership of the party (Robins 1991: 44). Until 1990, too, a member of the Naqşibendi order chaired the Union of Chambers of Commerce and helped to neutralize Demirel's small business constituency.

Özal's financial reforms also included reinvigorating the Istanbul Stock Exchange, so that it might alleviate the private sector's credit squeeze and facilitate the privatization of some state enterprises. As noted in the previous chapter, Turkish stocks enjoyed a minor boom in 1990. Inflation was so rampant that people preferred to invest on the stock market rather than in savings accounts. Mutual funds consisting mainly of government bonds also enjoyed some success, though the banks could manipulate their portfolios on their own accounts. Stocks were also risky: price-earning ratios in

1990 defied economic logic. Some banks and companies did raise useful sums on the market. Sabancı's Akbank, for instance, raised a staggering TL 500 billion (about $25 million) for an issue of 5 percent of its capital. But the market could not satisfy much of private sector's needs, and business figures resented Özal's rejoinder that they could sell their yachts if they needed cash. His wife's presence as an investor on the stock exchange added spice and speculation, for others followed her investment leads, with quick profits for all. Her explanations that their youngest son, Efe, a trader on the stock exchange, handled all her money hardly dampened press speculation about insider trading. When, finally, she entered politics and replaced an Islamist at the head of the Istanbul section of the Motherland Party in 1991, her husband's coalition imploded.

Financial instruments could not in the final analysis rescue the Motherland Party from defeat at the polls. Özal's reforms probably alienated more potential support in the business community than they attracted, and once Demirel's True Path (ex-Justice) Party was permitted to reorganize, disgruntled business magnates may have diversified their financial support. At least one of Demirel's key economic advisers enjoyed personal connections with a major conglomerate that Özal's policies had harmed, and eventually Prime Minister Demirel appointed a senior Koç executive to the key position of undersecretary of the Treasury and foreign trade. If Özal's tactics had failed him, however, the strategy of reform might yet succeed. He used Turkey's tried and true financial instruments to stay in power but may have sabotaged them for his successors. How far his reforms have really eroded Turkey's oligopolistic structure will be addressed in the following chapter.

Conclusion

Without any strong economic base, North Africa's opposition parties, with the major exception of the Islamists, lacked credibility in the 1980s. Serious strategies of political transition in fact had to place financial reform at the center of their agenda. Only by reforming the financial system could sufficient patronage be freed up for durable opposition parties, without which talk of "transition to democracy" sounded like hollow justification for an untenable status quo.

Sadat had carefully tailored economic to political strategy and unleashed a host of unruly banks against a hidebound and corrupt administration, but he did not consistently liberalize either finance or politics. Privatizing patronage did not build up a comfortable screen of opposition parties, as in

Turkey or Morocco, but instead exposed the Sadat family and intensified the difficulties of maintaining a patrimonial regime. He set in motion a dynamic of credit allocation that might constrain his successor's control of the economy. Mubarak, indeed, moved so cautiously on both the political and economic fronts that it was not clear whether the reform process was stalemated or quietly irreversible until the Second Gulf War jolted him into a second infitah.

With an economy and financial system less distorted by state socialism, Tunisia had embarked on a simultaneous effort of financial and political liberalization that was more carefully controlled than the Egyptian infitah. But both processes seemed stalemated within a year or two of Bourguiba's enforced retirement. Perhaps no middle way of incremental reform was possible. Without more democracy, perhaps no regime could really clean out its black box of bureaucratic clienteles, short of deliberately inducing financial anarchy as in Egypt. Yet anarchy seemed only to give new life to a patrimonial regime, rather than to support a Turkish-style transition to real multiparty politics with at least one strong opposition party. Algeria tested a bolder path of simultaneous political and financial reform, but the political experiment unraveled, and the economic and financial reforms drifted. The apparent affinities between the Islamist opposition and the financial reformers, however, raise questions about possible roles for Islamic financial institutions in other, financially more developed crescent contexts. Might they help, in Egypt if not Tunisia, to concentrate sufficient finance capital to empower political oppositions? And could they contribute toward a deepening of political pluralism in Turkey, where banking already enjoys relative autonomy?

Turkey and Morocco were the most successful at exploiting financial reform for political ends because their durable oligopolistic legacies offered their rulers the greatest flexibility. Their black boxes lay partly outside the state bureaucracy. In Turkey, Turgut Özal relied on big business to shift from import substitution to a strategy based on export-oriented growth. In Morocco King Hassan encouraged a similar shift and lifted credit restrictions once his business group had bought into leading banks. Financial reforms actually promised to strengthen his patronage networks in the private sector even while diminishing administrative power bases. In Turkey, by contrast, Özal's blatant use of the banking system may have enhanced its relative autonomy. If so, might Turkey be undergoing another major transition? How durable, in fact, is business and financial oligopoly in the face of established multiparty politics? Could these replicas of Hilferding's finance capitalism be as strong as the original model?

The following studies of the crescent's commercial banking structures will further explore their relationships to political structure and illustrate relationships between financial and political development. Two major hypotheses will be reviewed; namely, that a financial oligopoly rooted in the private sector is more likely than a more competitive banking system to pressure a patrimonial regime toward greater accountability and political pluralism, and that once a commercial banking system achieves a measure of autonomy and structural power, competition with Islamic financial intermediaries may deepen political pluralism in Muslim countries.

Chapter 4

Turkey: The Financial Levers of Power

Father had a particular interest first in soldiers, then in bankers.

(Sakip Sabancı 1988: 80)

The German banking system still places a powerful central bank in a bargaining relationship with a highly concentrated system of privately owned universal banks, but they no longer monopolize finance capital as Hilferding had predicted (Zysman 1983; "World Banking Survey," *The Economist*, 2–9 May 1992: 41, 49). His model better suits countries like Morocco and Turkey, where stock markets are thin and potential investors deterred by the poor quality of business information. Like their early-twentieth-century Berlin prototype, these banking systems are the principal source of finance capital, and they enjoy relative autonomy, a high degree of concentration, and a significant degree of private ownership. In Turkey they supported a remarkable succession of Center-Right coalitions after 1950 (Rustow 1987: 69), once Bayar had successfully challenged the Republic People's Party. While capitalism has perhaps not generated as much heavy industry in Turkey as in Germany a century ago, the bankers have been rising to the commanding heights of the economy.

Decision-making, to be sure, does not exclude state actors, such as finance ministries, but they may be at loggerheads with relatively autonomous banking systems. The state actors bargain with the banking sector, in which a small number of privately owned universal banks wield significant influence over credit allocation and other major economic issues. The banks are usually responsive to government, but they have independent bargaining power and can wield a collective veto to protect their common interests. While individually vulnerable to central banks and political authorities, they collectively allocate credit and may decisively influence government policies as well as the business strategies of their borrowers. Bankers generally avoid confrontations with governments, but they may economize on their financial support. In Turkey they supported Prime Minister Özal's reforms until electoral economics became too expensive and he had hurt too many of them. Even if the bankers do not personify advanced capitalism, they wield substantial structural power.

For Hilferding they were powerful because they controlled vast industrial conglomerates through holdings and interlocking boards of directors; indeed, the concentration of the banking industry had come about as a defense against monopolistic trends in iron and steel and other industries (Hilferding 1981 [1910]: 223). But financial power need not be based on the ownership and direct control of other enterprises. As long as a banking industry is highly concentrated and remains the preponderant source of finance capital, without significant competition from other potential sources such as stock exchanges, it can still command the economic heights. The secret of the bankers' power lies in the concentration of their industry. If, as in an iterated prisoner's dilemma game (Axelrod 1984), they continually resolve dilemmas of common interest, they may retain their oligopoly and keep control of credit allocation.

For an oligopoly to sustain itself, the price setters have to take a long-term view of their business interests. In a two-player game they may be expected to "cooperate" or collude as long as the expected future values of cooperation outweigh the present value of "defecting," or grabbing greater market share by shaving prices. By this token bankers seem to be natural oligopolists, expecting steady rates of return under a long shadow of future relationships. Their discount rates, or costs of capital, have to be just low enough to offset temptations for quick profits at the expense of their fellow oligopolists.

If oligopoly is to work, however, game theory points to the requirement for a clan of healthy, financially solvent players with relatively low costs of capital. In the real world bankers are all too tempted (or pressured by their governments) to load up their portfolios with dubious loans, and only the strongest of them manage, as in the international debt crises of the mid-1980s, to keep resolving their dilemmas of common interest (Lipson 1985). Inflation (but not necessarily civil war) may, as in Lebanon, blow out the model's underlying parameters (Moore 1987). In banking, as in the international oil industry, any enduring oligopoly presupposes real "surveillance procedures" to monitor the key players, "mechanisms for imposing discipline," even on state companies, and "real penalties for deviation" so as to engender automatic patterns of compliance, "rather than the 'softer' idea of shared norms, principles, and [rational] expectations" (Moran 1987: 578n.10).

Lenders of last resort, central banks try to perform these functions, even if they cannot always guarantee that leading banks will be financially fit, with costs of capital low enough to make them good oligopolists. In Turkey and Morocco, the independent states protected their rich nineteenth-century banking legacies rather than attacking them as in Algeria, Egypt, and Tunisia. Their central banks were relatively strong and autonomous by regional standards. But fifty years of import substitution in Turkey (1930–80) gave rise to many risky debts from highly leveraged private as well as public enterprises. There were all too many temptations for banks to overextend themselves and give up any pretense of command over the economy to the state planners and the Treasury. In fact the private oligopolists did not acquire much structural power until the 1980s. Turkey's reformers subsequently tapped big business to command major economic changes. Although the changes were supposed to induce greater competition and more open economies in finance as well as in other sectors, the reforms initially reinforced the oligopoly and helped sustain the reformers. The fragile bases of oligopoly in this developing capitalist system deserve further examination, however. Financial liberalization did eventually encourage trends toward a less concentrated commercial banking system. By encouraging Islamic financial institutions, moreover, Özal not only cemented his ruling coalition but perhaps anticipated further financial liberalization and a deepening of political participation.

The German Financial Legacy

While Germany no longer directly influenced Turkish finance after World War II, its legacy had already been institutionalized. Though British and French banks penetrated the Ottoman Empire several decades before Deutsche Bank's arrival in 1888, the German presence would decisively alter Turkey's financial climate, including the other European banks originally attracted by lucrative opportunities to finance the Ottoman state debt. As the Ottoman Empire was gradually stripped of its European and North African possessions, Europe's "sick man" staggered to the tunes of the Concert of Europe, continuing "to borrow and spend with the laxity of despair" (Feis 1930: 331). European diplomacy successfully resolved dilemmas of common interest in favor of formal Ottoman independence until 1914. The Ottoman Empire had perhaps enjoyed a marginal advantage over Egypt and Tunisia until 1875, when it, too, fell into arrears on its debts. Britain was not only committed to defending the integrity of the Ottoman Empire, *faute de mieux,* but also on occasion to financing it. The first loan, in 1854, was guaranteed by Egypt's annual tribute to the Ottoman overlord, but the second, in 1855, for the Crimean War against Russia, was directly guaranteed by Britain. Its immensely larger and more efficient financial markets made London, not Paris, "the greatest combination of economical power and economical delicacy that the world has ever seen" (Bagehot 1978 [1915]: 3), but British bankers subsequently became almost as reticent as the parsimonious Germans two decades later to pump money directly into the Porte's treasury. Once more, in 1865, Istanbul received a megaloan from London's financial market that was a good 5 percent cheaper than smaller bond issues floated by the Imperial Ottoman Bank and the Comptoir d'Escompte at about the same time in Paris.

After 1862 the Porte usually turned to Paris, where finance houses readily mobilized French savings purely for governmental lending. Small French rentiers, enthusiastic about "valeurs à turban," took over the floating debt earlier assumed by Istanbul's local Galata bankers at rates of 12 to 15 percent. But although the rentier would receive only his 6 or 7 percent coupon, the Turkish government still had to pay effective interest rates of 13 to 15 percent (calculated from Corm 1982: 41 and Owen 1981: 104). Defending its empire against Russia and others, Turkey had financial needs far greater than Egypt's, but little of the money went for productive purposes: until 1874 only 9 percent of loans were for railroads—exclusively in European parts of the Ottoman Empire (Bouvier 1982: 22).

Istanbul's banking scene acquired a distinctly French look after 1863, when a consortium led by Crédit Mobilier doubled the shares of the Ottoman Bank. This bank had been founded originally in London by British investors responding to an Ottoman decree of 1856, inspired by Her Majesty's Government, calling for "banks and other similar institutions" to promote and monitor overseas loans to the Ottoman treasury. Earlier British efforts in Ismir in 1842 and in Istanbul in 1847 had failed to take root, but the Ottoman Bank, renamed the Imperial Ottoman Bank in 1863, has survived as the Osmanli Bankası to the present day. Its very size and its special contacts with Paris ensured order among the greedy French banks pushing for a place at the Porte's high table. The orderly banquet at its expense stood in sharp contrast to "the anarchy of English finance" stirring up the Nile at this time (Landes 1958: 67). Many of Istanbul's aspiring European competitors left the field or amalgamated with the Imperial Ottoman Bank in the wake of a financial crisis in 1873 (Issawi 1980: 340–41). The bank was so closely identified with the Quai d'Orsay that modest French entrepreneurs tried to steer clear of it (Bouvier 1960: 29–30). Imperial Ottoman cashed in on usurious state loans and cranked out steady dividends of 12 to 13 percent to its shareholders between 1863 and 1873.

When the Porte, faced with a debt service amounting to 60 percent of its revenues, unilaterally halved its debt in 1875, it was careful not to cut payments on bonds which Britain and France had officially guaranteed. Neither the great powers, except Russia, nor bond underwriters, who had already skimmed off their fabulous profits, had any interest in seriously infringing on Ottoman sovereignty. Coming to power in 1876, however, Sultan Abdul Hamid was so unsuccessful in 1877 in raising a defense loan in London that he turned to the Imperial Ottoman Bank for short-term credits and hoped to strengthen its hand for further bond issues by encouraging divisions among the foreign bondholders. The Congress of Berlin, held in the summer of 1878, seemed to dash these hopes (while preserving part of Bulgaria for the Porte) by issuing the July Protocol, expressing official concern for the bondholders and recommending a financial commission of "specialists" from the various powers to examine their complaints and "the most efficacious means for satisfying them as far as is compatible with the financial situation of the Porte" (Blaisdell 1929: 85). When the Porte wavered, the British fleet, having intimidated Russia into signing a peace treaty the previous year, returned through the Dardanelles to effect a change of government in Istanbul. The new viziers quickly reached agreement in November 1879 with the Imperial Ottoman Bank on a scheme to "begin to satisfy its foreign creditors, while safeguarding the rights of local bankers, and avoiding official European intervention in the state finances" (88). When the accord failed to open up the European money markets, however, the Porte acceded to the Decree of Moharrem, 1881, establishing a Public Debt Administration (PDA) under multinational management in exchange for slightly more generous debt relief.

Because the major powers Britain, France, and Germany agreed to keep the sick man alive, the Porte was spared Tunisia's and Egypt's fate of colonial occupation. The PDA was "an alternative to the formation of a colonial apparatus: it reflected a compromise among rival imperialist powers in establishing a degree of stability in the financial relationship of the Empire with European sources of credit, while the commercial sphere remained open to competition" (Keyder 1987: 40). The PDA was also a logical outcome of a gradual reduction of Ottoman financial authority, beginning in 1855 and reaching "practically to zero" by 1879 (Blaisdell 1929: 26, citing Lord Derby). Although only the French at that point were enthusiastic about establishing a *tutelle* over the country's public finances, various British and Anglo-French councils had previously monitored the public debt and "advised" the Porte, much as the IMF presented diagnoses, recommendations, and prescriptions in the 1970s. Not only short-term stabilization but long-term structural adjustment, too, was in vogue. The Hobart and Foster mission of 1860, for instance, had urged the Porte to sell off its properties, including fisheries, forests, mines, and land, and to "lay aside all jealousy of private enterprise, whether national or foreign and throw doors open to free competition, . . . [for] it is by foreign capital that the land would be made most valuable" (Kiray 1990: 258, citing the Report of 1862).

Put in charge of collecting over one-quarter of the Porte's most liquid revenues, the PDA was a real "mark of Ottoman subjection" (Bouvier 1982: 25) despite pretenses that it was merely a vehicle for bondholders, operating under the full supervision of the Ottoman authorities (Blaisdell 1929: 95). The French representative of the bondholders, in fact, was appointed by the Imperial Ottoman Bank with the approval of the Quai d'Orsay, and if the British creditors underwent a more cumbersome selection process through meetings of bondholders, the effect was the same: an informal Foreign Office presence. Bismarck's personal banker designated the German representative with the approval of the Auswärtiges Amt (Stern 1979: 419); subsequently Deutsche Bank, enjoying a monopoly of German representation in Turkey, would appoint its man.

Despite their official ties to home governments, however, the managers acted more like international civil servants, pioneering one of the most successful ventures of the time in international organization. Though it was the most conspicuous mark of Turkey's semicolonial status, to be discarded by Atatürk in 1928, it protected the Ottoman Empire's international credit and developed new functions. It farmed out the tobacco monopoly to an independent agency jointly managed by the French and the Austrians, but it also administered new sources of revenues, such as customs surcharges accepted by the powers in 1907. It also monitored railroad concessions, including Deutsche Bank's line to Ankara, begun in 1888. The administrators in fact developed overlapping interests, sitting on the boards of various banks and railroad companies. Even when the powers quarreled, harmony reigned among these servants of the Ottoman debt until 1912; then, despite Italy's takeover of Tripolitania, the Porte expelled the representative of the Italian bondholders only after he defended his country's action to the German ambassador (Blaisdell 1929: 182–83). The British and French teams withdrew voluntarily in 1914, only to return in 1918 to expel the Germans and Austrians. Until World War I, the PDA had offered an ideal environment for the serious work of European finance capital.

Germany moved into railways. By the eve of World War I, the latecomer had accumulated 19.3 percent of the Turkish debt, most of it productive, being invested in the Baghdad Railway and other industries. In fact the Germans had acquired most of Turkey's productive assets, as only one-fifth or so of the 26 bonds issued before 1914 were for productive purposes (Feis 1930: 316). Britain nonchalantly ceded its share of state lending to France, which possessed more than 58.5 percent of these Turkish "assets" by the end of 1912 (319). Though the British, with better opportunities elsewhere, apparently lost interest in their Ottoman agribusinesses (in the region of Ismir), the little French investor remained enamored of "les valeurs à turban."

The Imperial Ottoman Bank tried to emulate Deutsche Bank—and Paribas for that matter—in the industrial field, but it lacked any "global systematic vision" (Thobie 1983: 472) and seems to have been torn between its official mission of underwriting the lucrative state bonds and a new interest in opening up the Near East to French capital. Perhaps it was easier for the bank to make money under French diplomatic protection than to place it sparingly and productively like the Germans. The French ambassador complained in 1893, when the Imperial Ottoman Bank refused to finance a loan for importing military wares manufactured by Le Creusot: "It is in the unity of German capitalists and industrialists that one can discover the cause of their success" (Bouvier et al. 1982: 30). In this case, the bank had refused the loan for fear of perturbing Ottoman bonds on the Paris Bourse. The bank did, however, cut a deal with Deutsche Bank in 1894 whereby each agreed to participate roughly 20 percent in the other's projects "to avoid any haggling detrimental to profits" in Turkey (37). Accordingly, the Imperial Ottoman tried to sustain a friendly competition with the Germans by investing in French railroads, utilities, and other projects, especially in the Levant. Only occasionally was there any serious rivalry between the French and the Germans until 1903, when France sent in gunboats to wrest concessions from the Porte to match those of the Germans. If the Germans were to build the Haidar-Pasha railway station on the Asian side of Istanbul, then France had to have the contract to refurbish the Galata quais on the European side, as well as various guarantees for its schools and cultural activities.

The Baghdad Railway became a major issue in 1903. Traversing rugged Anatolian terrain required huge capital outlays that were within the reach of only British or French capital markets. Germany had on occasion been allowed back into Paris markets closed to it after France's defeat in 1870, but in 1903 the Germans also appealed to London for official help, since any new Turkish customs duties needed for new debt service required consent of the major powers. British Foreign Secretary Landsdowne, who favored buying into the railway in order to neutralize it, asked the Baring brothers to study British participation issue in bond issues. Much to the chagrin of the financiers, however, the project attracted immense public hostility, whipped up by a patriotic press, leading Prime Minister Balfour to drop it. Apparently the timid bankers were the first to run. Lansdowne later recalled: "If it had not been for the scuttle of the financiers I should have been in favor of sticking to our position" (cited by Feis 1930: 351). In that tortured sense, maybe Hobson was right to argue that financiers stimulated imperialist rivalries (Hobson 1938 [1902]: 60–61).

Such rivalries would further complicate any industrial strategy of the Imperial Ottoman Bank. One result of the entente between Britain and France in 1904 was that the Quai d'Orsay obliged the bank to withdraw support for the Baghdad Railway. Though distressed by this turn in French diplomacy, the bank would no longer support any projects not controlled by French enterprises and would push for Le Creusot's arms deals with the Porte (Bouvier et al. 1982: 31–38). As cooperation broke down between France and Germany in the decade preceding World War I, their rival banks sponsored an economic partition of the Ottoman Empire that reflected the different railroad concessions. The French concessions would eventually be recognized in the Sykes Picot agreement of 1916, the basis for French mandates of Syria and Lebanon after the war. Alarmed by German inroads, the British had meanwhile encouraged Sir Ernst Cassel to found a new bank in Istanbul in 1909, only to stop him in 1910 from underwriting a new state bond issue (Feis 1930: 326). Though the British easily remained the Ottoman Empire's largest trading partner until 1914, their main political concerns were oil and passage to India: to ensure that the Baghdad Railway, were it to reach its destination, would respect the British sphere of influence in southern Iraq, Deutsche Bank was given a minority interest in the Turkish Petroleum Corporation.

With French investments diverted in part to the Levant, the Imperial Ottoman Bank did not constitute a model of industrial banking for Turkey. It had at best begun to fuse industrial and banking capital as Hilferding's model called for (Thobie 1983: 483), but lacking the relatively free hand or industrial substance Paribas would gain in Morocco. Its major legacy to Turkey was the control it had exerted over the Galata bankers and their joint ventures. Until 1888, when the Deutsche Bank arrived, the Ottoman Imperial enjoyed a virtual monopoly over state finances. It served until 1931 as the official state bank, with the power to issue currency, and survived to become by far the largest if most old-fashioned of Turkey's plethora of foreign banks and joint ventures in the 1980s.

The model with the greatest influence on Turkey, however, was the latest to arrive. Deutsche Bank had penetrated Anatolia in league with the

German railroad builders and other industrialists. As Herbert Feis explains, "The Deutsche Bank took the lead . . . in securing financial support for virtually all the German enterprises which combined into a network of power in Turkey. Its representatives wielded control over the Baghdad and Anatolian railways in Asiatic Turkey, the Oriental railways in European Turkey, over the Port Company at Haida[r]-Pasha, the Tramways Company at Constantinople" (Feis 1930: 64). By 1924 almost half of Turkey's foreign investment was of German origin (Hershlag 1968: 41), a network of influence that came directly out of the pages of Hilferding's *Finanzkapital.* Its Turkish emulators would spearhead Turkey's drive to multiparty politics after World War II.

The Turkish Transition to Multiparty Politics

Economic issues seemed to be behind the famous call of Celal Bayar, Adnan Menderes, Mehemed Fuad Köprülü, and Refik Koraltan on 7 June 1945 to remove wartime restrictions on democracy. Perhaps Turkey's need to cultivate the Western democracies against potential Soviet incursions, once Germany had been defeated, also encouraged a degree of political pluralism: the government permitted a rich Istanbul industrialist to form a token opposition party in July 1945. The really significant opposition, however, developed from the nucleus of dissidents within the ruling Republican People's Party (RPP). Already the Land Reform Act of 11 June 1945 had provoked bitter dissension within the RPP. Adnan Menderes, representing Aydin (in the West, just south of Ismir), opposed the act on the grounds that it destroyed medium landholdings and undermined agrarian modernization in the more advanced western parts of Anatolia. He also pushed for more credits to help the landowners modernize their enterprises. At about the same time the RPP was also divided over the budget for the Ministry of Commerce. Celal Bayar, one of Turkey's most senior leaders under Atatürk, founded the Democrat Party on 7 January 1946. The original idea was that it would organize only in the advanced western parts of the country and that it would enroll members one by one for 40 or 50 years before gaining real power (Karpat 1959: 152). In the July 1946 general elections it won just 62 seats, enough to be a vocal opposition without seriously endangering the RPP's majority.

If the government had initially financed the Democrat Party, as one disenchanted member claimed in 1948 (Kenan Oner, cited by Karpat 1959: 213), no personal understandings between President İsmet İnönü and former Prime Minister Bayar prevented real competition in the 1950 campaigns for resources as well as votes. The RPP and the DP had already agreed to limit the effects of agrarian reform and to reorient the economy in favor of private enterprise. Governments before and after the elections welcomed a major mission by the World Bank to advise on the necessary reforms (Barker et al. 1951: xi). Despite the bipartisan consensus in favor of liberalizing the economy, the elections of 14 May 1950 were a watershed in Turkish history: the Democrat Party's overwhelming victory, while reflecting general discontent with Turkey's traditional political machine, also marked an effective alliance among landowners, peasants, and emerging private sector business interests. Crumbs of government finance to support a token opposition surely could not have sufficed to break the RPP machine.

The victory reflected its venerable founder's remarkable influence. Bayar (1882–1986) had personally crafted many of the economic forces that made the victory possible. Furthermore, this son of a provincial mufti had started his long career at the turn of century, after graduating from Bursa's Alliance Israelite, by joining Deutsche Bank's local branch office. He came to embody Republican Turkey's legacy of German universal banking and ensured that it grew indigenous roots under Atatürk's independent regime. Bayar would try to replicate the model in the new regime. After serving as Atatürk's minister of economy in the provisional Republican government, he enjoyed Atatürk's full backing, including personal financing, in founding in 1924 a key project for national recovery, İş Bankası. Bayar managed the bank until 1932. The legacy of Deutsche Bank would live on, with interesting political repercussions.

İş Bankası "represented the central intelligence behind private capital" (Keyder 1987: 106). When, in the world depression, Turkey adopted "statism" and tried to build up industry and mining, it was again Bayar who served as minister of the economy and eventually prime minister. As minister of the economy he was determined that Turkey refuse "to accept colonial status" implied by any international division of labor that confined his country to agriculture (Wålstedt 1980: 66). The statism practiced by Turkey in the 1930s, however, built upon İş Bankası and its German legacy rather than trying to supersede them. The new parastatals imitated the German model of financial holding companies. Although Bayar held no formal administrative office after 1939 and resigned from parliament and the RPP in 1945, he still enjoyed residual clout within the banking system in 1950. It might even be argued that his variant of economic dirigisme had preserved the integrity of Turkey's weak private sector and enabled it to expand. In the 1930s "industrialists regarded [İş Bankası] as their platform when bargaining with the bureaucracy" (Keyder 1987: 106). The bank became greatly overextended in 1935 when its equity investments dramatically increased from TL 1.6 million to 12 million, backed by capital and reserves of only TL 7.8 million (İş Bankası 1974: 51). The more heavily capitalized public sector banks spared it, however, from further increases in industrial investments. İş Bankası thus escaped the fate of the Middle East's other private bank modeled along German lines at this time, Egypt's Banque Misr. The Turkish bank was presumably a centerpiece of the RPP patronage system.

Credit, in such demand by Menderes and his followers in 1945, remained scarce in 1950. In the private sector new banks were forming, such as Yapi ve Kredi, Türkiye Garanti, and Akbank, which would service the needs of emerging business conglomerates. Turkey was already moving toward a more competitive "multi-bank system" (İş Bankası 1974: 52), but in the early postwar years İş Bankası remained the champion of the private sector. In 1949 it collected TL 234.6 million, or 24 percent of the entire banking system's deposits, including those of foreign banks and the giant government-owned Ziraat Bankası (İş Bankası 1974: 51; Barker et al. 1951: 22). Deposits were scarce because the government kept interest rates well below the rate of inflation. Other sources of funds for lending to the private sector were extremely scarce. The Central Bank rediscounted a total of only TL 40 million to all the banks that year, even as it financed state enterprises to the tune of over TL 600 million (Barker et al. 1951: 216). Bayar could turn his banking connections to good use. In addition to all the careers he had helped along during his many years as the founding manager of İş Bankası, he had fathered most of the state enterprises as minister of the economy in the 1930s, while continuing to support the private sector. One disenchanted ex-Democrat claims in his memoirs that an influential businessman had urged him to preside over the DP's Istanbul headquarters (Karpat 1959: 317). In 1938, when Bayar was prime minister, the businessman in question (Onis) had founded Denizbank, the only new bank to get a permit from 1932 to 1944. It is no wonder that he supported the Democrat Party.

Further research would undoubtedly uncover many more connections between the business leaders who were the backbone of the Democratic Party and the patronage networks woven by Bayar's clients in Turkey's "nebulous banking and credit structure" (Hershlag 1988: 40). Evidently Bayar had opened up Turkey's "black box" to an emerging bourgeoisie. The new business elites possibly preferred electoral politics, "open to monetary influence" (Keyder 1987, 142) to coping with the traditional bureaucracy of a single-party regime, but they depended above all on Bayar's credit networks. Their enterprises in turn contributed to an organized opposition party and other political structures. Possibly, too, it was Bayar's residual influence, as much as old age, that saved him from the gallows after the military coup that overthrew Menderes on 27 May 1960. He was pardoned in 1966 and lived on another two decades, to the ripe old age of 104, writing voluminous memoirs. Despite periodic crises, Turkey retained its multiparty system.

Turkey's regime remained authoritarian in two respects. First, its human rights record, tarnished by the judicial murder of Adnan Menderes and others, "cruel and excessive by any standard" (Rustow 1987: 63), remained uneven. Without an adequate data base it is not possible to compare the respective performances of the crescent regimes along any quantitative dimension of repression and human suffering, but qualitatively Turkey, like Morocco, seems as authoritarian in this respect as the one-party systems included in this study, although probably not those of Syria or Iraq. Second, the military, guarantor of constitutional government, periodically intervened to reorganize political life, in 1960, in 1971, and in 1980. The transition of 1945–50 to multiparty politics obviously did not ensure stable democracy. After the coup of September 1980, the military authorities kept multiparty politics but abolished the old parties and banned their leaders from political life. After 1986, however, the old parties and leaders resurfaced, and Suleiman Demirel, who had been prime minister under two previous constitutional regimes, returned to power in 1991. Bayar's legacy endured, as did his patronage networks. Big business supported Turkey's authoritarian brand of multiparty politics, and the relatively competitive elections, in turn, provided a measure of legitimacy and capacity for reform that the crescent's single-party regimes no longer had in the 1980s.

Hilferding in Contemporary Turkey?

Contemporary Turkey obviously deviates from the German model in at least one key aspect: the Turkish Treasury owns eight banks controlling roughly 40 percent of the assets of the Turkish commercial banking system. In 1990 they held almost as many deposits as the 25 privately owned national commercial banks. Turkey's commercial banks collectively disposed of over 85 percent of the commercial bank deposits in 1990; four of them, Ziraat, Vakiflar, Halk, and Emlâk (Konutbank), were state-owned, and two of them were among Turkey's top five deposit-takers. The state is thus a major player as well as regulator of Turkey's financial oligopoly.

Turkey's four biggest commercial banks held from two-thirds to three-

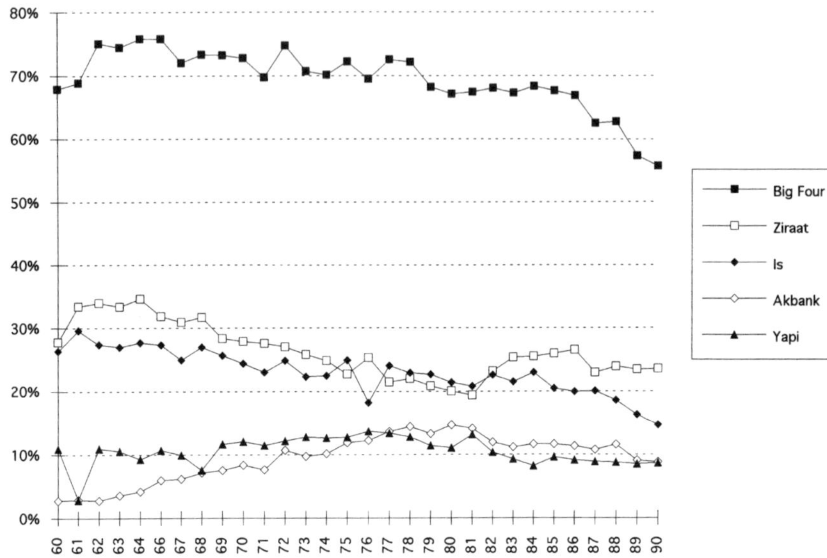

Fig. 4.1. Deposits of Turkey's top four banks as percentage of commercial bank deposits, 1960–90. *Source:* Banks' Association of Turkey.

quarters of the deposits continuously from 1960 until the mid-1980s, and they still held more than half in 1990 (fig. 4-1). Their very high market share was prime facie evidence of oligopoly, but it was eroding in the 1980s. Few of the players, in fact, fitted the profile of a strong oligopolist. Bayar's Türkiye İş Bankası was hardly Deutsche Bank, much less a vehicle for transmitting turn-of-the-century Berlin banking to contemporary Istanbul. The Turkish bank's official fiftieth anniversary history is revealing. It mattered less that "Atatürk opened up the way leading to the founding of T.I.B., supplied its initial capital and acted as its godfather, . . . a cause for pride and moral strength," than that "the majority of the bank's founders were men who figured prominently among the founders of the Turkish state and some occupied important positions in the administrative hierarchy. As was expected of them, they would put national interests before anything else in the decisions adopted by the Bank, and in the enterprises launched by it would make the authority of the State felt and obtain its assistance. This attitude persisted in the years that followed and T.I.B. was always helped along by the State" (İş Bankası 1974: 29).

İş Bankası became so weighted down by import substitution projects that it could hardly have survived without strong political support. Technically it remained a private sector bank, private persons and legal entities holding 28 percent of its shares, and the bank's Personnel Pension and Mutual Aid Fund an additional 33 percent in 1973. Only a minority of shares belonged to the Treasury. The state took over the shares of the Republic People's Party, heir to Atatürk's personal shares, after the military coup of 1980. But the bank seems to have performed very much like Turkey's lackluster public sector banks. In 1960, the year the military overthrew Menderes, İş Bankası was earning well below 1 percent on its total assets, and the bank's capital, which covered less than 5 percent of the assets, was hopelessly overextended. Almost twice the capital was tied up in fixed assets and in the equity of other companies—a pattern that was still sustained in the late 1980s. Despite its German legacy, İş hardly seemed in a position to set prices and manage an aggressive banking oligopoly. It was steadily losing market share in the late 1980s rather than offering higher interest rates to depositors. Despite a major capital revaluation in 1989, increasing its ratio of capital to total assets from 2.8 to 7 percent, well over 100 percent of its capital remained tied up in liquid assets. It had managed to ward off the attempt by a foreign company to acquire one-quarter of the total porfolio of the İş Group: its wholly owned Türkiye Şişe ve Cam Fabrikalari A.Ş., a conglomerate of 28 glass companies. To protect Şişe, however, the bank had to buy back T. Diş T.B., a bank it had earlier founded with Bank of America and subsequently spun off to the Turkish subsidiary.

Turkey's other dinosaur was the Ziraat Bankası. In the 1980s it still consistently raked in 20 to 25 percent of Turkey's commercial bank deposits, down from 33 percent in the early 1960s. Owned by the Treasury, it loyally served the government of the day and projected Turkey's "electoral economics" to the provinces on command through its 1,248 branches—19 percent of Turkey's entire banking network—distributed throughout the country. The bank also subsidized grain and other agricultural inputs as a normal part of government business. Like a number of other state banks, it needed a fundamental restructuring if it were to compete in liberalized financial markets. Yet the Treasury Ministry habitually called upon Ziraat to bail out other banks. In 1982 it absorbed two small private sector banks that had failed in the wake of the Kastelli affair, and then in 1987 it was obliged to join the Treasury and two other public sector banks in rescuing Türkiye Öğretmenler Bankası (the Turkish Teachers' Bank, or Töbank).

Being so burdened with government chores, Ziraat seemed in even worse position than İş Bankası to be a strategic player and price-setter. Prime Minister Özal appointed one of his "princes" in 1987 to modernize Ziraat. Against tremendous odds, working in the dark without an effective management information system, Dr. Şerif Coşkun Ulosoy tried to turn the unwieldy giant around. Ziraat had not tied up quite as much of its capital as İş Bankası in other shareholdings, but its huge branch network immobilized up to 90 percent of its capital in fixed assets, and Ziraat's new management had to keep increasing the number of branches as a public service, moving into villages that other commercial banks shunned. Although Ziraat managed to increase capital liquidity, the World Bank delayed release of a tranche of its structural adjustment loan for the financial sector, pending further reform of the bank. Finally, in May 1992, a law was passed that effectively wrote off the public sector debts of Ziraat and a number of other public sector banks (*MEED*, 22 May 1992: 32).

Under its new management, Ziraat's interest revenues increased more than its interest payments on deposits, and net income reached 3 percent of the bank's total assets, compared with barely 1 percent generated by İş. Both banks, undergoing restructuring, were developing nontraditional sources of income. Ziraat, for instance, was second only to İş in generating revenues from capital market transactions on Istanbul's renovated stock exchange. The bank remained undercapitalized, but of course the Treasury would always be obliged to support its flagship bank. It was clearly more of a government tool than İş Bankası.

Once Özal resumed the experiment of liberating interest rates in 1987, the banking oligopoly was at risk. Ziraat astonished the business community in the autumn of 1988 by launching a price war for deposits; the bank seemed prepared to stem the erosion of its market share, whatever the cost. Alarmed by the inflationary implications of the price war, the Central Bank quietly called a halt to it, but the message was clear: the banking oligopoly was vulnerable because its public sector component did not need to be concerned with the bottom line. A government intent on breaking the oligopoly might do so by calling upon the public sector to flex its muscle. One arm of government close to the prime minister had wanted higher, more realistic interest rates, and Ziraat had obliged. But in the final analysis the price war demonstrated the futility of the Sampson option and would encourage better coordination between the public and private sectors.

The other pair of oligopolists, privately owned, attended to their bottom line. Akbank was Turkey's strongest commercial bank. Five Adana families had founded it in 1948, but the Sabancı family gradually bought out the others after hiring Ahmet Dallı in 1962 to manage the bank. Dallı had been general manager of İş Bankası in 1960, when the military imprisoned him for having collected funds for Menderes. The Sabancı Group, which grew up in the shadow of the Bayar-Menderes regime, duly rewarded their ally upon his release from prison. As Sakip Sabancı recalls, "By acquiring Ahmet Dallı, we gained the opportunity of attracting his contacts also to the Sabancı Group. . . . It was in Ahmet Dallı's time that Akbank's significant participation in industry was achieved. Because of his close relations with Suleiman Demirel, who was all for development, public works and construction, he grasped the importance of cement. Our cement company, Akçimento, was Ahmed Dallı's creation. Ahmet Dallı provided one of the country's first examples of founding an industry by selling shares to the public. In addition, he brought Akbank into partnership with the Koç family in [various projects]" (Sabancı 1988: 83–84). In 1969, when Dallı entered the Demirel cabinet, the Sabancı family selected another banker-politician as general manager.

"We knew Medeni Berk from the reputation he had made for himself in banking over the years. Later he entered politics and served for many years as a minister and Deputy Prime Minister alongside so outstandingly able a Prime Minister as Adnan Menderes. . . . In those days [when he managed Akbank], although Adnan Menderes was no longer alive, the influence of the Democrat Party, covert or overt, was still felt throughout the country. The assumption of responsibility for the bank by a respected administrator of the Democrat era with banking experience increased confidence in it. And with his vast experience Medeni Berk established an excellent managerial structure" (Sabancı 1988: 84–85). Just as Demirel had inherited the Bayar-Menderes political legacy, so his friends and associates were co-opted into the Sabancı business empire. The most famous of them was Turgut Özal, a rising technocrat who had headed the State Planning Organization until 1970. Frustrated at the time in his efforts to liberalize the Turkish economy, he took a job at the World Bank until Sakip Sabancı wooed him back in 1972 to restructure the Sabancı Holding and to be a managing director of Akbank (Sabancı 1988: 86).

The 1970s were the golden years for a big holding company with a large retail bank, and the Sabancı Group was the first to enjoy this competitive advantage. Inflation averaged over 30 percent annually from 1971 to 1980, yet interest rates were kept artificially low—the discount rate hovering at 9 to 10 percent until the end of the decade—in vain efforts to stimulate development. With its market share rising to exceed 10 percent of the banking system's total deposits, Akbank was a major strategic asset—a cheap source of funds. But the Sabancıs did not milk the bank: they were clever oligopolists. Their leading son may be taken at his word: "A misconception held in some quarters is that the Sabancı Group engages in new investments with credits from Akbank and that it uses cheap credit. If the Sabancı Group had tied up the bank's resources in its own activities and had used cheap credit, how would Akbank have grown? How would it have made a profit? For years now, Akbank has been one of the most profitable banks, with the fastest-growing resources, of any in the public or private sectors. If every firm of the Sabancı Group takes cheap credit from Akbank, then Akbank will lose. If they use dear credit, then the Sabancı companies will lose. Our family policy has always been to seek the credits of our community's commercial and industrial enterprises from other banks on the most advantageous terms" (Sabancı 1988: 135–36). In other words, the strategy was to squeeze other banks into granting cheap credits—giving money away—to the Sabancı Group. Akbank kept a relatively lean portfolio—and very little equity investment—during most of those years and probably preferred lending to Koç, Turkey's most senior and credit-worthy group, to compounding the risk assets of Sabancı Holdings. The bank had every incentive to sustain its position in Turkey's financial oligopoly. It could deploy its market power to make other banks service the Sabancı interests.

The negative cost of money, however, had attracted other groups into retail banking in the 1970s. They fought epic struggles for control over commercial banks in the private sector, although Sabancı managed for a time to ward off the other majors, Koç and Çukurova. The prime prize was Yapi ve Kredi Bankası, founded in 1944 and Turkey's third-largest retail bank until 1978, when Akbank overtook it (fig. 4–1). Yapi's many shareholders, including Sabancı, gave its founder wide latitude to run the bank professionally. While it does not appear to have been as profitable in the 1960s and early 1970s as Akbank, Sakip Sabancı had considered it a model for Akbank to emulate (1988: 131). When its founder retired, the conglomerates competed to gain control of a majority of the shares. The rivalry between the Çukurova and Sabancı, both families from the Adana region, recalled Yachar Kemal's 1,200-page novel, *Les seigneurs de l'Aktschazas* (Gürsel 1986), about two families, aristocrats and upstarts, fighting to exploit the postwar cotton boom. The Çukurova group, scions of an ancient family, finally gained control of the bank in 1980, but by then it was too late. Interest rates were soon liberated, limiting the group's competitive advantage. Earlier Çukurova had gained control of Pamukbank (the Cotton Bank), which it had helped to establish in 1955. It also acquired a controlling interest in a venerable little bank, Ulusalararası Endüstri ve Ticaret Bankası, founded in 1888. Interbank, as it was known in the 1980s, became one of Turkey's four or five highly profitable banks specializing in international trade finance, the niche developed by Citibank in the early 1980s. The niche had become too big for the small foreign banks to occupy alone.

Another major battle pitted the Sabancı against Koç Holdings for control of Türkiye Garanti Bankası. With over 3 percent of the deposits, Garanti was the private sector's next largest retail bank, after Yapi ve Kredi. Sakip Sabancı naturally insisted in his autobiography that his group was not trying to consolidate a banking monopoly or keep major competitors out of the business. The family merely wanted to protect the quarter of the shares of a Sabancı tire company that Garanti owned. But whatever its real motives, the Sabancı Group acquired a third of the bank's shares and kept the Koç majority on the board of directors in check. Koç Holdings had acquired a 62 percent interest in the bank in 1977, but profits collapsed in the early 1980s (see fig. 4–2). Discouraged by the minority shareholders from consolidating control over the bank's management, Koç finally sold out to Ayhan Şahenk, a contractor. Şahenk then acquired full control of the bank by swapping shares in the Sabancı tire company for Sabancı shares in the bank and other financial assets. The contractor's Doğuş Investment Co. subsequently founded a second bank, Körfezbank, in a joint venture with investors from Qatar. In 1992 it acquired the Istanbul branch of the Bank of Bahrein and Kuwait (*MEED*, 29 May 1992: 32).

Owning a bank or at least part of one was a mark of business status that tempted many of the conglomerates. A major incentive, once interest rates were readjusted, may have been that banks were taxed less heavily than other businesses and might help to shelter a group's income. Owned by the Colakoğlu steelworks, for instance, Ekonomi Bankası consistently reported exceptionally high returns in the 1980s. The Yaşar Group from the Izmir region acquired Tütenbank. The Özaket Group, also from Izmir, owned Egebank. Enka, a big contracting group, was Chemical Mitsui Bank's Turkish partner. A couple of years before the collapse in London of Polly Peck, Asil Nader developed a high profile in Turkey and bought a bank (Titibank) to complement his other businesses.

Koç, too, returned to the world of banking, but in a much smaller way after the mishap with Garanti. In 1986 the Koç Group acquired a 50.6 percent interest in American Express, which was withdrawing from retail banking as part of a global strategy. For both parties the new joint venture, Koç-American Bank, was a very minor sideshow, involving less than 0.7 percent of the Koç Group's capital. With deposits equal to only 4 percent of

Akbank's, Koç-American was not about to be an oligopolistic price setter. Its major use to Koç in 1990 was floating modest offerings of some Koç companies on the Istanbul Stock Exchange, not in accumulating finance capital by forcing other banks to lend funds cheaply.

Despite being a latecomer to banking, Vehbi Koç had pioneered the concept of the holding company in Turkey when he established the Koç Group in 1963 along the corporate lines of some of his European and American business partners, such as Siemens, Ford, and General Electric (Koç 1977: 111–19). In the late 1980s the Koç Group was still the largest of the holdings, with turnovers topping 8 percent of the gross domestic product, and some of its companies were part of a fund quoted on the New York Stock Exchange. The group's minute presence in the Turkish banking community therefore seemed anomalous. Vehbi Koç's memoirs offer a possible explanation.

The group's founder seems to have distrusted banks. When made a director of the Industrial Development Bank of Turkey, founded with the support of the World Bank in 1950, Koç recalls: "I objected to the suggestion of paying a thousand liras to the directors and four and a half thousand to the chairman, on the grounds that if the compensation was set at such a high figure, many would covet these positions and vie for them. It was customary to appoint losing candidates at general elections, or retired high officials, to various boards of directors" (Koç 1977: 122). True to form, the new Menderes government made all the existing directors resign so that it could appoint new ones. Turkey's first modern capitalist distrusted banking because he tried to stay aloof from politics. When subsequently pressured by the Menderes regime to give up his People's Party card, he claims in his autobiography to have responded: "It would have been all right for me to join the Democrat party before 1950. If I join now people will say, 'This man is insatiable. He has changed parties now to make more money.' I don't want to bear that stamp. I have no active part in the People's Party. I am a businessman absorbed in my work, and that is my sole interest. If you want to avail yourselves of my knowledge and experience I am at the command of the Prime Minister. I am even prepared to work for one lira a year. In the elections I gave money to both parties. It is not the time for me to be forced into a change in my party affiliation" (162).

Of an older school, Koç had kept his distances from Menderes and Demirel, the politicians Sabancı cultivated. Rather than owning a bank, he would occasionally, as a large depositor, pressure a government bank for trading concessions or building permits (Koç 1977: 162). Furthermore, the Koç Group appeared to be well capitalized, with relatively little debt. And once Turkey underwent serious financial reforms in the 1980s, interest rates were driven up above the rate of inflation in order to encourage new savings and persuade wealthy businessmen to place their money in Turkey rather than on international markets. Consequently commercial banking lost some of its strategic luster for the diversified conglomerates.

In 1990 Istanbul bore some resemblance to Hilferding's Berlin, where "taking possession of six large Berlin banks would mean taking possession of the most important spheres of large-scale industry" (Hilferding 1981 [1910]: 368). Finance capital in the narrowest sense is the equity of the leading commercial banks invested in industry. No properly managed commercial bank, however, invests much of its capital, much less substantial proportions of its deposits, in the shares of other companies. For Hilferding, finance capital referred to loans to industry, working capital in effect, as well as equity investments. The universal banks were the major players because they were natural oligopolists. "Banks of the same type use the same technical methods, [the difference being] simply the size of their competing capitals. It is this quite distinctive type of competition which makes it possible for the banks alternately to compete and cooperate with one another in such varied and changing ways" (179).

Playing tit-for-tat (Axelrod 1984), the banks' growing concentration could protect stable, high margins between the interest rates charged to borrowers and those paid to depositors, the key to profitability. Indeed, they were immune to business cycles because the margins remained constant, whatever the prevailing interest rates. Here was the real reason for the modern tendency noted by Hilferding "to concentrate all capital in the form of money capital, and to make it available to producers only through the banks" (Hilferding 1981 [1910]: 180). Thus "bank capital was the negation of usurer's capital and is itself negated by finance capital" (226). The money capital became finance capital as bankers deployed their funds in the most profitable segments of the economy. Such sectors had tended in Germany to be industrial cartels, which were also protected from business cycles. In Imperial Germany as in Özal's Turkey, a solicitous government could tip the balance by providing the right incentives.

Despite Turkey's structural reform of the banking sector in the late 1980s, encouraged by an adjustment loan from the World Bank, the major banks apparently still colluded on interest rates to protect their margins, once the Central Bank intervened to halt the price war launched by Ziraat Bankası in 1988. In one sense the abrupt halt to the price war in 1988 concluded Özal's effort to liberalize Turkey's financial system. But if the immediate reason for the Central Bank's intervention had been to stem inflation, the major consequence was to strengthen the private sector components of the banking oligopoly. Two of Turkey's three top business conglomerates, Sabancı and Çukarova, had major stakes in the system. As long as Turkish governments remained responsive to big business, a few public and private banks could continue to control and deploy much of Turkey's finance capital.

Özal's reforms in fact strengthened the Turkish banking oligopoly. "Structural adjustment" in the financial sector served the oligopoly by obliging the weaker sisters to shape up. Akbank clearly remained the strongest cartel member and a model for the others because the Sabancı group had not milked it for cheap loans. The bank appeared so strong that it raised TL 500 billion on the Turkish stock market in 1990, reaping Hilferding's "promoter's profits" on its own account. If the public paid the full TL 500 billion for the 5 percent of the shares Akbank offered, the implicit market value of the bank was TL 10 trillion, compared with the shareholders' equity book value of only TL 1.4 trillion, about $500 million. The bank consistently registered high returns on assets while keeping up its share of deposits until the late 1980s because it did not clutter its portfolio with many risky loans. Then, as interest rates rose, it preferred to lose market share and keep up high rates of return. When Ziraat "defected" in 1988, Akbank temporarily held on to its share of deposits (fig. 4–1) but then gradually surrendered them in 1989 and 1990 rather than pay high rates of interest. Consequently it maintained high rates of return and a strong capital base. Akbank, in short, was the strongest oligopolist, the Turkish bank with the greatest incentive to resolve dilemmas of common interest with the other big banks. Its healthy image was essential to the Sabancı group, for the group as a whole was heavily leveraged and its financial performance was therefore very vulnerable to fluctuations in the interest rate. Figure 4–2 compares Akbank's profitability with that of Turkey's other major banks.

Before the financial sectoral adjustment was undertaken, the cartel had been a government artifact buttressed by an alliance between Özal and Sabancı. But with the exception of Sabancı, Turkey's highly leveraged conglomerates had fed off banking rather building it up. The Çukarova group, for instance, was considerably more heavily indebted than Sabancı. Many of its assets were deployed in capital-intensive heavy industry. The only big conglomerate, in fact, that was not highly leveraged was Koç Holdings. Table 4–1 compares the financial performance and capital structures of Çukarova and Sabancı with those of Koç Holdings in 1988.

The first thing to note about these conglomerates is that their total vol-

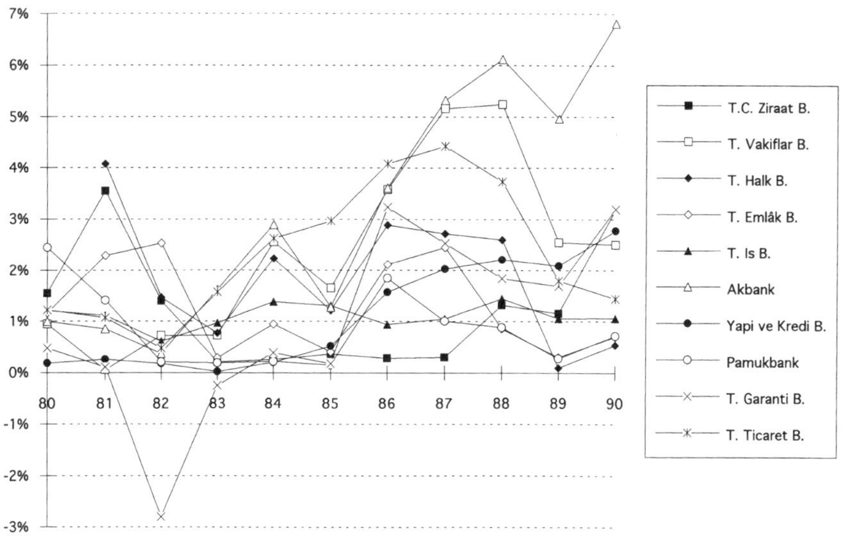

Fig. 4.2 Turkey's top ten banks: return on assets, 1980–90. *Source:* Banks' Association of Turkey.

ume of activity was immense. With Koç in the lead, they generated a collective turnover amounting to almost one-quarter of Turkey's GDP. Çukarova's assets were triple those of Koç, but they produced much less sales turnover and net income than the Koç Holdings assets. Sabancı also had a larger base of total assets than Koç, but its ratio of net income to total assets, although exceeding Çukarova's, was still only 5.2 percent, compared with Koç Holdings' 10.1 percent. Koç was considerably less indebted than the other conglomerates. Koç Holdings financed 18 percent of its total assets with its own capital and limited its long-term debt to only 7 percent of them. Çukarova was the least well capitalized of the three conglomerates. Without the capital invested in its three banks, Yapi ve Kredi, Pamukbank, and Interbank, the group's capital would have been negative. As it was, its shareholders' equity financed less than 3 percent of the consolidated balance sheet. Covering almost 12 percent of its assets, Sabancı was better capitalized than Çukarova but not as strong as Koç. Finance capital in the form of long-term debt from banks supported over one-third of the assets of both Sabancı and Çukarova. But Çukarova seemed in more desperate shape because its leverage factor, the ratio of long-term debt to shareholders' equity, was much higher than that of Sabancı. Its net income as a percentage of

Table 4.1. Financial indicators of Turkish business groups, 1988

(TL billions)	Çukarova	Koç	Sabancı
Total assets	8,818	2,909	7,046
of which banks	4,655	23	5,001
Property, plant, and equipment	975	423	533
Shareholders' equity	241	534	823
of which banks	277	7	519
Long-term debt	3,104	202	2,548
Turnover	3,825	13,637	6,033
Net income	89	295	368
Turnover/GDP	3.8%	13.5%	6.0%
NI/TA	1.0%	10.1%	5.2%
Equity/TA	2.7%	18.4%	11.7%
LTD/TA	35.2%	6.9%	36.2%
NI/equity	37.0%	55.2%	44.7%
LTD/equity	12.9	0.4	3.1

Sources: Annual reports. LTD, long-term debt; NI, net income; TA, total assets; GDP, gross domestic product.

shareholders' equity was not much lower than Sabancı's, but the conglomerate appeared to be financially more vulnerable.

Years of financing Çukarova enterprises had taken their toll on its banks. In particular, Pamukbank seemed from available balance sheet information to be in dire straits. It was one of two private sector banks relying on special handouts from the Central Bank to stay afloat (the other, getting much less, was Şekerbank). The special funds displayed in its 1990 balance sheet exceeded its entire capital by 10 percent. Only Ziraat Bankası and Bulent Şemiler's Konutbank, had received more special government support. Pamukbank seemed financially too weak and dependent on the government to be an active oligopolist, and the situation of the Çukarova Group's other major bank, Yapi ve Kredi, must have also been of some concern to bank regulators. Though their ratios of capital to total assets were increasing, the capital still did not cover these banks' fixed assets and investments in other companies. Figure 4–3 compares their capital shortfalls to those of İş Bankası and Ziraat. By international standards, no more than half of a commercial bank's capital was tied up in fixed assets and shareholding in other companies, but well over 100 percent of Yapi ve Kredi's and Pamukbank's capital, as well as İş Bankası's, was so committed.

With financial adjustment, however, other major players seemed slowly

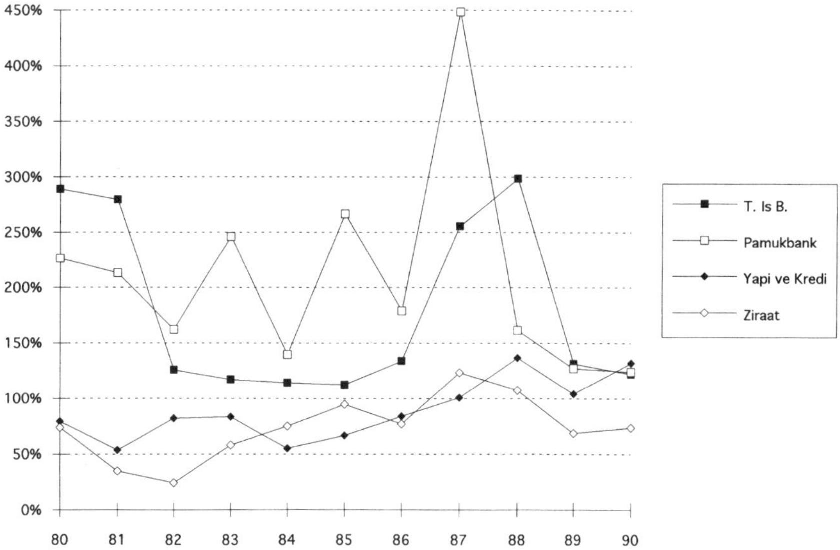

Fig. 4.3. Participations and fixed assets as a percentage of bank capital, 1980–90. *Source*: Banks' Association of Turkey.

to be adopting to new prudential norms and capital ratios. Strong banks, whether public or private sector, could make the oligopoly less dependent on the government. Garanti Bankası, which the Doğus Group had acquired from Koç, had expanded its share of deposits to about 5 percent and was Turkey's fifth-largest privately owned bank in 1990, just behind İş, Ak, Yapi, and Pamukbank. Two other commercial banks in the top ten also displayed relatively robust balance sheets. Türk Ticaret Bankası was the only leading private sector bank that was not identified with any of the major holding companies. The public sector's Vakiflar, a bank created in 1954 on the German model to manage Turkey's religious endowments (*vaqf-s*), was noted for its fine olive oil produced from some of the endowed properties, but its outside businesses did not hurt the bank.

The ultimate financial indicators of a "good" oligopolist are the interest rates paid to depositors and charged to lenders. Akbank bought its funds cheaply and sold them to the highest bidders, thus maximizing its "spreads" between interest received and paid and sustaining high profitability. İş Bankası, by contrast, was charging significantly less interest on its loans than the other oligopolists, while paying more for deposits until 1990. In order to control their costs of funds, the three biggest private sector oligopolists were collectively losing market share, apparently eroding their oligopoly. But

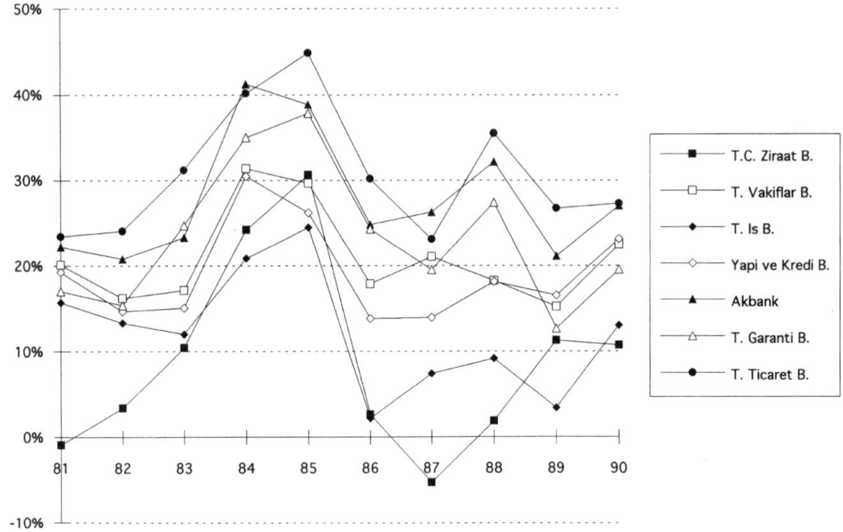

Fig. 4.4. Seven leading Turkish banks: interest rate margins, 1981–90. *Source:* Banks' Association of Turkey.

Garanti Bankası, Vakiflar, and Türk Ticaret Bankası were gradually gaining market share without forgoing profitability. Figure 4–4 shows that they were maintaining relatively high interest rate margins, or "spreads," keeping up with the leading private sector oligopolists. Türk Ticaret Bankası and Akbank were in the lead, followed closely by Yapi, Vakiflar, and Garanti Bankası. As expected, T. İş B. and Ziraat enjoyed lower margins. Ziraat fared especially poorly in 1987, a busy election year for the government's patronage machine.

Turkish banks, to be sure, did not directly control Turkey's conglomerates, but they still met Hilferding's expectation that the principal owners of the shares of banks and of industries become the same people (Hilferding 1981 [1910]: 225). The capital ratios being enforced by the Central Bank, however, were encouraging the banks to divest their capital holdings in the companies of their respective groups. They were also cutting back on their lending and diversifying their portfolios, thereby limiting the finance capital in the extended sense of loans and working capital, as well as formal equity, that they might offer their respective groups. Financial reform was pushing the others to emulate Akbank's strategy by serving their respective conglomerates indirectly. As long as they preserved their margins and their command of the financial markets, preventing the conglomerates from milking the banks, finance capital had a new lease on life. Financial oligopoly might thus reinforce the conglomerates in the long run.

Turkey's "liberal" reorientation of the 1980s was rendering the banking industry less concentrated, but the core of private oligopolists was strengthened. A future reformer might find the banking system less amenable to government manipulation. If not always in command of economic policies, the commercial banks were in a stronger position to bargain with the government, just as the German model specified. Liberalization was propelling their banks toward the commanding heights of the Turkish economy, backed by big business.

The Special Finance Houses: Economic and Political Deepening?

Authoritarian rule had relied in the early 1980s on three major sources of support: the army, state bureaucracy, and big business. Oligopolies controlled by a small number of holding companies facilitated symbiosis between the state and big business. While the holdings enjoyed some autonomy, they also simplified problems of economic coordination and political control. A tight coalition had enabled Özal to enact his various economic reforms, and the close ties between the generals and the oligopolists may also have helped to contain the severe economic and political crises of the late 1970s. Özal, however, had also developed another political strategy that, while not incompatible with relying on big business, also offered an alternative source of support. He admitted Islamic banking into Turkey.

The long-term consequence of admitting Islamist business interests into ruling combines could be greater competition among oligopolists, and ultimately less oligopoly. More competition—for credit as for other economic privileges—may temporarily threaten Turkey's political stability but deepen political and economic participation. Özal's policies, continued by Prime Minister Ahmet Demirel and his successor, Tansu Çiller, apparently favor greater competition. Reform is already nibbling away at the market shares of Turkey's largest banks, even while reinforcing private sector oligopoly and enhancing its autonomy. As markets alter the scope of bureaucratic interventions, the economic actors become more autonomous, multiplying the sources of potential support for politicians (radical and liberal as well as conservative and fundamentalist) and political parties. Islamist parties, too, may be more amenable to constitutional order, the greater the diversity and autonomy of economic interests supporting them.

Under temporary military dictatorship, Turkey's climate in 1981 had hardly seemed propitious for Islamic banking. The military establishment, imbued with Kemalist ideals, supported secularism with a zeal reminiscent of Muslim "fundamentalism." Turkey's leaders wanted to attract Arab capital, however. By 1988 Turkey was receiving more than its fair share of financing from the Islamic Development Bank, established in Jiddah by the Conference of Islamic States, which included Turkey. Holding 8.2 percent of the capital, Turkey received 12.6 percent of the bank's technical assistance and financing, but capital investment amounted to only 0.3 percent of foreign direct investment in Turkey in 1988 (Islamic Development Bank 1988: 99, 129, 204, 271). Islam's private sector banks were a larger, more attractive target of opportunity. By 1988 two of Turkey's newly established Islamic banks, Al Baraka and Faisal, would collectively outperform Islam's public sector and finance Turkish oil imports to the respective tunes of $150 million and $50 million annually. Korkut Özal, the prime minister's younger brother, was alleged to have had an interest in the oil deals. Most of the Islamic commercial banks belonged to one of two transnational networks: Prince Mohammed Al-Faisal's Dār al Māl al Islāmi or Sheikh Salah Kamel's Al Baraka Group. Unlike the Islamic Development Bank, which was owned by a consortium of governments, most of the banks in these groups were owned by private shareholders. On the international side, the principal owners were Saudis acting in a private capacity. Though son of the late King Faisal, Prince Mohammed did not enjoy official Saudi government support. Nor, despite close relations with Saudi authorities, did Sheikh Salah, a self-made businessman who developed his international network in tandem with his business enterprises. Each was a determined and principled innovator, noted for his piety as well as his entrepreneurship. Prince Mohammed had once suggested harnessing icebergs to meet Arabia's water needs—an idea that some engineers now believe should have received more serious attention.

The prince and Sheikh Salah sought local private investors in each country that permitted Islamic banking. Prince Mohammed Al-Faisal, Al-Baraka's major competitor, arrived in Istanbul in 1981 as the guest of a prominent Turkish banker. The banker recalls that Korkut Özal, Turgut's younger brother, was eager to meet the prince. The younger Özal developed a warm business relationship with Sheikh Salah Kamel as well and introduced him to his older brother Turgut. By 1982 Sheikh Salah was negotiating an agreement "line by line" on behalf of the Islamic banks with Özal's senior civil servants. In the wake of the Kastelli affair, however, Turgut Özal resigned from the government. The draft agreement was filed away, only to be reopened when he returned to power 18 months later, on 8 December 1983, elected this time to parliament as leader of the dominant Motherland

Party. As noted in the previous chapter, the agreement was immediately signed, and the banks opened for business in 1985.

Turkish secularists pointed to "a dangerous relationship between these finance houses and . . . fundamentalist forces in Turkey" (Yeşilada 1993: 188). A number of Turkish directors and stockholders of Al-Baraka Türk and the Faisal Finance Institution (FFI) were close business and political associates of President Turgut Özal and his enterprising younger brother, Korkut. A deputy of the National Salvation Party, Korkut Özal had served as minister of agriculture under Bülent Eçevit in 1974, then as interior minister under Suleiman Demirel in 1975–77. He drew on many of his Islamist connections. For instance, Eymen Topbas served as chairman of the Istanbul branch of the Motherland Party until 1990, and his brother was on the board of Al Baraka. Salih Özcan, on the board of FFI, was a former National Salvation Party member of parliament, as well as being a Naqşibendi and one of the leading Turkish figures associated with the World Muslim League, based in Saudi Arabia. Tevfik Paksu, a former minister of labor who had also represented the National Salvation Party, was another FFI board member. Moreover, Korkut's close friend Dr. Nevzat Yalçintaş had introduced many of the Arab investors to Turkey, including the promoters of the Islamic banks. Dr. Yalçintas had served as director of research of the Islamic Development Bank in Jiddah, and eventually Korkut Özal became the Turkish member of the board of directors, a position usually reserved for the Turkish finance minister. Through such connections the Özal family was connected to a Turkish core of Islamically minded investors, the World Muslim League, the Naqşibendi religious order, and Turkish foundations that have financed a new ideology of Turkish-Islam Synthesis (TIS) and the substantial growth in the 1980s of the Imam Hatip Okullari, or religious teacher training schools (Yeşilada 1989: 5–6).

Initially, however, Islamic banks worked almost exclusively with the established oligopolies. Blue chip corporations, as bankers claimed, lined up for cheap (in effect subsidized) trade financing. The decree that established the "special finance houses" had given them a competitive advantage. It reserved to the Prime Ministry the right "at all times" to supervise them, and, once Al Baraka and Faisal had opened their banks, a law specifically exempted them from the provisions of the banking law (Al Baraka Finance House 1987: 10, 52). The special finance houses were required to keep only 10 percent of their current accounts and a mere 1 percent of their much larger participation accounts as required reserves with the Central Bank, whereas other banks lost the use of 10 to 15 percent of their deposits. The special finance houses were also authorized to deal in commodities and were exempted from lending limits and deposit insurance applied to other commercial banks. Furthermore, they were given permission to advertise over state television despite a general moratorium in 1984 on television advertising for banks in the wake of the "bankers" (brokerage houses) crisis of 1982 (Öncü 1989). In the eyes of Uğur Mumcu, a liberal journalist who would subsequently be assassinated, the privileges amounted to a new "form of Capitulation" (Mumcu 1988). Playing upon secularist feelings, TÜSIAD even argued against a new corporate tax law disallowing deductions for interest payments on the grounds that it would favor the special finance houses (*MEED*, 10 November 1989: 29).

Most of the conventional banks also complained of unfair competition. The Banks Association of Turkey (BAT), officially mandated by Turkey's banking law (no. 57, 1985) "to take any necessary steps to stop unfair competition among banks" (Kandiller 1986: 87), was not consulted when the finance houses were established, and BAT complained of their "unfair privileges" (interview with Dr. Riza Kandiller, 4 August 1988). These new institutions were so potentially profitable, in fact, that the Turkish public sector bank Vakiflar, which managed the nationalized assets of Turkey's religious foundations, preferred to join rather than contest them. Both Al-Baraka and FFI had commissioned Vakiflar's extensive branch network to market deposits into its "investment" accounts. When Vakiflar discovered the potential of the market, it hired away FFI's manager to found its own Islamic subsidiary. At first Vakiflar was denied permission on the grounds that other Turkish banks would then enter the market (Öncü 1989). Only joint ventures would be permitted. Conveniently, however, the Kuwait Finance House (KFH) returned to negotiations, interrupted in 1982 by the Souk al Manakh crisis, for establishing a joint venture in Turkey. When KFH renewed its interest, the willing Turkish government found a ready partner in Vakiflar.

Consequently a third Islamic finance house opened its doors in 1989: the Kuvayt Türk Evkaf Finans Kurumu (Kuwait Turkish Evkaf Finance House). Its manager was expecting "to capture 60–70 percent of the Turkish market for Islamic customer deposits." He projected a fourfold increase in the total market to some TL 1 trillion, or 3 to 5 percent of all Turkish bank deposits (*MEED*, 28 October 1988: 4). No further Islamic banks were expected to receive permission from the Turkish authorities. The powerful secretary for Treasury and foreign trade explained that Turks could not be permitted, for lack of experience, to set up such ventures without foreign technical assistance, and the foreign technology had already been adequately transferred (interview with Yavuz Canevi, 18 August 1988). Yet in

1991, while Özal's ANAP was still in power, a fourth "special finance house" received permission to enter the market.

In the early years, the special finance houses posted extraordinary profits. Despite their "special privileges," however, their profitability steadily decreased after 1987 and fell below that of other foreign branches, joint ventures, and medium-sized Turkish banks operating in the foreign trade sector. Figure 4–5 compares the Islamic banks' respective returns on total assets with those of the entire sets of joint ventures with Middle Eastern and OECD countries as well as with the ancient Osmanli Bankası, which was still owned by French and British interests, and a sample of extraverted, trade-oriented Turkish private sector banks.

Most Turkish banks were highly profitable by international standards; over 1 percent return on total assets is considered quite high in most countries with which the writer is familiar. The banks with foreign business connections were even more profitable than the others, registering returns on assets in 1988 of 4 to 5 percent, compared with average returns of 2.3 and 3.0 percent, respectively, for the commercial public and private sectors as a whole. In 1988 and 1989 the Islamic sector fell behind the banks and groups of banks with foreign trade interests shown in figure 4–5, although Al-Baraka was still performing slightly above the average rate of return on assets of the entire Turkish public and private sectors. Despite its special privileges and promising beginnings, the Islamic sector was lagging well below the Middle Eastern average, not to mention the OECD banks or even Osmanli Bankası, which had evidently benefited far more from Turkey's financial liberalization. The two banks in question, Al Baraka and FFI, perhaps preferred to defer profits, lessen margins, invest in infrastructure, and increase market shares. Al-Baraka also claimed to the writer in 1990 that "the company gives priority to the utilization of participation account funds at the expense of idleness of its own company funds" (Letter from Adnan Büyükdeniz, 26 February 1990). At the Central Bank, however, the director of the service in charge of supervising the banks said that one of his major responsibilities was to ensure depositors of the full 80 percent of "profits" earned by their participation (i.e., time savings) accounts.

In 1989, a difficult year for Turkish banking, Al-Baraka slightly improved its performance, while Faisal apparently vegetated, falling well behind all of the Turkish banks included in figure 4–5 because they specialized in foreign trade. Al-Baraka had been quick to exploit the opportunity of leasing equipment (sharing certain tax advantages with the borrower), which a politically well-connected owner of a conventional bank had created, whereas Faisal, despite having idle funds, hesitated to commit short-term

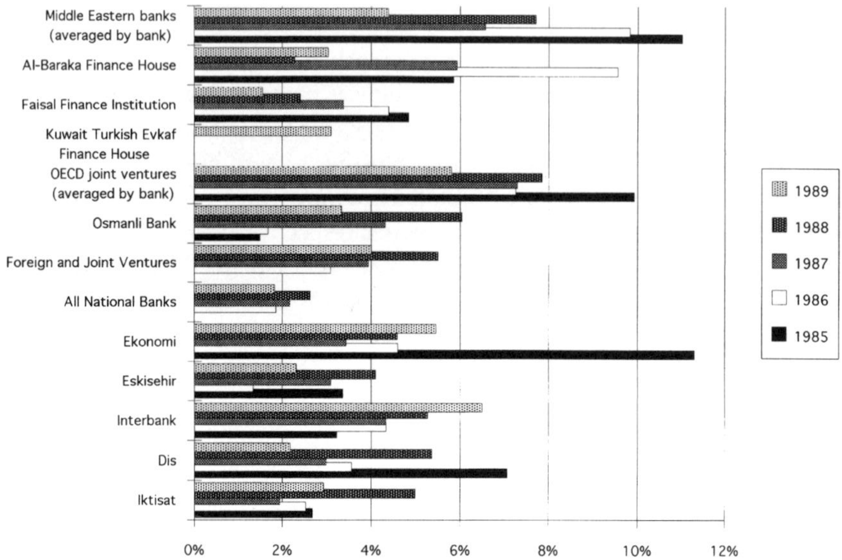

Fig. 4.5. Return on assets, Turkish Islamic and conventional banks, 1985–89. *Sources:* Banks' Association of Turkey; annual statements of special finance houses.

deposits to medium-term investments. The profitability of the Islamic sector continued to decline in 1990 and 1991.[1]

FFI, moreover, had been involved in a serious financial scandal. Salih Özcan, who was instrumental in Prince Mohammed's choice of the 94 other Turkish stockholders, had put his son, Hüseyin Sait Özcan, in charge of one of the bank's subsidiaries. The son is alleged to have financed imaginary exports. The bank's general manager (a professional banker who had previously served Koç as a manager of Garanti Bankası) discovered the tax evasion scheme, reported it to the Central Bank, and eventually resigned to become general manager of the Kuwait Turkish Evkaf Finance House. Prince Mohammed removed Özcan's son from the bank's executive committee, and the latter fled the country when an official investigation of the imaginary exports began (*Hürriyet,* 5 July 1989).

Islam's banks were increasingly regulated by the Central Bank and the Undersecretariat of Treasury and Foreign Trade; Al-Baraka, with more than 100 shareholders, also reported to the Capital Markets Board. In a private communication of 16 February 1990 addressed to the writer, Adnan Büyükdeniz of Al-Baraka Türk insisted that the regulations applicable to the special finance houses "are at least as stringent as those applied to conventional banks." Later in the year the Central Bank in fact sent its auditors into the special finance houses to take an unprecedented inside view of their operations. Although the finance houses retained their special privileges with respect to liquidity and reserve requirements, they were negotiating new regulations concerning lending limits equivalent to those imposed on conventional banks. In 1992 they were being pressured to raise their capital to meet the international ratios that the other Turkish commercial banks were obliged to meet.

The Islamic finance houses deployed about 19 percent of the total foreign sector's capital at the end of 1990—less than 1 percent of Turkey's total banks' capital. A year later they had improved their share, but it still constituted only 1.2 percent. Even so, they were developing an impressive financial surface. Despite diminished profitability, they were steadily expanding their share of the market. It is not so much their capital as their lending that may have political implications, knitting powerful combinations of business leaders and politicians together, and in the lending field the Islamic sector was more than holding its own, accumulating loan portfolios that appeared on 31 December 1989 to be 29.5 percent of the commercial loans accorded by the foreign sector and joint venture banks.[2] By 30 November 1991, their "sum of the funds used through profit/loss sharing, production support, and leasing was 2.2 percent of total bank loans," the Central Bank noted in its *Annual Report* (1991: 54). With only 1.2 percent of the capital, they were getting almost twice as much leverage as Turkey's other commercial banks. Moreover, they were developing new deposit bases among Islamically minded Turks who avoided interest-taking institutions. As of November 1993 they had accumulated 2.1 percent of the consolidated deposits of the banking sector and were making 2.7 percent of the total loans (Central Bank of the Republic of Turkey, *Annual Report* 1993: 69).

Al-Baraka, with over half of the special finance houses' consolidated balance sheet, had branched out from its main office in Istanbul to Ankara, İzmir, Bursa, Kayseri, and Konya, with plans for further branches in Gaziantep and Samsun. FFI was also present in Konya, an electoral bastion of Muslim fundamentalism (see fig. 4–6), as well as in Ankara, İzmir, Bursa, Adana, and Şanhurfa (Ş. Urfa). Their representative offices also competed with those of conventional Turkish banks in Germany and Saudi Arabia for workers' remittances.

In time, closer ties between Islamic banks and political clienteles might support more musharaka and mudaraba contracts, as distinct from trade financing. Al-Baraka engaged in slightly more mudaraba and musharaka than Faisal, but these distinctively Islamic forms of lending constituted only 8.2 percent of its placements as of 31 December 1987. They then dropped to a

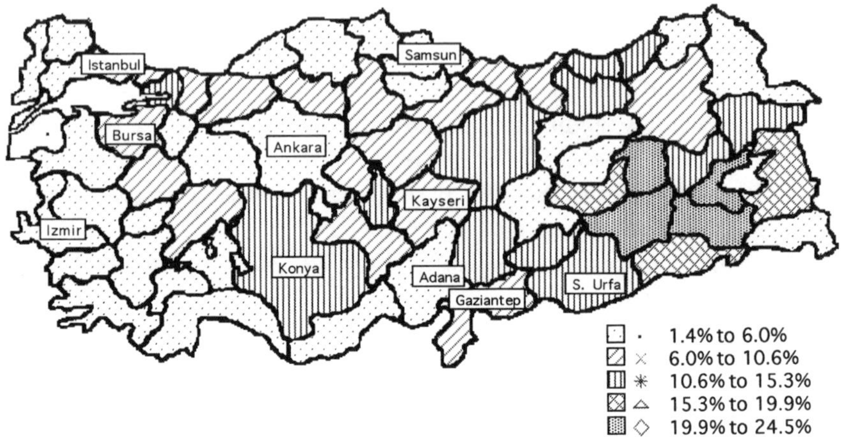

Fig. 4.6. Electoral map of Turkey, Welfare Party vote by province, 1987. *Source:* Republic of Turkey, Prime Ministry, State Institute of Statistics, Ankara; drafted with the help of Mark Supko.

mere 1.7 percent in 1989, but leasing then comprised an additional 7.4 percent of the bank's placements (*Annual Report* 1989: 13). A Turkish economist underlined these banks' potential to attract venture capital and urged "new legislation compelling the Islamic banks to devote, let's say, at least 15 percent of their investment portfolio to 'mudaraba' and 'musharaka' within a year . . . then [to] be increased to 35–40 percent within a few years" (Çizakça 1987: 89). As they deepened their deposit bases and developed greater familiarity with short-term borrowers, they might become more willing to venture capital in long-term lending. Leasing was a step in this direction. Al-Baraka had set aside a special investment fund, in effect deposits of over one year, to finance four-year leases. To improve their profitablilty, the Islamic banks would have to develop new market niches. Only Al-Baraka appeared in 1989 to be generating revenues from its investment portfolio equivalent to the interest revenues of conventional commercial banks. These revenues amounted to 20 percent of the bank's total assets, slightly above the average for all Turkish commercial banks. The newly established Kuwait Turkish Evkaf Finance House managed its first year to generate only 15 percent. FFI did not disclose its total revenues. Generating more revenue might require tying up more funds in mudaraba and musharaka as well as leasing, but the banks could not risk (nor would the Central Bank allow) any grossly mismatched maturities. Applying short-term deposits to long-term loans—in effect, equity financing—was a sure recipe for bank failure. A substantial increase in mudaraba and musharaka lending would require corresponding infusions of capital.

Whether or not more private foreign capital became available, Islamic finance survived the defeat of Özal's "Holy Alliance" in the 1991 elections. The temporary, somewhat unnatural coalition he had forged in 1983 between elements of Demirel's old Justice Party and Erbaken's Salvation Front had become institutionalized in the financial sphere. The quid pro quo for vital Islamist support over the years seems to have been a more open economy, permitting the further financing of religious causes: more scholarships for religious training, propaganda for the Turkish-Islamic Synthesis (TIS), and even a television documentary, sponsored by the FFI, that commemorated the Gallipoli campaign but excluded one of its heroes, Mustafa Kemal (Mumcu 1988: 47). Kemalists understandably feared the erosion of their ideological hegemony. But the consolidation of Islamic banking had further economic and political implications for Turkey. If ANAP was becoming past history, the special finance houses remained a potential tool of any republican regime against anticonstitutional Islamist forces—or a vehicle for integrating some of their key economic leaders into the constitutional regime. The greater their successes, the greater their stakes in the existing system and thus their willingness, for fear of undermining the system, to tolerate ever extended delays in the full application of the *shari'a* (Islamic law).

The moderating influence of the Islamist business community became visible during the Gulf crisis of 1990–91. Islamist political activists were sharply divided between their traditional loyalties to Saudi Arabia and rage against the American imperialists, alleged to have used and possibly even to have provoked the Iraqi seizure of Kuwait as part of a long-term strategy to occupy the holiest lands of Islam, including their oil fields. While the Saudi regime mobilized a number of Islamic scholars to support the American military presence in the face of a greater evil, much articulate Muslim world opinion, including some distinguished Saudi scholars, was urging immediate withdrawal of all non-Muslim military forces. In Turkey the fundamentalists of the National Salvation Party clearly opposed the American presence, and "Saudi-America" as well, but so also did a number of Muslims in the Naqşibendi order. As the leftist *Yüzyil* (30 September 1990) commented, the Gulf crisis split Turkish Islamists into "the partisans of Big Capital and America," the radical partisans of Iran looking favorably on Iraq, and a narrow middle ground. Özal's political investment in the Islamic banks facilitated his astonishing leadership during the crisis. He managed by 5 September 1990 to obtain from parliament a ringing endorsement for his staunchly pro-Western policy. Two hundred forty-six ANAP deputies voted the government full powers, refused earlier, to send Turkish troops abroad, if necessary, and to station foreign troops on Turkish soil. In August only 216 of them voted for a compromise proposal, but the Holy Alliance obviously supported the president. Korkut Özal tried to shore up support and legitimacy among the Islamists in private meetings featuring Eymen Topbas and Salih Özcan. During the war the president's younger brother continued to appear on panels sponsored by various Islamist factions (*Zamam,* 27 February 1991).

If civil society was being (very) gradually Islamized in Turkey, practical Islam was also adapting to civil society, perhaps "corrupting" or civilianizing some of its militants in the interests of "Saudi-America" or other moderate causes. If Islamist political tendencies could, as in 1991, attract 16 percent of the vote in a general election, there was probably room for financial intermediaries to distribute more than 2 to 3 percent of the credit in distinctively Islamic ways. Financial integration into civil society, involving the sharing of a capitalist ethic, is not political integration, of course. But *Islamic* business touches another chord: it can occupy some of the cultural space that might otherwise be seized by other, less benign expressions of authenticity—those traditions, residues, roots, and elements of community left out of civil society. Perhaps pluralistic regimes in contemporary Muslim societies now need to preempt cultural space from unconditional oppositions. Islamic financial institutions could play an important mediating role. Integrated into civil society, they could become part of the state and help it to manipulate cultural spaces. If "civil society itself is the major source of the dynamism of the fundamentalist movement in Turkey, . . . the groups that seem to hold the upper hand are not the splinter radical groups but the neo-traditionalist Islamists, who . . . pursue nonconfrontationist policies in their relations with the state" (Ayata 1993: 59).

Many Turkish secularists still fear or despise these cultural residues, whether in the form of religious orders, parochial schools, or financial institutions. But the Islamic financial intermediaries have tended for the sake of business to encourage moderate Islamic factions inside and outside government. They could strengthen political forces in Turkey committed to more democratic forms of pluralism.

Conclusion

Turkey offers a baseline against which to compare the experiences of other Mediterranean Debt Crescent countries. Spared from colonial occupation, it experienced a rich financial legacy of German universal banking and institutionalized it after independence. While its single-party regime, preceding the others on the crescent by more than three decades, may have encouraged the private sector more than the others, the circumstances of World War I and the independence struggle against Greece had decimated Turkey's business community. Yet business and banking elements within the regime were behind the transition to multiparty politics in 1950. The German model articulated in İş Bankası offered a network of support for political dissidents within the ruling party.

A closer look at Turkey's commercial banking system in the 1980s reveals major differences, however, between the German model and Turkish practice. Most of the leading banks were not "good" oligopolists, that is, strong competitors ready to sacrifice current windfalls for steady streams of future earnings. Özal's political coalition had included big public sector banks as well as Turkey's strongest private commercial sector bank. Under the impact of his financial liberalization policies, the banking system was becoming slightly less concentrated, but the strong competitiors were increasing their market share, suggesting the development of a stronger and more autonomous financial oligopoly. Any future reformer might have to be more beholden than Özal to the big conglomerates controlling the largest private sector banks.

Özal's strategy had other interesting long-term implications, however. By recognizing "special finance houses" and incorporating them into the banking system, he gave Islamic forces a potential foothold in Turkish finance capital. Turkey's new Islamic banks had a very minor share of national markets, but their share was growing steadily and possibly offered a way for Islamist political forces to acquire new financial stakes. There was no organic connection between the special finance houses and Erbaken's mainstream Islamist Welfare Party. The bankers kept their distance from the politicians and preferred to work with the big established business conglomerates. They established branches seeking out deposit bases, however, in areas of the country where the Welfare Party was strong. The further expansion of these banks might contribute not only to further financial liberalization, in the sense of developing a less concentrated, more competitive banking system, but also to stronger economic roots for the Welfare Party. So far as the Islamic financial institutions displayed any political color, however, they tended to reinforce the moderate pro-Saudi wing of the Islamist movement that Özal had co-opted. To deepen its economic base, the leadership of the Welfare Party might also be moving in this direction. Erbaken himself, so outspoken against "Saudi-America" during the Gulf crisis of 1990–91, seemed to be changing course. The Turkish case offers some evidence that the rise of Islamic banks encourages moderate liberal elements within Islamist movements. Financial "deepening," associated with a more competitive banking system including Islamic banks, may lay the groundwork for a deepening of political participation, incorporating Islamist forces into the mainstream political economy. Mediated by Islamic institutions, increases in the structural power of finance capital may contribute to a dispersion of political power consonant with democracy.

The evidence from Turkey is hardly conclusive, for the special finance houses still occupy a very small share of the market—much smaller than the Welfare Party's share of the national vote in recent elections. It may have important comparative implications, however, for other Muslim countries where Islamic financial institutions have made greater inroads. In Turkey, a multiparty system and relatively autonomous financial and business oligopolies had preceded Islamic banking. By contrast, finance capital remained fragmented and political pluralism relatively underdeveloped in the other crescent countries that permitted Islamic banking. In Egypt this form of banking acquired a much greater share of the market than in Turkey. Simultaneous efforts in Egypt to Islamize finance capital and to promote political pluralism will be examined in chapter 8. Morocco, by contrast, did not permit Islamic banking, although it displayed the greatest degrees of capital concentration and political pluralism in North Africa.

Chapter 5

Finance Capital in Morocco

> The smallness and introversion of the elite are crucial to the throne's ability to divide it, manipulate it, and use it for its own defense.
>
> (John Waterbury 1970: 162)

Like Turkey, Morocco illustrates a "German" model of financial development despite the fact that France and Spain eventually occupied it. By remaining nominally independent and open to international competition until 1912, Morocco absorbed a German financial legacy both directly and indirectly, mediated through French banks that competed with the Germans. In Morocco as in Turkey, the independent states protected their banking legacies rather than attacking them, as in Algeria, Egypt, and Tunisia. Most banks remained under French control well into the 1970s and offered a base for indigenous oligopoly, once commerce was Moroccanized. As noted earlier, the Moroccans kept up credit restrictions until 1991. Although the reforms were supposed to induce greater competition and more open economies in the financial and other sectors, the reforms seem instead to be reinforcing the oligopoly and the political order that sustains it. The case of Morocco is especially significant because it illustrates not only relationships between financial oligopoly and political pluralism but also the preemptive strategy of an astute patrimonial ruler.

Capitalism Triumphant in Morocco

Late to be opened up, Morocco became French North Africa's California—or its Prussia. With the help of the British, the makhzan (Morocco's royal household) withstood a variety of French and Spanish threats in the course of the nineteenth century. The Spanish invasion of 1859, reminiscent of France's Algerian adventure, was successfully parried when the British helped Morocco to pay the required tribute without recourse to international bond markets. Moroccan money, like Tunisia's, was in a virtually chronic state of devaluation; from 1822 to 1848 the piaster lost 80 percent of its value against the French écu (silver five-franc piece) and the Spanish douro (Miège 1961 III: 97–99). Instead of experimenting with paper money, however, Morocco blocked all monetary reform in 1869 and then tried in 1877 to stabilize the value of its silver coins (142, 431ff.). Foreign trade did not offer opportunities for a futures market like Tunisia's licenses for exporting olive oil. Morocco's first bank, founded in 1844, three years before Bin Ayad opened Tunisia's short-lived Central Bank, was merely a little trading house tied to the Anglo-Egyptian Bank based in London and Gibraltar; Moses Pariente, a Moroccan Jew, operated under British consular protection out of Europe's trading entrepôt of Tangier. Various banks and European trading houses followed him but also restricted themselves to foreign trade finance, in keeping with the country's gradual opening to outside markets guaranteed by the Anglo-Moroccan treaty of 1856. At least two of the institutions tried unsuccessfully to convince Sultan Hassan to let them establish a Moroccan central bank and issue paper money. In 1894 Hassan, the last of Morocco's truly independent sultans, seconded by his wise black vizier, Ba Ahmed, was able to wriggle out of yet another tribute to Spain without yielding to the entreaties of Crédit Lyonnais or the Comptoir d'Escompte to float a bond issue.

Morocco would not enter the sorts of financial deals that had ruined Tunisia until 1902, almost forty years after Tunisia's bankruptcy. Meanwhile, if industry and banking remained separated in France, high finance was taking a new shape in the form of the industrial banking group. The Banque de Paris et des Pays-Bas (Paribas), founded at France's hour of defeat in 1871, would compete, to be sure, with France's speculative finance houses to underwrite lucrative bond issues for spendthrift governments, and France would continue until 1914 to place a good half of its surplus capital in these unproductive financial instruments. But back in the metropole Paribas represented a new development, correcting the mistakes of the original Crédit Mobilier (Feis 1930: 40). It grew slowly and carefully, investing in new industry as well as in other banks, pioneering a French version of those trusts and holding companies that Rockefeller and J. P. Morgan were constructing in the United States. When Morocco finally became vulnerable, Paribas powered its way past old finance houses and retailers like the Comptoir d'Escompte, whose Moroccan branches were too gaudy to support themselves, and took the market. In Morocco, as in much of late-nineteenth-century Europe, Émile Zola's Gundermann, who represented rational finance capital in *L'argent,* "vanquished Saccard" (Hilferding 1981: 180), Zola's principal character, who was a traditional speculator.[1]

Paribas's only serious French competitor, in fact, was another industrial group. Eugène Schneider, France's leading armaments manufacturer, competing with Krupp for Moroccan business, had formed a syndicate to seek mining and railroad concessions. In 1902 he bought France's principal trading house in Tangier and renamed it the Compagnie Marocaine. He made his acquisition only after being encouraged by the Quai d'Orsay (Guillen 1971: 33). Foreign Minister Théophile Delcassé seems to have felt France's strategic objective of "peaceful penetration" of Morocco could be better furthered by working through an industrial group dependent on French government contracts than through a more independent international bank (Thobie 1983: 136). Once Ba Ahmad died, in 1900, the lid on the Moroccan makhzan lifted. Sultan Abd al-Aziz quickly surpassed the Tunisian Ahmad bey's profligate expenditures: in 1901 Schneider's military-industrial complex, Le Creusot, sold him a miniature train with 10 kilometers of track to play with in the royal gardens of Fez. Since it was now inevitable that Morocco would have to borrow on international markets, the French foreign minister wanted to make sure of a reliable debt tool for chiseling away at Moroccan sovereignty before the Germans, British, or Spaniards got at it and possibly threatened the French stranglehold over Algeria. After its victory over France in 1871, Germany had briefly toyed with plans to set up a naval base on the Mediterranean shores of Morocco in order to monitor its neighbor.

The Quai d'Orsay, however, was quickly disabused of its financial schemes. Paribas wielded sufficient influence over other banks to squeeze Le Creusot's cash flow if necessary. The cash-poor armaments manufacturer was not prepared to tie up its own funds, even a paltry 7.5 million francs, in an unguaranteed commercial loan to Morocco. Delcassé could not prevail upon any other bank to finance Le Creusot's Moroccan subsidiary because Paribas had already passed them the word and could depend, if need be, upon the minister of finance, himself a banker in Paribas's network, to sabotage his cabinet colleague's scheme. Delcassé shifted his ministry's support to Paribas within days, once it became clear, in November 1902, that Schneider's group could not raise funds from other Paris banks. With some help from the finance minister, Paribas quickly assembled a lending syndicate; in return, some of Paribas's directors received promotions in the Légion d'Honneur as well as approval for a Serbian bond issue (Guillen 1971: 58).

Heavily in debt for merchandise, including Le Creusot's armaments and the toy train, the sultan overspent his loan within a month and used up equal amounts of commercial credits from Spain and Britain. He was unable to collect taxes from tribesmen who usually complied, so discredited was the makhzan by defeat in the autumn of 1903 at the hands of a pretender whom unofficial Algerian interests had probably backed (Guillen 1967: 644). He could not generate a fraction of the revenues he had expected from minting new coinage because the subcontractors—British, French, German, and Spanish banks—were all insisting on being reimbursed at high rates of interest. By 1904, as the commercial loans fell due, the only way out of the impending anarchy was a long-term bond issue, involving guarantees that might seriously infringe upon Moroccan sovereignty.

Paribas was quite prepared to join forces with British and German banks to float an issue, but Delcassé was determined to preserve Morocco for France. Until complex diplomatic negotiations between France and Britain were sealed by the entente of April 1904, however, neither the London or Paris markets were ready for any lending, despite entreaties from the makhzan and local European banks. Berlin banks, approached in 1902 and again in 1903, had no appetite for Moroccan risk despite concern by the Auswärtiges Amt (German foreign ministry) over France's growing influence, no longer checked by Britain. After April 1904, the stage seemed set for Paribas to complete its conquest of Moroccan finances. The bank had already prevailed upon a chastened Quai d'Orsay to stop a rival, Crédit Mobilier, from concluding negotiations with the makhzan on terms more favorable than Paribas was ready to offer. Instead, Paribas brought the other bank into its syndicate (Guillen 1971: 122). But the battle among bankers and industrialists was not over.

Creusot's Compagnie Marocaine struck back. In complete secrecy it arranged a rival consortium with private Protestant banks and L'Union Parisienne, a half-Belgian banque d'affaires ready to compete with Paribas. Instead of insisting that French functionaries run the Moroccan customs, it called for a private sector public works monopoly. The Compagnie Marocaine would manage the country's infrastructure for 35 years and, supervised by makhzan officials, organize a customs treasury that would serve also as a central bank of issue. No European state, France or any other, would be permitted to infringe on the sultan's sovereignty. When Creusot's emissary arrived in Fez for the final negotiations in mid-May of 1904, high officials of the makhzan, so distrustful by then of the official French lending parties, welcomed Monsieur Brun as Allah's gift from the skies (Guillen 1971: 135n.4). But the apolitical dreams of the Compagnie Marocaine quickly evaporated.

After six days Brun begged off further negotiations with Mohammed Tazi, the Moroccan finance minister. News of the impending deal had leaked, infuriating official France as well as Paribas. Whether or not Schneider had intended all along to cut a deal with Paribas (Guillen 1971: 129), vicious press campaigns obliged him to come immediately to terms with the consortium. While getting a small slice of the lucrative loan, he lost the public works monopoly. One consolation, perhaps, was that Paribas's new loan to Bulgaria assured him repayment of debts totaling 30 million francs. The press campaign so embarrassed him, however, that he even requested an interview with the president of the republic to prove his patriotism. It still took a few more days of frantic telegraphing between Fez, Tangier, and Paris to convince Brun to stop negotiating with the Moroccans, whom both the French legation and Paribas's representatives were simultaneously besieging.

Not that any force was needed: Finance Minister Tazi pocketed a bribe of 500,000 francs from Paribas (Guillen 1971: 146) that set a new record for Moroccan business. The makhzan received 10 million francs of fresh cash at an effective interest rate of 57 percent (a nominal 5 percent on a loan of 62.5 million)—a "risk-free hold-up," as the sultan's grandson, King Hassan II, put it (El Hassani 1988: 82, citing S. M. Hassan II, *Le Défi*, Paris: Albin Michel 1976)—and almost all of it was spent by the end of the year. The details of the loan virtually ensured a French protectorate over Morocco: French officials were to collect up to 60 percent of the customs revenues for 35 years, and Paribas was poised to set up a Moroccan central bank as soon as official discussions between France and the makhzan could iron out the details. Neither Britain nor Germany seemed to stand in the way any longer, though in 1901 they had entertained the idea that Britain take Tangier for strategic reasons and Germany the Atlantic coast for its economic potential, leaving France the interior for the sake of Algeria and a possible interest in Moroccan archaeology and tourism (Fieldhouse 1973: 299).

But Germany remained a loose cannon in *Weltpolitik*. Unable to whet the appetites of the Berlin banks, still recovering from the credit crunch of 1900–1902, the Auswärtiges Amt interested the Kaiser in a voyage to Tangier in 1905 to defend an open and independent Morocco. While German dipolomacy failed to split Britain from France, the Algeciras Conference the following year effected a facade of internationalization, featuring among other measures a multinational ownership for Morocco's projected central bank. Paribas would manage the bank, however, just as France continued to advance its troops, first allegedly to protect its Algerian borders, then to protect French citizens from a "xenophobic mob," and finally to save the sultan (Fieldhouse 1973: 307), until they reached the Atlantic in 1911. Although one sultan had meanwhile been overthrown for collaborating with the infidels, his successor was persuaded of the need for an additional loan on the remaining 40 percent of the customs revenues and various other taxes. Paribas accorded German and Spanish banks, respectively, 20 percent and 10 percent of the 1910 loan, and meanwhile the Union Minière, half of which was allotted to Creusot, welcomed Krupp's 20 percent participation. Mannesmann was the only major German industrial interest to be excluded, and its ties with right-wing groups at home would encourage a final German gesture, the sending of the battleship *Panther* to Agadir, for Moroccan independence. In the end, however, Germany accepted an exchange France had offered five years earlier: territory in Central Africa in return for a French carte blanche in Morocco.

The French takeover of Morocco was hardly the peaceful affair that the Quai d'Orsay had expected. Marshal Lyautey and his successors fought proud tribesmen until 1934 whereas Tunisia had been fully pacified within a year of its invasion. The gentle bankers, however, wielded considerably more influence in Morocco. Prior to 1912 Paribas enjoyed relative autonomy in bargaining with the Quai d'Orsay. It was certainly no parasite like the speculators set up in Tunisia as an instrument of French foreign policy. To be sure, Paribas did not determine France's strategic objectives. Once selected as the Quai d'Orsay's instrument for the "peaceful penetration" of Morocco, it also respected Delcassé's compulsive urge for a French monopoly. Cautioned, it dropped plans in 1903 for a jumbo loan with British and German participation. It also used its influence with the Quai d'Orsay to humble Schneider, but it did not, like an earlier generation of French bankers, become subservient and dependent upon state patronage. The high finance of advanced capitalism had in the meantime graduated from dreamy speculation to strategic thinking. Marxists and their critics may argue over fine questions of historical interpretation—just how much impact speculators had on Léon Gambetta's crucial vote to invade Tunisia or precisely how "the interest of our banks tends today to be confounded with those of our policy," as the French minister to Morocco observed in 1903 (Guillen 1971: 91). Historians may argue over the causes of imperialism and the weights to be assigned to capitalist interests, diplomatic objectives, and even—why not blame the victim?—the misbehaving natives themselves (Fieldhouse 1973: 306). Of greater import for the future, however, was the nature and structure of the financial intermediaries to be implanted. Not only a generation but an entire capitalist mentality separated the European speculators in Tunisia, to be discussed in the next chapter, from the calculating financial sharks and captains of heavy industry in Morocco.

High finance and industry never quite fused in France into Hilferding's model based on the giant German universal banks. Capital remained too abundant in the stagnant but happy Third Republic of small investors to require rationing by a Germanic money monopoly. The German model did, however, make its way into Morocco. Trade was considerable by the turn of the century, with German ships sometimes outnumbering those of Britain, and German imports outstripping the French if not the British (Fieldhouse 1973: 276, 277). By 1903 German industralists were also becoming seriously interested in Morocco, and Diskonto Gesellschaft's proposal for a mining consortium (Guillen 1967: 641) suggested that the banks, though unwilling to engage in state lending unrelated to projects, were pushing the Auswärtiges Amt as much as they were being pushed. In chronic need of capital, the German banks were quite ready to cooperate with the French in Morocco so long as it did not become "a second Tunisia, that is, a country closed to free traffic among peoples" (Guillen 1967: 746, citing *die Post,* 23 October 1903). In 1905 Deutsche Bank may have negotiated with Paribas for French investment in the Baghdad Railway in exchange for the Germans staying out of Moroccan public finance (Guillen: 1967: 737). But Deutsche Bank, along with Krupp, had retained one of Morocco's largest commercial banks, the German trading house of Haessner, as an agent and correspondent. In 1909 Deutsche Orient Bank, owned by Dresdener and other large German banks, set up branches in Tangier and Casablanca. Deutsche Orient also had branches in Istanbul, Cairo, and Alexandria, but of course not in Tunis or Algiers.

Paribas, not the Germans, would manage the economic affairs of the protectorate, but national origins made little difference in the new world of capital-intensive mining and heavy industry. Morocco remained technically more open to international trade and investment than Tunisia, though British and American businessmen often complained of discriminatory French practices. Real closure was informal, an exaggerated practice of monopoly capitalism. Paribas perfected the form of the industrial financial conglomerate in Morocco's open spaces, not in the constricted metropole. One early fruit was the Omnium Nord Africain (ONA), engineered in 1919 and renamed in 1934. It not only survived Morocco's independence struggles but helped, in conjunction with the protectorate's other financial and industrial interests, to attenuate them. Bankers did not care about politics. One of them expressed his neutrality in this revealing passage: "Le banquier qui fait les gouvernements, impose ses créatures, achète les consciences, dicte sa loi, c'est du roman . . . la réalité est plus subtile et plus simple à la fois. . . . L'intérêt bien compris est de s'adapter à chaque étape au stade nouveau atteint par l'évolution dans des conditions telles que personne ne puisse nous tenir grief de notre attitude pendant l'étape précédente. . . . Il est dangereux de tenter de s'interposer pour l'indépendance, la retarder ou l'accélérer au risque de se voir accuser ensuite des plus sombres machinations" (El Hassani 1988: 142, citing Stéphane Bernard, 1963 III: 246–47). [The banker who makes governments, imposes his men, buys consciences, dictates law is a fairy tale . . . the reality is subtler and at the same time simpler. . . . Well understood, his interest is to adapt at each stage to the new set of conditions in ways that will not allow anyone to bear us a grudge for our stance during the previous stage. . . . It is dangerous to try to advocate independence, delay it or accelerate it, at the risk of subsequently being accused of the darkest machinations.]

Such cool and calculating mentalities could be far more easily reconciled to independence than the hotheaded and shortsighted French settlers who made the Tunisian national struggle so bitter and so petty, and the Algerian one so bestial, that capital would flee, baring gentle bankers of their usual defenses. Paribas's ONA, by contrast, became the jewel in the makhzan's crown, radiating new beams to transport royal patronage into the 1990s.

The Seven Sisters

By 1991, when Morocco finally elected to accelerate financial liberalization by lifting credit ceilings and most controls on interest rates, its banking system was more concentrated than Turkey's and considerably more secretive. Unlike the Banks Association of Turkey, the Groupement Professionnel des Banques du Maroc (GPBM) published neither balance sheets nor income statements, much less analyses of comparative financial performances. Individual banks rarely advertised interest rates to the public, and until 1989 their glossy annual reports displayed the least informative income statements published in any crescent country, including Algeria. But private conglomerates were less developed in this citadel of oligopoly than in Turkey. The Omnium Nord Africain was the only major Moroccan group that really compared in size and scale of organization with the major Turkish groups. As indicated in chapter 3, financial reform was postponed until the ONA, controlled by the makhzan, had in turn acquired a major stake in several Moroccan banks. Like Sabancı in Turkey, the ONA could be expected to support a strong banking oligopoly rather than milk the system. Financial liberalization would reinforce the oligopoly and propel the banks directly to the commanding heights of the economy. They could become the prime movers and allocators of finance capital, developing other groups of enterprises in spaces allowed by the ONA.

Two public sector banks controlled almost half the total assets of Morocco's commercial banking system, and five privately owned banks controlled more than four-fifths of the remainder. Morocco's central bank, founded in 1907, was as strong and autonomous as Turkey's. Though publicly owned and Moroccanized in 1959, the Bank Al-Maghrib had been governed continuously over the following 25 years by a member of the royal family and thereby retained its relative independence, whereas the predominantly privately owned Central Bank of the Republic of Turkey had bowed to the dictates of the Treasury and the State Planning Organization until the 1980s. In ostensibly liberal Morocco, state planners had never directly intervened in the allocation of credit. The Bank Al-Maghrib had tightly circumscribed the commercial banks' interest rates and quantities and types of credit, but it did not oblige any bank, public or private, to lend to particular customers. By Mediterranean standards, the banks appeared to have relatively clean portfolios when various credit restrictions were lifted in 1991.

Independent Morocco had carefully preserved its colonial financial legacy. To be sure, only 16 of the 69 banks counted in 1954 still existed in 1966 (Berrada 1986: 30–32; Benothmane 1985: 89), but in 1954 at least 48 had been located in Tangier, an international city until its return to Morocco in 1958 and finally, in 1960, to the jurisdiction of the national banking system. The monarchy carefully protected Morocco's French businesses, and the "Moroccanization of commerce," provoked in part by its neighbors' examples, was conducted in 1973 so as to preserve much of the substance of French control. Despite modest increases in Moroccan shareholding (to reach the required 50 percent), only one of the five large commercial banks was unambiguously managed by Moroccans in 1975, and control was strictly formal in at least two of them. Three other fully Moroccanized banks were small and would remain marginal to the system, while others were incorporated into one of Morocco's two public sector banks, the Banque Marocaine de Commerce Extérieur (Saâdi 1989: 84, 226; El Hassani 1988: 177n. 56).

With formal Moroccanization, the oligopoly took its present form. Credit ceilings imposed in the mid-1970s essentially froze existing market shares of loans and deposits. The Banque du Crédit Populaire (BCP) was Morocco's largest commercial bank. Founded by royal decree in 1961, the central headquarters was an exclusively public sector bank, owned by the Moroccan Treasury, the Bank al-Maghrib, and a number of specialized public sector agencies. This bank, however, coordinated an extensive network of regional cooperatives and European affiliates. The cooperatives accounted in 1990 for 38 percent of the consolidated bank's capital. The bank's board of directors included eight representatives of the regional boards, alongside 16 officials and two representatives of artisans, professionals, and small industries. Directed for many years by a prominent leader of the Istiqlal Party, the BCP represented one of many successful royal initiatives to co-opt elements of the nationalist opposition. Though a disproportionately large share of its huge deposit base was lent to the government, the bank also earmarked important sums for loans to artisans and small businesses, traditional constituencies of the Istiqlal Party.

Next in size as well as in the degree of state ownership came the Banque Marocaine du Commerce Extérieur (BMCE). Founded in 1959 as Morocco's flagship bank for foreign trade, the BMCE gathered a diverse set of public sector enterprises, foreign banks, and private Moroccan entrepreneurs on its board of directors. In 1990 the public sector held almost 60 percent of the capital, the foreign banks 12.5 percent, and of the remaining 28.7 percent more than half was held by an insurance company (El Amane). Abdellatif Jouahri, who took charge of the bank in 1986 immediately after being dismissed from his post as minister of finance, had earlier controlled credit ceilings in the Bank al-Maghrib. Once he took charge of the BMCE, he also presided, as Morocco's leading banker, over the Groupement Professionnel des Banques du Maroc. In effect he managed the oligopoly—including periodic negotiations over interest rates—while also tightening up the BMCE's management structures and cutting back its excessive costs so as to render it more competitive with private sector banks. By 1990, in fact, little distinguished it from the private sector, apart from the formal capital structure. The public sector board members tended to be silent partners, and the king was implying, as early as his speech formally opening the spring session of parliament in April 1988, that the bank could be privatized. The speech was formally incorporated into the law on privatization passed in 1989 (*L'Opinion,* 13 December 1989), and both the BCP and BMCE were on the list of "privatizable firms" circulated by the Ministry of Economic Affairs and Privatization in 1991. Jouahri declared in mid-1994 that the BMCE would be privatized by the end of the year (*MEED,* 24 June 1994).

The other core members of the oligopoly were five medium-sized privately owned banks, each of which had at least 6 percent of the loans and deposits in 1990. All of them, originally branches or subsidiaries of French banks during the protectorate, had been merged or fused before being Moroccanized in the 1970s. The Banque du Crédit Marocain (BCM) was the largest and most consistently profitable of the five. For some years after formal Moroccanization it remained under the management of its largest French shareholder, the Credit Industriel et Commercial, until a cadre of young Moroccans could take over. Employed by the bank since 1969, Abdelaziz Alami rose through the ranks to become Morocco's premier private banker in the 1980s. A published poet as well as banker, he competed both personally and professionally with Jouahri, the central bank bureaucrat turned banker. They jousted over market share in the late 1980s; in Casablanca banking circles it was said that the poet accused his rival of considering himself still the finance minister.

In fact the market shares of the banks changed little in the 1980s. Figure 5–1 shows the major winner of deposits to be the BCP, Morocco's biggest bank and the only one that was wholly government-owned. It increased its share of deposits by almost 8 percent, at the expense of all the other banks except BCM and Wafabank. But an inspection of the BCP's deposit structure shows the gains to have come from time deposits rather than sight deposits. Most of them were workers' remittances from France. In 1982, when the French franc slid below parity with the Moroccan dirham, the king insisted on full parity for his subjects residing in France. The effect was to saddle the BCP with a monopoly on these remittances. The other banks preferred not to offer premiums for foreign exchange; moreover, they preferred cost-free sight deposits to time deposits. The real competition between commercial banks in the 1980s was over sight deposits. Strategic planners carefully analyzed their competitors' deposit structures as well as their own to detect minute variations. Gaining even a fraction of a percentage point in one's share of sight deposits could be touted to one's management as a major victory, whereas more time deposits simply meant a higher cost of funds, hence lower margins and profits.

BCM gained about 1 percent over the decade, but Wafabank was the clearcut victor, increasing its share of sight deposits from 7.6 to 10 percent between 1981 and 1990. Though not the largest of Morocco's five privately owned banks, Wafa was first to be fully Moroccanized. In 1968 Moulay Ali Kettani, a Fassi textile magnate who enjoyed close relations with the palace, acquired a majority stake in the Compagnie Algérienne (subsequently "Marocaine") de Crédit et de Banque and gradually Moroccanized its management after 1970. He put Abdelhak Bennani in charge of the bank in 1976. This trusted member of the family (on Kettani's mother's side) had French banking experience and was also the half-brother of the vice governor of the Bank al-Maghrib. In 1978 Bennani introduced Morocco's first privately generated innovation, a carte blanche to guarantee checks for skeptical merchants. He opened Africa's first automatic teller in 1981 and led the other banks in introducing credit cards, various other financial

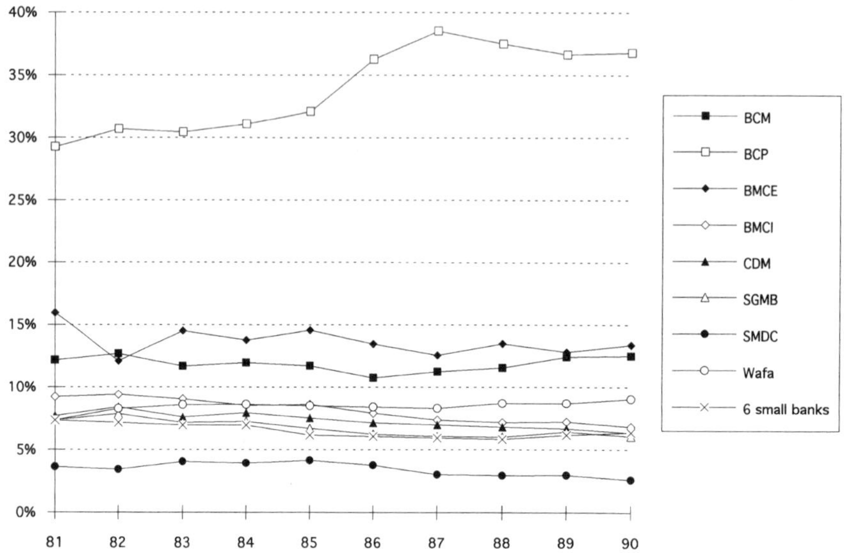

Fig. 5.1. Moroccan commercial bank deposits, 1981–90. *Sources:* annual reports of the commercial banks.

"products," and on-line computing facilities. Image building was also part of the strategy: the Compagnie Marocaine de Crédit et de Banque was renamed "Wafa," signifying fidelity, in 1982, and the bank blitzed the Moroccan press with advertisements. To further its image, the affluent new Casablanca headquarters housed a chic art collection. For all its efforts to generate more sight deposits, however, Wafa gained only half a percentage point in its shares of loans. As long as credit restrictions were enforced, competition remained an artificial exercise.

Under credit rationing the banks marched lockstep, deploying much of the country's finance capital. Figure 5–2 presents their steady distributions of loans between 1981 and 1990. In theory, specialized financial institutions offered most of the medium- and long-term credits (some 75 percent of them in 1990) whereas the commercial banks concentrated on short-term credit. In practice, however, many Moroccan enterprises were undercapitalized and relied on short-term loans to service their working capital needs. Shortly before being appointed minister of finance (1986–93), Mohammed Berrada succinctly summarized his academic research: "The study of bank accounts of enterprises which were visited shows that the accounts are permanently in the red. This signifies that the enterprises are transforming a provisional short-term credit into a permanent long-term one. Such a practice, were it

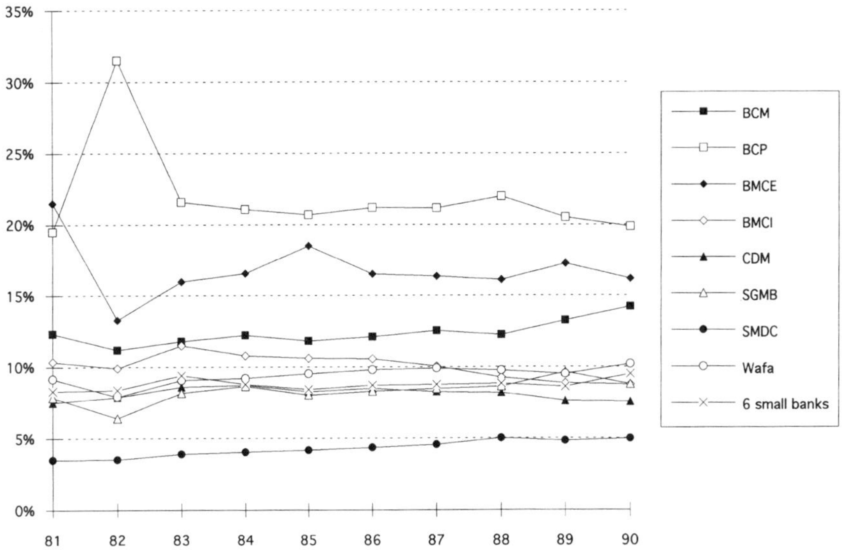

Fig. 5.2 Moroccan commercial bank loans, 1981–90. *Sources:* annual reports of the commercial banks.

adopted by all the bank's clients, would endanger the equilibrium of the bank's balance sheet" (Berrada 1986: 198–99). Cursory analysis of *Kompass,* Morocco's annual business directory, shows that most enterprises shared their business with more than one bank. Consequently the banks shared dilemmas of common interest. Were one bank to insist that a client settle his account, the burden of paying off the bank would fall upon the other bank(s). As long as the Bank Al-Maghrib restricted the lending of each bank, however, competitors could not be expected to rescue clients. In the 1980s prevailing regulations helped to ensure that the bankers would remain good oligopolists, peacefully "cooperating" to roll over short-term loans.

Another practice was pooled lending. In Morocco large loans were usually contracted by a consortium of local banks. Bankers estimate that pooled lending accounted for about half the value of the commercial banking system's outstanding credit (compared with about 30 percent in Tunisia). Shared risks thus enhanced common interests. Pooling practices also helped to concentrate commercial banking in the hands of the seven largest banks. Smaller banks, with less capital and lending capacity, tended to be excluded from most of the pools. Citibank was perhaps atypical in that corporate practice discouraged it from pooled lending unless it had adequate information about the credit risk. It still exemplified the dilemma of the smaller banks. Without a sufficiently large capital base, Citibank could not play a lead role in any lending syndicate and consequently could not get the necessary information.

Credit restrictions had trained Morocco's seven sisters to be "nice," tit-for-tat players. Bankers may be natural oligopolists in theory, ever ready to resolve dilemmas of common interest as if they were playing iterated prisoner's dilemma games, valuing an indefinite rosy future over temptations to cash in present values. But real bankers are not always so magnanimous, so immune from scandal, as amply demonstrated by the savings and loan crisis in the United States or the BCCI affair. In Turkey, bankers could be free-wheeling entrepreneurs, sometimes setting up new banks at the expense of their former employers. In Turkey, moreover, inflation rates were high and tended to diminish expected values of future cooperation. Powerful conglomerates were needed in Turkey to hold the system together, once the government proceeded with formal liberalization.

In Morocco, by contrast, the parameters were more favorable to cooperation and continued oligopoly, once the government finally went ahead in 1991 with significant steps to liberalize its financial system. To be sure, when the credit ceilings on individual banks were lifted in 1991, their initial responses lived up to the reformers' expectations of greater competition. Anticipating the lifting of the ceilings, the BMCE and BCM were competing for deposits in 1990, before the GPBM reached an informal understanding on interest rates. Once the ceilings were lifted, the banks then rushed to satisfy pent-up demand for loans. They collectively increased their loans by at least 30 percent during 1991, roughly triple the increase that the Bank Al-Maghrib had planned. Surprised by the credit surge, the central bank increased the required reserves on sight deposits from 15 percent in January 1991 to 16 percent in July, 18 percent in November, and 20 percent in 1992, with threats to hit 30 if the banks did not cut back on their lending. Once the banks had repositioned themselves, however, it seemed likely that they would once again settle into a comfortable oligopoly. Inflation rates were much lower, encouraging a bank to discount the values of future cooperation less than in Turkey. There were fewer actors, and Moroccan liberalization apparently did not include opening more doors to joint ventures as in Turkey or Egypt. Other, more primordial bonds also held the Moroccans together.

The top management of some banks was almost exclusively Fassi (Tangeaoui 1994: 141–42). Family connections cut across banks, including the Bank Al-Maghrib, managed for over two decades by Vice Governor and subsequently Governor Ahmed Bennani, the half-brother of the manager of another leading bank. Junior managers without "the right origins for the right post" complained of being shunted aside when their Berber or non-Fassi background was discovered. "Fassi," to be sure, no longer meant originating in Fez, the most important of Morocco's four traditional capital cities. Since the nineteenth century many important Fassi families had migrated to other business centers, especially Casablanca (Waterbury 1970: 94). The term "Fassi" had acquired an independent sociological meaning, connoting business interests and proximity to power as well as family lineage; though not unconditionally loyal to the sultan, Fassis, unlike tribesmen, had never been in a position to wage a campaign of dissidence against him. Not all bankers had the right lineage, but the marginal ones apparently did not enjoy much success unless they had special connections with the palace. A banker with the right connections might mismanage a loan portfolio and remain a top manager in the system. Indeed it was almost impossible, if one was a member of the club, not to make steady profits in the 1980s.

Within a given bank, the managers were much less likely to defect than some of their Turkish counterparts. Each bank had built up a housing fund for its employees, especially high-ranking ones; indeed, visiting Tunisian managers marveled at the lifestyle of their Moroccan counterparts. Banks did not seem to compete with one another for talent, and opportunities in the foreign sector were limited. No new banks were founded in the 1980s. Apart from the French, the foreign sector consisted of only four banks, Citibank (USA), Algemene (Holland), Arab Bank (Jordan), and UNIBAN (Spain); in 1991 Spanish banks were also permitted to acquire 50 percent of BMAO. Unlike "secular" Turkey, the monarchy rejected Al-Baraka's overtures in 1987 to set up an Islamic bank. Although an Islamic offshore leasing company was permitted to operate, the existence of an Islamic bank might have implied that the economy of the Commander of the Faithful was not itself Islamic.

The principal threat to the oligopoly, in fact, was an emerging bourgeoisie of private entrepreneurs. Nascent "groups" of Moroccan investors might acquire control of some of the banks and milk them for cheap credit to their related enterprises. Real competition could then drive down interest rates and the spreads between interest received on loans and interest expenses for deposits. As a result of "Moroccanization," two groups of Berber investors had acquired commanding interests in a couple of small banks. Being small, they did not have sufficient market power to diversify their risks in pooled lending. Each was on the brink of bankruptcy in the mid-1980s. Both banks appear to have overextended credit to some of their investors' other enterprises, compounding the leverage of their respective groups to the breaking point. Fortunately for the system, however, the banks were too small to have a major impact.

Moroccan bankers shivered, however, when they first heard the news in 1988 that ONA had acquired a major stake in the BCM (Ziady 1989: 52). Abdelaziz Alami, the bank's chief executive officer, tried to reassure them that the request for the investment had come from him and not the ONA. The major foreign owner, the Crédit Industriel et Commercial, had sought to reduce its stake as part of its global strategy, and the ONA was merely a convenient source of capital. Fouad Filali, the king's son-in-law, who was also chief executive officer of the ONA, corroborated Alami's story, but there was another interpretation. A number of insiders diplomatically praised Alami for his "clever" handling of the situation, as if he had put the best spin on an uncomfortable development. Filali denied that the ONA had any intention of interfering in the bank's management, but his talk of "synergy" between "Africa's premier private group and the kingdom's premier private bank" included potential lending of the bank to the ONA's growing hotel and tourism sector (*Maroc conjoncture 1988/1989* [1989]: 67–68). Alami seemed in fact to retain a relatively free hand in managing the BCM, for the ONA's major objectives were to gain better access to the entire banking system and to enlist BCM's assistance in improving the ONA's internal financial controls.

Were the ONA to play a role in Moroccan banking comparable to Sabancı's in Turkey, BCM and the other banks under its influence would pass much of the business risk to other banks in the system. Financial reform in fact required all the banks to diversify their portfolios and to limit their lending to a single individual or enterprise to 10 percent of the bank's capital, and in 1992 the Bank al-Maghrib was beginning to make an inventory of the banks' borrowers with a view to enforcing portfolio diversification. Morocco was also committed to meeting international banking standards of capital adequacy by the end of 1993, but loans to shareholders had to be deducted from a bank's capital. The reform therefore served to protect the banks from the ravages of other groups that were less structured, more highly leveraged, and perhaps less committed to Morocco's financial oligopoly. Seen in conjunction with the financial reforms, ONA's acquisition of substantial holdings in the BCM and a number of other banks could best be interpreted as a preemptive measure to block the emergence of other groups. Table 5–1 analyzes the capital structure of the commercial banking system at the end of 1990—on the eve of the major reforms and ONA ac-

Table 5-1 Capital structure of Moroccan commercial banks, 1990

Bank	Total assets (million dirhams)	Capital (million dirhams)	Percent shares held by: Public sector	Moroccan private sector: Groups	Moroccan private sector: Misc.	Foreign
BCP	35136	2340	100.00			
BMCE	22817	1262.6	58.73		28.71	12.56
BCM	13930	1049		32.72	42.52	24.76
Wafa	10011	617		100.00		
BMCI	7235	321		2.31	44.69	53.00
SGMB	7785	506		32.00	18.00	50.00
CDM	6713	455	26.46	10.02	20.32	43.20
SMDC[a]	3152	174			50.00	50.00
UNIBAN	1979	182				100.00
SBC	1556	99		some ONA	100.00	0.00
Algemen	1502	99			50.00	50.00
BMAO	1448	109			100.00	
Arab Bank	794	106	50.00			50.00
Citibank[b]	303	56			50.00	50.00
Total	114361	7376				

Source: Groupement Professionnel de Banques du Maroc, Annuaire des Banques du Maroc, 1991–92
a. Total assets are for 1989.
b. Total assets are for 1985.

quisitions. The official listings of the banks offer information about the distribution of their shareholders among the public sector, the private Moroccan sector, and foreign banks. The Moroccan private sector, including semipublic companies, held 36 percent of the capital, an increase of only 3 percent since 1983 (Saâdi and Berrada 1992: 344). Identifying the "groups" within the private sector, however, presented theoretical as well as practical difficulties. They were not officially identified as units, and Moroccan conceptualizations of a "group" were in the same state of evolution as the assemblages themselves.

The Moroccanization of commerce had encouraged a variety of "groups" to acquire French assets. Holding companies became a kind of "fever" in the mid-1970s (El Hassani 1988: 277), and Saâdi discovered that 58 "groups and dominant families" controlled 55 percent of the private Moroccan capital and almost 20 percent of the country's total industrial capital in 1978 (1989: 190–92). When confronted with these data, however, an experienced Moroccan banker identified fewer than ten of them as real conglomerates operating as business entities. Another Moroccan author included six official Moroccan government investment vehicles but no private sector entities, not even the Omnium Nord Africain, in his "repertory" of groups like Hoechst, Mitsubishi, Unilever, and Fiat (Sagou 1987), whereas Saâdi argued that the government holdings were sleeping partners of the Moroccan private sector. The "group" in the sense of a business conglomerate (Leff 1979a, b) was not as easy to identify in Morocco as in Turkey, for it did not exist in the corpus of Moroccan business law. Indeed the most balanced work on Moroccan groups had to refer to German law to develop a working definition of a group (El Hassani 1988: 35), whereas Koç had pioneered the concept of a holding company and sponsored appropriate Turkish legislation in the mid-1960s. This form of capitalism was obviously less developed in Morocco.

The group could be envisioned either as a "coalition of capitalists developing a network of personal matrimonial and business relations . . . animated by a leader" (Saâdi 1989: 163) or as a "set of enterprises enjoying legal autonomy but subordinated to a common direction . . . by means of financial control or a contract . . . or *de facto*" (El Hassani 1988: 35). The second definition is more general, including the public as well as the private sector, but leaves open the scope of authority or control. Government agencies tended to be relatively passive portfolio investors, not active holding companies of the sort that could be found in Algeria or Egypt (Saâdi 1989: 90–110, but cf. El Hassani 1988: 196–97). A number of companies originally started up by the government for lack of private investment were slated for privatization, which was finally, after many delays, beginning to be implemented in 1992. If it proceeded, privatization would have a cascading effect upon the government's portfolio, eventually affecting some 40 percent of its companies (Saulniers, forthcoming). Privatization was also designed to discourage acquisitions by the biggest private groups. Criticized earlier for acquiring a sugar refinery, the ONA prudently disqualified itself. In keeping with royal business strategy, the leaders of Morocco's other two most prominent groups were named to an independent valuation authority, which equally disqualified them from any purchases.

Most private groups were informal "coalitions of capitalists" who were the principal beneficiaries of Moroccanization and would presumably drive any future privatization. With the major exception of the Omnium (ONA), however, few Moroccan groups fit the organizational criteria. Many of their holdings were shell companies that had been devised to "Moroccanize" foreign firms so that their foreign owners could retain them. The simplest way to do this was for the foreign firm to keep 49 percent of the equity and transfer the other 51 percent to a "Moroccan" shell company in which it had a minority share. Other, more complex interrelationships produced the same effect (El Hassani 1988: 220–29; Saâdi 1989: 74–75). Obviously a "group" consisting of a principal holding, a network of shell companies, and their foreign affiliates did not constitute a group in the Turkish sense of a set of companies subordinated to a common direction. Most of the Moroccan "groups" appeared to be ethereal constructs of financial and political analysts, largely consisting of tax havens and leveraged cross-holdings; like a tribe, a group was above all a name, a shorthand for a system of fluid alliances, but not necessarily a corporate actor.

Many bankers, journalists, and academics put the Mohammed Karim Lamrani Group and the Ali Kettani Group in the same league as the venerable Omnium (ONA). They were supposed to be the strongest privately owned groups operating in Morocco in the late 1980s. In the case of Lamrani, however, there was significant disagreement. One prominent knowledgeable banker denied the group's very existence, while another argued more generally that groups were "too theoretical" to enjoy any significant competitive advantages. At issue was the degree to which these newer Moroccan groups were organized. In the most careful empirical analysis of Moroccan groups to date, Mohamed Saïd Saâdi inferred from data available in the late 1970s that Lamrani's network of financial companies had assembled more financial power than the ONA (1989: 190). But on Saâdi's own analysis, Lamrani was clearly a one-man show, playing the role of "federator and animator, which permits him to shepherd capitalists of various horizons" (147).

Of Sharifian lineage (Waterbury 1970: 97), Lamrani had become a royal adviser after making his fortune in Africa. Though reputed to support Morocco's radical opposition party, the UNFP, he was put in charge of the Office Cherifienne des Phosphates (OCP) in 1967 and served as prime minister in the mid-1980s while retaining the OCP. He meanwhile built up a personal business empire—the so-called Lamrani Group—through a variety of financial holding companies. Already a core member of economic elite in the mid-1960s (Waterbury 1970: 106–7), he was alleged by the late 1970s to control one bank, the Crédit du Maroc, which he had managed before 1967, and to exercise significant influence over the Banque Commerciale du Maroc and the Société Générale Marocaine de Banque as well as some thirty other enterprises (Saâdi 1989: 147). As chief executive officer of the OCP he also sat as the largest single shareholder, with one-fifth of the capital, on the board of directors of the Banque Marocaine du Commerce Extérieur (Groupement Professionnel des Banques du Maroc 1991: 22). Here indeed was a highly influential, wealthy, and presumably talented individual who had served the king for three decades. But his private "group" appeared to be an academically constructed set of interlocking portfolios, not a corporate headquarters (apart from the state-owned OCP).

Groups like Lamrani were supposed to serve as proxies for underdeveloped financial markets by allocating and deploying scarce capital. Indeed, Saâdi concluded his pioneering analysis with the demand that the private groups be nationalized to prevent their misuse of Moroccan finance capital. His only concrete evidence of any financial management within the Lamrani Group, however, concerned the credit policies of a bank allegedly affiliated with the group. At some time in the late 1970s or early 1980s the bank apparently accorded evergreen facilities (short-term credit rollovers) far in excess of legal limits to certain enterprises associated with the group (Saâdi 1989: 175–76). While such banking practices were apparently widespread, as noted previously (Berrada 1986), it does not necessarily follow that "centralized treasury management is frequently practiced, although in a pragmatic manner, within the Lamrani Group" (Saâdi 1989: 181). Crédit du Maroc (CDM), the bank in question (149), drastically reduced its credit portfolio, relative to total assets, in the early 1980s, and was reputed subsequently to run the tightest credit checks of all Moroccan banks. While banks might favor clients associated with wealthy and well-connected individuals, such as Mohamed Karim Lamrani, they were better off diversifying their portfolios in the absence of legislation that defined groups and their constituents' liabilities. The ownership and control of the CDM also deserves further analysis. At best, the putative Lamrani Group had only 10.02 percent of the bank's equity, whereas Crédit Lyonnais held 43.2 percent in 1990 (Groupement Professionnel des Banques du Maroc 1991: 36). Any Lamrani control depended more on the man's influence over insurance companies and the BMCE, which controlled 26.5 percent of the shares, than on his private holdings. Moreover, the private shareholder was the Société Financière et de Participations (SOFIPAR), a financial company in which Ali Kettani had a 30 percent interest, supplementing Lamrani's 43.14 percent, in 1981 (Saâdi 1989: 147, 150). While recognizing the interloper in the Lamrani Group's core, Saâdi dismissed it in a footnote: "This participation would seem to confer upon the M.A. Kettani group a certain influence on the orientation of SOFIPAR. We have unfortunately not been able to integrate this 'potential influence' in our analysis in so far as interviews we conducted with the leaders of this group made us lean toward the hypothesis of a simple financial placement" (1989: 150n.16). In other words, Moulay Ali Kettani, the most dynamic of Morocco's exclusively private sector businessmen, let some of his scarce capital idle in a sleeping partnership with a principal competitor. Supposing Saâdi's informants to be correct, Kettani must have considered the capital to be a strategic investment. Returns for other business favors perhaps offset returns on capital invested in the fixed assets of his expanding empire.

The Kettani Group, however, had a more tangible base than Lamrani's pervasive webs of personal influence and investments. Also of Sherifian lineage, Kettani had been a cloth merchant before independence and then invested in an Italian textile manufacturer to gain experience, encouraging him to invest further in textiles in the 1960s. From this industrial base he moved into banking and also diversified into insurance, navigation, electrical household goods, industrial carpentry, engineering, public works, and real estate. His principal holding company, SOPAR, was created in the early 1970s, however, purely for tax reasons (El Hassani 1988: 291). Saâdi's informants observed that the Kettani Group's treasury operations were even less systematic and less integrated than Lamrani's. It seemed, in fact, that Kettani's son, who had studied modern business organization, was continually frustrated in his attempt to rationalize his family's holdings (El Hassani 1988: 292n.245). It was far from clear how this group, despite its ownerhip of Wafabank, could take advantage of the principal competitive edge that a conglomerate theoretically affords its members in a Third World society, namely, better business information. Of the groups studied by Moroccans, in fact, only the ONA appeared to have an extensive corporate headquarters, an efficient treasury that could allocate capital according to the group's needs, a financial strategy, and presumably ways of exchanging information between its various strategically located enterprises.

Though second to the Lamrani Group in the total financial surface constructed in Saâdi's study (190), the ONA was clearly the largest and most articulated of Morocco's conglomerates. Total sales of the group in 1990 constituted 5.5 percent of Morocco's GDP, about as much as the Sabancı Group's share of a much larger Turkish economy. The ONA's strategic planners were projecting growth rates of 20 percent in the early 1990s, accompanying investments of 5 billion dirhams. In 1992 the conglomerate was restructured along four lines of business, agro-distribution, mining, high technology, and finance. High technology appeared to be focused mainly on the media, including a satellite television monopoly reminiscent of Özal's efforts in Turkey to control the most politically strategic of the mass media (Poindexter 1991: 30; *L'Economiste*, 16 April 1992). The finance "pole" included the ONA's shares in a variety of industrial enterprises but significantly excluded the BCM, which, like ONA's philanthropic foundation (also reminiscent of Turkish groups) reported directly to the chief executive officer, the king's son-in-law.

The monarchy was too astute, however, to interfere directly with Morocco's finely tuned banking system. Instead, it seemed ready through the ONA to help recapitalize the bigger banks and to merge some of the smaller ones so as to reinforce the oligopoly. Thus it increased its holdings in the Banque Marocaine pour le Commerce et l'Industrie (BMCI) to 15 percent in 1991. This bank appeared to be the weakest and, until 1991, the least capitalized of the Big Seven. Its principal shareholder, the Banque Nationale de Paris Internationale, had been allowed to acquire a majority of the shares and full control of the bank after application of the Moroccanization decree of 1973 was suspended in 1990. In 1992 the ONA encouraged the merger of the Société de Banque et de Crédit (SBC) with the BCM. Earlier the little bank had been the object of takeover bids by the ONA and another Moroccan group backed by a Kuwaiti investor. The ONA had acquired the bank but had kept it under the provisional management of a banker close to the palace rather than incorporating it into the holding, for it was too small to play any significant role in financing large enterprises. Another bank, managed until late 1991 by the same banker (who subsequently became deputy manager of the BMCI), also faced prospects of being merged.

The bank in question was the Société Marocaine de Dépôt et de Crédit (SMDC), Morocco's eighth largest. Product of the merger after Moroccan independence of the Banque Ottomane and Crédit du Nord, the SMDC was still half-owned by Paribas and Worms until the ONA repurchased their shares in 1992 (*MEED*, 5 June 1992: 19). The other Moroccan shareholder was Abdelkader Ben Salah, owner of the Holmarcom Group. The group was reputed to be among Morocco's largest, with total sales amounting to over half those of the ONA and 70 percent of the Kettani Group's. Seven of the eight companies listed in Kompass that could be identified with the group indicated that the SMDC was their lead bank. The bank had projected itself as a *banque d'affaires* in the tradition of its French owners, and its manager had enjoyed close ties with both Paribas and the ONA. But its evident ties with the Moroccan group had perhaps stretched its financial capacities. The bank did not keep up with the other predominantly French banks in the 1980s. It had lost a full percentage point of the market during the decade. It had been obliged to rely more heavily on costly time deposits to finance its portfolio. Unlike the other banks, it had few provisions for nonperforming loans and was seriously undercapitalized. Though much bigger than Citibank, the SMDC further illustrated the dilemmas of a small bank in the

Moroccan marketplace. Unless a bank had a special foreign niche like Citibank or UNIBAN, it was hard to survive in Morocco without being one of the Big Seven.

Among the seven sisters, Wafabank was the only one tied to a tangible external group that was not in turn directly governed by the palace. The Kettani Group was hardly in a position, however, to subvert the oligopoly by doling out cheap credits. Financial reform undertaken in 1991 in tandem with a loan package from the World Bank placed Wafabank under the same microscope as the other banks. Internal sources in the bank claimed that the total credit accorded the Kettani group of companies was less than the bank's exposure to the OCP and amounted to about 4 percent of the bank's total portfolio (Interview, 30 December 1991), but the exposure was equivalent to about one-quarter of the bank's capital, well over the 10 percent ceiling allowable to a single enterprise. Under discussion was how the ceiling was to be applied to groups of enterprises. Another issue concerned the bank's capital. Kettani was under some pressure to limit his total holdings to 30 percent. Wafa was delaying raising new capital to meet the required capital adequacy ratios until agreement with the Bank al-Maghrib could be reached concerning the definition of a shareholder and his related holdings. Loans to shareholders owning more than 5 percent of the bank had to be deduced from the capital counted in the new ratios, but did the loans to enterprises in which a shareholder held no controlling interest also count as items to be deducted from the core capital?

The Bank al-Maghrib was vigorously pressing reforms upon the banks that would eliminate any remaining ties to groups by requiring greater diversification of their portfolios. The central bank required monthly reports of loans to all shareholders, however remotely connected they might be to the corporate borrowers. Gradually it seemed to be assembling the information needed to define the intricate webs of financial relations that constituted "groups" in the sense of personal relationships, alluded to earlier. The reform process was thus continuing the work accomplished earlier with credit ceilings: institutionalizing the banking oligopoly. The World Bank was also contributing to the process by granting the oligopoly an international recognition of sorts: its loan package was reserved exclusively for the seven sisters and a development bank, leaving out all the smaller banks.

With international help, then, capitalism in Morocco was being channeled into structures reminiscent of Hilferding's Germany. But reform also consolidated a major difference between Imperial Germany and contemporary Morocco. It detached commercial banking from industrial holdings, as required in Anglo Saxon practice. Unlike the German universal bank, the reformed Moroccan bank was cut off from any industrial or commercial bases. Detached from the groups emerging in the private sector, the individual Moroccan bank wielded less financial power than the large commercial banks in Turkey that were joined to major conglomerates. The deregulated Moroccan banking system was indeed ascending to the commanding heights of the economy, but the command was strictly collective. While directly or indirectly deploying most of Morocco's finance capital, the bankers would also be collective hostages to their largest borrowers, above all to the ONA and to state enterprises such as the OCP, which were not to be privatized. Various other groups would vie for loans, but a secretive and vulnerable financial oligopoly also shared the monarchy's interest in keeping the private sector loyal and subservient. In Morocco finance capital would be controlled by the makhzan, not an emergent industrial bourgeoisie.

Financial Adjustment and Political Order

Whether or not financial adjustment leads to greater economic efficiency, it helped to consolidate finance capital in Turkey and Morocco. Though the reforms were intended to encourage competition for scarce capital resources, they reinforced oligopolistic tendencies in the respective banking systems. Since commercial banks remained the principal sources of capital, they seemed bound to stimulate ever greater concentrations of private capital side by side with their respective public sectors. With further reforms and cuts in the public deficits, public borrowing might diminish, leaving greater room for private borrowing. But whether the government kept crowding out the private sector, as in Turkey, or dramatically reduced its deficit, as in Morocco, the respective oligopolies would channel their available funds to the larger, established borrowers.

Though transplanted from Imperial Germany, the banking system's deployment of finance capital did not reproduce a German industrial bourgeoisie in either Turkey or Morocco, much less turn the respective states into its executive committees. Though financial reform strengthened Turkey's finance oligopoly, it did not eliminate the state's heavy hand inside it. Transposed to Morocco, Hilferding's finance capital had a different effect. As in Turkey, financial reform sharpened oligopolistic tendencies within the banking system. But in Morocco the concentration of finance capital served the makhzan, not an emerging bourgeoisie. Through the ONA's investments in Morocco's leading banks the royal household has achieved a dominant position within the banking oligopoly and can place its men in key positions in leading banks. Holding the credit strings, the makhzan continues to manipulate patronage systems and political parties by controlling the socioeconomic status of business and political elites. Financial oligopoly has helped shrink the elite to a manageable size. By streamlining patronage, finance and banking help to explain why Waterbury's *Commander of the Faithful,* cited at the outset of this chapter, still so superbly conveys the flavor of Moroccan politics, more than two decades after it was written. In different ways, growing concentrations of finance capital have constituted foundations for political order in Morocco as well as Turkey.

Chapter 6

Algeria and Tunisia: In Search of Financial Power

> Si j'avais voulu me lier à certains groupes d'intérêts, j'aurais bénéficié de leur soutien, de leurs forces! Il suffisait de travailler avec cinq ou six personnes et on aurait mobilisé toute une force. [If I had wished to tie myself to certain interest groups, I would have benefited from their support, their power! It would have sufficed to work with five or six people to mobilize a real force.]
>
> Un homme d'affaires, quand vous le touchez, il est là. [A businessman, when you touch him, is there.]
>
> (Belaid Abdesselam, interview, in Bennoune and El-Kenz 1990: 2:378)

> Modern methods of drawing up balance sheets not only make it possible to conceal doubtful undertakings from the average shareholder, but also allow the people most concerned to escape the consequences of unsuccessful speculation. . . . The balance sheets of many joint stock companies put us in mind of the palimpsets of the Middle Ages from which the visible inscription had first to be erased in order to discover beneath it another inscription giving the real meaning of the document.
>
> (Ludwig Eschwege, cited by Lenin, *Imperialism* 1939 [1917]: 50)

Algeria and Tunisia stand in sharp contrast to Turkey and Morocco. The structural power of Algeria's finance capital is virtually nil. Though highly oligopolistic in a formal sense, Algeria's commercial banking system enjoyed virtually no autonomy and consequently could not provide Chadly Benjedid any backing for his simultaneous financial and political reforms. This chapter will therefore devote more space to Tunisia, where the simultaneous reform processes initially appeared to be more promising, to examine whether bankers might quietly acquire structural power, preparing the way for multiple centers of political power. But the similarities between Algeria and Tunisia are greater than the differences: in Tunisia the structural power of finance capital was almost as limited as in Algeria. Tunisian finance capital, too, had been circumscribed by provincial nineteenth-century French practices and by a single-party regime after independence which, while displaying more subtle tactics than its Algerian counterparts, suffocated the commercial banks. There was also a striking political similarity: by the early 1990s, each country in its own way was replicating the struggle for national liberation against French colonialism. The Islamists occupied the political ground that the nationalists had successfully contested several decades earlier, against states now dominated by indigenous rather than foreign elites. Just as Algeria's military republic recalled the military regime of French Algeria beefed up by the Mollet government in 1956, Ben Ali's regime was reminiscent of the Corsican police state managed by hard-line French Residents General such as Marcel Peyrouton in 1934 and Jean de Hautecloque in 1952.

Financial Legacies

At the beginning of the nineteenth century, bankers on both shores of the Mediterranean tended to come from minority groups, and they performed similar functions on a relatively level playing field. If not quite the "virtual rulers of Algiers" (Fieldhouse 1973: 107; cf. Sahli 1986: 187), the Bacri and Busnach families strongly influenced the economic and foreign policies of the Ottoman rulers. These Sephardic Jews purchased and exported grain with the help of their networks of local moneylenders even in times of domestic shortages. Originally from Livorno, Italy, they had connections so extensive that one of Napoleon's ministers concluded that "all the commerce of the Mediterranean has fallen into their hands" (Julien 1964: 19, citing Jean Bon Saint-André). Financing French grain purchases, they enjoyed as much access to Napoleon's Foreign Minister Talleyrand as other court bankers.

Their very success would be Algeria's undoing. The French government delayed repayment of debts accumulated from Algerian wheat shipments during the Napoleonic wars. By his arrogant behavior, the French consul eventually provoked the dey of Algiers, egged on by his bankers, into impatiently grazing him with a fly swatter (Sahli 1986: 181). After three more years of dilatory negotiations about repaying part of the debt in return for other concessions, the French government exploited the incident by invading the country in 1830. Henceforth Algerian banking would be French.

Sandwiched between French Algeria and a rising Italy, Tunisia managed to stay independent for another half-century in an increasingly dangerous environment. Then as now, Tunisia was a "relatively wealthy society, with an increasing taste for European products—capital, consumer goods, and military equipment—which wanted to modernize itself and was prepared to cooperate with European finance and technology" (Fieldhouse 1973: 112). It also displayed a genius for financial survival that reflected some of the southern shore's rich legacies, even if it eventually fell victim to the profligacy and corruption of some of its political leadership and the sheer greed of European speculators.

The story of the Tunisian debt, however, was hardly one of a triumphant European imperialism carving out more space for greater profits. Fieldhouse is on sound ground in arguing that "economic enterprise would become the tool rather than the motor of political imperialism" (1973: 115)—at least for relatively backward French capitalism. The British capitalists could never get interested in Tunisia, however much the resilient British consul, Richard Wood, tried to involve them. In 1856, shortly after arriving in Tunis, he secretly sounded out bankers in London about establishing an Anglo-Tunisian Bank as a Tunisian joint venture. He even persuaded the bey to sign a treaty on 21 March 1858 giving the proposed bank the right to issue money and the British consul the right to supervise the bank. But faced with strong opposition from the Quai d'Orsay, his superiors in London had him tone down the project, just as they also watered down the traditional British strategy of encouraging Tunisia to be more independent (from France) by strengthening relations with its nominal suzerain, the Ottoman Empire. British businessmen promptly backed out of the banking project, and their little project of a suburban railway to La Goulette was put on hold until Wood found another British contractor willing to take the concession in 1871. The three-mile line was not profitable, and the British were happy to sell out to the highest bidder—to Italy's short-lived triumph in 1880 (Ganiage 1959: 63–66, 422, 566, 580). Capitalism in Tunisia was very small scale, driven by diplomats. The country "was not worth a five-cent cigar," French President Jules Grévy exclaimed in 1881, on the eve of the colonial conquest that his brother Albert, governor general of Algeria, helped to organize (Guillen 1984: 135).

Tunisia's public debt was also manipulated to diplomatic ends. Once London had clipped Wood's wings in the late 1850s, the French consul consolidated an informal veto power over Tunisia's international finance. In 1862 Kheireddine Pasha, the Tunisian minister closest to the French, was persuaded to block an impending deal with London. Instead, the government of the day accepted a short-term loan at a higher rate of interest from an indigenous financier on the grounds that "Il vaut mieux payer cher l'argent que nous emprunterons dans notre pays, en conservant notre liberté d'action, que d'obtenir des avantages matériels au prix de notre indépendance" [It is better to pay dearly for money borrowed in our country, conserving our liberty of action, than to gain material advantages at the cost of independence] (Ganiage 1959: 202). When, within a year, Tunisia was obliged to get long-term financing, which was available only on international markets, the French consul made sure that Paris, not London, would get the business. It went to a "tenth-rate" (Ganiage 1959: 208, citing Auguste Chirac) Paris underwriter, "Baron" Emile Erlanger, a Prussian Jew newly immigrated from Frankfurt, where his family had served the Péreire brothers' Crédit Mobilier. Despite various offers promoted by Wood and others, the Tunisians floated the bond issue with Erlanger, assisted by the Oppenheims, who had just promoted a lucrative loan to Egypt with help from a Frankfurt syndicate including Raphael Erlanger (Landes 1958: 116–17). Tunisia gave Emile Erlanger his real start in lucrative international public bond dealings, much to the surprise of his Paris competitors. He made contact with agents of the infamous Mustapha Khaznadar, the Tunisian prime minister who by 1863 had shoved Kheireddine to the sidelines and consolidated power over Tunisia's public finances. Over the years their deals would illustrate "les moeurs diplomatiques de ces pays d'Orient où la corruption musulmane et la corruption européenne se combinent de façon à donner des résultats exceptionnels" [the diplomatic practices of these Oriental countries where Muslim and European corruption so combine as to give exceptional results] (*Le Figaro* 16 December 1881, cited by Ganiage 1959: 693).

Theoretically, the terms of the 1863 loan were little worse than those Egypt was getting at the time. Bonds to these countries sold at deep discounts, and the bankers and underwriters also took fat fees and commissions they then shared with various politicians. Erlanger's terms, bribes and all, were actually slightly better than those offered by another French group in 1860 or by Wood's people from London in 1862. Although the nominal 39,346,000-franc bond issue, discounted to 37,772,160, did not quite reach Tunisia's goal of 35 million, the final produce of 30 million did not compare too unfavorably, at an effective interest rate of 12.4 percent, with Egyptian loans of the period (see chapter 7), even after bribes to Khaznadar, to some of his agents, and to various local businessmen and administrators, including the complaisant husband of a beautiful and influential Italian courtesan. But the Tunisian government did not receive the full proceeds. Erlanger colluded with corrupt Tunisian officials, and the French consul may also have received some pecuniary as well as strategic satisfactions. Erlanger never really raised the funds he had promised; perhaps the bond issue had been slightly overpriced, given the market's perceptions of Tunisian risk. Instead, he secretly and illegally kept more than one-third of the issue and subsequently sold the paper back to the Tunisian government at an inflated price—splitting kickbacks with the Tunisian prime minister. In Tunis the remainder of the bond's proceeds, some 20 million, were squandered.

Up to one-quarter of it was embezzled, and the rest was used to buy off the short-term debt that was immediately rolled over, in effect doubling it (Ganiage 1959: 213). After inciting a national rebellion the following year by raising taxes to service the debt, the Tunisian Treasury was in quick need of another loan. Behind a veil of apparent neutrality, French Foreign Affairs Minister Drouyn de Lhuyz must have been pleased about his prey's growing vulnerability (Ganiage 1958: 329–33).

A second bond issue, floated in 1865 with a face value of about 37 million francs, produced 17 million after bribes and commissions, on which Tunisia was supposed to pay annuities at an effective rate of about 25 percent. This time Erlanger and Oppenheim contracted with a supposedly respectable French retail bank, the Comptoir d'Escompte et de Crédit, whose director, Alphonse Pinard, also worked with Erlanger on Mexican loans (Ganiage 1959: 290). The Tunisian bond issue was priced to be fully subscribed, enabling Khaznadar and Erlanger to split a further 750,000 francs on ostensible redemptions of the 1863 loan (293). Erlanger then promoted a few military sales to Tunisia with the remnants of the loan, pocketing more commissions. Finally, in 1867, he tried to float another loan for Khaznadar. This time he did not dare "buy" 95 percent of his bond issue; it would have saturated the secondary markets for Tunisian debt, which he and Pinard now controlled.

If these bankers had controlled the French government, Tunisia would have been annexed to Algeria in 1867. The bankers were buying up Tunisian 500-franc bonds at well under one-third their nominal value in the hope, obviously not shared by the public, that France would bring order to Tunisia and quickly redeem the bonds at par value. But the regime, to fall to the Prussians in 1870, was already distracted, and Khaznadar, too, had other designs. As cholera, typhus, and famine ravaged Tunisian populations in late 1867 and early 1868, the prime minister, holding on to power, had at least five rivals strangled, decapitated, or otherwise eliminated (Ganiage 1959: 310–11). He had the bey sign a desperate measure in 1868 to reconvert the debt and establish a National Bank of Tunisia with the help of a dubious new "établissement sans crédit," the Banque de Crédit International de Paris; but Pinard and Erlanger enlisted the Quai d'Orsay to block the deal (320–29). In 1869 Tunisia became the first Islamic Mediterranean country to be pushed into international receivership.

Virtually all of Tunisia's 26 sources of revenues were conceded to an International Financial Commission on which the three European powers most interested in the country were accorded equal representation. The huge majority of bondholders were French, but the British and Italian consuls dissuaded the bey from accepting the original French proposal for a Joint Franco-Tunisian Commission. Their clients had engaged in local reconversions of short-term debt that the original French scheme would have neglected in favor of the bondholders. It was finally agreed that a French inspector of finances would head the commission's executive council, on which he was joined by an Englishman, an Italian, a Tunisian, and an outside European (Sammut 1983: 46). The final arrangements worked out in early 1870 did not fully satisfy the exaggerated claims of either the bondholders or the local holders of the short-term debt, but the principal players, including Prime Minister Khaznadar, translated their inside information about the various negotiations into further profits on the debt. Pinard parlayed investments of 5 million francs in 1867 into paper worth about 13 million (Ganiage 1959: 391–93). Erlanger was less happy because the French inspector of finances had discovered some of his swindles. The Prussian still extracted a further 5 million out of the Tunisians with the support of the German consul (395–96). Tunisia remained nominally independent, however, until 1881.

Bondholders could not make their state act unilaterally, nor could an imperially minded state make its bankers a decisive weapon in rivalries with other states. Not until the Congress of Berlin in 1878 would France get the green light to take over Tunisia. To alleviate the bitterness of France's defeat by Germany in 1870, the loss of Alsace-Lorraine, and the payment of an enormous tribute to the victor, Bismarck considered Tunisia expendable if it gave French morale an imperial boost and helped to cement good relations with Germany. To Britain, with its eye on Cyprus, Tunisia was also expendable.

Apart from the state loans that enriched a few Parisian affairists, Tunisia was of as little economic interest to French as to British capitalists. The only industrialists of any note to seek concessions were the railroad magnates of the Compagnie Bône-Guelma who wanted to extend lines from Algeria. Although linked to French industrial capital, however, the railroad itself was utterly dependent on state subsidies. It was a tool of French foreign policy, not its dynamic determinant. Only after 1878 did the business rivalries really heat up in Tunisia. A casualty of the Berlin Conference, Sir Richard Wood finally retired at the age of seventy-three, leaving the field open to the French and the rising Italians. The French consul went ahead with plans to promote French investment, but the only takers were the Péreires and—by the spring of 1881—that old Tunis hand, Baron Emile Erlanger. He had acquired even more Tunisian debt at bargain prices, now that Berlin augured good profits (Ganiage 1959: 644–45). "Le banquier allemand n'apportait-il pas avec lui la fructueuse expérience de dix ans aux affaires tunisiennes, la connaissance des hommes et des choses, une solide pratique de la corruption orientale?" [Did not the German banker bring with him the fruitful experience of ten years in Tunisian business, knowledge of people and things, a solid working knowledge of Oriental corruption?] (654).

But the French Third Republic dithered over Tunisia instead of taking Bismarck's bait. Léon Gambetta, whose forces of the moderate Left were the backbone of France's problematic new Republic, was opposed to any military intervention in 1878. In April 1880, the French finally sent three gunboats to hasten the bey's approval of various concessions. Coincidentally, Kheireddine Pasha, who was retiring to Istanbul after serving as Tunisia's reforming prime minister between 1873 and 1877, signed over his vast Enfida estate to the Société Marseillaise de Crédit rather leave it to a pro-Italian Tunisian rival. This bank had opened a branch in Tunis the previous year to service the various railroad, steamship, and land speculation schemes hatched by the zealous French consul. It then officially merged with Eugène Péreire's Société Transatlantique.

The conservative French government still hesitated to move more decisively on the ground, much to the frustration and embarrassment of the French consul and the Quai d'Orsay's director of political affairs. The Italians, possibly with British help, waged their counteroffensive, not only purchasing the Goulette railroad but also sabotaging various French attempts to grab land concessions, including Enfida. After a change of government in Paris in September 1880, Gambetta's influence would be decisive. The Republican leader seems to have changed his mind about intervening in Tunisia after hearing from a French journalist of their ambassador's report from Berlin. Bismarck had expressed doubts about France's "will" and "determination" and was thinking of shifting Germany's support to "younger and more enterprising nations," that is, Italy. Historians now agree that Gambetta had already made up his mind to support a more energetic Tunisian policy some weeks before late March 1881, when a French foreign ministry official, sidestepping the formal government hierarchy, claimed to have converted him (Guillen 1984: 133–34). France manufactured an incident with border tribes in April, moved some forces from Algeria, and made the bey sign the Treaty of Bardo legalizing the French protectorate in less than a month.

The reasons for Gambetta's conversion, however, are still controversial. As early as June, France had to send a second expedition of 50,000 troops to put down rebellions. In late September London's *Pall Mall Gazette* published an article, "The real origin of the war in Tunis," which may have caught John Hobson's fancy. It accused Baron Erlanger of trying to "galvanize Tunisian Bonds" by enticing a number of French delegates to the Congress of Berlin to press for a free hand in Tunisia. The status of a French protectorate would mean that France would take charge of the Tunisian public debt and fully repay the bondholders. And indeed, Baron Erlanger and his friends made killings on the Paris Bourse when their bonds shot up to almost par value in May 1881 (Ganiage 1959: 642–46). Since the baron and others in his circle were on familiar terms with Gambetta, some critics hastily inferred that he had facilitated their "coup de bourse." Perhaps "there were too many contacts and the interests in play were too obvious for the speculators of the Tunisian 'group' who had so many friends in parliament not to have intervened at an opportune moment" (656). But financial interests in the French takeover represented pure opportunism, not finance capital. Imperialism in Tunisia was better explained by John Hobson than by Rudolph Hilferding. In Hobson's words, the stock speculator's "interest lies in the oscillations of paper values, which require fluctuation and insecurity of political conditions as their instrument" (1938 [1902]: 359).

The financial legacies of the speculators survive in the 1990s. The Banque Franco-Tunisienne is in government receivership, but a second Tunis branch, established in October 1880 and renamed the Banque de Tunisie, is Tunisia's most profitable bank. Both were owned by the same combine of French promoters and bankers that had sent the country to its ruin in the 1860s. They would proceed after the establishment of the French protectorate in 1881 to implant more banks and reorganize the country's finances, but they hardly represented more than a mix of money and land speculators. Bank capital never evolved into finance capital promoting industry (Mahjoub 1983: 108–15). Once the protectorate took hold, eliminating the International Finance Commission and other possible sources of competition among foreign capitalists, the local bankers developed a cartel, which indifferently served the country's European settlers (Sebag 1951: 49–52). The Bank of Algiers, founded in 1851, shunned Tunisia because it appeared too international, yet offshore capital also stayed away. The Tunisian banking system would be a backwater like Algeria's at independence.

Nationalizing the Colonial Banking Systems

The continuity between the former colonial system and independent Algeria's banking system was perhaps more formal than real, for virtually the entire cadre of colonial bankers were foreign settlers and assimilated indigenous Jews who departed for their summer holidays in 1962, never to return. Algerians inherited the colonial carcasses of banks and other institutions and then learned to operate them with French technical assistance. Various little banks were consolidated into three big state enterprises; in 1971 each was allocated a mutually exclusive portfolio of other state enterprises. The system of state monopolies was of course perfectly compatible with highly centralized military rule. Lending to a residual private sector virtually ceased, and half of its credits (which did not exceed 2 to 5 percent of the total in the 1980s) were earmarked for veterans of the war for national liberation.

In Tunisia the nationalization of the colonial banking system took more subtle forms than Algeria's. Unlike the Algerians, Tunisian nationalists had previously assimilated French financial practices. In 1906 Tunisians opened the Credit Foncier de Tunisie, but it was amalgamated with a French bank in 1908. Although three predominantly Tunisian banks founded in 1934 also failed after a few years (Bistolfi 1967: 65), the Coopérative Tunisienne de Crédit, founded in 1922, would subsidize Habib Bourguiba's breakway nationalist movement until 1936, when the Coopérative was restructured. Under Mohammed Chenik's leadership, it had given Bourguiba a financial base. The first congress of the Neo-Destour was held in Ksar Hellal in March 1934, in the home of one of Chenik's clients. The delegates overrepresented Tunis and the Sahel, the very regions in which the Coopérative was most heavily implanted. In its early years the Neo-Destour "was a party based on extensive patron-client networks. The wealthy, like Chenik, provided the party with funds for leaflets and automobiles, aid to the indigent, and support for the families of jailed militants" (Anderson 1986: 172–74). However big a moral and religious explosion the charismatic leader ignited, he needed selective incentives—patronage grounded in financial obligations—in order to build an enduring organization. Bourguiba understood financial power, and Hedi Nouira, his first governor of the Central Bank of Tunisia, would carefully oversee a "Tunisification" of the protectorate's banking system that preserved old forms while ensuring state control.

Bourguiba and Nouira were not able immediately after independence—with French soldiers still camped in Tunisian territory and waging war on its borders against Algerian guerrillas—to break financial ties with France. The Banque de l'Algérie et de la Tunisie not only continued to serve as Tunisia's central bank but also to facilitate the repatriation of settler capital to France until September 1958, when the Central Bank of Tunisia was finally founded to stem the hemorrhage. While avoiding a head-on collision with France, however, the Tunisian government as early as 1957 became the majority shareholder of a new, completely Tunisian bank, the Société Tunisienne de Banque (STB). This national enterprise was to be both a retail deposit bank and an industrial investment bank. Within a year it became the largest bank in the marketplace, with 17.5 percent of the country's deposits. On 1 June 1959, the fourth anniversary of Bourguiba's historic return from French prisons to Tunisia, the Banque Nationale Agricole was founded. This bank, too, was a predominantly state-owned enterprise. Despite its ostensibly agrarian vocation, it also became a "bazaar bank" like the STB (Bistolfi 1967: 201), engaged in all lines of activities at the expense of adequately servicing the farmers and peasants. By 1963 the two parastatals had replicated France's colonial system of oligopolistic control. They had accumulated 45 percent of the deposits and 68 percent of the loans (from Bistolfi 1967: 241). The STB also acquired a controlling interest in Tunisia's oldest bank, the Banque Franco-Tunisienne, in 1964 (235). A Tunisian inspector recalls that its European owner, Monsieur Daninos, was framed in a foreign exchange transaction and then permitted to leave the country in exchange for his shares in the bank. Indirectly the STB also acquired control of a new bank, the Union Internationale des Banques (UIB), formed in a merger of a French and a private settler bank. As Bistolfi concluded, "Tunisification occurred without the creation of a single properly Tunisian private bank. Alone, state intervention ended the monopoly exercised by French banks: Tunisification and parastatallism went hand in hand" (236). One private Tunisian bank, the Banque du Peuple, founded by the UGTT in 1964, was soon bought out by a fourth public sector bank, the Banque du Sud, because the government was determined to curtail trade union autonomy.

The STB was quickly overextended, accumulating a portfolio of participations in other enterprises amounting by 1961 to almost half its capital and financing long-term real estate loans and home mortgages with short-term deposits. By then, however, the Central Bank could cover any financing excesses—at the cost of any significant autonomy for the banks. When Ahmed Ben Salah (minister of planning and finances, 1962–69) began implementing grandiose designs for a command economy, Bourguiba was careful to keep Nouira at the Central Bank. The governor opposed Ben Salah's version of state socialism, monitored his economic policies, and limited the commercial banks' contributions to the government's deficit financing. In agreement with the International Monetary Fund, he introduced a stabilization plan in 1964 that devalued the dinar and imposed rigid controls on the banks. The Central Bank would limit its rediscounting of banks' loans and require its prior approval for any discountable loan exceeding 10,000 TD and for any loan exceeding 50,000 TD. Moreover the banks were required to place at least 30 percent of their deposits in treasury bills, 10 percent in development loans, and an additional 10 percent in reserves with the Central Bank. Thus all the banks, whether privately owned or parastatal, were so closely regulated that they effectively became state agencies. While favoring private enterprise, Nouira also shared Bourguiba's vision of the state as a monument without cracks.

Algeria's Public Sector Oligopoly

Algeria's bunker state seemed peculiarly immune to endogamous reform processes, whether toward a market-oriented economy and a significant degree of political pluralism or back to a purified command economy and one-party system. Military clan politics offers more immediate explanations of reform failures than any economic explanations, but a key obstacle to any coherent economic reform lay in the commercial banking system. Algeria's system could not offer reformers any political leverage. Finance capital's structural power was minimal.

Algerian domestic credit had mushroomed in the 1980s, as figure 2–1 indicates. It was distributed by five state banks, which each enjoyed sectoral monopolies. The banks, however, were mere cash registers, doling out the credit allocations determined by the Ministry of Planning. Algerian lending to the public sector enterprises was supplied principally in the form of overdrafts—open checkbooks on the banks, in other words. Despite declining oil and gas revenues, the checkbooks remained open in the late 1980s. Just as Algeria's five commercial banks were called upon to become responsible autonomous lenders, their balance sheets drifted further out of control. Collectively the banks were carrying a greater disproportion of loans relative to deposits on their balance sheets on 30 September 1991 than at any other time since 1981. Over two-thirds of them were nonperforming, and all of the deposits held by the entire commercial banking system covered only 56.2 percent of them.[1] Examination of the balance sheet of each bank reveals that most of the loans were in the form of overdrafts. Figure 6–1 charts their progress during the 1980s in current dinars and as a percentage of the respective loan portfolios. Figure 6–2 plots the total loans, in turn, as a percentage of each bank's sight and time deposits.

The Banque Nationale d'Algérie, which financed most of Algerian heavy

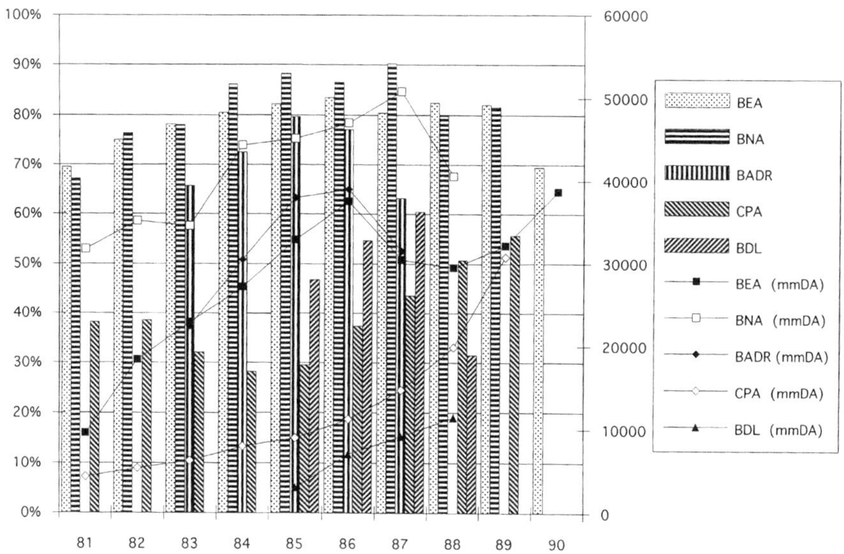

Fig. 6.1. Algerian overdrafts (mm DA and as percentage of bank loans), 1981–90. *Source:* author's database of commercial banks.

industry outside the petrochemical sector, carried the largest percentages of overdrafts. It reduced them by 20 percent in 1988 but they still amounted to 80 percent of the bank's outstanding loans at the end of the year—and to more than 120 percent of its deposits. Since the public sector enterprises accounted for about 40 percent of the deposits, they seemed on average to be leaving only one dinar in the bank for every three that they extracted. Of course the Bank of Algeria had to refinance the commercial banks so as to make their books balance. The one bank that was not being heavily refinanced as reform got underway in 1990 was the Banque Extérieure d'Algérie (BEA), which held the accounts of Sonatrach, the national petroleum company. Nevertheless, its outstanding loans exceeded its deposits by 30 percent at the end of 1990, and its overdrafts climbed to 70 percent of its loans and 90 percent of its total deposits. The only Algerian bank that had managed to keep its overdrafts under relative control (in the 30 to 40 percent range of overdrafts to total loans) was the Crédit Populaire Algérien. The secret of its success, as a former director general of the bank explained, was that it had been shortchanged in the allocations of banks to public sector enterprises in 1971. Even so, its overdrafts jumped by 50 percent in 1989, reflecting a sharp downturn in the construction industry. Its smaller public sector enterprises also had to be serviced, and by 1990 this relatively

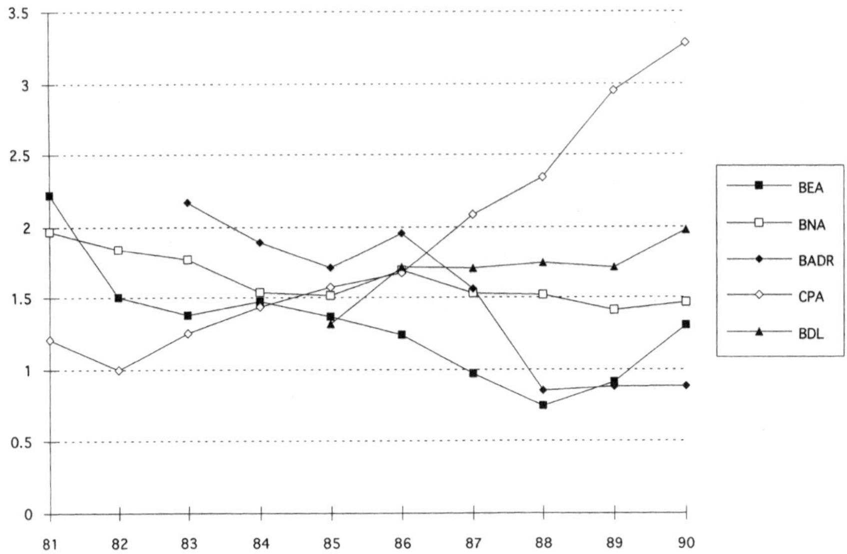

Fig. 6.2. Algerian bank ratios of loans to deposits, 1981–90. *Sources:* Bank of Algeria; author's database of commercial banks.

well-managed bank had a less favorable loan-to-deposit ratio than the other state banks.

Algeria's economic and financial reforms were already in serious trouble before President Benjedid was dismissed in 1992. The years 1990 and 1991 were to have been the crucial ones of transition to a market-oriented economy. Most public enterprises, including the banks, had officially become autonomous, that is, free to manage their own affairs like private enterprises responsible primarily to shareholders. But paper autonomy could not transform the public sector overnight into self-reliant, market-oriented enterprises. The new "participation funds," the state shareholder's fiduciaries, were too understaffed and poorly equipped to be of much help to management. After years of doling out credit on command, Algeria's five commercial banks could not suddenly become "responsible" lenders, carefully diversifying their loan portfolios and evaluating their credit risks. At the end of 1990 they still carried roughly 140 billion dinars (over $13 billion at the official rate of exchange) of nonperforming loans on their books. Almost one-fifth of the nonperforming loans were a dead loss because the enterprises had been dissolved. But an additional one-fifth concerned public enterprises that had "passed" to autonomy despite their weak financial condition. Worse, 80 enterprises, including 22 big ones, were in such bad financial shape that they did not "pass," yet still had to pay their employees. The commercial banks had to keep servicing these companies, even the 22 that had already accumulated half of the nonperforming loans (*Al Watan,* 11 January 1992: 4).

Instead of cleaning up their portfolios and becoming more market-oriented, the banks were sucked into a black hole. While they were permitted after some delay in 1991 to write off 30 billion dinars of bad debts to nonexisting enterprises, chancy new loans further disequilibrated their balance sheets. For all its vaunted autonomy, the Bank of Algeria in turn had to keep the banks alive by refinancing them. Its handouts doubled in less than a year, reaching 137.9 billion dinars on 21 November 1991 (*Al Watan,* 11 January 1992: 6). Credit ceilings worked out with the IMF were continually breached and revised, even as a new standby went into effect in July. By the end of the year inflation was running at 45 percent or more (an economist at the Bank of Algeria unofficially estimated it to be 60 percent), and it threatened to spiral out of control. The Bank of Algeria officially reproached the banks for ignoring its instructions, especially concerning the 22 nonautonomous enterprises, which had received 2.2 billion dinars above their planned quotas. The government had undermined its authority.

The central bank lost control of the reform process when the army pressured President Benjedid to change governments in July 1991. Although Governor Hadj Nasser successfully defended his reforms before parliament in late August, the new government criticized its predecessor for having centralized too much power in the Bank of Algeria. The Money and Credit Law had given it control not only over monetary policy but also over foreign investment. Economics Minister Hocine Benissad had criticized the law and attacked Algeria's "monetarist-type program without the Chicago boys" as a "false opening" in a book published shortly before Prime Minister Ghozali selected him to be minister (1991: 139–41, 145, 149). While urging further steps toward a market economy, the new minister argued that "those who were in charge of introducing the economic reforms were still governed by the reflexes and concepts of an administrated economy" (Carnevale 1991: 5). One consequence of the standoff between the Ministry of the Economy and the Bank of Algeria was that government allocations to the banking sector, promised in April, were held up until the end of 1991.

Prime Minister Ghozali assembled an impressive team of technocrats apparently determined to pursue the reform process—"a profound structural adjustment," in Benissad's words (Carnevale 1991: 6). The economics minister addressed a letter of intent to the IMF on 30 September 1991, which essentially reconfirmed the broad outlines of the standby negotiated by the previous government while admitting that delays in bank reforms were "creating difficulties in the conduct of monetary policy" (*Alger Républicain,* 31 October 1991). The letter requested revisions in "performance criteria" with respect to credit ceilings that could no longer be met (*Alger Républicain,* 2 November 1991). The government sweetened the pill by carrying out another small devaluation of the dinar and increasing prices on kerosene, wheat, propane, tomato paste, and sugar while deregulating prices of other commodities. Prime Minister Ghozali, who had taken over the Economics Ministry, succeeded in an informal rescheduling ("reprofiling") of Algeria's foreign debt with the help of a $1.5 billion loan managed by the Crédit Lyonnais. But political uncertainties paralyzed the reform process. Symptomatically, there were no further devaluations of the dinar, and the gap between the official and unofficial rates of exchange increased at the end of the year amid political uncertainties following the initial FIS victory in the December elections.

Algeria's attempt in 1992 to revert under the leadership of Belaid Abdesselam to a command economy was equally short-lived. Many Algerians looked back with nostalgia to the Boumédienne-Abdesselam era of "industrializing industry," and were perhaps convinced that it need not have ended. Abdesselam himself had vigorously argued in *Le gaz algérien: Stratégies et enjeux* that his successors had deprived Algeria during the 1980s of an annual $5.1 billion of oil and gas revenues (1990: 303). By insisting on inflated prices, they had lost natural gas sales to the United States (finally resumed in 1990) that would have earned Algeria annual revenues of $800 million (289).[2] While objecting to Abdesselam's version of the facts, Abdelhamid Brahimi, who served as planning minister during the "gas battle" and as prime minister from 1984 to 1988, tried in his book, *L'Economie algérienne: Défis et enjeux* (1991), to document the sensational claim he had made in 1990, widely reported in the press, that Algeria had wasted at least $26 billion in "wealth transferred to foreign companies without any real countervalue" except commissions and bribes to Algerian officials (155). On either Brahimi's or Abdesselam's interpretation, Algeria's command economy could have been viable had it been "correctly" administered.

Administration, however, remained the Achilles' heel of the planned economy. To be sure, it was within any government's capacity to lock up or even execute a few "criminals," as long as a sufficiently powerful coalition of janissaries was unwilling to protect them. But the issue of corruption ran far deeper. Algeria's command economy had unraveled even before Boumédienne's death in 1978. At the time there did not appear among high officials to be much criminal behavior of the sort that was standard practice in Nasser's Egypt or Hassan's Morocco. I recall as a participant in the U.S. State Department's Scholar-Diplomat Program reading a classified document on the airplane industry in 1975: Algeria was the only state in the Arab world that did not insist on "commissions." Official practices deteriorated under Benjedid's more easygoing rule, but much of the "corruption" lay deeper. The other face of the command economy was Algeria's informal economy. This sociological reality, "which escapes statist organicity" (Henni 1991: 155), made a mockery of official efforts to set quantities and prices and to erect financial barricades around the bunker state. Yet those who benefited the most from the command economy, namely those in command, were also the chief beneficiaries of the informal economy. They risked losing the most in any sort of reform designed to eradicate it, whether by purifying the command economy or by making the transition to a market economy.

As Ahmed Henni explained, there were really two kinds of dinars in circulation, those that bought goods and property at official prices and those that served unregulated markets. The official dinars were certified as a medium of exchange, not by the central bank, but by the authorities who controlled access to the officially priced goods. The greater the shortages, the greater their influence. Dinars denied access to officially priced goods flooded the informal economy. Making reasonable assumptions about the velocities of official and unofficial money, Henni estimated that the informal economy was generating revenues amounting to 60 percent or more of Algeria's official private household consumption by 1988. Originally, in 1973, agrarian reform had stimulated this economy by enabling some Algerians to gain control of land at ridiculously low, politically negotiated prices. The subsequent oil boom, by contrast, like Benjedid's consumer boom in 1981–82, reduced the relative importance of the parallel market. The collapse of oil prices then increased it (Henni 1991: 91). Henni argued that the "surplus" dinars financed workers' remittances—the savings of Algerian workers in France, which were in fact never remitted—and subsequently masked capital flight he estimated to total some 100 billion French francs by 1989, "the equivalent of Algeria's external debt" (125).

Henni admits that his estimates are only "order of magnitudes," as an informal economy by definition eludes state statistics. In 1990 Algeria's National Planning Council estimated that "nominal informal private consumption amounted to some 28 percent of official private consumption, and . . . of this 28 percent, only some 4 percent was due to resale of official goods at higher prices on the parallel market" (Khadr and Parks 1991: 14). Under

Henni's assumptions, by contrast, informal consumption amounted to 51 percent of official private consumption in 1989 (and 45 percent in 1990). Whatever its real size, however, the parallel economy fueled interests opposed to any reform, whether toward a sustainable command economy or a market-oriented one.

One very rough indicator of the parallel economy's size was the amount of currency in circulation relative to GDP. Algeria's circulation was much larger than those of the other crescent countries, as figure 2–6 depicted in chapter 2. Another indicator, presented in figure 6–3, is currency in circulation as a percentage of the broad money supply (M2), consisting of the currency and total deposits held in the banks other than those of the central government. Both data series show Algeria to have been largely in the lead by the late 1980s, but they also reveal interesting comparisons with Egypt. Both command economies—Egypt in the 1960s and early 1970s and Algeria starting in 1970—displayed inordinately large amounts of currency in circulation. Not until the mid-1980s did this indicator of the informal economy significantly diminish in Egypt, even as it moved to new heights in Algeria. In Egypt, however, the explosion of the banking system associated with infitah significantly diminished the amount of currency in circulation as a proportion of the broad money supply between 1977 and 1979. In the early 1980s, Egypt's informal economy expanded with black market money-changers, fueled by remittances from workers in the Gulf states, but the deposits in the official banking system more than kept pace. Banking scandals involving collusion between the money-changers and some of the infitah banks foiled government efforts to control foreign exchange markets, but the web of interests tied the informal economy to the official banking sector. By recognizing private sector banks, the authorities acquired a handle on the informal economy. The official system then gradually absorbed the floating currency associated with it.

In Algeria, by contrast, the banking system could not mediate between the administered and the parallel economy. In 1982 and again in 1990 the authorities took heavy-handed measures to suppress black markets. In 1982, the year Egyptian black market activities peaked, the Algerians suddenly called in all 500-dinar notes in a vain effort to halt smuggling. The move shows up as a small blip in figures 2–6 and 6–3. In 1990 the authorities launched a massive campaign against trabendo (contraband) merchants by searching meticulously through every single suitcase entering ports and airports. The growth of Algeria's currency supply after 1982 suggests the futility of such measures. In the 1960s the Tunisians had launched a similar operation against 5-dinar notes (the equivalent of only 50 Algerian dinars),

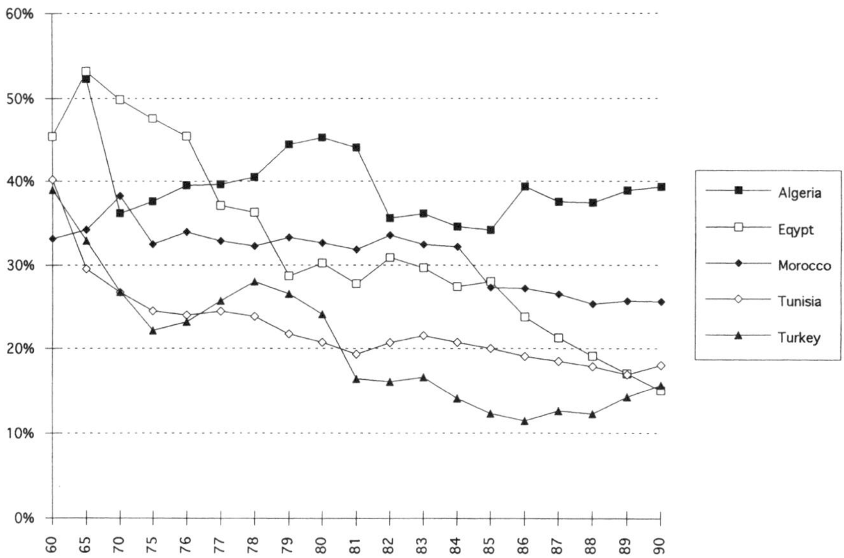

Fig. 6.3. Currency as percentage of broad money supply (M2). *Source:* IMF, international financial statistics.

but their command economy never gave rise to an antithetical informal economy of Algerian or Egyptian dimensions.

Tunisia's Public Sector Oligopoly

Tunisia appeared to be a much more promising candidate for financial liberalization than Algeria. On the surface, its commercial bank structure resembled Turkey's far more than Algeria's and suggested that finance capital already had latent structural power that could serve the reformers. At their peak in the early 1970s, the four public sector banks commanded 70 percent of the deposits of commercial banks and allocated up to 85 percent of the loans. At the end of 1986, as Tunisia's adjustment program took effect, these four public sector banks still held 63 percent of the deposits and 78 percent of the commercial bank loans. The STB and the BNA dominated the market, much like Türkiye İş Bankası and T.C. Ziraat Bankası in Turkey. Figure 6–4 gives a summary picture of the distribution of deposits among Tunisian banks from 1972 to 1990.

Despite its substantial presence, however, the Tunisian public sector was hardly monolithic. The state did not own any bank outright but preferred patterns of mixed ownership associating parastatals with private investors,

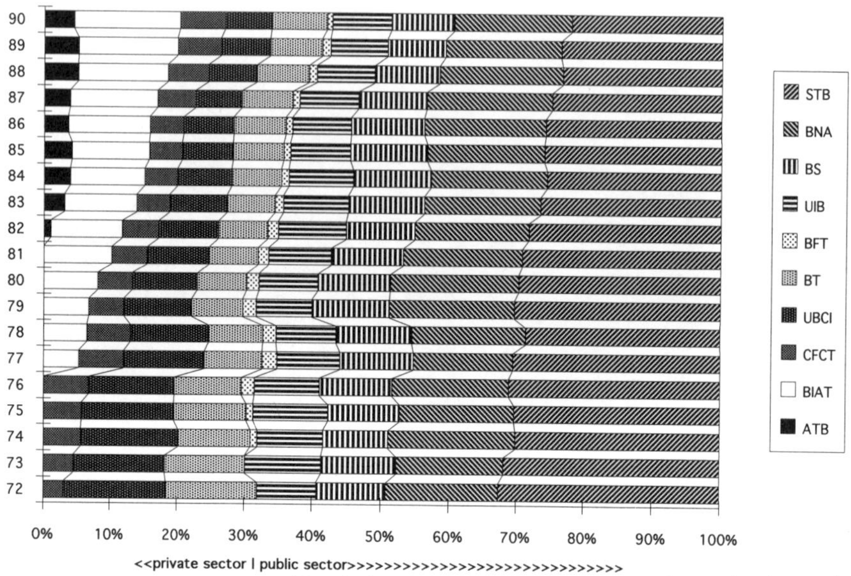

Fig. 6.4. Tunisian commercial bank deposits, 1972–90. *Source:* author's database of commercial banks.

Tunisian and foreign. Table 6–1, which presents the ownership structure of the Tunisian commercial banking system in 1987, shows that public capital, had it been distributed evenly throughout the banking system, would have controlled barely more than one-third of its total assets. In 1988 the dynamic new chief executive officer of the Banque du Sud was calling for the "privatization" of his bank, barely half the capital of which was public money.

Just as private Tunisian and foreign investors participated in public sector banks, the public sector also invested in the private sector. The STB held a minority ownership of the venerable Banque Franco-Tunisienne (BFT) but managed it like a public sector bank, except for a brief period from 1987 to 1989 that will be discussed later. In figure 6–4 the BFT is placed on the border between the public sector and private sector banks. The Banque Internationale Arabe de Tunisie (BIAT) had also attracted public capital, but was business oriented and had pursued its interests with a significant degree of autonomy, becoming Tunisia's leading private sector bank. It is situated in the private sector.

Within the private sector relics of the old French colonial system endured, in Tunisian hands. The Banque de Tunisie (BT) survived the transition to independence intact, its ownership being gradually altered with increases in

Table 6-1 Ownership of Tunisian commercial banks, 1987

Bank	Assets (1987) (mm T dinars)	Percent shares held by		
		Public sector	Private sector	Foreign sector
BNT (BNA)	1184	58.2	41.8	
STB	1173	56.7	43.3	
BIAT	545	8.5	56.1	35.4
UIB	433	57.7	25.6	16.7
BS	430	51.5	33.9	14.7
BT	379		61.2	38.8
UBCI	299		48.6	51.4
CFCT	262		100.0	
ATB	147		36.6	63.4
BFT	60	27.7	20.3	50.0
All banks	4912	38.4	46.2	15.3

capital to reflect a Tunisian majority. The Union Bancaire pour le Commerce et l'Industrie (UBCI), which had resulted in 1961 from a fusion of French banks, became a joint venture in 1979, half-owned by a leading French bank, half by private Tunisians headed by a businessman from Sfax. Coexisting with these relatively conservative banks was a newer Tunisian private sector, consisting, along with BIAT, of the Crédit Foncier et Commercial de Tunisie (CFCT) and the Arab-Tunisian Bank (ATB). The CFCT, created in 1967 from remnants of the colonial private sector, was acquired by the Ben Yedder family, a Jerban business group. BIAT was established in 1976 by a former Tunisian minister who could attract Arab capital and Tunisian public sector funds as well as private Tunisian capital. With some Arab Gulf backing, BIAT acquired the local branches of the British Bank of the Middle East and the Société Marseillaise de Crédit (Signoles 1985: 497–98). ATB was a Tunisian joint venture with the Arab Bank, headquartered in Amman, Jordan.

Most of the private sector banks were content to follow the public sector's lead. Like that of Turkish banks in 1981, the first collective Tunisian response to reform was to collude on interest rates to be offered depositors. When the rates were deregulated, as of 5 January 1987, the competition lasted only a couple of weeks before an agreement was reached by the Association Professionnelle des Banques de Tunisie (APBT) to put a halt to competitive bidding. According to some bankers, the Société Tunisienne de Banque used its market power to impose fixed rates. Deposits actually changed hands less between banks in 1987 than in many years prior to deregulation. By agreement, too, all banks stopped paying any interest on sight deposits, so that average rates most banks paid for deposits actually diminished slightly in 1987. Ironically, the STB ended up paying slightly more than BIAT, although BIAT gained almost a percentage point of market share at the expense of the STB. The BNA and CFCT also registered slight gains, suggesting some slippage in the monitoring of the cartel's decision, but there were no overt price wars. No Tunisian bank broke ranks as Ziraat did briefly in Turkey in 1988.

The Tunisian cartel, however, did not have strong price-setters like Turkey's Akbank to give it backbone. Years of indifferent management had made the public sector banks as unwieldy and unprofitable as their Turkish counterparts. In 1992 outside consultants were called upon to help the overstaffed STB organize its daily ledgers so as to make the information available on a timely (overnight) basis like most other banks. The STB was experiencing delays of up to a month in getting the information to internal management and to the Central Bank. The only large aggressive Tunisian bank was BIAT, but it did not have Akbank's strong capital base or high profitability. In Tunisia the cartel depended upon its members' financial vulnerability, not on their strength. During the early years of the reform, the banking system as a whole remained seriously undercapitalized, and fixed assets and shareholdings in other companies immobilized much of the capital.

Figure 6–5 shows that the commercial banks' capital as a percentage of total assets was decreasing, and their fixed assets and shareholdings as a percentage of capital increasing until 1989, contrary to the international standards that banks were expected to reach by 1992. The Cooke Committee recommended that banks reach an overall capital to total risk asset ratio of 8 percent, only half of which could be tied up in illiquid assets (Kapstein 1989: 344), but their equity amounted to only 4.1 percent of total assets at the end of 1990 and all of it was tied up in investments (fig. 6–5). Roughly half of the banks' equity was invested in business properties, the rest in shareholdings in other companies. By this time nonperforming loans amounted to some 15 percent of their collective portfolio, and less than one-third of them were provisioned by reserves. Total deposits of TD 3,954 million barely covered their loans (TD 3,824 million, excluding special state-funded credits), so that some banks obviously faced liquidity as well as solvency problems.

Examination of the Tunisian banks' individual balance sheets revealed significant variations with respect to the banks' capital adequacy, the extent to which it was tied up in fixed assets and shareholdings, and the quality of

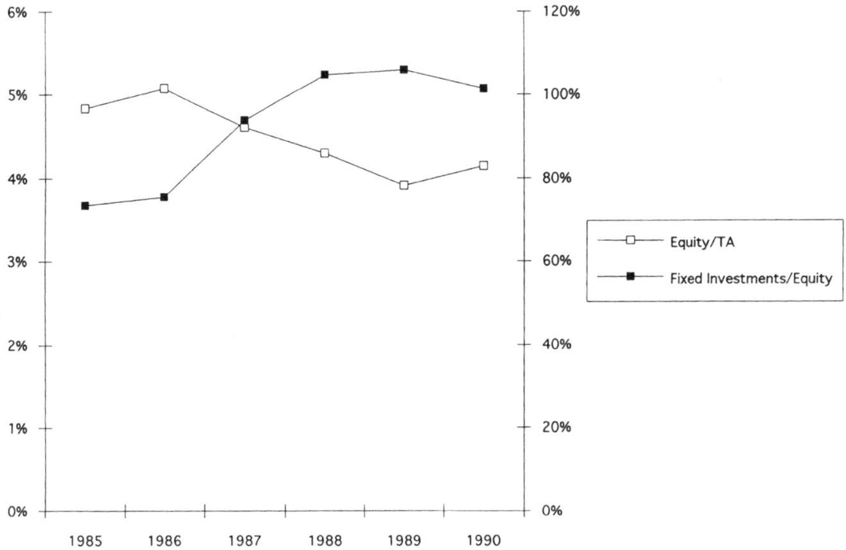

Fig. 6.5. Capitalization of the Tunisian commercial banks, 1986–90. *Sources:* Banque Centrale de Tunisie, Statistiques Financieres, March 1990: 5–6, September 1991: 6–7.

their respective loan portfolios. All four public sector banks were seriously undercapitalized. The UIB was particularly poor, its capital covering barely 2 percent of total assets. Most of the private sector banks were also in need of more capital; only the smallest ones, ATB and BFT, seemed at the end of 1989 to be within reach of the international norm of 8 percent. The Central Bank obliged each bank to publish data about its loan portfolios by 1989 (STB, *Annual Report* 1987: 9); table 6–2 offers a detailed analysis of the capital, reserves, and troubled loans for each bank at the end of the year.[3] UIB's capital did not cover its investments, much less the gap between its nonperforming loans and the provisions that were supposed to cover them. Fixed assets (buildings and equipment) and shareholdings in other companies had immobilized all of the bank's capital and some of its deposits as well.

Renowned in the early 1980s for its advanced international department, the UIB had fallen on hard times as a result of too many soft loans handed out to various friends and family members of Ouassila Bourguiba. When President Bourguiba turned against his wife, the UIB's chairman was jailed and Habib Bourguiba Jr., chairman of the APBT, was dismissed from the palace as well for defending the poor banker. In 1987 problem loans

Table 6-2. Capital, reserves, and troubled loans, 1989 (in millions of Tunisian dinars)

Bank	Problem loans[a]	Problem loans (%)	Equity[b]	Provisions[c]	P Loans/(E+P)	Immobilized/equity[d]	Capital shortfall
STB	244	25.9	68	42	2.2	84.2%	190.8
BNA	135	11.9	83	50	1.0	49.8%	43.8
UIB	92	23.3	14	14	3.3	113.2%	79.7
BS	71	20.3	23	27	1.4	57.1%	34.0
BFT	21	32.8	6	4	2.2	30.2%	13.0
BT (1990)	54	16.5	30	26	1.0	72.4%	19.7
CFCT	23	8.8	19	4	1.0	77.4%	14.2
BIAT	37	8.8	32	17	0.7	87.7%	15.7
UBCI	23	9.1	22	20	0.5	74.1	−2.5
ATB	13	11.0	18	0	0.7	74.2	8.7
Totals	712	15.8	316	204	1.4	71.3%	418.1

a. "Autres credits" from Reports of APBT, reduced by weightings to total of Statistiques Financières.
b. Includes net income for 1989.
c. Projected from APBT data and verified by Statistiques Financières.
d. Capital funds tied up in fixed assets on 31 December 1989 and in shares in other companies. Since some of the shareholdings data were unavailable, the capital shortfall was actually higher.

constituted 22.1 percent of the bank's portfolio; in 1985, the last year when the bank's provisions for credit risk were published, reserves covered only 12.7 percent of the problem loans.

Problem loans seemed very unevenly distributed. They were held for the most part by the public sector banks, suggesting greater pressure on them than on the private sector banks to book credits to poorly managed state enterprises or well connected individuals. The private sector, however, was not immune, for its managers enjoyed close ties with the political elite. The banks were often involved in consortium lending with the public sector. The conservative Banque de Tunisie, for instance, had been tricked into lending a Tunisian contractor, Moncef Bouzguenda, funds for a fictitious public project. The Banque de Tunisie's large exposure to problem loans was revealed only in 1990. While it claimed in its *Annual Report* of 1987 (p. 11) to have fully provisioned the exposure to Bouzguenda, it evidently accumulated other nonperforming loans.

Though the UIB was known to be saddled with many nonperforming assets, it had not been suspected that the STB or its little subsidiary, the BFT, was in serious trouble. The Banque du Sud also had a checkered portfolio. Each of these banks was carrying a portfolio of troubled loans far greater than its capital and reserves, including the woefully inadequate provisions that had been made to cover such loans. Table 6–2 presents the ratio of problem loans to capital and reserves in 1989. On the optimistic assumption that half of the troubled loans could be recovered (i.e., dividing by two the ratio of problem loans to capital and reserves), the STB, the UIB, and the BFT still appeared to be insolvent. As the BFT will illustrate later in this chapter, many of the problem loans had been on the books for years, and only very persistent internal auditors could define the magnitude of the problem. Much of the public sector banks' capital, moreover, was already tied up in fixed assets and investments in other companies. In the final column of table 6–2 the banks' capital shortfall is estimated by subtracting their "free" capital and provisions from the bad loans.

If this picture of Tunisia's public sector banks is even half correct, it heavily constrained any financial liberalization. Large banks could not be permitted to go out of business, especially not the flagship STB. By rigging the rates on deposits, the Association Professionnelle des Banques de Tunisie reassured these banks that they could preserve their market shares with a minimum of effort. The banks most hungry for deposits normally paid slightly higher rates for their savings and time deposits, but differences were actually less in 1987 than in 1986. The UIB's rates on savings accounts actually dropped from 9.8 percent (two full percentage points above the average) in

1986 to 7.7 percent (just over half a percentage point above the norm) in 1987—as if it were being specially protected. Public enterprises helped to sustain these banks with their deposits, even though they were under no legal obligation to do so. The relatively wealthy Banque de Tunisie, on the other hand, lamented in its annual reports that it was unable to attract more deposits from the state enterprises. They had constituted only 8.3 percent of the bank's sight deposits in 1985 and had decreased from 12.2 million to 11 million dinars by 1988 (*Annual Report* 1985: 7; 1988: 7).

Under the new Ben Ali regime there were strong political pressures to lower interest rates. Coordinated through the APBT, the banks "volunteered" to charge no more than 2.5 percent over the variable borrowing rate on the money market in 1988. The Central Bank obliged, too, by lowering the money market rate from some 10 to 8.5 percent (while also, to the benefit of some banks, turning a blind eye to the requirement that 25 percent of a bank's deposits be placed in poorly paying government bonds). One banker took great delight in showing how the Central Bank reformers were manipulating the market. He also poked fun at amateur bank dealers who changed their minds about telephone operations concluded "more than half an hour earlier." He observed that some banks had simply quit the market, resorting instead to "other much simpler mechanisms giving the same results"—presumably, direct bilateral relationships between banks (Saidane 1988: 58, 57). Most bankers remained skeptical about the Central Bank's partially deregulated markets. As for efforts to expand the stock market or in other ways to securitize debt, one leading banker commented that newfangled commissions could never make up for standard spreads.

Financial deregulation did, however, squeeze the banks' margins, or "spreads" between the interest they earned on loans and paid on deposits. By 1989 the Banque de Tunisie, which had always enjoyed high margins, was paying slightly higher rates for its deposits but receiving lower revenues. One secret of its profitability had been to encourage a high proportion of overdrafts among reliable clients, then charge up to 15 percent interest. In 1988, revenues were not keeping pace with its burgeoning loan portfolio (*Annual Report* 1988: 9), and again in 1989 it greatly increased its loan portfolio, so as to sustain relatively healthy spreads. At that time, some of the other banks were hurting much more, after having experienced relatively bountiful spreads in 1987, the first year of the reforms. Most of the big public sector banks seemed particularly hard hit. Their spreads all fell from 3 or 4 percent of total assets in 1986 to less than 2 percent in 1989. While interest rates for certain categories of loans remained regulated, the bank's cost of funds rose under the pressure of the partially deregulated money market.

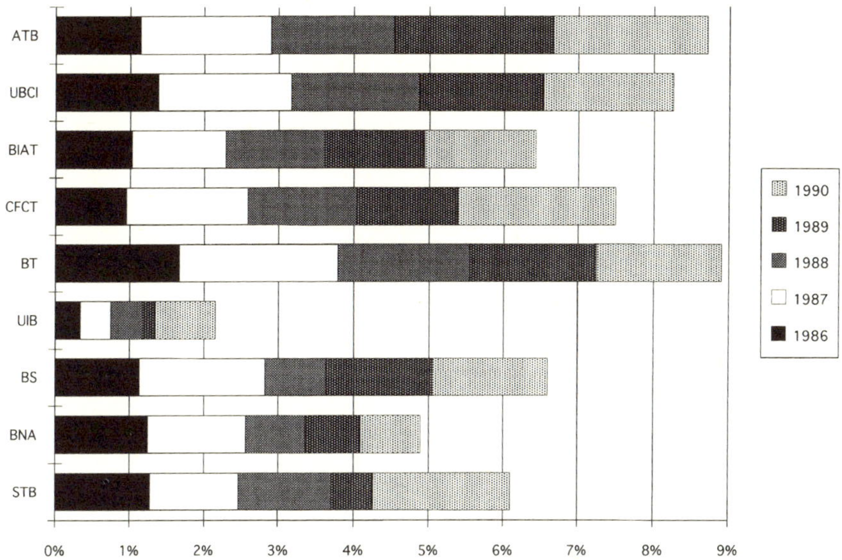

Fig. 6.6. Cash flow of commercial banks as a percentage of total assets, 1986–90. *Source:* author's database of commercial banks.

Cash flow, the sum of net income and allocations to provisions and the depreciation of fixed assets, sheds further light on the banks' profitability.[4] Figure 6–6 measures the cash flow of each bank as a proportion of total assets at the end of each year after 1986. Leading the pack, in cash flow as well as in spreads, the Banque de Tunisie consistently generated close to 2 percent of its total assets every year during the 1986–90 period.[5] In fact this bank, unlike the others, preferred to squirrel away as many provisions and reserves as possible to escape taxes, rather than maximizing net income. To encourage more provisions, the Central Bank prevailed upon Tunisia's tax administration in 1988 to exempt up to 20 percent of a bank's revenues from corporate tax if they were saved as provisions.

It is readily seen from figure 6–6 that the UIB's cash flow remained just barely positive, but it did not offset the annual growth in problematic assets, much less increase coverage of them. Neither the STB nor the BNA was enjoying the comfortable cash flows of the mid-1980s; they were particularly hard hit in 1989. The Banque du Sud (BS) apparently adapted more readily to the financial reforms. Evidently the Central Bank relaxed its pressure on the banks in 1990 and let their spreads and cash flows improve slightly. But their financial performance suggested that Tunisia's public sector, left to the free play of financial markets, would take years to recover. The STB, BS, and UIB were carrying many more nonperforming loans than their provisions and capital could cover (table 6–2). At the rate they were generating cash flow in 1989 and 1990, the STB and the BS would have each required four or five years to balance their books, and the UIB many more, assuming that half of the loans were recoverable and that all of the new funds went toward covering the loans rather than for new equipment, upkeep on buildings, and the like. Among the private sector banks, the Banque de Tunisie and CFCT carried the biggest proportions of nonperforming loans, but their hypothetical "workout times" were twelve and ten months, respectively, a shorter time than for the troubled public sector banks. Obviously the latter needed not only more cash flow generated by higher spreads, but also an infusion of capital.

The UIB, in the greatest need of additional capital, unsuccessfully tried to enlist Crédit Lyonnais, its principal foreign bank shareholder, to participate in a major restructuring. Although the French bank was expanding its operations in North Africa, it refused to sink more capital into the UIB. Nor could the STB, the principal Tunisian shareholder, afford more capital. Finally the Tunisian authorities prevailed upon Tunis Air and the Tunisian Social Security Fund to acquire a 50 percent interest in the bank by covering much of a 250 percent capital increase (*MEED,* 6 December 1991: 36). The chief executive officer of the UIB was transferred to another bank when it was discovered that the bank had been buying its own stock on the Tunis Bourse to inflate its apparent value—a tactic reminiscent of the financial chicanery depicted in Émile Zola's *L'Argent.*

If the public sector banks were so troubled, the others could be fairly confident that their margins would be protected. Enmired in financial difficulties, the major public sector banks could not be price-setters, for all their theoretical autonomy, without help from the Central Bank. They needed the protection of supposedly deregulated markets. Financial reform therefore opened up interesting prospects for the private sector, since all the banks could depend upon government protection. An aggressive mover like BIAT could pursue a risky strategy of growth. The success of financial reform at instilling real competition would ultimately depend on the strategies of the relatively healthy players, whether to compete head-on with their sicker sisters or to live comfortably and dependently off the rents reserved for keeping them in business.

Capital barriers to entry meanwhile helped to keep out newcomers, while capital requirements rose flexibly so as not to disturb existing members of the club.

Barriers to Entry

The government in theory welcomed foreign investment in banking, as in other sectors of the economy, as part of the official effort to encourage healthy competition. Even in the early 1980s the governments of Kuwait, Saudi Arabia, Qatar, and the United Arab Emirates had been successfully encouraged to set up development banks under reliable Tunisian management. They were too small to disturb the official oligopoly and, despite efforts to integrate the development banks into Tunisia's financial markets (the second pillar of reform), did not seem actively to compete for deposits. The Tunisian chief executive officer of the Banque Tuniso-Qatari d'Investissement was fired in 1991, together with a senior Central Bank regulator, for permitting losses of over $30 million in offshore foreign exchange transactions (*MEED,* 20 September 1991: 22). Tunisia had also accepted a number of offshore banks, but it rejected the BCCI's application for an offshore license despite the latter's alleged efforts, in Tunisia as in a number of other countries, to bribe Central Bank officials (*New York Times,* Texas edition, 30 July 1992: C5).

Entry into the commercial core of the Tunisian banking system was more problematic. Influential bankers opposed the granting of an onshore license to Citibank, but the Central Bank, supported by Prime Minister Baccouche, overrode their objections in 1989 because Citibank might invigorate the money market by developing secondary markets for government securities and commercial paper. A private Saudi financier, however, was less welcome to the Tunisian club: Sheikh Salah Kamel, the self-made Saudi businessman, who had launched the Al-Baraka Group of Islamic banks in the early 1980s. Outside his Saudi base, where his Al-Baraka Investment and Development Company was not recognized as a commercial bank, it held controlling shares of banks in Bahrain, Sudan, Tunisia, Turkey, and the United Kingdom by 1984. The Bank of England licensed the British subsidiary to take deposits like any other commercial bank until 1993, when the license was withdrawn, ostensibly for technical reasons (*MEED,* 16 April 1993: 4). The group expanded in the mid-1980s to create banks as far afield as Thailand, Mauritania, and Bangladesh, and it enjoyed special relationships with "sister institutions" in Jordan, Denmark, and Luxembourg. It acquired control of Al-Ahram Bank in Cairo and established a new Islamic bank in Lagos.

Entry into Bourguiba's Tunisia, however, was fraught with difficulties. His son, who chaired the Association Professionnelle des Banques Tunisiennes, initially objected to Sheikh Saleh's request for a license even as an offshore bank. Any bank labeling itself as distinctly "Islamic" raised political objections. Finance Minister Mansour Moallah, who had tapped Gulf funds to finance his rapidly growing private sector bank, also initially opposed the Islamic initiative, though Prime Minister Mohammed Mzali was in favor. The decisive support finally came from President Bourguiba himself. Public Works Minister Mohammed Sayah had interested Sheikh Salah in one of the president's favorite projects, drying up part of Lake Tunis for real estate development, and had persuaded the Saudi that the Tunisian state should keep title to the land around the lake. In return for investing in the project, the Al-Baraka Group received an offshore bank license, pending legislation passed in the fall of 1985, that was tailored specifically for the new bank: it allowed offshore banks to raise deposits onshore, denominated in Tunisian dinars, up to an official limit of 1.5 percent of Tunisia's total dinar deposits (Moore 1990: 243, 246).

Officially named Bayt Al-Tamwīl Al-Tūnsi Al-Sa'ūdi ("Beit Ettamwil Saoudi Tounsi" in the French transliteration), BEST Bank quietly promoted "participatory" financing but downplayed its Islamic character and any association with Tunisia's political Islamists. During the bank's first four years of operation, from 1984 through 1987, BEST had a hard time fending off requests from Bourguiba's palace for loans if it was not to be associated with the regime's victims. Once the bank was raided, in vain, by security police in search of evidence linking it with the Islamists, but Ben Ali, then serving as Bourguiba's minister of the interior, denied the existence of any official investigation and protected the bank from further raids. The bank had to be loyal to a regime that outlawed Islamists. Though he was not a member of the governing party, the bank's general manager was one of two Tunisians on the board who together represented the 20 percent of the shares belonging to Tunisia's Central Bank. He also served, until 1990, as deputy mayor of Carthage, the seat of the presidential palace, and, with academic degrees from the United States as well as France, was active in business circles that advocated greater competition and deregulation of the economy. The new "participatory" banking techniques were promoted in conjunction with the bank's expertise in project finance, which was equally unfamiliar to most of Tunisia's traditional French-trained bankers. Further efforts to seek out local deposits and lending opportunities would probably have associated the bank with Islamist sympathizers, whom the government indiscriminately viewed in the early 1990s as a threat to national security.

The bank opened new branches in Sfax and the Tunis medina in 1988, while Tunisia was still enjoying Ben Ali's political opening. But when official relations with the Islamists deteriorated, the bank's plans to open branches in Kairouan and Sousse were indefinitely postponed. A confidential marketing study had concluded that Islamic banking might attract an additional 100 million dinars, equal to about 2.5 percent of total bank deposits, from pious savers who rejected the existing commercial system (Barbulesco 1989: 11). By 1990, however, BEST's dinar deposits failed to exceed 17 million—barely one-half of 1 percent of the deposits of the commercial banking system and well short of its legal limit. Yet its paid-in capital of $25 million rivaled that of the Banque du Sud and the Banque de Tunisie, and an additional $25 million could be called upon. While the new player did not face formal barriers to entering the competition for onshore loans and deposits, the political climate encouraged discretion in the early 1990s. The contrast between Tunisia and "secular" Turkey was striking. By the end of 1990 the Islamic banks' share of Turkish commercial banking deposits was more than triple BEST's share in Tunisia, although BEST had opened for business a year earlier than Turkey's special finance houses. Al-Baraka's international network benefited from trade relations and other offshore activities, and BEST Bank showed consistent profitability and steady increases in the returns on equity. In 1990 the return on equity reached 11 percent, and dividends distributed to the shareholders amounted to a healthy 9.5 percent return on investment. But expansion inside Tunisia would require a more receptive political climate.

Though BEST Bank retained a marginal presence onshore, the Tunisian government and the Central Bank drew the line against banking acquisitions by private Tunisian investors who were not members of the club. Struggles over the ownership and management of the Banque Franco-Tunisienne (BFT) exposed the limits of Tunisian liberalization. This bank is by far the smallest, as well as the oldest, of Tunisia's commercial banks, but its story, suppressed by the authorities after 1988,[6] illustrates the determination of the Central Bank and the STB to defend the regime's black box from intruders.

The Banque Franco-Tunisienne

In 1981 the Central Bank called upon all commercial banks to increase their capital to at least 5 million dinars each, thus dashing any hope that the STB might sell off the BFT to members of Tunisia's banking establishment. In early 1982 the STB agreed to sell 50 percent of BCT's shares for 2.5 million dinars to Arab Business Consortium International Finance and Investment Company (ABCI), a firm registered in the Cayman Islands and apparently owned by Prince Bandar Bin Khalid, a son of the Saudi king. The sale, supported by the Mzali government, was in keeping with Tunisia's policy of attracting Arab capital. Commercial as well as development banks had been beneficiaries; in fact the incumbent minister of finance had earlier founded BIAT with the help of Arab capital. Much to the consternation of the Tunisian authorities, however, the ABCI official who arrived to take his bank shares was not a Saudi dignitary but a brash young Tunisian lawyer from Kairouan who claimed to be the prince's equal partner. Abdelmajid Bouden was not connected to the Tunisian banking or political establishment; a distant relative would run for parliament as an Independent (Islamist) in 1989. Bouden's career and his money were a mystery to the Tunisian authorities, for he had spent thirteen years abroad after graduating from a French university. The Saudi contracting company that he represented lived off princely connections. The ABCI had gained the contract for the construction of the causeway to Bahrain, for instance, before King Khalid's death in 1982. Bouden purported to be in partnership with the prince and to represent the ABCI. He clearly intended to take an active role in management of the bank rather than serve as the STB's sleeping partner.

The authorities quickly acted to annul the sale, although by most legal interpretations it had been completed on 27 July 1982, when the BFT received a telex for $4,139,072.85 (2.5 million TD at the prevailing exchange rate) from the ABCI's Swiss bank. Mohammed al-Riahi, who was the BFT's general manager at the time, claims he was instructed over the telephone by a Central Bank official to stall the sale but to cover the foreign exchange by reconverting the dinars to dollars. Apparently under instructions, Riahi then telexed ABCI on 29 July that one further formality was required to complete the transaction for purchase of the shares. In November the same Central Bank official instructed Riahi to keep ABCI's funds in a non-interest-bearing account pending resolution of the problem. At an extraordinary general assembly held on 30 December 1982, the BFT's shareholders, consisting primarily of the STB and some of its subsidiaries, voted to annul the capital subscription, thereby in their view undercutting any legal basis for a transfer of shares to ABCI. To ensure that ABCI could not get a hand in management, they also revised categories of shares for voting purposes at general assemblies (which elect boards of directors).

Bouden, however, was determined to wrest control of the bank from the STB. He litigated some sixty cases before Tunisian courts in the following six years. On 27 July 1984, two years after the original dollar transfer, he was permitted as ABCI's agent to buy half of the shares on the Tunis

Bourse for 2,125,000 TD. The STB's rearguard action after losing legal battles was essentially to offer Bouden's company, in addition to the shares, an interest payment of 375,000 TD (7.2 percent compounded annually, about the going rate for Tunisian savings deposits) on the 2.5 million TD that had been frozen two years earlier. Bouden was given only one seat on the BFT's board of directors in 1985, and he contested both aspects of the compromise.

Objecting that he was receiving inadequate information about the bank, Bouden resigned from the board in December 1986 and called for an emergency meeting of the BFT general assembly. He and his brother had meanwhile bought extra shares on the Tunis stock exchange, at inflated prices, and had made alliances with other dissatisfied small investors by promising them to build a much bigger and more dynamic bank, with branches throughout the country. Controlling 53.6 percent of the seats at the BFT general assembly, Bouden appointed a new board of directors and took charge of the bank. General Manager Riahi, 63, retired. On the recommendation of Tunisia's ruling Destour Socialist party, which vetted all important personnel decisions, Tahar Bourkhis was named to replace him. Not only was Bourkhis an experienced public sector banker, having arrived at the BFT from the Banque du Sud, but he also came from the hometown of the party's director and was a trusted element of the "nomenklatura," as Bouden put it. As a nonresident, Bouden was himself disqualified from signing on the bank's behalf.

Now president of the BFT and in control of its policies, however, Bouden quickly moved to regain ABCI's frozen funds and also to delay closing the BFT's 1986 accounts, pending his appeal. Instead of doing further battle in Tunisian courts, he persuaded Habib Mallouche, general secretary of the Association Professionnelle des Banques de Tunisie (over which Habib Bourguiba, Jr., still nominally presided), to arbitrate the respective claims of the BFT and ABCI at the Paris Chamber of International Commerce. The bank, described in the proceedings as both coplaintiff and defendant, named Samir Annabi, one of Tunisia's most respected international corporate lawyers, to be its representative on the three-man arbitration board. ABCI selected a French law professor.

After two months of deliberations, the tribunal unanimously concluded on 23 July 1987 that the BFT owed ABCI over $3.2 million, plus its half of the legal expenses, $55,945, which ABCI had advanced. Their reasoning was that the BFT, under its old management controlled by the STB, had acted wrongly in keeping the original dollars transferred to purchase the shares. It should have either delivered up the shares or returned the dollars to Switzerland. By the time the share purchase was consummated, two years later, the dollar had appreciated in value, so that the price of 2,125,000 TD charged for the shares amounted to only $2,772,962 at the prevailing exchange rate. BFT owed ABCI the balance of $1,366,110 as well as interest on the original $4,139,072.85 over the two years that it had been frozen. Two outside Swiss banks consulted by the tribunal agreed that an interest payment of $1,088,606.47 (12.4 percent compounded annually) was a conservative estimate of the interest that would have been received at the international market rates prevailing during 1982–84. In addition, the BFT owed ABCI interest on the remaining dollars unspent by the stock purchases in 1984, a further $750,000, which represented the Eurodollar rates prevailing from July 1984 to July 1987, when the tribunal issued its verdict.

These details presented here illustrate the vast discrepancy between a fair international understanding of the transactions between ABCI and the BFT and the Tunisian understanding. The international perspective, which the BFT's arbitrator recognized by signing the agreement, integrated Tunisia into international capital markets. From this perspective, the Tunisian authorities had obviously blundered and should pay the price exacted by the Shylock from Kairouan. To many Tunisians, especially the STB shareholders, however, the arbitration seemed inequitable because the STB had already admitted errors committed in 1982 and had permitted Bouden to purchase the shares at a discount that renumerated frozen Tunisian dinars at a fair Tunisian market rate. Were he so seriously interested in rejuvenating Tunisian banking, he might be extending and developing the BFT as he had promised other shareholders, rather than waging vendettas over legal technicalities. Once the dollars had entered Tunisia, they fell under Tunisian, not international jurisdiction. Bouden arguably had no right to engage the bank in international arbitration.

Even if the Central Bank and the STB had blundered in 1982, Tunisia's top banking officials were incensed by the arbitration. Mohammed Bouaouaja, who had meanwhile become chief executive officer of the STB, was originally involved in the case while serving as the Central Bank's director of research in 1982. With the full support of Central Bank Governor Ismail Khelil, he attempted after the tribunal's decision to neutralize Bouden's board of directors by requesting that Bourkhis be named judicial administrator (freed of control by the board). Bouden got wind of the scheme and fired his manager, who had signed the arbitration agreement in Paris, for playing a double game. On 14 November 1987, just one week after Ben Ali's coup overthrowing Bourguiba, Bouden was indicted for betraying his country and the interests of the BFT's shareholders by resorting to international arbitration. While the case dragged on, however, he continued to run the bank, parry legal actions by the STB, and preside over two general assemblies of the shareholders.

If Bouden seemed primarily intent on getting fair value for his dollars, he also opened up Tunisia's black box. In retrospect it would seem that the STB and the Central Bank had been less concerned about the foreign exchange than about an independent economic actor gaining full information about a Tunisian bank. Even after Bouden got access to the bank, in early 1987, it took him more than a year to unravel the mess he found. So little did he know about the bank's true condition in the summer of 1987 that, in rejecting the STB's argument that the shares acquired on the Tunisian Bourse in 1984 had been a bargain, his lawyers insisted they had been fairly valued. Taking Tunisia's liberal facade as the reality, the ABCI had ingenuously argued that the lower stock price simply reflected the BFT's decline in market value from 1982 to 1984. In a transparent market, in fact, the shares would have been worthless—for the privilege of holding a banking license in Tunisia was offset by mountains of nonperforming loans towering over any remaining capital.

Bouden had delayed closing the bank's books for the calendar year 1986 in order to include in them the bank's retroactive losses as determined by the international arbitration tribunal. When the bank's auditor, Mourad Guellaty, refused to recognize these losses, Bouden finally, in January 1988, hired another team of auditors. He then managed, despite opposition from the STB, to convene a general assembly on 31 March 1988. It approved his new version of the accounts for 1986, fired Guellaty, named the new team of Radhouane Nagbou and Mohamed Habib Landoulsi as the bank's official auditors for the years 1986 and 1987, and expressed its lack of confidence in all of the board members who had directed the bank in 1986 with the exception, of course, of Abdelmajid Bouden, who represented ABCI. Fought tooth and nail by the STB and its allies, the series of resolutions passed by narrow majorities of 10,047 to 9,019 (each vote representing one of the BFT's outstanding 20,000 shares). The chairman's report presented to the general assembly mentioned in passing that close to 10 million TD of the bank's loans were without collateral or guarantees, but the worst was still to come.

Bouden chaired an emergency session of the general assembly on 9 May 1988. The STB and its allies objected that the meeting was illegal, since no auditors were present to provide evidence. As usual, the STB delegate refused to sign the minutes of the meeting, but in them he is recorded as remarking an "improvement" in the minutes of the March meeting over previous ones. In fact the resolutions of the May meeting are worth citing in some detail because by this time Bouden's auditors had uncovered serious patterns of mismanagement that neither the STB, the Central Bank, nor the rest of Tunisia's banking establishment wanted to see exposed. Bouden publicly announced that the loans that were "recoverable with difficulty and which are becoming doubtful" totaled almost 14 million TD (out of 33 million booked as of 31 December 1987). He immediately incurred the wrath of almost all of Tunisia's leading bankers, concerned about the reputations of their own loan portfolios. (Bouden reports that a number of them urged him at one of their meetings of the APBT to keep silent in the future. It is not possible for an outsider to judge how general the BFT's practices in fact were, apart from the circumstantial evidence reported in table 6–2).

The first resolution at the May 1988 emergency session, noting the problematic 14 million TD and "deploring this dramatic situation which has been carefully and knowingly hidden, recommends that all efforts be mobilized to recover whatever can be and to determine the responsibilities for this faulty negligence and behavior which exposes the bank's patrimony to grave difficulties . . . and that this question receive top priority." In its second resolution the general assembly could no longer "tolerate" accounts that had been sitting on the books "for more than fifteen years"—from the time the late Hassan Belkhodja had run the STB, from 1971 to 1982—without the accounts being cleared or justified. Another resolution, addressed to "all the shareholders who irregularly benefited from free shares" that the bank had improperly distributed in 1983, appealed to them to return the shares or pay for them to avoid legal action. Bouden's auditors had discovered that some 700,000 TD of provisions for nonperforming loans had been diverted between 1982 and 1984 to the capital holdings of the STB group. The general assembly called upon the STB to reimburse the BFT for all of the nonperforming loans booked prior to 19 February 1987 by previous boards of directors "which were none other than an emanation" of the STB. Further, the STB was to take back at historical cost plus interest all shares of other companies held in the BFT's securities portfolio. Most of these shares were investments in the STB's group of companies. The BFT's new auditors estimated that the shares had lost almost half their book value of 708,153 TD. The general assembly warned the STB that legal action would be undertaken unless it reimbursed the BFT for the nonperforming loans and securities. It also accused the former auditor, Mourad Guellaty, of "calumny" and concluded that "contrary to the affirmations of the Order of Accountants and Company Auditors of Tunisia, the revocation of

Guellaty is not abusive but is founded on his serious professional errors . . . justice will be taken against the Order . . . and against Guellaty." In citing Guellaty, who had accused Bouden's regime of accumulating the nonperforming loans, the handful of shareholders who controlled the little bank broadened their judicial attack against Tunisia's largest bank to include the country's entire professional leadership in the field of accounting.

As in 1984, further efforts were made to settle the disputes between Bouden's BFT and the STB out of court. Bouden claims to have reached an understanding on 19 January 1989 with the minister of finance and the vice governor of the Central Bank that he buy out the balance of the STB's equity in the bank for a new capital injection of about $3 million. But then, just as the dollars arrived from Switzerland, the bank was sequestered. The police raided the central office because of suspicious movements near the vaults in the basement, which turned out to be workmen repairing a water leak. Bouden lost access to the bank. Then, in March 1989, the Tunis Municipal Court finally reached a verdict on the STB's case initiated against him in November 1987: Bouden was convicted of evading foreign exchange regulations and of mismanaging the bank to the detriment of its minority shareholders. He, his brother, and another shareholder were sentenced to six years in jail. The court also waived the damages awarded by the international arbitration tribunal and ordered the three instead to pay a fine of five times the amount, or 13,761,000 TD. Just as these Draconian sentences were being handed down, other leading bankers were confiding to me that the "Bouden problem" had been "solved."

Prime Minister Hedi Baccouche had earlier favored the compromise whereby Bouden would buy out the STB, but Khelil and Bouaouaja had persuaded Gery, Ben Ali's secretary, to reverse it. Baccouche then arranged another compromise whereby Bouden was to give up his shares in exchange for proper compensation and exoneration, along with his associates, from any fines and prison sentences. Implementing such an agreement was another matter. The STB's lawyer handed Bouden's lawyer an ultimatum. Under threat of the jail sentence, Bouden and his associates signed the settlement. It offered compensation for the shares in Tunisian dinars, at ABCI's original cost of 4.250 dinars per share. In addition, Bouden was granted 1 million TD for renouncing the arbitration, a sum that could be interpreted as the difference between the dinar value of 1982 dollars and the price paid for the shares in 1984, plus interest. But he was also called upon to pay 2,125,000 TD (the cost of the shares) for ABCI's half of the bank's nonperforming loans. In other words the STB was confiscating Bouden's shares on the grounds that he, not they, had mismanaged the bank. Bouden described the deal as pure "extortion" and insisted he had signed it under duress. While there is in fact strong evidence that nonperforming loans had accumulated under the prior management, an outsider cannot rule out the hypothesis that some of the loans contracted after February 1987 were also nonperforming handouts to friends and allies.

The BFT's ostensibly performing loan portfolio increased by about 6 million TD between 1986 and 1987 (table 6–3). The financial statements of 31 December 1987, which were officially contested by the STB, claims nonperforming loans totaling "more than 11 million TDs, and of course much more in actualized value" because they had been rolled over for years on the bank's books. As noted earlier, Bouden claimed in 1988 that the loans amounted to almost 14 million. The first official information to be released about the bank after 1985, however, was its balance sheet as of 31 December 1989. Under the heading "Other Credit to Clients," which has served most banks since 1987 mainly as a euphemism for nonperforming loans, the BFT reported almost 23 million TD. Interestingly, it also carried over the 2,114,000 TD of "losses in 1986" that Bouden had inserted into the 1986 and 1987 books to recognize ABCI's arbitration award.

The Bouden affair thus reached a theoretical conclusion, only to reopen shortly after the prime minister was dismissed from office in November 1989 and the Central Bank governor retired, pending his reassignment as minister of foreign affairs. While the two disagreed with each other on many matters, Bouden perceived them as responsible for his demise but now collectively weakened by other elements in President Ben Ali's entourage. Although the bull in Tunisia's china shop had apparently lost the crucial final case after winning so many against the STB, the slow wheels of Tunisian justice continued to grind. On 30 November 1989 the Ministry of the Interior's "Brigade" for economic and financial investigations subpoenaed the retired general manager of the BFT along with Mourad Guellaty, Mohamed Landoulsi (one of Bouden's auditors), and the sequestrator of the BFT. In official testimony taken over the following six weeks, Riahi and Guellaty confirmed the essentials of Landoulsi's analysis, including the irregular freezing of Bouden's dollar funds, the existence of some 10 million TD of nonperforming loans contracted prior to his administration, and the illegal use of provisions to inflate the capital of the bank, not to mention side payments to the complaisant Guellaty. On 29 March 1990, the Court of Appeals (Cassation) rejected the ruling that the international arbitration had been illegal. Litigation would continue, and the legal tide seemed to be turning again in Bouden's direction.

Whatever the outcome, the story can be read as a microcosm of the forces

	1984	1985	1986	1987	1989	1990
Total assets/liabilities	43.24	46.89	51.09	63.84	87.96	96.6
Deposits	25.08	25.21	24.77	29.38	46.87	29.2
Capital and reserves	5.5	5.54	5.9	5.9	5.9	5.9
Provisions	1.15	1.57	2.05	3.35	3.5	3.6
Loans						
Commercial loans	14.39	15.51	17.21	23.11	26.3	32.5
Overdrafts	9.33	9.6	9.88	9.51	14	15.6
Subsidized term loans	0.11	0.15	0.26	0.33	0.77	0.88
"Other credits to clientele"	0.57	0.53	0.54	13.9	22.9	26.4
Investments in other companies	0.63	0.5	0.39	0.68	0.7	0.7
Fixed assets	0.72	0.72	0.8	0.92	0.84	0.84
Losses 1986			2.114	2.114	2.114	2.114
Total revenues[a]		3.8	4.09	4.983	6.36	7.99
Interest revenues	3.28	3.186	3.45	4.09	4.95	3.235
Interest expenses	1.12	1.74	2.225	2.184	3.09	2.138
Administrative expenses	0.9	1.07	1.145	1.41	1.69	1.84
Salaries	0.7	0.76	0.815	0.96	1.19	1.43
Provisions and amortization	0.62	0.58	0.91	1.39	0.099	0.144
Net income	0.033	0.359	0	0.0023	0.14	0.333
(Net income reported to APBT)	0.94	0.83				
Personnel	126	143	153	154	182	183
Capital/total assets	12.72%	11.81%	11.55%	9.24%	6.71%	6.11%
Spreads/TA	5.00%	3.08%	2.40%	2.99%	2.11%	1.14%
Cash flow/TA (lines 24+25/line 2)	1.51%	2.00%	1.78%	2.18%	0.27%	0.49%
Workout time (years)[b]				2	31	19

Sources: Financial statements of BFT, 1985–87 (Annual Report 1985; internal audits 1986, 1987); Reports of APBT 1984, 1985, 1989.

a. BFT Annual Report of 1985 is used to correct inflated APBT estimates of 1984 and 1985 income.

b. The time required to pay off half the uncovered nonperforming loan exposure by expected cash flow.

at play in the struggles to liberalize the Tunisian economy. The dominant player is a powerful state banking bureaucracy. At the apex stands the Central Bank, which is also a reservoir and training ground for managers of the parastatal commercial banks. The architect of Tunisia's facade of liberalization also took the lead in crushing one of its consequences, a genuinely autonomous private commercial bank. Tunisia's accounting profession was a willing accomplice, for the accountant Guellaty had the full backing of the official organization's leadership. The Association Professionnelle des Banques de Tunisie went along with the Central Bank, firing its general secretary—a veteran technocrat who, like Bouden, was a native of Kairouan—when he incurred the displeasure of the authorities. Despite an apparent openness to direct foreign investment, Tunisia refused its corollary of integration with international capital markets under international law. Once dollars entered the country, they were treated as dinars falling under jealously guarded Tunisian sovereignty.

The country's top political leadership was also involved in many of the bank's management issues, despite the bank's tiny size and relative insignificance. In the final months of the Bourguiba regime, the ruling party had to be consulted about the new bank manager, for companies with a minority of public shareholdings were still treated as parastatals, in effect sources of patronage for the party-state machine. Ben Ali's coming to power does not appear appreciably to have modified these practices. The politicians involved in the case tended to defer to the Central Bank, as if the matter were a technical issue. On the two occasions when Prime Minister Baccouche intervened, he took general positions that were never implemented. The public has been kept in the dark by a news blackout since 1988. There were some efforts in June 1988 to mobilize the BFT's staff against its president, but he neutralized them through a bonus scheme based on performance that penalized the few still loyal to the old management. Other bankers almost universally detested Bouden; whatever principles he might represent, he appeared to be not a banker but a conniving lawyer out to milk the system. These perceptions had some impact upon an otherwise immobile political leadership, usually content to let Tunisia's economic team run technical matters.

Many personal interests were also at work, and in the hothouse environment of Tunisia's political and business elites it is often difficult to separate personal from political or professional interests. Bouden's observations consistently fused them. He explained his legal difficulties by citing the balance of political forces, which could in turn be reduced to personal relationships between key individuals, sometimes revolving around their wives and mistresses. Street gossip reflects the reality that economic and political power are held in Tunisia by a small and interconnected establishment, much as in Machiavelli's Florence.

The economic substance of the Bouden tale, however, is supported by documents that include the official minutes of police investigations as well as internal audits of the bank. No doubt they do not tell the whole story. STB's allegations of Bouden's mismanagement may prove as well founded as his allegations of their fraud. Whatever the final outcome of the various lawsuits, the story also reveals a relatively autonomous system of Tunisian justice. The Tunisian authorities seem unable, in the final analysis, to escape the realities of the country's opening to international capitalism. If the Tunisian facade of financial liberalization is still in need of stronger foundations, the Four Pillars constructed in the late 1980s may nevertheless augur the "radical transformation" to which its exponents verbally aspire—eventually. Other private sector banks have been gaining some autonomy.

Private Sector Strategies

Though the banking system remained heavily regulated, the protective barriers served the interests of the established private sector banks as well as the STB. Relatively stable margins enabled them to pursue distinctive strategies and to keep gaining market share at the expense of the public sector banks if they so chose. The dramatic entry of the Banque Internationale de Tunisie (BIAT) into the Tunisian marketplace is documented in figure 6–4. From the 2.3 percent share of the market it had inherited in 1976 (BIAT 1986), BIAT advanced to almost 16 percent of the commercial banking system's deposits by 1990.[7] The strategy of rapid growth was risky because the bank became undercapitalized as a result of investing in so many new branches. Conversely, the old colonial banks, the Banque de Tunisie and UBCI, steadily lost their shares of deposits until the 1980s and began to increase their shares of lending only in the late 1980s, when the financial reforms cut into their margins. The Banque de Tunisie, in stark contrast to BIAT, implemented a conservative strategy, generating good profits, supposedly with relatively little risk, from a quality clientele. As noted earlier in this chapter, however, the quality of the clientele apparently increased rather than reduced the risk of nonperforming loans: some well-connected people either did not pay up or lost their good connections in political reshuffles. The private sector banks nonetheless enjoyed some discretion in their lending as a result of the financial reforms. Although the public sector banks had to dole out credit to ailing public sector enterprises as a matter

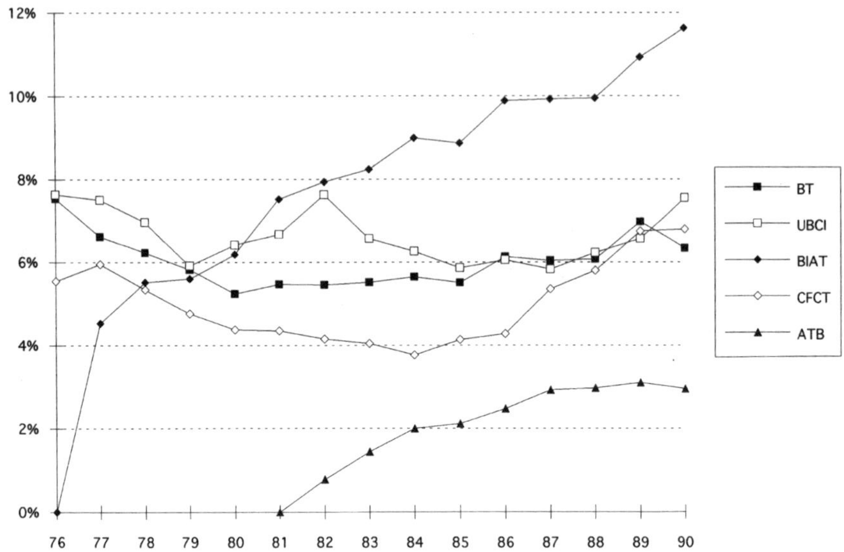

Fig. 6.7. Private sector shares of bank loans, 1976–90. *Source:* author's database of commercial banks.

of practical politics, the influence of the private banks over credit allocation was increasing, as figure 6–7 indicates. In effect they might one day serve as monitors, reducing the costs of state supervision. Enterprises refused by BIAT as well as by BT might in the future be refused elsewhere.

BIAT projected the image of a "solid, profitable, and battle-hardened institution," a determined competitor (*Rapport Annuel 1990:* 9). It had solid roots in both the public and private sectors, for its founder, Mansour Moallah, served as minister of finance from 1980 to 1983, before returning to the bank as honorary president. Habib Bourguiba, Jr., had also been a founding member of the bank's board of directors. The excellent political contacts of the two enabled BIAT to grow rapidly, attracting deposits from the public sector as well as from a core of Sfaxi businesses. Chairman Mansour Moallah and many of his top cadres came from the city of Sfax, although the Tunisian shareholders were a diversified group of some 350 individuals, and there was also a significant minority of Kuwaiti and Saudi bank shareholders. Managers claimed that the bank's loan portfolio was fully diversified, not particularly skewed toward Sfax businesses. While Moallah was minister, his bank surged into third place, surpassing the Banque du Sud and the Union Internationale de Banques as well as the UBCI in deposits, loans, and total assets. BIAT's strategy was one of all-out growth, carefully projected in five-year business plans. Like the BT's general director, Abderrazak Rassaa, Moallah injected his years of experience as an economic planner into the bank's strategy. Unlike the BT, however, BIAT was prepared to sacrifice profits for market share.

BIAT rarely paid out dividends of more than 6 percent and retained 60 to 75 percent of its annual earnings, whereas the BT usually paid out more in dividends and directors' fees than it retained. Before declaring its net income, however, BT reserved more provisions than BIAT. In the 1980s it plowed an average of 85 percent of its cash flow back into the bank, compared to BIAT's 87 percent. Since BT had the better cash flow (see fig. 6–6), proportionately more funds were available for investment. It chose, however, to build up hidden reserves rather than to invest in more branches for greater market shares. BIAT, by contract, was hard-pressed to sustain its growth. It was seriously undercapitalized: its ratio of shareholders' equity to total assets fell to slightly below 3 percent in 1982, and in 1987 it hovered slightly above the 3 percent mark. The bank's annual report for 1987 tried to "show undeniably that BIAT performed better in 1987 than all banks" (p. 32), for it had to persuade shareholders of yet another capital increase. It also claimed to be in the forefront of Tunisia's computer revolution, developing on-line capabilities so that branches could act more autonomously. Its computer planning dovetailed with an organizational strategy that encouraged greater autonomy at the regional and local level. By pioneering decentralized management systems, BIAT was diffusing more flexible forms of credit allocation that might indirectly affect future political development.

The strategy of rapid growth had not allowed BIAT to be as discriminating as the old colonial banks in its choice of clientele. Almost 9 percent of BIAT's loan portfolio was nonperforming in 1989, but it was improving. According to Saidane (Interview, 11 June 1990), problem loans constituted only 17 million of the 40 million TD of "Credits divers" listed in the BIAT balance sheet and reweighted to 37 million in table 6–2. If so, the troubled loans were already covered by provisions. Saidane made the further point that only 69 percent of the bank's equity was immobilized, an improvement over the 88 percent reported in table 6–2. As long as much of Tunisia's banking system was less viable than BIAT, this aggressive newcomer could continue to push. Politically it was part of the club, yet it also challenged the state oligopoly. There were plans in 1990 to spin off five regional banks from the parent, so as better to penetrate the markets for loans and deposits.

Regional banks would be less susceptible to central government pressures. The Central Bank showed initial interest but then refused to grant BIAT permission.

The CFCT also demonstrated its relative independence. The only bank whose shares were not traded on the stock exchange, it was privately held by a family of Jerban entrepreneurs. Its behavior anticipated Central Bank efforts to make banks truly autonomous. It was an outsider, occasionally refusing to participate in lending packages promoted by the Central Bank before such shows of independence became acceptable, as a high official of the Central Bank explained (Interview, Ahmed Karm, 5 June 1989). The bank's basic strategy seemed to be to support its owners, the Ben Yedder business group, as a ready source of loans. Consequently it competed with BIAT as well as other banks for deposits. CFCT was in the vanguard of banks designing new instruments to attract household savings. Like BIAT, it had substantially expanded its branch network. BIAT undoubtedly had its principal competitor in mind when it urged Ismail Khelil, as part of his effort to rationalize Tunisian banks, to make them diversify their loan portfolios. As of 18 December 1987 a Central Bank circular stated that no more than 10 percent of a bank's capital was to be lent to a single client, but implementation would be gradual. In 1991 the limit was to be set at 40 percent, and meanwhile the CFCT was undergoing a painful transition. In 1990 its loans exceeded its deposits. However, its cash flow was stronger than BIAT's, relative to total assets, because operating expenditures and salaries were lower.

The old colonial banks also showed new signs of life after 1987. The UBCI's share of loans steadily increased, although its share of deposits remained stationary after steady decline in the 1970s and 1980s. After being brought under partial Tunisian ownership in 1979, its ratio of equity to total assets also diminished steadily until 1984; evidently, the bank did not generate sufficient profits to finance both growth and dividends for the shareholders, yet the remaining French owner, the Banque Nationale de Paris, was loath to increase its stake. UBCI's ratio of capital to total assets improved in 1985 and 1986, however—due to a doubling of paid-up capital that the Central Bank had obliged the French and Tunisian partners to contribute. Like the UBCI, the BT also preferred to keep equity stakes low, so as to generate high returns on investment to the shareholders. Each of these old colonial banks kept its capital ratio at 4.5 to 5 percent of total assets, 65 percent of which was tied up in stocks and fixed assets. BT consistently paid out 12 percent dividends.

The ATB, half Palestinian-owned, was the most strongly capitalized of all

Tunisian banks, public or private, its equity constituting 6.7 percent of total assets in 1989. In 1995 it easily raised more capital from its shareholders to meet international standards (*MEED*, 26 May 1995; 27). This newcomer, reorganized out of a branch of the Arab Bank established in Tunis in 1959, had debarked onshore with the PLO in 1982. It tried to generate attractive dividends although it was more heavily capitalized than the former colonial banks. In 1986 it managed to distribute 9 percent dividends, half its net income, but it reserved much less of its cash flow to cover problem loans than the UBCI did. It had branched along the coast as far south as Gabes by 1986 and Mednine by 1988, but its growth in deposits seems to have reached a plateau, just keeping up with the market, and future growth perhaps depends on Tunisia's commercial relationships with Arab neighbors. In 1989 it added three more branches and continued to generate the biggest cash flows, relative to its size, of any Tunisian bank. Its structure mirrored that of its Arab Bank parent in Amman, Jordan: a relatively lean loan portfolio, relative to total assets, and a strong deposit base. The Arab Bank insisted that the local management conform to the parent's conservative strategy and keep up its good reputation. When, for instance, the Tunisian general manager leaked to the press the private accounts of a senior military politician who had fallen from political favor, the head office in Amman promptly fired him.

As the banks strove to be more independent, their credit decisions might gradually cover the state's disengagement from public enterprises. As the reforms took effect, the private sector's share of credit steadily increased, from 62.5 percent in 1986 to 69.1 percent in 1989 and 83.5 percent in 1990.[8] Competition among the banks was spreading geographically, too, as branches proliferated.

Branching into Civil Society

Setting up a new branch required the approval of the Central Bank, but it also reflected the strategy of the bank in question. From 1971 to 1988 the number of branches quintupled, finally totaling 496, or one branch for every 16,000 inhabitants.[9] Figure 6–8 shows how these branches have been distributed by region since independence. Tunisia's traditional colonial estates of the Northwest were neglected in favor of Tunis. Large urban centers attracted the most branches per capita. Greater Tunis alone supported 119 branches, or one for every 7,000 men, women, and children, in 1988. By contrast, Tunisia's Center, the governorates of Kasserine, Siliana, and Sidi Bou Zid, were neglected as in colonial times. The region averaged one

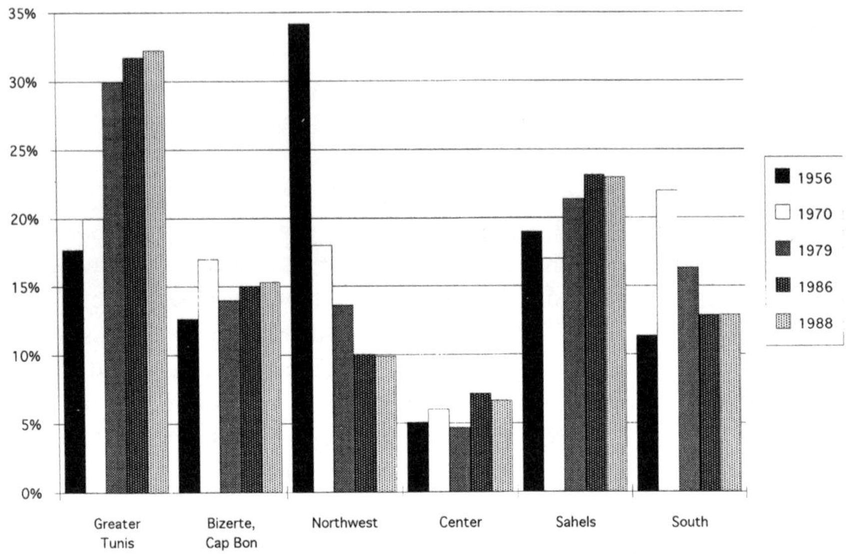

Fig. 6.8. Bank branches by region, 1956–88. *Sources:* Signoles 1985; Central Bank of Tunisia.

branch for every 35,000 inhabitants. Branches in the poor areas of the country seemed to be a luxury that few private sector banks could afford. UBCI and BT had implanted a branch in Sidi Bou Zid and Siliana, respectively, in 1983, but the other 23 branches were all public sector. The private sector stayed away completely from Zaghouan and from Kebili and Tataouine in the far South, and certain of its presences in the Northwest seemed to be relics of the colonial era rather than signs of a competitive strategy.

In the early 1970s the BT still had one of the largest branch networks, rivaling those of the younger, more vigorous STB and BNT, but by 1988 the BS, BIAT, and even the UIB had forged ahead. In the 1980s, however, the private sector banks as a whole regained the ground lost by BT to the public sector. They focused their attention on the coastal areas, leaving the poorer, peripheral parts of the country to the public sector. Figure 6–9 maps their penetration of the country, revealing a sharp cleavage between the coastal regions and the interior. Private sector branches were concentrated along the extended Sahel between Bizerte and Jerba; elsewhere their presence was minimal.

From 1981 to 1988 the total number of bank branches increased by 82 percent, and those of the private sector by 237 percent—BIAT and CFCT being the most dynamic, more than tripling their networks. Their main tar-

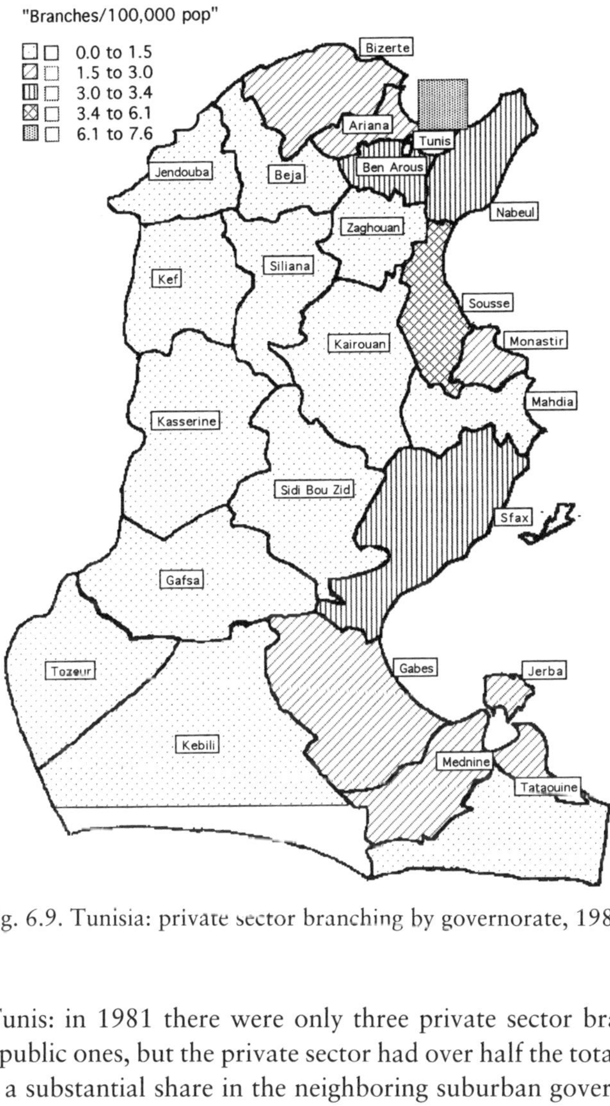

Fig. 6.9. Tunisia: private sector branching by governorate, 1988.

get was Tunis: in 1981 there were only three private sector branches for every five public ones, but the private sector had over half the total by 1988, as well as a substantial share in the neighboring suburban governorates of Ariana and Ben Arous. In Sfax, too, the private sector banks had gained a slight majority, as table 6–4 indicates. Nabeul, Sousse, and Monastir, homes of much of the political-administrative elite, were more heavily banked than Sfax, but the private banks, having accumulated little over one-third of the total number of branches, did not compete as much as in Sfax. Perhaps the degree of economic activity in the coastal provinces did not justify more forceful presences. In fact the governorate of Monastir was home to only one private bank branch in 1981. But the more politically attuned of the

Table 6-4. Bank branches by governorate, 1988

Banks	STB	BNA	BS	UIB	BT	CFCT	BIAT	UBCI	ATB	BFT	Total	% private sector	Population per branch
Tunis	15	10	10	20	14	20	17	8	3	2	119	54	7,000
Nabeul	9	13	6	4	4	4	4	3	2		49	35	10,000
Sfax	7	6	3	3	1	3	11	5	1		40	53	17,000
Sousse	7	6	3	5	4	3	4	1	1		34	38	11,000
Bizerte	6	6	3	3	3	1	3	1	1		27	33	16,000
Monastir	7	5	7	1	4	0	3	0			27	26	12,000
Ben Arous	5	5	2	2	2	2	2	1	1	1	23	39	13,000
Medenine	5	4	4	2	3	3	1		1		23	35	15,000
Kairouan	2	5	1	1	2	1	2	1			15	40	31,000
Ariana	4	4	2	0	2	3	2	1			18	44	25,000
Jendouba	4	5	0	2	3	0	1				15	27	26,000
Gabes	1	3	1	1	2	2	1	1	1		13	54	22,000
Other	20	35	19	7	6	1	3	2	0		93	13	27,000
Totals/averages	92	107	61	51	50	43	54	24	11	3	496	37	16,000

Source: Central Bank of Tunisia, 1984 Census (projected estimate 1988).

private sector banks remedied their relative neglect by 1986. BIAT opened two branches, and the BT added three to its original presence, although CFCT and UBCI preferred to stay away from Bourguiba's paradise.

In Bizerte the private sector's share declined in the 1980s, whereas it held a majority of the branches in Gabes, the center of Tunisian petrochemical industries. If Sfax was the major focus of competition outside Tunis, private sector banks varied their emphasis in light of particular strategies. BT preferred Monastir, for instance, and even built on historic strength in Jendouba, a former *colon* stronghold in the northwest of the country, rather than develop its modest presence in Sfax. By contrast, BIAT increased its three branches to eight to service its extensive network of Sfaxi businesspeople, overtaking not only UBCI (whose Tunisian business partner was from Sfax) but also the government's own STB. The CFCT, on the other hand, tied most of its expansion to Tunis and also dominated private sector activity in Mednine, where Jerba is located.

Off the coast, Tunisia's Islamic capital of Kairouan also attracted some private sector attention, though presences remained symbolic. Whether in search of Islamic (interest-free) deposits or merely a measure of Islamic respectability, three of the four private sector banks descended upon the city, and CFCT caught up with the herd in 1988.

Political Implications

Obviously, financial liberalization has not yet generated sufficient structural power to help opposition parties. The 1989 elections, discussed in chapter 3, marked the end of any transition toward greater democracy and a turning point back to authoritarian rule. The Tunisian experience does not invalidate the hypothesis, however, that financial liberalization gradually generates the resources for a more pluralistic politics. Structural adjustment of the financial sector is a lengthy process, as is the emergence of autonomous business groups capable of collective action. Indeed, the Tunisian authorities appear to be aware of the political risks; Tunisia illustrates increasing tensions between a patrimonial authoritarian regime and structural adjustment.

The beneficiaries of credit constituted a tiny but influential minority of Tunisians. Figure 6–10 indicates that barely more than 30,000 Tunisians or firms enjoyed access to any credits classified by the Central Bank in 1986, though these did not include either loans of less than TD 3,000 or various other farm or home financing credits. Of the beneficiaries, only 1,017 received loans of more than TD 500,000. The number of beneficiaries had in-

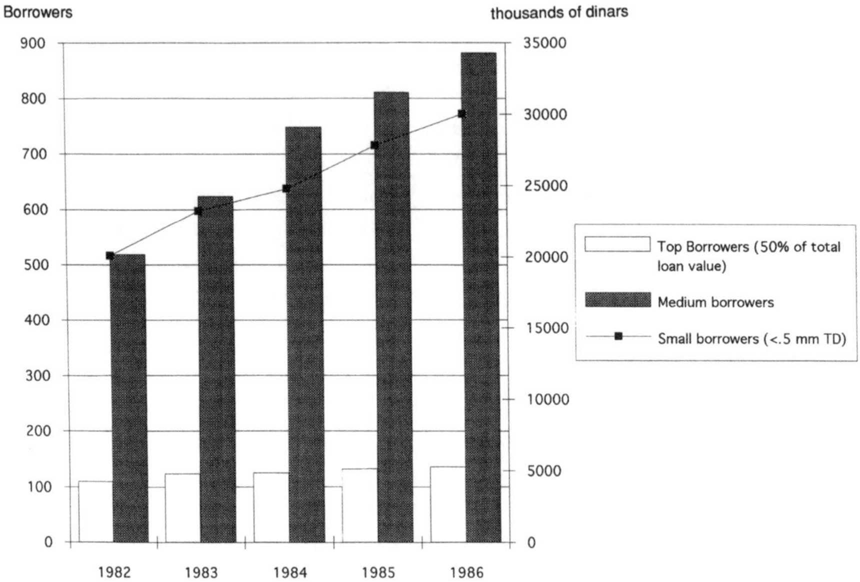

Fig. 6.10. Tunisian borrowers, 1982–86. *Source:* Central Bank of Tunisia.

creased by roughly 50 percent since 1982, but the distribution seemed increasingly skewed, in that the small borrowers received only one-fifth of the total value of the loans in 1986, compared with one-quarter in 1982. Major potential contributors to political organizations—those firms and individuals borrowing TD 500,000 or more—had almost doubled, but the number of top borrowers shown in figure 6–10 remained almost stationary. In 1986, 136 firms or individuals took half the credits.

While the banks' branching strategies presumably reflected economic rather than political concerns, the provinces they targeted also tended to display the politically most active oppositions. Figure 6–11 maps the votes for opposition lists (including null ballots) by governorate as a proportion of those voting. The opposition, notably Islamically minded Independents, was strongest in the southern part of the country most exposed to Libyan media and in the coastal, more urbanized regions. Excluding the south, the governorates with the greatest per capita number of private bank branches tended to be those with the highest proportions of opposition voters—with Tunis and Sousse taking the lead. The branches were most frequent in those urban and coastal parts of the country where organized oppositions, notably the Islamists, were most likely to flourish.

Bourguiba had taken advantage of provincial credit networks to organize

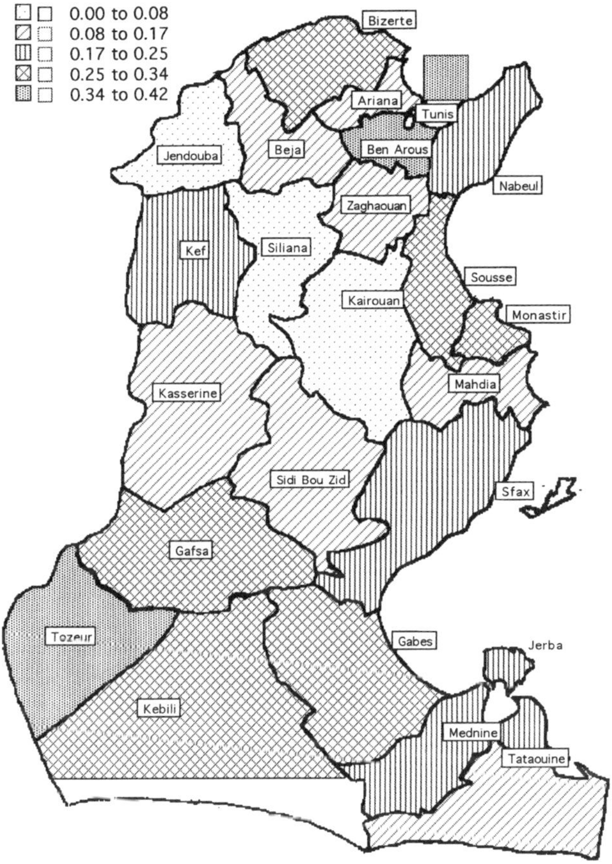

Fig. 6.11. Oppositions' share of votes, Tunisia, National Assembly elections, 1989.

the Neo-Destour Party in 1930s, but the authorities, perhaps aware of the party's history, acted preemptively against any similar developments in the 1980s. Although "participatory" Islamic banking was permitted a marginal beachhead onshore, BEST Bank's plans to develop its branch network had to be shelved after 1988. Potentially autonomous private sector banks were also discouraged from becoming more independent. BIAT, in particular, had nourished plans to develop autonomous regional banks but was in the end refused. The CFCT, the other most autonomous of the private sector banks, recruited to its top management an official from the Central Bank who had no prior commercial banking experience, and the move was interpreted in some quarters as a control measure. A more plausible interpretation might be that Ahmed El Karm, the talented official in question, had simply opted for a more promising career with the private sector, but the conspiracy theory was widespread in banking and political circles.

BIAT suffered a sharp setback in 1993 that sheds further light on the limits of Tunisia's financial and political liberalization. Buttressed by private enterprise based in Sfax, the bank threatened the government's informal control over the private sector through selective credit incentives. A pretext was found to clip its wings. On 11 May 1993, *Le Monde* cited its chairman, former Finance Minister Mansour Moallah, as calling Tunisia "more IMF than the IMF." By 19 May parastatal organizations like Tunis Air began to withdraw their deposits from the bank, obliging Moallah to resign from the honorary chairmanship of the bank as well as other public positions in order to save the bank. BIAT lost 20 percent of its deposits within a week but managed to survive by borrowing extensive funds from the Central Bank. The real issue behind the affair was that BIAT, Tunisia's third-largest commercial bank, had grown too powerful, but there was a political interpretation that sheds further light on the link between political and financial reform. Some weeks earlier, Moallah is reported to have responded to a former French prime minister in an informal conversation overheard at a reception that yes, he supposed he, too, might be "présidentiable." Moallah's elimination from public life was viewed by many Tunisians as part of Ben Ali's preelectoral campaign to preempt any presidential opposition in the 1994 elections (though Moallah's associates indicate that he did not harbor any presidential ambitions); two other aspiring candidates were subsequently jailed. In the elections Ben Ali, uncontested, received 99.9 percent of the vote.

Financial reform had obviously not given rise to an independent business sector committed to greater government accountability, much less willing to finance a multiparty system. Some opposition parties were permitted to compete in the parliamentary elections held in 1994, but they fared poorly. They had little time to campaign and only token access to the media. Private businesses were perhaps less loath in 1994 than in 1989 to be perceived as supporting these parties, now that the regime had officially endorsed the token oppositions and entitled them to a small share of the parliamentary seats. Collectively, they won less than 3 percent of the vote in 1994—even less than the weak showing of Tunisia's principal opposition party in 1989. For electoral and other purposes, the ruling party's patronage networks remained largely in place, channeled through a state banking sector that still held well over half of the total assets of the commercial banking system and through a largely complacent private sector as well. The structural power of finance capital remained almost as limited in Tunisia as in Algeria, despite modest increases in the market shares of the private sector banks. The system clearly lacked the autonomy of its Turkish counterpart, and the patrimonial regime seemed determined to contain it.

Ben Ali ostensibly remained committed to a middle way of carefully calibrated economic and political liberalization, but his commitment to the "irreversible process" of "democratization" appeared hollow and hypocritical in the face of continuing repression of Tunisia's leading opposition party. Tunisia had clearly lost an opportunity to emulate Turkey's transition to multiparty politics. The elections of 1989 could have been a critical turning point, but if Ben Ali was no Inonü, neither had a credible opposition arisen from within Tunisia's old single-party establishment. Ahmed Mestiri had enjoyed moral authority as a politician who had stood up to Bourguiba's personal power and founded the Tunisian League of Human Rights in 1977. But by his own admission he lacked economic muscle, though Tunisia's private sector was surely no weaker than Turkey's in 1950. Bourguiba's one-party system had not projected a Tunisian Celal Bayar. The closest candidates might have been Hédi Nouira, who had served as governor of the BCT before becoming prime minister, or Habib Bourguiba, Jr., who founded two banks and the Association Professionnelle des Banques de Tunisie. Neither man was in a position to engage in competitive politics, and the opposition politicians lacked roots in Tunisia's private sector. Political and financial strategies thus remained bifurcated.

Perhaps, however, the economic reforms were less reversible than Ben Ali's political promises. The banks could not yet, as in Turkey, scale the financial heights and command credit allocation, but some of the private sector banks might still hold the key to incremental change, despite temporary reverses at the hands of the authorities. A tougher oligopoly of private sector banks will be needed for finance capital to acquire enough structural power to fight back.

Chapter 7

Egypt's Fragmented Finance Capital

> The owners of [Egypt's] wealth are those who gained power or influence, or both simultaneously.
>
> (Sāmia Sa'īd Imām 1986: 215)

> Ordinary business transactions are . . . based upon the idea that a continuing relationship allows cooperation to develop without the assistance of a central authority. . . . The fairness of the transactions is guaranteed not by the threat of a legal suit, but rather by the anticipation of mutually rewarding transactions in the future. It is precisely when this anticipation of future interaction breaks down that an external authority is invoked. . . . Without the shadow of the future, cooperation becomes impossible to sustain.
>
> (Axelrod 1984: 178–79, 182)

Egypt's commercial banking system is considerably more developed and diversified than Tunisia's and Algeria's. In keeping with Sadat's political strategy, financial infitah encouraged multiple centers of power that facilitated patrimonial rule. From the late 1970s until the late 1980s, the commercial banking system appeared to be relatively autonomous and competitive, featuring a multitude of free-wheeling, undisciplined banks. For much of the period its market concentration of deposits was lower than Turkey's, Morocco's, or Tunisia's (fig. 2–9), despite earlier concentrations as high as Algeria's. The Egyptian infitah raised the possibility that financial pluralism might offer an easy and direct road to political pluralism, bypassing the concentration of finance capital into banking oligopolies and business groups experienced by Turkey. Despite the Nasser interlude, Egyptian banking still seemed to reflect a British financial legacy that encouraged greater financial diversity and competition than the Continental models that had oriented banking in the other crescent countries.

Legacies of Financial Pluralism

Egypt was only briefly a British protectorate, during the emergency of World War I until 1922, when it became conditionally independent. To be sure, it had in Milner's well-known words been a "veiled protectorate" after the British occupied it in 1882, and although it was no longer in any monetary sense a protectorate after leaving the Sterling Zone in 1948, the last British troops did not evacuate the Suez Canal until 1954 (only to return, very briefly, during the futile invasion of Egypt in 1956 by Britain, France, and Israel). Some argue that Egypt had become a "colony" of the West much earlier than 1882, in the senses that Europeans enjoyed "extra-territorial immunities and privileges," that "a nominally autonomous Egyptian Government . . . [was] subject to usually irresistible pressures from the governments of the European Great Powers," and that "its culture, its techniques, and the ambience of its ruling class had been infiltrated by . . . the civilisation of Western Europe" (Marlowe 1975: 7; cf. Mitchell 1988). But these aspects do not encourage useful comparisons between Egypt and the more heavily colonized parts of North Africa, including Tunisia, where capitalism was frozen in the nineteenth century.

Egypt was never to be as exclusively British as Algeria and Tunisia became French. In Egypt there remained a certain permeability between peoples as well as between their kinds of banking. Some Egyptians became foreigners who from 1876 to 1948 enjoyed the special jurisdiction of the Mixed Courts as well as their consular courts; subsequently, however, foreigners would find it more difficult to acquire Egyptian nationality. Egypt's government enjoyed considerable autonomy as late as May 1882, perhaps more so than its nominal Ottoman overlords. In 1879 an apparently "bewildered" Sultan Abdul Hamid had acceded to British and French pressure to depose the Egyptian khedive in favor of his son rather than a favored uncle (Cromer 1908: 129), and by 1882 Egyptians were taking decisive steps toward constitutional government after almost a century of autocratic rule under Mohammad Ali (1803–49) and his successors. While their bureaucracy fell under the control of British advisers between 1882 and 1922, it subsequently—as in the turbulent period between 1878 and 1882—became a battleground for three contending forces, the nationalist movement and the palace as well as the British high commissioner (who reverted to being an ambassador, a little more equal than the others, with the signing of the Anglo-Egyptian Treaty in 1936). Egypt was, to be sure, a "colony" in the sense that the ruling classes, their oppositions, and broad segments of the population had been acquiring aspects of Western culture and techniques ever since Napoleon's invasion of 1798, if not earlier, but in this sense virtually the entire world was a colony.

By 1882 Egyptian banking was considerably more developed than Tunisia's, and "informal" British rule would keep it open to foreign capital and new financial models. After one failure in 1837 (Crouchley 1938: 105), European trading houses began to found banks as early as 1842, shortly after the British had obliged Muhammad Ali to dismantle his state monopolies. The Pastrés of Marseilles, who made at least one loan to the bey of Tunis, seem to have been among the first to test the Egyptian market. Public debt floated on cotton futures, just as olive oil had served the Tunisians, but it remained seasonal. Despite his extensive efforts to industrialize Egypt and field a modern army, Muhammad Ali left the country without a significant accumulation of foreign debt. Only under Said (1854–63) did short-term debt servicing become so onerous that Egypt was finally persuaded, in 1862, to convert some of it into long-term bond issues. The European bankers' debt feast lasted only from 1862 to 1873, interrupted by the crash of 1866, in which a number of new entrants quickly expired. No single bank could keep order, as in Istanbul, for the largest of them, the Bank of Egypt, was too encumbered with floating debt and advances on cotton in 1861 to play the role of the Imperial Ottoman Bank.

Whereas only one European bank entered Tunisia, very shortly before 1881, Egypt had already experienced four decades of banking by the time of the British occupation. Jules Pastré and an associate raised British capital in 1864 to found the Anglo-Egyptian Bank, and when the British investors were ruined in 1866, the Crédit Foncier replaced them (Landes 1958: 205, 305). Again reorganized in 1887, and returned to British ownership, the bank survived to be nationalized after 1956, whereas the Bank of Egypt, despite British ownership, collapsed in 1911. Edouard Dervieu, immortalized in David Landes's classic *Bankers and Pashas,* promoted the loan of 1862 but "lost his place at the banquet table" (1958: 310) by 1868. The "true wizards" (306) who feasted the most, the Oppenheims, never established the national bank in Egypt that had once been their ambition and Pastré's, as well as Dervieu's. Their successes, like subsequent coups of Ernest Cassel at the turn of the century, depended on personal connections across the major houses of Europe, not on institutions. Egypt nevertheless acquired an impressive infrastructure of commercial banks and finance houses. Crouchley indicates that "in the report for the newly established Caisse de la Dette for 1877 we find that 'the following banks furnished telegraphic exchange on Paris and London: The Commercial Bank of Alexandria, the Crédit Lyonnais, The Imperial Ottoman Bank, the Anglo-Egyptian Banking Co., Limited, the Banque Franco-Egyptienne, Cattaui Fils et Cie., M. Ismalum and the Bank of Egypt'" (1977: 30). If originally attracted by the debt feast, many in addition to the Bank of Egypt and the Anglo-Egyptian would remain long after Ismail was deposed: Société Générale,

Comptoir d'Escompte de Paris, Paribas, Crédit Lyonnais, Crédit Foncier, and of course the Imperial Ottoman Bank (Bouvier et al. 1982: 207), as well as the Banque Franco-Egyptienne, directed by the brother of Jules Ferry. The Rothschilds were also represented, through the Banque Austro-Egyptienne.

While "the pecuniary interests of European creditors . . . led directly to European intervention" in the khedive Ismail's (1863–79) finances, it does not necessarily follow that they "without doubt, changed the whole course of the country's political history" (Crouchley 1977 [1936]: 20). From the outset of the crisis in 1876, the British government remained officially aloof from the various schemes of Anglo-French control over Egyptian finances put forward by French and British bankers. The first scheme, elaborated by the French in the spring of 1876, failed not so much because the British government refused to nominate its representative to the Caisse de la Dette as because London's financial markets refused to buy the bond issue promoted by the Crédit Foncier, with official backing from the Quai d'Orsay, for unifying the Egyptian debt. The scheme blatantly favored the floating short-term debt held by Crédit Foncier. New negotiations led by Goschen and Joubert, respectively representing powerful London and Paris finance houses, resulted by late 1876 in a more equitable arrangement for British as well as French bondholders, but the debt servicing requirements were out of Egypt's reach. The British government again refused to become officially involved in the administration of the dual control. Sir Evelyn Baring (later Earl of Cromer), for instance, was named the British commissioner of the debt by a representative of British bondholders, not by the government (Cromer 1908: 14–15). In his words, "The tendencies and traditions of the British Government . . . ran counter to any endeavour to enforce the claims of the foreign creditors at whatsoever cost to the population of Egypt. . . . Moreover, the influence of the bondholders in England was limited" (41).

Despite the Law of Liquidation of 1880, however, the Egyptian debt service remained far too high, consuming some two-thirds of expected government revenues (Cromer 1908: 173). Consequently the bondholder interests expressed in the dual-control regime certainly help to explain the internal Egyptian political crises of 1879–82. Possibly a more generous settlement would have enabled the Egyptian government to fend off Colonel Arabi's revolt in the army by paying off the troops and government administrators, thereby postponing the rise of nationalism. But bondholders' interests do not seem to have influenced any of the crucial decisions that led to the British military occupation. Wilfred Scawen Blunt, a contemporary observer sympathetic to the Egyptian nationalists, claimed (1907: 160, 182) that the French bondholders drove French Prime Minister Léon Gambetta to take the first decisive step, getting the British to sign on to his joint note of 8 January 1882, which enraged the nationalists and which Cromer likens to a candle igniting a mixture of hydrogen and air (Cromer 1908: 234). But Gambetta did not need friends among the bondholders to convince him of the need to tighten French control over Egypt, much as he and his predecessor, Jules Ferry, had consolidated the French hold over Tunisia. Gambetta feared Egypt-based pan-Islamism much as Guy Mollet would fear Nasser's pan-Arabist threat to French North Africa in 1956. By the summer of 1880, moreover, Crédit Foncier had already sold off its Egyptian unified bonds—leaving no more "fundamental obstacle, on the side of the big French interests, to the English take-over of Egypt," according to the most refined Marxist analysis of the French interests (Bouvier 1960: 100). Finally, on 29 July 1882, as the British prepared to strike, Freycinet's government resigned when the French National Assembly by a vote of 417 to 75 rejected its plea for the necessary credits to hold up the French side of an Anglo-French military intervention (Guillen 1984: 163). Ironically, Gambetta's faction voted with the majority against too little too late.

Once Britain had occupied Egypt unilaterally, it still had to accommodate the financial interests of other European parties. The French government, having lost its preeminent position, waged a rear-guard action in the name of the bondholders against British financial planning. However, the incumbent authorities also brandished the French threats before Egyptian government officials as a way of justifying the British presence (Milner 1899: 334–48; cf. Owen 1981: 221). The British in fact did a superb job of putting some of Muhammad Ali's original irrigation investments to good use. The occupier alleviated taxation rates yet doubled government revenues from 1882 to 1913 (Feis 1930: 397) and cut the debt service ratio from 40 to 23 percent of the revenues (Owen 1981: 223). The Anglo-French entente of 1904 put an immediate end to the fuss about the bondholders; meanwhile, French investors, after taking only one-fifth of the loan of 1885, actively sought out other issues on the secondary markets after 1890 or so. After 1904 foreign investment became an "avalanche" (Crouchley 1938: 179), thrusting into joint stock companies as well as the public debt. By 1914 the French held 53.1 percent of the public debt—a greater share than in 1880—together with 50.3 percent of the capital of foreign-owned private companies, and 70.9 percent of the Suez Canal shares (Bouvier et al. 1982: 206; Crouchley 1977: 22, 72). On the eve of World War I, after occupying Egypt for almost 32 years, Britain could claim no more than one-third of the capital invested in joint stock companies, followed by Belgium with 15.5 percent.

More than half the capital of banks and financial companies by this time was in British hands. The French kept about one-quarter of it but preferred to concentrate most of their capital in speculative mortgage companies through which they simply bid up the cost of land and "sucked abroad" part of Egypt's agricultural capital (Owen 1981: 233); Crouchley (1977: 193) estimates that joint stock companies remitted an annual average of more than LE (Egyptian pounds) 3 million over the years 1903–14. Crouchley found it "remarkable" (66) that none went bankrupt in the crash of 1907; England's new financial order was generous to the foreigners. Retail banking was mainly if not exclusively handled by British-owned banks: the National Bank of Egypt, founded in 1898, and the Anglo-Egyptian, reorganized in 1887 (31–32). One result of the war, however, was that the National Bank of Egypt began to issue paper backed by British treasury bonds rather than gold, thereby discouraging hoarding in favor of deposits.

The stage was thus set for an indigenous bank. Grand Mufti Muhammad Abduh had issued a *fetwah* (a formal legal opinion) in 1901 to the effect that interest on commercial loans and deposits was legal. The great irony was that the new Egyptian bank, Banque Misr, would be established in 1920 along the lines of Rudolph Hilferding's model rather than that of the National Bank of Egypt or the Anglo-Egyptian Bank. The Egyptian founder, Talaat Harb, had switched his own deposits to a German bank in 1906 or so, and his original finance company worked in 1911 out of the offices of the Deutsche Hypotheken (German Mortgage) Bank (Davis 1983: 70–76, 93–94). Perhaps the enemy of the British enemy must be the Egyptian nation's friend, but only a relatively liberal "colonial" framework, attuned to the business needs of various great powers, could have tolerated such an experiment. As such, Banque Misr, too, became part of the Egyptian financial legacy that subsequent generations of nationalists would attack or defend on political grounds. But the model was misplaced for other reasons.

Transplanted from an advanced capitalist system to a dependent semicolonial one, the model presupposed the conditions it purported to create: a system of industrial cartels against which the universal banks as described by Hilferding had perfected their oligopolistic defense. Such a system made some sense in semicolonies like Ottoman Turkey, structured around state monopolies. Britain's Egypt, however, was too soft a terrain. It featured too much competition across industries between groups of companies. Some market segmentation by nationality existed; some of the smaller private banks, for instance, catered to particular communities like the Greeks in Alexandria or the Jews in Cairo, but competition also cut across such lines (Vitalis 1995: 32–37). Indeed Talaat Harb, the founder of Banque Misr, owed much of his prominence in business circles before the war to the Suares and Qattawi families of Cairo, and a Qattawi would become vice president of the bank. A further barrier to a Germany on the Nile was Egypt's political structure: from the 1880s until the 1950s, power remained divided among the palace, the British government, and successive generations of nationalists, some of whom could be co-opted by the other poles of power. Political pluralism became too expensive for a single national bank to serve with easy credits.

Other "structural" arguments may partially explain Banque Misr's collapse and reorganization of 1939–40. Imperialist rivalries fueled expectations of war that drew down deposits, leading to the liquidity crisis of August 1939. Egypt's class structure, dominated by large landowning interests, stacked the cards against protection for Misr's fledgling industries. The workforce was undisciplined, and hungry graduates needed jobs. To compensate, the bank was obliged to spend enormous amounts of energy and resources buying political support. But these "structural" factors, while explaining some of the Misr Group's problems, may also explain away too much without specifying why this particular model of banking proved so disastrous. The essential point is that there was too much political pluralism, necessarily overextending the bank's resources when it engaged—as most banks do—in political activity. A number of smaller competing Egyptian banks would not only have been more congruent with the rest of Egypt's economic structure but would also have enabled each to limit its stake in the various political clienteles in the interests of portfolio diversification—as Lebanese banks did from 1970 to 1982 (Moore 1987). Banque Misr and its affiliated enterprises suffered the paradox of having to compete in the economic field with other banks and enterprises while suffering the monopoly of a cow being milked by all its national constituencies.

These generalizations, however, should not obscure the bank's flawed business strategy and systematic falsification, after 1930 or so, of its balance sheets. Using hitherto unpublished documents, a recent study by the bank's former legal counselor confirms earlier allegations of "criminally responsible" management with newly available evidence (Tignor 1984: 164, citing independent British auditors). It is now known that the bank for years had claimed fictitious income (interest on nonperforming loans) and had paid out dividends that eroded first its reserves, then its paid-in capital, and finally some of its deposits by 1939. By the end of 1939 the bank had lost over LE 4 million—double its paid-in capital and reserves (Sālim 1982: 17,

20). Banque Misr's portfolio of securities was tied up in evergreen (i.e., rolled over year after year) short-term advances to companies in the Misr Group, a risky subsitute for capital. Harb might have strengthened his group's capital base in 1927 had he not insisted on keeping 91 percent of the shares of the Misr Spinning and Weaving Company (Tignor 1989: 14–15). The bank retained some of these and other shares of Misr companies to bid up values on the Bourse—a practice more reminiscent of Paris's fabled Banque Universelle described by Émile Zola than of German banking. Salim's data indicate that over LE 5.6 million was tied up in illiquid Misr companies' stock, nonperforming loans, and real estate. Quite contrary to the rosy picture projected in the bank's *Golden Jubilee Report* of 1970 (Tignor 1984: 166), the bank had simply used some of its deposits to set up new companies and pay out dividends to the shareholders (Sālim 1982: 45). Its basic problem was not liquidity—a matter that a central bank might have been able to handle—but solvency.

Yet many Egyptians blamed the British management of the National Bank of Egypt for not bailing out Banque Misr in 1939. British interests were presumed to have plotted the bank's downfall—with the help of an unlikely pro-Italian ally, Ali Mahir, who became prime minister in 1939 and who supposedly held a grudge against Talaat Harb for not having favored him with a board directorship in the past. If British imperialism was at work, however, surely it had worked harder in Palestine, where foreign immigration was actively encouraged, as in Algeria and Tunisia. Despite operating in a far more intensive colonial situation than Banque Misr, the Arab Bank, founded by the Shoman family in Jerusalem in 1930, survived the same difficult period to become one of the largest and most soundly managed banks of the Arab world in the 1990s. Banque Misr received exceptionally favorable treatment from both the British-run National Bank of Egypt and an Egyptian parliament full of the bank's shareholders and other interested parties. Other banks failed. In 1911, in fact, Britain's original Bank of Egypt had been liquidated for committing some of Banque Misr's errors on a much smaller scale. The Bank of Egypt had financed long-term mortgage loans on short-term deposits.

Credit, as Talaat Harb knew well from his experience in selling off the khedivial domains of the Dairah Sanieh Company to Egyptian notables, could be a major weapon in Egyptian politics. As early as 1908, after leaving Mustafa Kamil's National Party for Lutfi al-Sayyid's People's Party, Harb persuaded one of his big clients to cut off all financial aid to the former (Davis 1983: 104). Harb might also have suspected that Egypt's biggest investor, Sir Ernest Cassel, principal financier of the Aswan Dam as well as of the Daireh Sanieh, had engineered the removal of the British high commissioner, Sir Eldon Gorst (Tignor 1966: 369–73). He certainly could not have been unaware of how Prime Minister Ismail Sidky, his principal political supporter in the early 1930s, used the Banque de Crédit Agricole to build up support for his party against the Wafd (Davis 1983: 139–40; Binder 1978: 127). Despite Harb's "profound disenchantment" after 1908 "with what he referred to as *hizbiya* (party factionalism)" (Davis 1983: 105), his Banque Misr became the motor of a vast patronage machine that protected the group's companies and collected subsidies for ill-advised ventures such as the Misr Navigation Company and Misr Airworks. His dreams of monopolist hegemony, however, could have been achieved only in a single-party regime; it is sometimes said that he was a visionary ahead of his time, anticipating Nasser's state capitalism. Banks do indeed reflect the social and political order of which they are a part, in rather specific ways. A competitive banking system reflects a pluralistic capitalist order. Banque Misr became fully reconciled to this order after 1939 and recovered sufficiently to launch one more major project after the war, the Misr Rayon Company. To achieve a monopoly of political power, Nasser would therefore have to disaggregate the very institution that had once embodied nationalist aspirations for monopoly capitalism.

Egypt's pluralistic legacy was as antithetical to an aspiring political monopolist as to monopoly capitalism. It was also antithetic to populist aspirations. Much was amiss in semicolonial Egypt, and neither its competitive economic system nor its political reflections in banking and patronage served the people. However well intentioned their efforts, for instance, the British had lamentably failed to extend credit to broad categories of peasants. The Agricultural Bank, spun off in 1902 from the National Bank of Egypt, had lent usurers most of the funds earmarked for small landholders. As an official of the National Bank of Egypt explained its role: "We are the bankers' bank, in other words we are the usurers' bank. Go to the usurer, pay him from 36 to 60 percent and he will supply you. Next day the Bank takes over the bill or note of the native with, of course, the signature of the usurer or so-called banker on it, and gives him very extensive credit of 5½ to 6½ percent and this is shown in the accounts as 'Bankers' accounts. . . . Twelve of those local usurers are the relations of one of the Directors of the National Bank" (Owen 1981: 232, citing Walid Kazziha). Bankers thus circumvented interest rate restrictions by shifting to the informal sector the relatively low risks but high administrative expenses of making many small loans to poor people. Such phenomena were in no way special to Egypt. As late as 1983, a year of relative peace, none of Lebanon's 80 banks cared to administer a USAID program for small loans, despite records of almost perfect repayment. In semicolonial Egypt, as in much of the Third World today, commercial banks steered clear of consumer lending in favor of elites and expressed few affinities with democratic development. But the Egyptian system had supported political pluralism.

Nasser could not simply abolish political parties, bribe the masses with petty cash to demonstrate for the revolution—as was done at a critical juncture in his showdown with General Naguib in 1954—and expect politically to survive in a pluralistic system. Despite the great popularity he gained as the political victor of the Suez War of 1956, he had no political base outside the military and security services. Efforts to build an official government party from above, through inner circles of Free Officers, their friends, friends of friends, and so on down the line, were not successful. The spoils of war, nationalized French and British enterprises, were managed by the public sector's Economic Organization, which resembled the Misr Group of companies, and until 1960 Nasser tried to placate Egypt's principal capitalists, the 'Abbud group and Misr. A pluralist, autonomous system of private enterprises posed a potential political threat, however, because its resources were available to potential dissidents. It was not in the name of some abstract concept of socialism but for very pragmatic reasons of political defense that Nasser seized these assets in 1961 and reorganized them as sectoral state monopolies rather than as potentially competitive holding companies. As Robert Mabro observed, the slide to socialism was inexorable but probably not premeditated, once Nasser had made his break in 1954 with Egypt's constitutional tradition (Mabro 1974: 128; Waterbury 1983: 77–79; Migdal 1988: 230). The banking system was not only nationalized but also "rationalized" into four big state banks, each to specialize in different forms of credit—sectoral monopolies, in effect. Yet if Egypt's pluralistic legacy was thus almost refracted into its opposite by the victorious nationalists, the new monolith still contained managers whose previous experiences would not be lost. Consequently Egypt's national system would not be quite as impervious to reform in the 1970s and 1980s as Algeria's. Nasser's state socialism only temporarily made its banking system appear more "French" than "English," as if propelling Egypt back to earlier Napoleonic legacies.

High Noon on the Nile

It will be recalled that Sadat's infitah was part of a political strategy that coopted disaffected political elites and multiplied power centers, unleashing them to feed upon the carcass of a stagnating bureaucratic economy. The sharks at the cutting edge, so to speak, of Sadat's attack against Nasser's old order were Egypt's joint venture and private Egyptian commercial and investment banks, the principal beneficiaries of infitah. They escaped the net of Central Bank regulations and infested Egypt's sovereign if murky waters of economic policy-making. Collectively, they sabotaged government policy in areas of vital national interest, such as foreign exchange and domestic credit allocation. But these new banks did not enjoy ties with major business groups, as did their Turkish or Moroccan counterparts. The Egyptian private sector displayed nothing comparable to a Sabancı or Kettani. Trimmed during the Nasser years, the other enterprises of the bourgeoisie remained as fragmented as its banking system. The banks lacked the muscle and discipline of methodical oligopolists. Established during the boom years of the late 1970s and early 1980s, few of them had long-term strategies, much less the low discount rates of oligopolists who work prudently in a long shadow of future expectations. Egypt's banks had opened at high noon.

The Research Department of the National Bank of Egypt (NBE), Egypt's oldest bank, recently reviewed the impact of the new banks on Egypt's banking system: "The increase in the number of banking units had some positive effects, . . . improved banking services as a result of tough competition and the introduction of modern technology. However, . . . some of the banking units . . . plunged into rash competition to attract the biggest number of clients . . . [regardless of] transgressing established practices and conventions of the banking business. . . . A large number of adventurers with no prior experience entered the market, stimulated by the desire to make quick profits [and encouraged by the direct and indirect effects of the second oil boom, 1978–82]" (National Bank of Egypt 42:4 (1989): 242–43). The result was financial pluralism, but much of the new private finance capital was at risk. While it supported multiple power centers under Sadat and in the early Mubarak years, some of its adventurous manipulators faced bankruptcy in the early 1990s, once the new financial reforms discussed in chapter 2 took effect. In fact the principal beneficiaries of Mubarak's "second infitah" might be foreign banks, not private sector Egyptian establishments. The only commercial private sector banks that might have been sufficiently big and healthy to promote political pluralism were the Islamic banks.

Table 7–1 offers a snapshot of Egypt's new commercial banking system as it appeared at midyear 1989. The infitah banks are classified by capital structure rather than by the Central Bank's more formal categories of "commercial banks" and "investment and business banks." The investment and business sector, devised in 1975 to mobilize foreign capital and domestic savings for financing long-term investment, had "failed to perform the role assigned," concentrating instead on financing foreign trade and short-term lending to the trade and services sectors, just like most of the new commercial banks (National Bank of Egypt 42:4 (1989): 255). After 1976 there was little to distinguish the investment banks from the commercial banks. Law 97 of 1976 granted Egyptians the right to have accounts in foreign currencies and thus gave the commercial banks equal access to foreign exchange. The investment banks' special exemptions until 1985 from other regulations were perhaps more theoretical than real because the Central Bank had lost much of the staff that, with more experience and incentives, might have implemented them.

The first category of infitah banks listed in table 7–1 are the major joint ventures established by public sector banks with major American banks in 1975 and 1976. Commercial International Bank, Misr International Bank, and the Egyptian American Bank were in a special league. Each was relatively profitable, professionally managed, and committed to modern techniques of credit analysis and strategic planning. A second category consisted of other joint ventures between Egyptian public sector and foreign banks. They tended to be smaller and more focused on particular foreign trade niches—with Britain, France, Spain, Romania, and the like—though they also lent on the Egyptian market, with mixed results. Banks belonging in this category, essentially owned by other banks, merged almost imperceptibly into a third category, which included private Egyptian investors. Misr Exterior, for instance, was a joint venture of Banque Misr and various Spanish banks, but private individuals held 6 percent of the shares, and Hassan Sayed Marei was a board member. Cairo Far East, a joint venture of various Korean banks, the Banque du Caire, and a public sector insurance company, also grouped private investors, including its founder and chief executive officer, Dr. Ahmed Abou Ismail, a former finance minister and parliamentary spokesman of the New Wafd Party.

Banks in the third category were founded after 1977, when Egyptian shareholders were accorded the same protection granted to foreign investors in 1974. The Nile Bank was the only one exclusively funded by private Egyptian capital, much of it from a single family, but the others acted like private banks and could make public sector capital serve the interests of the private shareholders. The National Bank for Development, it will be recalled, became a slush fund for dubious projects of benefit to Osman Ahmed Osman, among others. Many of the "adventurers" observed by the NBE's

Table 7-1. Egypt's commercial and business banks, 1989

1989 Percentages of	Deposits	Loans	Equity
Public sector commercial banks	64.5%	56.9%	23.3%
Banque Misr	22.9%	21.0%	5.6%
National Bank of Egypt	21.0%	19.1%	7.8%
Banque du Caire	11.3%	8.4%	6.6%
Bank of Alexandria	9.3%	8.3%	3.3%
Infitah banks			
I. Big banking joint ventures	9.8%	8.2%	17.8%
Misr International Bank	4.5%	4.3%	4.9%
Commercial International Bank (ex Chase)	2.8%	2.1%	8.2%
Egyptian American Bank	2.6%	1.8%	4.7%
II. Other banking joint ventures	4.4%	6.8%	17.5%
Arab Investment Bank	1.0%	1.5%	1.6%
Cairo Barclays	0.8%	1.1%	0.7%
Misr Iran Development Bank	0.6%	0.8%	5.4%
Misr American International Bank	0.6%	0.8%	1.2%
National Société Générale	0.4%	0.7%	1.3%
Export Development Bank of Egypt	0.3%	0.7%	2.9%
Caire Paris	0.3%	0.3%	0.5%
Crédit International d'Egypte	0.2%	0.6%	1.0%
Misr Romanian	0.2%	0.2%	3.1%
III. Banks with some Egyptian private ownership			
A. General	13.5%	17.5%	24.9%
Suez Canal Bank	2.7%	2.8%	3.8%
Bank of Credit and Commerce Misr	2.4%	1.2%	1.1%
Delta Bank	1.2%	1.2%	1.4%
Nile Bank	0.8%	0.9%	3.3%
Alexandria Kuwait International Bank	0.8%	0.9%	0.9%
Misr Exterior	0.7%	0.7%	1.6%
Egypt Gulf Bank	0.7%	0.8%	0.9%
Egypt Arab African Bank	0.6%	0.9%	1.9%
Hong Kong Egyptian Bank	0.5%	0.5%	0.7%
Alexandria Commercial Maritime Bank	0.5%	0.5%	1.6%
Al Watany	0.5%	0.6%	0.9%
Société Arabe Internationale (SAIB)	0.4%	0.3%	2.0%
Cairo Far East	0.2%	0.3%	0.9%
National Development Bank	1.1%	1.8%	1.8%
(includes 17 provincial affiliates)	0.6%	0.7%	1.7%
Dakahlia Development Bank	0.3%	0.4%	0.3%
Housing & Development Bank	0.2%	3.8%	1.6%

Table 7-1—*continued*

1989 Percentages of	Deposits	Loans	Equity
B. Professional Unions	1.0%	1.7%	1.5%
BCD Tegariyoon	0.5%	0.7%	0.6%
Mohandes Bank	0.5%	1.0%	0.4%
Workers Bank	0.1%	0.1%	0.5%
C. Islamic	6.8%	8.9%	15.0%
Faisal Islamic Bank of Egypt	6.2%	7.1%	8.7%
Islamic International Bank of Investment and Development	0.5%	1.5%	4.3%
Egyptian Saudi Finance Bank	0.1%	0.3%	2.0%
Total of new banks (millions of LE)	19,888	15,167	2,447
Grand total	56,033	35,227	3,191
Central Bank of Egypt totals[a]	55,832	34,566	2,904
Big Arab "offshore" banks			
Arab African International Bank	1,443	3,288	253
Arab International Bank	4,478	1,425	637
Specialized banks			
Industrial Development Bank	365	0	65
Principal Bank for Develoment and Agricultural Credit	1,713	1,629	299
Arab Land Bank	778	753	42
Crédit Foncier	1,035	1,138	70
Nasser Social Bank	185	313	140

Foreign branches

American Express Bank	Oman Bank
National Bank of Abu Dhabi	National Bank of Pakistan
Citibank	National Bank of Greece
Bank of America	Jammal Trust Bank
Bank of Credit and Commerce International	Crédit Suisse
Bank Saderat Iran	Crédit Lyonnais
Banca Commerciale Italiana	National Bank of Oman
Arab Bank	Middle East Bank
Bank Melli Iran	Banque Paribas
Lloyds Bank	Rafidain Bank
The Bank of Nova Scotia	National Bank of Sudan
Manufacturers Hanover (offshore branch)	

Sources: Directory, Egypt's banks, 1990–91; author's database of commercial banks.
a. Central Bank of Egypt, *Economic Review* 31:4 (1990–91): 132, 140.

Research Department clustered in this third category and serviced influential business networks. Two subsets were of special interest: the banks established by professional syndicates and trade unions, which officially integrated key components of Egyptian civil society with the financial system, and the Islamic banks, equally rich in influence and potential business networks.

In addition to the commercial and "investment and business" banks, which were free to make transactions in Egyptian pounds as well foreign currencies, other banks, until 1993 permitted to operate only in foreign currencies, are appended to table 7–1. First come the two banks founded prior to 1975 as offshore consortia of the Egyptian government with other Arab states. Neither of the consortia was authorized to deal in Egyptian pounds, but both were major players on the local as well as regional scenes. The Arab African International Bank, founded in 1964, was integrated in 1982 into Egypt's investment and business sector, subject theoretically to the supervision of the Central Bank. The major shareholders in 1986 were the Central Bank of Egypt (43.6 percent), Kuwait's Ministry of Finance (43.6 percent), and Iraq's Rafadain Bank (10 percent), but Jordan, Algeria, Saudi Arabia, Qatar, and "other Arab individuals and authorities" also had fractions of the capital. The Arab International Bank (AIB), founded by treaty between Egypt, Libya, and Oman in 1974, remained exempt from all Egyptian banking regulations but competed with the others for foreign exchange deposits of individuals as well as other banks. Its capital included contributions from Abu Dhabi and Qatar as well as from the founders, and 8 percent of the capital came from private individuals, Egyptians as well as Gulf Arabs. AIB also participated in the capital of local banks. For instance, one board member, former Economics Minister Hassan Abbas Zaki, represented the private shareholders but also served as chief executive officer of the Société Arabe Internationale de Banque (SAIB), which AIB had helped finance. Various specialized financial institutions, wholly owned by the Egyptian state, complete the picture of Egyptian banking. None is a commercial bank, although efforts were under way in 1992 to detach the largest of them, the Principal Bank for Development and Agricultural Credit, from its home ministry. Also appended to Table 7-1 are the 22 branches of foreign banks in the order of their arrival to Egypt between 1974 and 1983. The notorious Bank of Credit and Commerce International, for instance, entered Egypt on the heels of Bank of America, with which it had been closely associated. Some of the foreign banks would become more integrated into Egypt's commercial banking system once they achieved their goal of operating in Egyptian pounds, permitted under the banking law of

1 June 1992. A 23rd foreign bank, Manufacturers Hanover, operated an offshore branch.

This snapshot of Egyptian banking in 1989 underlines the continuing preponderance of Egypt's four public sector banks: they held 64.5 percent of the deposits. At first glance it would appear that infitah had spawned Lilliputians quite incapable of tying Gulliver's hands and redirecting credit to their little clienteles. However, the public sector banks were providing only 57 percent of the loans, less than their share of deposits, while some of the privately owned banks, notably the development banks and the Islamic banks, were lending out more than their share. Credit allocation substantially shifted in the early 1980s from the public to the private sector (Moore, 1986: 641). Even so, from 1988 to 1992 the banks increased their lending to the public sector companies from 34 to almost 41 percent of the credits offered to business enterprises (Central Bank of Egypt, *Economic Review* 31:4 (1990/91): 136, 144; 33:1 (1992/1993): 112, 120). Public sector banks also lent substantially to the private sector, however, whereas infitah banks risked little of their funds in that area.

Under closer inspection, any formal distinction between private and public sectors is difficult to draw. Such a distinction implies that capital structure determines management and policies, omitting the thorny issues of principals, agents, and "agency costs," such as monitoring the managers. The actions of bank managers do not necessarily reflect the interests of shareholders—whether government ministries, parastatal enterprises, foreign banks, foreign public entities, private enterprises, or private individuals—Egyptian, Arab or foreign. A branch manager from an old landowning family told me that every loan in Egypt has its price and that every lending officer excepting himself was corrupt. His oblique confession need not be taken literally and should be put in context. His branch, affiliated with the BCCI, had been closed down, and the manager was besieged by creditors. Nevertheless, his comment highlights the issue of agency costs in Egyptian financial bureaucracies. The public sector holds a preponderant share of the capital but lacks any commensurate influence on the infitah banks. The internal management of the Big Four is also problematic. "The state" is not a unitary actor, and the Lilliputians have intensified its multiple schizophrenia.

The Structure of the Infitah's Finance Capital

Table 7–1 shows how undercapitalized Egypt's four public sector banks became: despite carrying a majority of deposits and loans, they held only 23.3

percent of the equity of the commercial banking system in 1989. In fact they were so undercapitalized—their core capital covering only 3.7 percent of their loans, not to mention other risky assets[1]—that the government finally, in 1991, injected into Banque Misr and the National Bank of Egypt LE 1 billion each of new capital, while their smaller sisters each received LE 750 million. The capital injection brought the public sector banks' ratio of capital to outstanding loans in mid-1991 up to 11.4 percent, and the Central Bank's chief bank controller claimed (interview, 28 December 1992) that their capital covered 8.3 percent of their risk assets, meeting international standards, while that of the other commercial banks covered 12.1 percent of their risk assets.

While the capital base of the formal public sector had been less than one-third that of the formal private sector in 1989, the state was nevertheless very much a part of the private sector's capital as well. It constituted 100 percent of the Egyptian capital of banks included in the first and second categories of infitah banks, and of course Egypt was the dominant partner, legally required to hold at least 51 percent of the shares in each of these joint ventures. As Table 7–1 indicates, the two categories of public sector joint ventures with foreign banks respectively aggregated 17.8 and 17.5 percent of the banking system's capital. In other words, the public sector still directly controlled 35.3 percent of the capital in addition to the 23.3 percent—greatly increased in 1991—on its own books. By contrast, the banks having some element of private Egyptian ownership had controlled less than 45 percent of the finance capital before the public sector increase.

Formal government control of finance capital, moreover, did not end with the Big Four and their banking joint ventures. The capital of the public sector banks was only part of the Egyptian state's investment in commercial banks. In addition to the capital of the Big Four reinvested in other joint venture banks, various other state enterprises contributed to their equity, and "the state" in this sense dominated the capital structure of most of the other "private sector" banks established under Law 43 of 1974 as well. Many of the "private and joint venture" banks were almost entirely owned by public sector institutions. The Suez Canal Bank ranked second, after Faisal Islamic Bank, in both loans and deposits among banks having some Egyptian private ownership, and its ownership was typical of third-sector banks. Its major shareholders, in order of importance, were Arab International Bank, Misr Insurance Co. (LE 1.45 million), Banque Misr (LE 1.25 million), Banque du Caire (LE 1.25 million), Bank of Alexandria (LE 1.25 million), National Bank of Egypt (LE 1.1 million), the pension funds of the Suez Canal Authority (LE 550,000), and the Arab Contractors Company (LE

550,000). Since the total paid-in capital was only LE 10 million, the remainder of capital belonging to the Arab International Bank and to 21 individual private shareholders (Gillespie 1984: 129) amounted to LE 2.6 million. Since AIB held at least LE 1.45 million, the private shareholders owned no more than LE 1.15 million, barely over 10 percent of the total shares. Osman Ahmed Osman personally contributed only LE 175,000, and Abdel Azim Lokma, the board member who represented the private shareholders, had LE 250,000 (Imām 1986: 242–48, 262, 266, 279–328, esp. 293–95).

Few of the banks in this category offered breakdowns of their ownership in published annual reports. Available evidence suggests that the bulk of the capital came from public institutional investors on the Egyptian side, not private investors. Figure 7–1 tentatively estimates the share of private capital in each of the banks. For purposes of analysis, subsidiaries of public enterprises that are legally considered to be private sector, such as the Arab Contractors Investment Fund, were counted as contributing public, not private capital. Technically the Arab Contractors Investment Fund was a private sector company, but 95 percent of its capital came from the public sector Arab Contractors Co. and only 5 percent from the private sector Arab Contractors Employees Fund. Noting that Arab Contractors Investment undertook most of its Law 43 private investment projects with the participation of one or both of its related companies, Kate Gillespie observed that "opposition could well question whether Arab Contractors, technically a public company, could have redirected such considerable money and management time into the private sector without Mr. Osman's political influence" (1984: 128).

Only the Nile Bank and the banks of the Islamic sector were purely private sector in the sense that they were wholly owned by private individuals. Al Watany Bank was almost exclusively private. Private Egyptians also held about 51 percent of the shares of the Hong Kong Egyptian Bank, a joint venture with the Hong Kong Shanghai Banking Corporation. Egypt Gulf Bank (EGB) probably came next, with roughly 47 percent of its shares in the hands of "Egyptian and Arab businessmen," an additional 9.5 percent held by Kuwaiti family companies, and 9 percent by the Tunis International Bank, an offshore bank set up by the Arab African International Bank to launder its losses. The Banque du Caire and Misr Insurance together owned only 19.5 percent of the EGB's capital. Alexandria Kuwait International Bank also had a strong dose of private capital, with 21 percent coming from "individuals mostly Egyptians working in Kuwait," 31 percent from the Egyptian public sector, and the rest from Kuwait. The Société Arabe Inter-

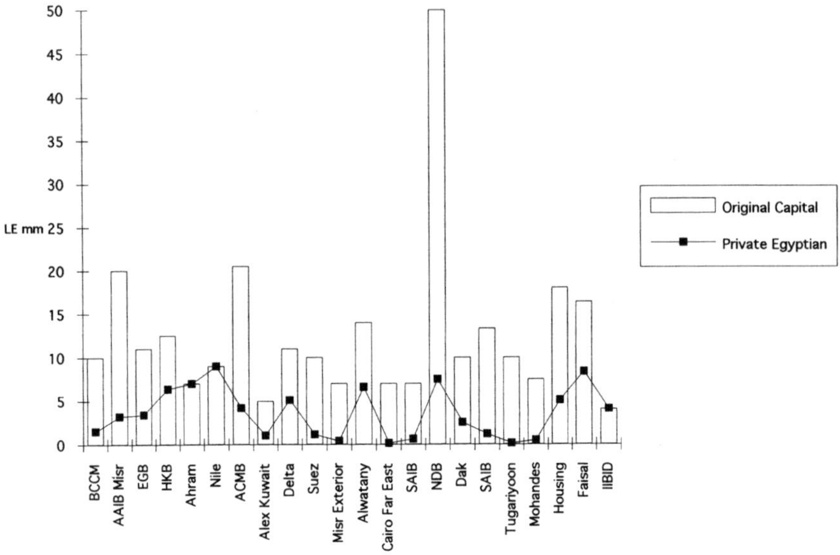

Fig. 7.1. Private Egyptian component of third sector banks. *Source:* author's database of commercial banks.

nationale de Banque, on the other hand, drew only 8.8 percent of its capital from private Egyptians, and 42.2 percent from the public sector (including the Arab Contractors Investment Fund). The Bank of Credit and Commerce Misr, a joint venture with the corrupt Bank of Credit and Commerce International, drew on the National Bank of Egypt more than upon private investors (Imām, 1986: 244). The Egyptian private sector capital invested in many of the third-sector banks seems to have been quite small, often under 10 percent of the total.

Yet this third sector had attracted most of the capital deployed into commercial banking by Egypt's new capitalist class. Private investors seemed quite willing to take minority positions in banks apparently controlled by the state's institutional shareholders. Perhaps tying up much of one's capital in a bank was unnecessary if the majority shareholders—"the state"—were sleeping partners. With only 1.7 percent of the shares, Osman Ahmed Osman could orient the credit policies of the Suez Canal Bank to suit his multitudinous business interests as long as he retained political influence. The chairman of the bank was one of his close associates (Springborg 1989: 84). Also at his beck and call, at least in his political heyday, were the Mohandes Bank, the National Bank of Development, and possibly two other banks in which he was a shareholder, Nile Bank and Delta International.

On a less grandiose scale, with just LE 50,000 (Imām 1986: 280), 0.7 percent of the bank's paid-up capital, Dr. Ahmed Abou Ismail controlled Cairo Far East until 1991.

In aggregate, the public sector joint ventures (categories 1 and 2) were much better capitalized than the other infitah banks. The leading banking joint ventures set the standard. One confidential bank rating service considered only the Commercial International Bank (CIB) and Egyptian American Bank (EAB) to be "strong. . . . [with] no cause for concern." If their loan portfolios were indeed the soundest, it followed that any bank operating in the Egyptian environment, including their principal competitor, the Misr International Bank (MIB), probably required capital cover of at least 25 percent of outstanding loans to meet international standards of capital adequacy, not to mention adequate provisioning for nonperforming loans. CIB and EAB both made such provisions but MIB did not.

The other joint ventures with foreign banks collectively met this standard, but there were big variations among banks, depending upon their lines of business and the quality of their risk assets, including contingent liabilities. The Misr Iran Development Bank seemed well capitalized but was burdened with many risky assets, including long-term investment projects. The Export Development Bank of Egypt was a well-managed joint venture of the four public sector banks. The other highly capitalized bank, Misr Romania, had apparently vegetated while Romania collapsed. Ahmad Fuad, Nasser's original political appointee to the board of Banque Misr in 1957, had been retired as chairman in 1982 but continued to preside over Misr Romania until 1986. Other banks in this category seemed to be almost as poor as their Egyptian public sector parents.

Cairo Barclays was not only the largest of the joint ventures but also the most undercapitalized. It had thrived in the early 1980s but then, like many of the new banks, it fell on hard times with nonperforming loans. It declared losses in 1985 and was still plowing much of its earnings back into provisions for nonperforming loans in 1990. Misr American, too, had experienced difficulties that may account for the low capitalization, and Arab Investment Bank was in dire straits. The French seem simply to have been more hesitant than the Americans to earmark more capital to Egypt, perhaps at the expense of more familiar hunting grounds in Morocco and Tunisia. Less easy to explain by purely banking criteria are the capitalization ratios of the banks that include private Egyptian shareholders.

Most of these third-sector banks were considerably less capitalized Commercial International bank, Egyptian American, or the Export Development Bank of Egypt. The total capital of the third sector covered less than 15 percent of its loans, although its loan portfolios tended to be much more problematic than those of the premier joint ventures. Among third-sector banks, only Nile Bank, Cairo Far East, and Alexandria Commercial Maritime Bank, together with the business and investment bank Société Arabe Internationale de Banque, had capital to cover more than 25 percent of their loans. Among the rest of the private sector banks, only the Egyptian Saudi Finance House was highly capitalized, being newly reorganized and converted to Islamic practices. The banks of the professional syndicates were as seriously undercapitalized as the four public sector flagships had been before the government refinanced them in 1991. Only the tiny Workers Bank was well capitalized. Given the chance, most private Egyptian investors apparently preferred milking banks for loans to investing in them.

Sāmia Sa'īd Imām's invaluable study, *Who Owns Egypt?*, offers further evidence of the investment strategies of Egypt's new capitalist class. She painstakingly extracted from the official records the names and shareholdings of the owners of 534 companies established between 1974 and 1982 under Law 43 of 1974. Of the 15,000 names, she selected 1,000 for closer scrutiny on the advice of knowledgeable informants. Her sample of companies, with an aggregate capital of LE 1,952 million, of which 1,363 million was Egyptian, almost precisely corresponded to the totals registered by Ministry of Investment and Industry (cf. Moore 1986: 639) of fully operationalized investment projects. The public sector was responsible for 53.2 percent of the Egyptian investment and placed 37 percent of its share into banking and an additional 10 percent into related financial services (Imām 1986: 168–69). Imām did not analyze the distribution of the rest of the Egyptian investment, amounting to LE 638 million, but she provided data on the shareholdings of the 252 individuals in her sample who had accumulated shares worth at least LE 100,000 between 1975 and 1982. The sum of these holdings turned out to be about LE 150 million, almost one-quarter of the entire private Egyptian investment in Public Law 43 companies during the period. The sample's investments in banks also approached one-quarter of the private Egyptian capital portrayed in figure 7–1.

Imām's sample is the closest approximation to the core of Egypt's new capitalist class that could be documented. It included Osman Ahmed Osman, in a league by himself, and many other prominent businessmen and -women. All of the "four sharks" (Ibrahim Ahmed Kamel, Medhat Mohamed El Tounsy, Moustafa El Beleidy, and Mohamed Abdel Mohsen Sheta) unanimously identified in 1992 as Egypt's leading private sector "group," were included, as was Said El Tawil, the head of the Egyptian Businessmen's Association. So was Hatem Niazi Mostafa, mentioned in American circles as one of Egypt's top entrepreneurs. The detailed appendices of shareholdings included most of the banks mentioned in figure 7–1. The only ones missing from Imām's listings were Al Watany, Misr Exterior, Société Arabe Internationale de Banque, some of the provincial development banks, those of the professional unions, and the Islamic sector, which had mobilized considerable amounts of Egypt private capital. Within Imām's sample, to be sure, some of the individuals who had purchased the requisite LE 100,000 worth of shares did not really qualify as core capitalists. The investments in banks made by a couple of engineering consultants personally known to the writer, for instance, could be best interpreted as public relations expenses to gain better access to credit for their consulting firm (Moore 1994: 174). But they, too, represented the financial logic of infitah. As another engineer explains, "The category of engineering-consultants and their satellites rejoins that of businessmen and bankers, as they are among the wealthy, upwardly mobile classes" (Hanna 1992: 54).

Evidently Imām's sample did not invest much of its funds in banks. Whereas the public sector had committed 37 percent of its Public Law 43 investment to banking, the private individuals and families included in the sample invested a bare 11 percent of their shareholdings in these risky ventures. Their investment portfolio mirrored that of Egyptian private capital at large, for the total private capital of these banks added up to about 10.3 percent of the total private capital invested between 1975 and 1982. In other words, the heavy investors identified by Sāmia Sa'īd Imām were no more likely than the general population of shareholders to invest in banks. Their allocations of capital further confirm their thirst for financial leverage, using banks not as nuclei of family holding companies, like Sabancı in Turkey, but rather as points of access to easy loans. The entrepreneurs of the infitah were out to milk the system. The ten heaviest investors, among them Osman Ahmed Osman, placed less than 4 percent of their portfolio with banks. Osman himself was on the high side, with almost 7 percent invested in the Suez Canal Bank, Delta Bank, and Nile Bank. He also wielded considerable influence in a number of other banks through his Arab Contractors Company, nationalized in 1963 and nominally still part of the public sector, but his financial strategy minimized his personal holdings in banks. Osman had also qualified as a founder of the Faisal Islamic Bank of Egypt by investing a mere $25,000 (Galloux 1993: 101).

Analysis of the sample also confirms that the private component of ownership in the infitah companies remained highly fragmented and dispersed.

Egypt's new capitalist class had apparently not concentrated much capital in large family holdings. Despite much talk in the local press of Egypt's new "fat cat" millionaires, the "new bourgeoisie" appears not to have concentrated much of its wealth in ownership of the means of production. Despite concentrations of capital prior to the nationalizations of 1961–63, Egypt's second wave had not yet caught up with Morocco's, much less Turkey's. While the sample does not shed light on the total holdings of the individuals concerned, it does offer a reasonably reliable cross section of shareholdings of Egypt's new capitalist class. Osman, who owned a paltry LE 3 million of the sample's shares, had obviously smuggled most of his fortune into overseas investments. Unlike a Sabancı or Kettani, he did not construct a major group in Egypt. Some combines of capitalists were emerging in the 1990s, but they remained small in comparison with Moroccan or Turkish groups. Osman's group was launched in 1973, when his eldest son, just graduated from Cairo's Faculty of Engineering, refused to take a routine company job. Established for his children, the group was smaller than many others—and rent with family discord by 1990—although Osman was reputed to be the richest man in Egypt. The new Egyptian capitalists had yet to concentrate their capital, much less develop the business empires of an Abbud Pasha (Vitalis 1990) or the original Banque Misr.

Taking some methodological liberties, it is interesting to compare the structure of emergent Egyptian capitalism with that of Morocco. Saâdi, it will be recalled, concluded that 58 Moroccan families held 55 percent of the industrial capital that was in private Moroccan hands. From Sāmia Saʿīd Imām's data it was possible to identify 252 Egyptian shareholders holding 23.5 percent of the private Egyptian funds invested in Public Law 43 companies between 1975 and 1982. While Saâdi focused exclusively on industrial and manufacturing capital, Imām included all Public Law 43 investment, of which only 23 percent qualified as industrial (Moore 1986: 639). In Morocco, as in Egypt and most other Third World countries, however, capitalists tended to diversify their investment portfolios rather than focus on a single sector. The Moroccan families controlling private industry could therefore be assumed to control other sectors as well. Clearly the acquisitions of the Egyptian capitalists between 1975 and 1982 were more widely shared than the French industrial capital that was Moroccanized in the mid-1970s, as figure 7–2 graphically demonstrates. Egypt's top 58 families in Imām's sample accounted for only 16.5 percent of the Egyptian investment, and the top 58 shareholders in third-sector banks had about 15 percent of the estimated total of private Egyptian capital.

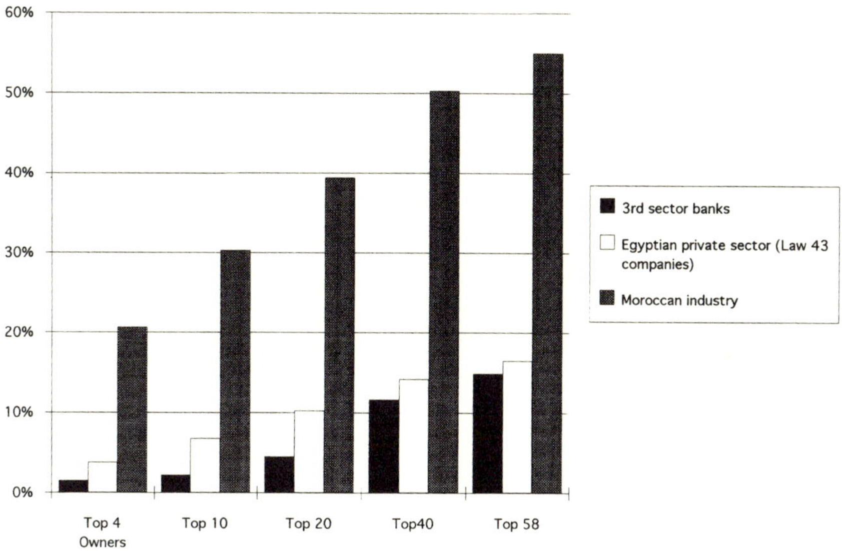

Fig. 7.2. Concentrations of private capital by top owners in Egypt and Morocco. *Sources:* Imām 1986; Saâdi 1989: 192.

Figure 7–3 compares the respective concentrations of capital within each of these samples of top private owners. The top 58 Moroccans not only acquired more private industrial capital than their Egyptian counterparts but also concentrated greater shares of it in their upper echelons. Figure 7–3 reflects the fact that the top four Moroccans owned 37.5 percent of holdings of the top 58 families, whereas Egypt's top four owned only 23 percent of the much smaller proportion of shares held by its top 58 families, and shareholding was further dispersed in the banking sector. If Morocco was the land of oligopoly and vast "group" holdings, there might be room for more competition in Egypt.

Further analysis of the Egyptian sample showed that there was no significant relationship—negative or positive—between investing in banking and in other shareholdings. Only one of the top 10 investors was also among the top 10 in banking. Osman, with a total personal investment of LE 210,000 in three banks, ranked only 22nd among the bank investors, was preceded by people like Hamed Sayeh, a former minister of the economy who became chief executive officer of the Hong Kong Egyptian Bank and received shares as part of his generous compensation package. But whether it was a quirk of the sample or part of its design, the bankers were more influential than their total volume of share acquisitions suggested.

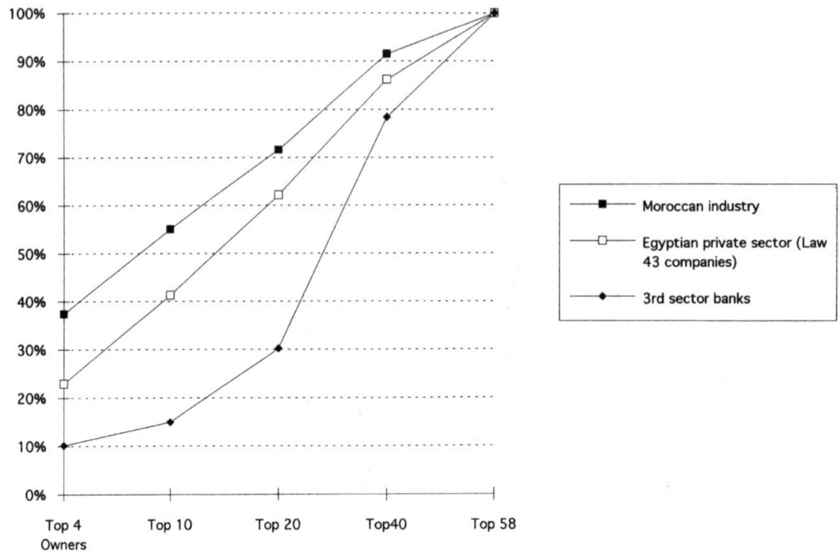

Fig. 7.3. Distribution of capital among top owners. *Sources:* Imām 1986; Saâdi 1989: 192.

Heading the list was Said El Tawil, the chairman of the Egyptian Businessmen's Association in 1992. His principal lines of business were dairy products; the design, production, and erection of steel structure and buildings; the import of industrial goods, sewing machines, and turnkey garment projects; and the export of juices and dairy products (Egyptian Businessmen's Association 1992: 1), but 77.5 percent of his investments recorded between 1975 and 1982 went into the Nile Bank, the Egyptian Arab African Bank, and the Hong Kong Egyptian Bank (HKEB). Indeed, all five of the top bank investors placed their money with the HKEB. Immediately following Tawil came Moustafe Beleidy, Ibrahim Ahmed Kamel, and Mohamed Abdel Mohsen Sheta, three of the "four sharks" mentioned earlier. The fourth, Medhat Mohamed El Tounsy, also had a share of HKEB's paid-in capital. They founded an export consortium, UNIMEG, to market their cosmetics, detergents, and other consumer goods. Sometimes also known as the Beleidy Group, they were unanimously considered in 1992 to be the private sector's leading group. Their political leader, Ibrahim Kamel, enjoyed close relations through Osama El Baz to President Mubarak and influential security officials. Kamel flew the government's economic team in his private plane to Russia and Central Asia to prospect for Egyptian export markets in late 1991. Moustafa Beleidy, with the largest business base in the group, had a less political image than Kamel but was no wallflower. He had been privileged to participate in Dar Mayo, Sadat's personal propaganda arm, with fellow shareholders Sadat, Mubarak, Osman Ahmed Osman, and various other business notables, as well as public and private sector banks (Imām 1986: 142).

While overrepresented among the sample's top 10 bank investors, Hong Kong Egyptian bank was clearly a magnet for high-powered money. So also were the Suez Canal Bank, Egypt Gulf Bank, Egyptian Arab African Bank, and the Nile Bank, to which the sample's top 10 in total shareholdings gravitated. The eleventh largest investor, who was not a member of the Egyptian Businessmen's Association, put his money into BCCI's Egyptian affiliate, as did a number of politicians whom BCCI had perhaps bribed as part of its entry fee into Egypt. Yet with the exception of the Nile Bank, which remained firmly under the control of one family, these banks seemed less interested in profits than in prestige and growth. Their rationale was perhaps more political than economic. Extending their patronage took priority over assessing risks and balancing risk with returns on investment. The banks competed vigorously for deposits that could then be doled out to their shareholders' networks of clients, patrons, and friends. The private shareholders paid in relatively little capital to enjoy the privileges, and institutional shareholders could be willing accomplices as long as key administrators were included in the networks. Private individuals simply wanted access to easy credit, not control of finance capital. Infitah produced lots of loose finance capital in the extended sense of bank credit, largely by converting trusting depositors' cash into short-term evergreen facilities for Egypt's new capitalist class.

Formal ownership was not a reliable measure of influence on credit allocation in any given bank, for management did not necessarily pursue the interests of all the shareholders, much less their collective interest in the long-term profitability of the enterprise. It favored influential private shareholders and administrators, not abstract institutional partners. A private entrepreneur could maximize credit by investing a small amount of capital in a set of banks. Buying into a bank was like a marketing expense; getting a piece of a number of banks purchased access to finance capital in the extended sense employed by Hilferding: working capital, often in the form either of overdrafts or of renewable short-term loans, those evergreen facilities favored across the entire debt crescent.

Buying into a private bank did not assure the entrepreneur of access to easy credits from that particular bank. In fact the Central Bank limited any given shareholder's access to credit, and by 1992 international financial institutions were developing the Central Bank's capacity to monitor and enforce the regulations. But commercial banks could promote their respective shareholders and favored clients to other banks. Moreover, the pattern of cooperation, as well as competition for good clients, cut across the various banking sectors to include public sector and joint bank ventures as well as banks having private shareholders. Public sector and institutionally owned banks deployed the lion's share of finance capital. The new bourgeoisie still depended primarily on public money to finance their private projects.

In 1989 the public sector disbursed most of Egypt's domestic credit. The bourgeoisie's third-sector banks had not yet acquired a financial surface large enough to cover the needs of private sector projects. Even if they had financed the private sector exclusively, they would have provided less than half the credit received in 1989 by the private sector. On the further assumption that the Big Four government banks were the sole purveyors of credit to the government and public sector enterprises, the Big Four would still have provided 27.8 percent of the private sector's loans, and their institutional joint ventures of the first and second sectors would have contributed an additional 25.3 percent.[2] On these stringent assumptions, the banks having some private Egyptian shareholders could not have produced more than 47 percent of the private sector's loans. In reality, investment and business banks, some of which were third sector, allocated about 22 percent of their collective loan portfolio to the government and public sector enterprises (Central Bank of Egypt, *Economic Review* 31:4 (1990/91): 144). To the extent that third-sector banks were involved, the amounts they could lend to the private sector were correspondingly diminished.

The public and private sectors, however, have never been distinct blocs of interests. Private entrepreneurs could also be public sector administrators. The "private" sector, as the dealings of Osman Ahmed Osman illustrate, largely served to convert political influence into personal wealth. In the banking sector the private investors perfected ways of converting power into money and "finance capital." They benefited from two sorts of leverage. Within the sectors they owned jointly with the public sector and foreign interests, they extracted most of the credit, and they then more than doubled their take by borrowing directly from the institutionally owned banks. In other words, they stretched their "private sector" banks' lending capacities and then obtained matching funds or better from the four big public sector banks and their joint ventures. Of course their myriads of transactions did not always reflect the aggregate picture, but private capital in general depended on "the state" much as little pins need a pincushion to stay upright. The Big Four's gigantic branch networks still attracted over half the deposits of the private sector (including private households) and together with the joint ventures commanded more than 70 percent of them. Private sector enterprises then fed upon them. In the last analysis, Egyptian capitalism has depended heavily upon "the state" for its finance capital.

Bankers' Strategies

A comparative analysis of the balance sheets and income statements of Egyptian banks sheds further light on the financial strategies serving Egypt's new capitalist class. Many of the banks seem to have allocated credits on personal or "political" rather than economic grounds. Private entrepreneurs were not on the whole interested in controlling bank management with their capital. Instead, they offered banks crumbs of their own capital, better understood as marketing expenses, to get access to cheap credit. Operating at high noon, rather than in the lengthy shadows of expectations, they sought quick returns, in the form of finance capital for other projects, irrespective of the impact upon the lending institutions. Osman Ahmed Osman had pioneered strategies of accumulating private profits and capital at the expense of public institutions. Under Nasser's old command economy, Osman had extracted surpluses from scarce materials and machinery, but the banking system offered greater leverage and scope for legitimate as well as fraudulent operations. Manipulating money was easier than cornering markets for scarce imports or falsifying invoices, and banking offered plenty of scope for many lesser Osmans. His National Bank of Development was a microcosm of the financial infitah. Not only did grateful provincial capitalists call on his services for purchasing marked-up machinery and materials, but they also spawned myriads of subcontractors. One of their escapades was an LE 2 million desert reclamation project. The first phase was to build a huge high concrete fence around the property (construction contracted out to a relative, of course). The entrepreneur went to the bank for more money to complete the project but then disappeared, money in hand, leaving a very big and well-protected sand lot. Writ large, here was the dark side of infitah, scandals of capital flight associated with Tawfiq Abdul Hay, Rached Osman (a shareholder in Dar Mayo and the Alexandrian Maritime Commercial Bank but no relation to Osman Ahmed Osman), and others, as well as various Islamic investment companies to be discussed in the following chapter. To be sure, friendly "political" bankers financed good schemes as well as bad, and relatively few of them were fraudulent. The more professionally managed banks were also occasionally swindled, as might be expected of any bank. I nevertheless expect that "political" credit practices would take their toll over the years on the balance sheets of the more complaisant, more "political" banks.

If a bank was "political"—in business to lend money to friends of friends rather than to make profits—its financial performance could be expected to deteriorate in the long run. While not burdened, like public sector banks, with loans to public sector companies, the "political" banks would exhibit lower rates of return than more professionally managed banks because more of their loans would become "nonperforming." It was common knowledge, for instance, that the Mohandes Bank was seriously over-extended. The third of its loan portfolio tied up with the Mohandes National Company for Alimental Products in a joint venture with Cadbury-Schweppes had to be written off. By the mid-1980s, Mohandes Bank's net income, and consequently its return on assets (net income divided by total assets), was nil.

One way, then, of spotting "political" banks was to identify the ones with low returns on assets. Of course banks could fare poorly for other reasons. Al Watany lost huge amounts in bullion trading in the early 1980s but was gradually recovering by the late 1980s. Tegariyoon lost $30 million in foreign exchange dealings concealed from the bank's chief executive officer in the mid-1980s. Poor financial performance, however, usually pointed to complaisant credit policies. A user-friendly bank would give its favored depositors high interest rates—and perhaps had to, in order to attract deposits—and would lend them cheap money. A tightly managed bank, by contrast, would maximize its spreads (the difference between interest received from borrowers and interest expenses to depositors), a principal indicator of profitability.[3] Virtually all of the private sector banks in Morocco displayed differences of 4 to 5 percent between their average rates on loans and on deposits in the late 1980s. Their closely regulated Tunisian counterparts appeared to do equally well, and in Turkey's more inflationary climate the leaders did much better, getting spreads on average of 20 to 30 percent in the late 1980s. Egypt's more competitive climate permitted much less. Despite much higher inflation rates in Egypt than in Morocco or Tunisia, its banks' spreads tended to be much lower.

For the debt crescent, any analysis of financial statements is hazardous. Well managed or not, Egyptian banks were no less artful than others in dressing up their balance sheets, and accounting practices were flexible. Until 30 June 1991, a commonly accepted practice was to inflate revenues by declaring as income the fictitious interest on nonperforming loans. When done "properly," by the public sector banks, this practice did not inflate return on assets because provisions for the fictitious income were deducted from the bottom line, but it did inflate spread rates. Some of the other banks claimed not to declare fictitious interest income, but they perhaps inflated their net income by omitting provisions. Without lending more credence to the data than it deserves, it is still expected that low returns on assets and low spreads point to "political" management practices. A bank's capital structure might also offer clues about management strategies. Though shareholders did not necessarily dictate credit policies, it was expected that the banks that included private shareholders were more prone to political networking than the joint ventures owned by institutions, unless the private shareholders were governed by a responsible core like the Nile Bank's El Ayouti family. All of the third-sector banks were potentially political in this sense with the exception of the Nile Bank, and the development banks and those of the professional syndicates also exemplified a capital structure that seemed propitious for political patronage, as did that of the Islamic banks. At the other end of the spectrum, the banks most insulated from politics were joint ventures like Egyptian American, managed by the foreign partner.

The data are presented in table 7–2. Each bank's return on assets is the average of returns for each year since 1985 for which income statements were available to the writer,[4] as indicated in the table. Averaging the returns gave a more reliable record of a bank than a single year, though gaps in the data meant that the averages were not strictly comparable. Average lending rates to borrowers and average spreads, the difference between lending rates and rates given to depositors, are also presented in table 7–2.[5] The average annual returns on assets and the average spread rates and interest charges were in turn averaged out by sector and by third-sector subcategories.

The four public sector banks fared poorest of all, averaging a return on total assets of only 0.37 percent and spreads of 1.19 percent, while the big banking joint ventures, especially Egypt American Bank and Commercial International Bank, consistently registered the highest earnings and spreads. The other institutionally owned joint ventures, however, did not post significantly higher spreads or returns on assets than the third-sector banks. The Export Development Bank was the only one to generate high earnings; some of the French joint ventures kept up high spreads but evidently failed to generate enough commercial loans or other sources of income to have high returns on total assets. Misr Romanian also kept high spreads, due to a relatively low cost of funds, but failed to generate much income. The Arab Investment Bank, Cairo Barclays, Misr Iran, and Misr American had all fallen on hard times, as noted earlier. They brought down the

Table 7-2. Financial indicators of Egypt's commercial and business banks, 1985–91

	Average for the years	ROA	Lending rates	Spreads
Public sector commercial banks		0.37%	7.11%	1.19%
Banque Misr	1986–91	0.44%	7.81%	1.79%
National Bank of Egypt	1986–91	0.27%	5.92%	0.89%
Banque du Caire	1986–91	0.54%	7.21%	1.26%
Bank of Alexandria	1986–91	0.24%	7.52%	0.81%
Infitah Banks				
I. Big banking joint ventures		1.53%	8.71%	3.09%
Misr International Bank	1988–90	0.68%	8.26%	2.46%
Commercial International Bank (ex Chase)	1985–90	1.71%	9.42%	4.39%
Egyptian American Bank	1985–90	2.18%	8.45%	2.43%
II. Other banking joint ventures		0.96%	7.94%	2.28%
Arab Investment Bank	1988–90	0.19%	8.72%	1.62%
Cairo Barclays	1985–90	0.17%	7.35%	0.94%
Misr Iran Dev Bank	1985–90	0.77%	8.59%	0.80%
Misr Amerian Intl Bank	1987–90	0.88%	7.41%	0.87%
National Société Générale	1985–89	0.76%	9.21%	4.34%
Export Development Bank of Egypt	1986–90	2.68%	7.48%	3.75%
Caire Paris	1987–90	1.12%	9.98%	4.27%
Crédit International d'Egypte	1988–89	0.98%	6.23%	0.87%
Misr Romanian	1986, 1988–90	1.10%	6.46%	3.02%
III. Banks with Egyptian private ownership		0.83%	8.28%	2.00%
A. General		0.86%	8.60%	2.32%
Suez Canal Bank	1985–90	0.50%	6.75%	0.81%
Bank of Credit & Commerce Misr	1985–90	0.50%	8.63%	3.03%
Delta Bank	1985–90	0.25%	7.86%	1.78%
Nile Bank	1985–90	2.00%	9.59%	3.49%
Alexandria Kuwait Intl Bank	1985–89	0.00%	7.21%	1.11%
Misr Exterior	1985–86, 1989–90	1.07%	9.06%	2.60%
Egypt Gulf Bank	1985–90	0.95%	9.08%	1.32%
Egypt Arab African Bank	1985–90	0.81%	8.11%	2.93%
Hongkong Egyptian Bank	1985–90	0.88%	11.63%	5.07%
Alexandria Commercial Maritime Bank	1985–86, 1989–90	2.41%	9.35%	2.09%
Al Watany	1985–90	0.77%	9.13%	2.85%
Société Arabe Internationale (SAIB)	1985–86, 1988–89	1.02%	7.03%	2.77%
Cairo Far East	1985–90	0.07%	8.36%	0.28%

Table 7-2—*continued*

	Average for the years	ROA	Lending rates	Spreads
B. Development Banks		1.01%	8.40%	1.89%
National Development Bank	1985–90	0.49%	6.42%	0.97%
Assiut	1987–88, 90	0.17%	8.80%	0.56%
Behera	1987–88, 90	1.76%	7.36%	3.00%
Damietta	1987–88, 90	−0.01%	8.41%	2.28%
Fayoum	1987–88, 90	−1.82%	5.76%	−1.29%
Gharbiya	1987–88, 90	1.25%	10.57%	2.65%
Giza	1987–88, 90	0.91%	7.43%	2.26%
Ismailiya	1987–88, 90	−0.17%	9.07%	−1.40%
Kafr el Sheikh	1987–88, 90	1.85%	9.40%	2.70%
Minya	1987–88, 90	0.74%	9.97%	3.61%
Mounoufeya	1987–88, 90	1.51%	7.77%	3.16%
Port Said	1987–88, 90	1.60%	8.82%	1.83%
Qalyoubeya	1987–88, 90	1.27%	6.65%	0.14%
Qena	1987–88, 90	3.53%	8.16%	4.50%
Sharqiya	1987–88, 90	0.81%	8.42%	1.64%
Sinai	1987–88, 90	5.23%	8.77%	7.69%
Souhag	1987–88, 90	1.62%	10.65%	1.95%
Dakahlia Development Bank	1989–90	−2.02%	3.79%	−3.71%
Housing & Development Bank	1988–90	0.58%	13.46%	3.41%
C. Professional Unions		0.64%	9.67%	3.33%
BCD Tegariyoon	1985–86, 89–90	−0.84%	8.14%	1.40%
Mohandes Bank	1985–86, 88–89	−0.70%	9.42%	2.58%
Workers Bank	1989–90	3.47%	11.46%	6.00%
D. Islamic		0.01%	5.21%	0.19%
Faisal Islamic Bank of Egypt	1985–90	0.50%	7.35%	1.24%
Islamic International Bank for Invt & Dev	1985–90	−0.60%	4.76%	1.20%
Egyptian Saudi Finance Bank	1987–90	0.13%	3.54%	−1.88%
Big Arab "offshore" banks				
Arab African Intl Bank	1985–86, 89–90	−1.83%	7.95%	−0.73%
Arab International Bank	1986–91	0.58%	8.36%	1.78%

Sources: Annual Reports of the banks; Egyptian Banks' Directory; author's database of commercial banks.

a. Central Bank of Egypt, *Economic Review* 31:4 (1990–91): 132, 140.

general averages of the banking joint ventures to third-sector levels, despite the fact that their shareholders were other banks, not free-wheeling private Egyptian shareholders. Obviously each bank was unique, and individual differences in management strategies and choices outweighed any abstract differences in their capital structure.

As expected, most of the third sector performed appreciably below the standards set in recent years by Egypt's leading joint ventures. The Ayouti family's Nile Bank was the only one that demonstrated consistent financial performance like that of the premier tier of infitah banks. The Alexandria Commercial Maritime Bank staged a higher average return on assets, but the bank was facing severe difficulties by 1990. Return on assets was still a respectable 1.6 percent, indicating either other sources of income or creative accounting, but spreads were squeezed to an infinitessimal 0.24 and 0.07 percent in 1989 and 1990, respectively. Perhaps one of the bank's founding shareholders, Rached Osman (Imām 1986: 145), had helped to lead it astray. The Société Arabe Internationale de Banque, the only other third-sector bank to average more than a 1 percent return on assets in recent years, was stagnating, generating returns on shareholders' equity of less than 9 percent, although its circumstances were not dire. SAIB had drastically reduced its loan portfolio after 1985 while backing up more than 40 percent of the remaining portfolio with provisions against nonperforming loans. In fact provisions and capital more than covered the entire portfolio. SAIB seemed to be prudently managed, but it did not engage in much financial intermediation. Its chairman, Dr. Hassan Abbas Zaki, had once served as Nasser's minister of the economy, and he was also deputy chairman of the wealthy Arab International Bank, working closely with Dr. Mustafa Khalil, Sadat's former prime minister and the AIB's chairman. Dr. Zaki also served on the board of governors of the Central Bank, and he enjoyed good relations with the Islamic banking community. If political connections had encouraged bad loans in the past, the bank seemed on the road to a modest recovery. Misr Exterior, a joint venture between Banque Misr and Spanish banks, was the only other third-sector bank (with 6 percent of its shares owned by private individuals, including Hassan Sayed Marei) to have averaged better than a 1 percent return on assets, with respectable spreads.

Most of the remaining third-sector banks were in difficulty. They had overextended themselves during the boom years and, burdened with many nonperforming loans, faced prospects of major restructuring in the 1990s. The largest of them, the Suez Canal Bank, was only barely keeping up with the public sector banks. Its average return on assets placed it at the bottom of its sector, just a bit above Delta International Bank, Alexandria Kuwait, and Cairo Far East; and only Cairo Far East seemed squeezed by tighter spreads. With an average lending rate of 6.75 percent, in fact, Suez seemed to be giving money away—or failing to collect on nonperforming loans. The connection with Osman Ahmed Osman had perhaps contributed to the bank's steady decline, despite Ahmad Fuad's efforts to revive the bank in the late 1980s. Osman's joint venture with Schweppes, for instance, the Mohandes National Company for Alimental Products, had ruined Mohandes Bank, one of his other financial strongholds. As Osman's political influence waned, so also did his projects. Might there be some correlation, in fact, between the contractor's political influence and the fates of his "political" banks, like the Suez Canal Bank? As usual in such financial matters, too many other factors intervene in ascertaining cause and effect, and the data are less reliable than discussions with Cairo bankers who encouraged such a hypothesis. But a correlation could be traced, whatever other explanations there may be of the decline of the Suez Canal Bank.

Osman's political influence had peaked by early 1981. Several months before Sadat's assassination, the president dropped him from his inner circle of closest advisers. Osman had become a political liability by choosing in his autobiography to attack both Nasser's family and Abd al-Aziz Higazy, countering similar charges of corruption against himself (Waterbury 1983: 378–79). Sadat seemed finally to have lost confidence in some of Osman's advice. The president's economic czar, Dr. Abd al-Razaq Abd al-Maguid, claims to have undermined Osman's credibility on at least two occasions in early 1981. He foiled a scheme to lease the Suez Canal to pay for Salahiya, one of Osman's pet agribusiness projects in his home province of Ismailiya, by obtaining USAID financing instead (Hinnebusch, 1985: 167; cf. Dr. Abd al-Maguid's interview in Hilāl 1987: 167), and he stopped a project promoted by one of Osman's close associates on behalf on Crédit Lyonnais to establish an Egyptian bank in France under French management. Deeming the bank project to be analogous to the original concession of the Suez Canal, Abd al-Maguid refused to sign the documents, turned Sadat against the deal, and knew he had won the day against Osman when Sadat mandated him later that evening to present the Crédit Lyonnais's chief executive officer with his consolation prize, a state medal (Interview with Abd al-Maguid, 20 February 1992).

When Hosni Mubarak succeeded Sadat, Osman appeared to be vulnerable as well as unpopular, discredited in parliament and in the press for much of Egypt's unprecedented high-level corruption as well as shoddy construction work. Yet, incredibly, the new president was apparently unable to discover sufficient evidence to prosecute the man. Osman's extensive patronage networks within Egyptian bureaucracy had covered up the paper trails. The best the president could do in 1982 to curb Osman should be to appoint a strong and wily prime minister, Fuad Mohieddine, and let him buffer the influence peddling. After Mohieddine's sudden death in 1984, Osman regained some influence before falling ill and suffering, too, from the unseemly squabbling of his children over the family's wealth. He finally retired in 1991 from the chairmanship of the engineers' professional syndicate, his symbolic power base since the late 1970s. He had been no more than a figurehead since 1987, when Muslim Brothers had packed the general assembly and controlled its elections. The Engineers' Syndicate conducted a confidential investigation in 1992 into the mismanagement of their Mohandes Bank. The financial "negligence" inherited from Osman's team of managers had put up to one-fifth of the engineers' pension fund at risk (Moore 1994: 232).

It seemed in Egypt that a bank's performance might mirror the influence of its principal power broker. The quality of a bank's investments and loan portfolio depends in the last analysis upon the viability of the projects being financed. If an entrepreneur had sufficient influence on the business environment and cared to exercise it, his projects would succeed. Osman surely wielded such influence with Sadat (as, previously, with Nasser), and under Mubarek, too, he seems to have carried enough vestigial influence within the Egyptian bureaucracy to regulate most of his business parameters. When attacked head-on, for instance, over the Salahiya project, which had escaped his control and should be poorly executed, possibly to discredit him, he benefited from its mistakes. In the desert to the north of Cairo he set up a similar project, Masr ed-Dina (named after his great-grandniece), partly financed by the emir of Abu Dhabi, and raided Salahiya's experienced personnel. Unfortunately for Egyptian banks, however, many of his pet projects were of interest to Osman only in their initial stages, while the machinery should be being purchased. Subtle ebbs and flows of his political influence may therefore not always be reflected by blips in a bank's balance sheet. Morover, there are time lags. Like Banque Misr in the 1930s, a bank may cover up its nonperforming loans for several years.

Table 7–3 presents the financial statements of the Suez Canal Bank published in its annual reports between 1980 and 1990. As mentioned earlier, this bank should be the second-largest in Egypt's third sector, surpassed only by the Faisal Islamic Bank of Egypt. Osman in his heyday helped the Suez Canal Bank in many ways, and the bank's annual reports feature him among its pantheon of founding fathers. The bank was founded on 9 March 1978, when Osman's influence was at its peak. The financial statements show that the bank had relatively few interest-free sight deposits. It nevertheless paid relatively little interest on its other deposits because it had easy access to the Suez Canal Authority, one of Egypt's few cash cows. Easy access survived Osman's political decline because he had arranged for the authority's pension fund, as well as that of his Arab Contractors Company, to be a shareholder of the bank. When Ahmad Fuad assumed management of the bank after retiring from Misr Romanian in 1986, its cost of funds remained slightly below the average for third-sector banks.

As Osman's influence declined, however, the Suez Canal Bank's spreads diminished, becoming negative in 1989. Provisions for nonperforming loans mounted after 1982, once Prime Minister Mohieddine curbed Osman's appetite for new projects. The bank's profits were steadily squeezed, compressing the return on total assets (ROA) reported in table 7–3. Net income steadily diminished after 1982, even though total assets steadily increased, more or less in line with Egyptian inflation. The bank tried to pay out consistent dividends each year, yet it also had to increase its core capital, which had amounted to only 2.6 percent of total assets in 1981. In the early to mid-1980s the Suez Canal Bank perhaps still enjoyed the leverage of a public sector bank because the Osman connection was as good as any state guarantee. But the bank had to increase its capital base once Osman's political influence waned. It raised more capital from its shareholders in 1988, the year Osman was reelected to a three-year term as chairman of the Engineers' Syndicate, but, still squeezed in profits, the following year it reduced the annual dividend. Although slightly higher profits in 1990 permitted the bank to restore the previous year's cut, the dividend amounted in real terms to less than one-sixth of the funds paid out to stockholders a decade earlier, assuming an average annual inflation rate of 20 percent. Income had similarly dwindled, reflecting the bank's contracting spreads. The shrinkage was caused by a steady decline in interest income, not rising costs of funds. If the blips in the bank's financial statements had closely mirrored Osman's political trajectory, the decline in interest revenues might have been visible in 1982, not 1984, but any bank's statements can be doctored for a time. A final cause for concern was the increase in 1990 of the bank's investments in other companies as a proportion of core equity, tying up scarce capital in illiquid shareholdings. Though still below the danger threshhold of 50 percent, the increase possibly indicated that nonperforming loans were being traded for equity in troubled enterprises. In 1991 a financial analyst raised the question of another capital increase for the Suez Canal Bank in the columns of *Al Ahram al Iqtisadi* (no. 1177, 5 August 1991: 58).

Table 7-3. Suez Canal Bank, 1980–90

Year (mm LE)	1980	1981	1982	1983	1984	1985	1986	1987	1988	1989	1990
Total Assets (TA)	343	670	790.6	855.3	867.6	1270	1484	1710	2036	2213	2551
Loans	179	385	418	388	379	584	730	791	938	972	1110
Investments	3	5		9	10	14	18			30.5	48.3
Clients' Deposits	269.6	530.5	570.9	587.7	602.6	873	1034	1204	1299	1531	1861
(Sight)				103	135	216	229	271		282	355
Interbank Deposits	28	42		100	99	159	191	176		265	200
Provisions	29	69		121	124	181	196	262			
Capital	10	10	10	10	15	15	15	15	15	15	15
Retained Earnings	6	7.2	25.3	32.5	32.6	37.5	42.6	48.4	106	107	113
Dividends	2.1	2.5	2.5	2	2.1	2.4	2.4	2.4	2.4	1.8	2.4
Net income (NI)	6.3	11.9	12.4	10.7	8.3	8.4	9	9.2	8.1	8.15	10.2
Interest earned	23	59		61	61	74	89			109.4	137.5
Interest paid	13	35		45	44	58	73			109.9	125.1
Sight/Total Deposits				17.5%	22.4%	24.7%	22.1%	22.5%		18.4%	19.1%
Cost of Funds	4.4%	6.1%		6.5%	6.3%	5.6%	6.0%			6.1%	6.1%
Spread rate	2.4%	2.9%		2.5%	3.5%	1.5%	1.2%			0.0%	0.6%
Spreads/TA	2.9%	3.6%		1.9%	2.0%	1.3%	1.1%			0.0%	0.5%
NI/TA (ROA)	1.8%	1.8%	1.6%	1.3%	1.0%	0.7%	0.6%	0.5%	0.4%	0.4%	0.4%
Provisions/Loans	16.2%	17.9%		31.2%	32.7%	31.0%	26.8%	33.1%			
Equity (Cap+RE)/TA	4.7%	2.6%	4.5%	5.0%	5.5%	4.1%	3.9%	3.7%	5.9%	5.5%	5.0%
Interest earned/TA	6.7%	8.8%		7.1%	7.0%	5.8%	6.0%			4.9%	5.4%
Investments/Equity	18.8%	29.1%		21.2%	21.0%	26.7%	31.3%			25.0%	37.7%

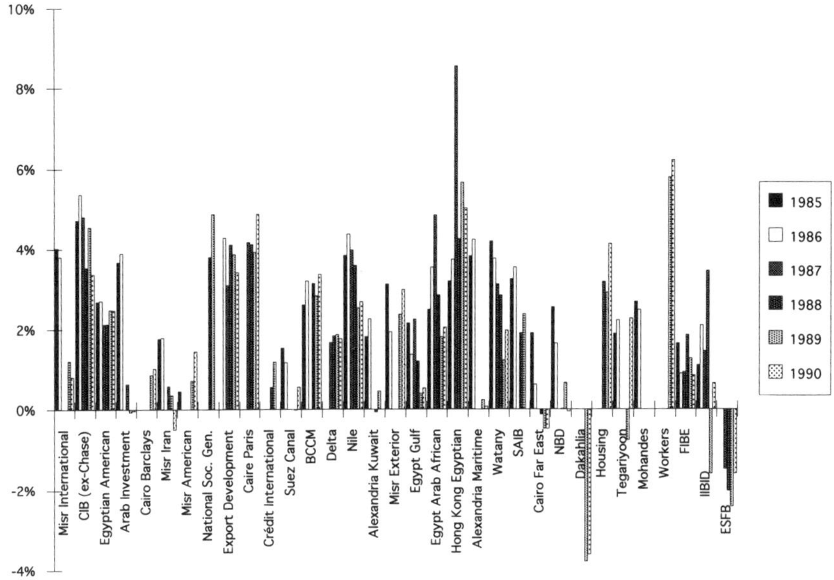

Fig. 7.4. Spread rates of Infitah banks, 1980–90. *Source:* author's database of commercial banks.

Osman was the prime embodiment of the "parasitary" capitalism that Mubarak had determined to bend to more productive purposes, and the Suez Canal Bank was the biggest of the non-Islamic third-sector banks milked by the new class. Since the banks were not required to declare how much of their loan portfolios were nonperforming—much less how devalued their investments in other companies had become—the clearest indicator of being milked was the decline in spread rates so vividly illustrated by this bank. Figure 7–4 depicts similar declines at other banks for which data were available, while confirming the consistent performance of Egypt's top two infitah banks, Egypt American and Commercial International.

The banks reputed in 1992 to be in the greatest trouble were the Bank of Credit and Commerce Misr (BCCM), those of the professional syndicates Mohandes and BCD Tegariyoon, the Dakahlia Development Bank,[6] the Islamic International Bank for Investment and Development (IIBID), and possibly the Suez Canal Bank and Delta International Bank. Some sources also mentioned Egypt Gulf Bank. Its chief executive officer, former Prime Minister Kemal Ali Hassan, and the vice chairman, Ahmed Mohammed Abbaza, a New Wafd notable, had coincidentally retired for reasons of health in January 1991 amid rumors of the bank's substantial exposure to a troubled Islamic money management company. Figure 7–4 confirms that most of these banks were indeed in trouble, together with others like Cairo Far East. Further inspection of their individual financial statements indicates that, except in the case of Tegariyoon, decreases in interest revenues were greater than increases in the costs of funds. The only "troubled" banks that still seemed in 1990 to sustain reasonable spread rates were BCCM and Delta. BCCM kept high spread rates because it lent little in Egypt. It was part of the international network of the Bank of Credit and Commerce International, which owned 49 percent of its shares. The strategy of the bank was to attract Egyptians' dollar deposits—those of other Egyptian banks as well as individuals—by offering premium returns. When the Bank of England, in conjunction with other central banks, closed down the BCCI in July 1991, the BCCM's foreign exchange deposits held with the BCCI were frozen, along with those of other Egyptian banks such as Faisal Islamic. That bank had parked $200 million ("a forward contract on goods," one bank official explained) with BCCI's international network, and it lost the use of at least $338 million in the debacle (*MEED,* 31 July 1992: 5; Faisal Islamic Bank of Egypt, *Annual Report 1411/1991*). Egypt-based individuals and enterprises lost up to $1.2 billion, plus at least that amount in overseas Egyptian accounts. BCCM lost $372 million (*Financial Times,* 21 January 1992), roughly two-thirds of its total balance sheet.

Though not part of the BCCI problem, squeezed spreads appeared to be a fairly reliable indicator of an overextended bank with a poorly performing loan portfolio. With the exception of Delta International, the banks reputed to be basket cases displayed steady declines in their spreads—reaching negative rates in the cases of Dakahlia, IIBID, Tegariyoon, and probably Mohandes, which ceased to disclose such sensitive matters in its annual reports after 1986. Delta inflated its spread rate by declaring interest income on nonperforming loans and then provisioning against it, reducing net income. Return on total assets dwindled to 0.05 percent in 1989 but recovered to 0.3 percent in 1990. The bank was seriously undercapitalized, with fixed assets immobilizing almost three-quarters of the core capital, while investments in other companies amounted to an additional 45 percent, some of which obviously had to come from depositors rather than shareholders. Administrative expenditures seemed high, possibly reflecting the "mediocre management" noted by a bank rating service. Changes were likely, however, after the 1992 appointment of a new chairman, former Central Bank governor Ali Negm, to raise new capital and turn the bank around.

A number of other banks were experiencing vanishing spread rates and poorly performing loan portfolios. Arab Investment Bank, Misr Iran Development Bank, Alexandria Kuwait International Bank, Alexandria Commercial Maritime Bank, Cairo Far East, the National Bank for Development and many of its local affiliates, and the Egyptian Saudi Finance Bank were all in similar straits. Of the banks displaying very low or negative spread rates, only Egyptian Saudi Finance Bank was in fact healthy, despite its portfolio of nonperforming loans. The bad loans were the legacy of the late Abdul Latif Abu Rageila, who had founded the Ahram Bank and had induced Zakei Shafei, a recently retired minister of the economy, to be its chief executive officer. Shafei had resigned when he discovered dubious financial dealings around him. Abu Rageila and some of his other bank managers were eventually implicated in a financial scandal involving the black market money-changer Sami Ali Hassan. In 1988 Sheikh Salah Kamel, the Saudi financier who had created banks in Turkey, Algeria, and Tunisia, was finally permitted to take control of the bank, recapitalize it, and convert it to Islamic practices.

The others, such as the Suez Canal Bank, stagnated under the burden of nonperforming loans. None of the public sector banks fared well, and their spreads worsened in 1992, when their income statements reflected new accounting practices. Banque Misr's balance sheet, weighed down by the controversial Ameriya project, a huge textile complex near Alexandria, seemed particularly overextended. Spread rates slipped from 2–3 percent in the mid-1980s to 0.33 percent in 1989 and 0.25 percent in 1990. Much of the public sector banks' difficulties stemmed from financing public sector enterprises, but a study by the National Bank of Egypt's Research Department reported that the banks were also carrying over LE 1 billion of nonperforming loans to 1,681 ailing private enterprises in 1989. Egypt's joint venture commercial and investment banks carried the brunt of these bad debts, however, some LE 2.2 billion distributed among 2,299 customers. In other words, 15 percent of their total loan portfolio was nonperforming, and much of it must have been clustered in the banks that suffered diminished spreads. The study also indicated that the total value of the "sick balances" in the banking system as of 30 June 1989 amounted to LE 5.3 million and that only 104 clients were responsible for 56.4 percent of it (National Bank of Egypt, *Economic Bulletin* 42:3 (1989): 143, 146). It would have been interesting to identify them and discover their connections with the ailing banks and with the shareholders on Sāmia Sa'īd Imām's lists. In addition to common shareholders like Osman Ahmed Osman, a number of these banks shared investments in a variety of companies. Alexandria Kuwait International Bank, for instance, listed projects in association with the Suez Canal Bank, Delta International, and Nile Bank. Clusters of debtors perhaps shared dilemmas of common interest with groups of banks. As long as each bank "cooperated" by rolling over the loans, all were apparently safe, but they were like bicyclists careening down a hill without brakes.

Some of the infitah banks were quite successful. Misr Exterior, connected with the Marei family, seemed to be getting spread rates as high as Egypt American's, even though the latter had other sources of income that boosted its return on total assets. Al Watany, too, was recovering from earlier losses, and SAIB seems to have restructured its portfolio successfully. The biggest stars were the Nile Bank and Hong Kong Egyptian, in which the "four sharks" of the Beleidy Group had placed their money. These rising groups of private investors did not seem to be exploiting their banks for easy money. Until 1991 the four relied instead on the Central Bank. In transactions described in general terms by Tahsin Bechir (1992), they exported cosmetics and other products at inflated prices to the Soviet Union. The Central Bank of Egypt reimbursed them from the "sterling equivalent" balances still owed to the Soviet Union. The Nile Bank, however, appeared to be a smaller version of Turkey's Akbank, the flagship of Sabancı's group of family companies. Both its spread rates and returns on assets consistently kept up with the high standards set by Commercial International Bank and Egypt American.

The collapse of the BCCI in London spelled the end of the bicycling act for Egyptian banks. Just as the Second Gulf War breathed new life into Egyptian macroeconomic reform, its financial aftershock triggered microeconomic changes that were a real tribute to BCCI's marketing skills. Eight Egyptian banks together lost between $1.2 billion and $1.8 billion—possibly equal to one-quarter of the total foreign exchange placed by commercial and investment banks in overseas banks (Central Bank of Egypt, *Annual Report 1990–91:* 64, 69). A shakeout of the commercial banking system seemed inevitable. The losers, BCCM, Faisal Islamic Bank of Egypt, and others, would not all be able to roll over their borrowers' loans without buying more money from other banks. Yet interest rates for local currency skyrocketed with the macroeconomic reforms introduced in 1991. Either spreads would be further squeezed or some of the banks would have to call in loans, with domino effects upon the borrowers and other banks alike. Restructuring the banking system became a central focus of Egypt's second infitah.

Egypt's Second Infitah

Decades of easy credit came to an end in April 1991, when an IMF standby loan imposed tight money policies on Egypt in return for a license to receive international debt relief—the reward for supporting the international coalition against Iraq. Egypt had already anticipated the agreement by liberalizing interest rates earlier in the year, but high money rates coupled with the BCCI losses that summer terminated any lingering access to easy political credits. The banks reacted quickly. In September they failed even to reach their credit ceilings for private sector lending, which the Central Bank imposed individually on each of them for lack of more subtle instruments of control. Subsequently, an informal market of ceiling quotas developed among the banks so as to utilize more of their collective lending capacity, but borrowers, however personally well connected with their bankers, could no longer play on their dilemmas of common interest. Although the regulatory capacities of the Central Bank had been cannibalized by the infitah, the banks were being brought to heel. They had to increase their capital to meet international standards, as well as diversifying their portfolios and tightening their credit policies, limiting loans to their friends, relatives, and political combines, just as banks from Morocco to Turkey had been obliged to conform, at least superficially, to conventional Anglo-Saxon banking practices.

Though some bankers questioned the need for yet another banking law, the BCCI affair propelled to the national agenda a draft that had been prepared by concerned government and Central Bank officials in response to previous crises. The BCCI's Egyptian joint venture, the BCCM, was temporarily closed in July 1991, when the Bank of England finally acted against its parent, provoking a run on the Cairo bank. The BCCM was put under a special administration, headed by the recently retired chairman of the Bank of Alexandria, but how might the depositors retrieve their funds, a good third of which had vanished? Hitherto the public sector banks had always bailed out banks in difficulty, but the costs were mounting. When the Ahram Bank had been about to fail in 1983, the Central Bank imposed a new management and called upon the public sector banks to increase its capital by LE 28 million, in two equal increments. Strained as they were, the Big Four were also required in 1989 to rescue, first, the Islamic International Bank for Investment and Development, adding LE 120 million ($48 million) to its capital, and then Tugariyoon, with a capital injection of LE 76 million and further increases planned for 1993. The Bank of Alexandria was exonerated on the grounds that it had to support its troubled joint venture, the Alexandria Kuwait International Bank. Any rescue of the BCCM, a bigger bank with much greater losses, would not be so simple, however. The Central Bank reacted to the crisis by issuing a directive to all the banks in late summer 1991 to contribute 0.5 percent of their deposits, in both local and foreign currencies, "in a spirit of solidarity and mutual support" to cover

BCCM's losses. While no bank could refuse the powerful Central Bank of Egypt, some raised questions. Was the contribution to be a gift, in which case shareholders had to be consulted? Or was it a loan, and, if so, at market rates of interest? Or was it to be part of a deposit insurance scheme that Egypt had not yet established? It was finally agreed that half the sum would be disbursed to the Central Bank as a one-time expense for a new deposit insurance fund, while the banks would keep the remainder on call for the Central Bank. Meanwhile controversy raged over the new banking law.

A consensus quickly developed that the Central Bank's regulatory authority had to be strengthened to prevent future crises. The bank was to be made more independent of the government by reinforcing the authority of the governor, to be appointed by the president on advice of the prime minister, not merely the minister of the economy. Since mismanagement and cronyism were endangering the entire banking system, the Central Bank was to be given the right to approve all boards of directors and managers. As in Tunisia, banks were to be independent, managing their own affairs in keeping with various financial ratios determined by Central Bank regulators. The regulators were also to receive explicit legal authority to enforce various liquidity and capital ratios—by closing down unresponsive banks or ordering mergers if necessary. By the end of September 1991 the key proposed amendments to Banking Law 163 of 1958 were published, with commentaries (Ghoneim 1991: 24–28), and they were extensively debated in the press in October and November. But the legislation was delayed until 1 June 1992, when President Mubarak finally pushed it through parliament after further discussions with contentious bankers and bureaucrats. The delay and the virtual news blackout between December and June were a victory of sorts for some of the bankers because, behind the scenes, they had gained time since the shock of the BCCI affair to temper the proposed Central Bank controls.

Extensive consultations orchestrated by the Banks' Association of Egypt had mitigated some of the powers initially proposed for the Central Bank. For example, it would be required to consult with shareholders before imposing mergers on local banks. The Central Bank was not in the end given the right to vet all bank employees of managerial rank. As bankers had pointed out, hundreds of them held the rank of manager, and the Central Bank did not have the competence to evaluate them. One bank manager quipped that the draft provision, had it passed, would have obliged his bank to demote several, including himself, rather than subject itself to the Central Bank's micromanagement.

The extended consultations also promoted the Banks' Association. Founded initially in 1981 as a voluntary association under the formal supervision of the Ministry of Social Affairs, the Banks' Association of Egypt achieved official recognition in the new law. Its vigorous president, Mahmoud Abdel Aziz, played a major role in articulating the heterogeneous interests of the banks included in the association—public and private sector, joint ventures and foreign branches, and various specialized public sector banks. Publicly Aziz urged passage of the law in his official Bank Day speech, 1 January 1992, while privately he met with each category of banks and helped to hammer out compromises. Although he was a public sector banker, he stood for professionalism as much as for government interests, and he advocated the maximum autonomy for banks consistent with prudent regulation. Together with other key public sector bank managers, he objected to bailing out any more banks. A banker literally to his fingertips—the right-hand middle finger calloused from holding the pen to inscribe the daily registers—Mahmoud Abdel Aziz had spent his entire career at the National Bank of Egypt and was looking for ways of privatizing it. He was promoted to the chairmanship of the bank in late 1992 and had already implemented a plan to sell off a small number of shares to the employees of NBE's prize subsidiary, the Commercial International Bank. CIB was further privatized in 1993, when individual shareholders acquired more than 50 percent of the bank's capital (*MEED*, 8 July 1994: 22).

Depending on how it was to be applied, the new banking law might help public sector managers to clean up their loan portfolios, as their banks would no longer be permitted to lend more than one-quarter of their capital and reserves to any single client, even to a big public sector company. The principle of portfolio diversification had given way in Nasser's time to sectoral specialization, whereby each of the four banks was allocated entire industries, and much of the public sector portfolio of LE 10.5 billion consisted of untradeable nonperforming loans. The public sector companies were highly leveraged and externally indebted as well (*Al-Ahram al-Iqtisadi*, 15 June 1992: 24–25). The system was inherently "corrupt" (in the words of a judicious insider) because a public sector company could perform unreimbursed services for another enterprise, make paper profits, and carry the loan giving the bank its paper profits. The Arab Contractors (Osman Ahmed Osman's public sector company), for instance, by itself had about LE 1 billion in loans in 1990, paying interest of about LE 123 million, which amounted to 88 percent of the total profits of the public sector banks. At least LE 4 billion ($1.2 billion) would be required to clean up their portfolios (Bakri 1991: 20, 23). The new credit ceilings put increasing pressure on banks and enterprises to settle their outstanding debts. Prodded by international donors, some public sector companies might have to sell off assets to meet their payrolls.

Although the Banks' Association president had tried to articulate the interests of the various categories of banks, one set was still dissatisfied when, after further delays, the Council of State finally approved the law's executive regulations in December 1992. The foreign bank branches had won permission to deal in local as well as foreign currency, but they objected to some of the strings attached. According to the draft of the executive regulations, which was published in the centerfold of *Al-Ahram al-Iqtisadi* (12 December 1992), dealings in Egyptian currency would require foreign branches to take Egyptian partners holding at least 25 percent of their capital; either the home office had to guarantee all local deposits or the foreign branch had to meet the capital increases being imposed on local banks. Apparently these conditions were so objectionable that the centerfold became a nonpublication. As late as 12 March 1993, the *Middle East Economic Digest* was reporting (p. 10) that "the executive regulations of the law have yet to be published." The Central Bank was holding firm to the capitalization and Egyptianization requirements. Led by Citibank's local manager, accompanied by the U.S. ambassador, the foreign bankers interceded with President Mubarak, whose signature was required to put the law into operation. While he hesitated, the People's Assembly was inspired in March 1993 to pass an amendment to the banking law eliminating the requirement that the foreign banks take Egyptian partners. The executive regulations were then duly revised and signed.

The second infitah might primarily benefit the foreign banks, in particular Citibank, Arab Bank, and Crédit Lyonnais (*MEED*, 19 March 1993: 7–8), although others, like Bank of America, departed in 1994. Despite a paucity of branch networks in Egypt, the foreign banks enjoyed competitive advantages over most banking joint ventures and third-sector banks. For one thing, the foreigners were relatively unencumbered with nonperforming loans. Further, they were not saddled with the staffing demands imposed on a joint venture by their public sector partners (or by "private" entrepreneurs, for that matter). Lateral transfers of public sector managers to their more lucrative private joint ventures threatened the organizational integrity of the best-managed banks in town, unless, like the Egyptian American Bank, the foreign parent happened to hold a management contract to shelter it against dead wood. The foreign branches could quickly lose their competitive advantage some day, however. Having scorned the protection of any local partners, they became more exposed to the winds of political change.

Further progress in reforming the banking sector depends in the final analysis upon the entire package of structural adjustment measures to be implemented in exchange for international debt relief between 1992 and 1994. A shakeout and cleanup of Egypt's banking system seemed inevitable. Its autonomy proved illusory; finance capital had not acquired much structural power after all. A number of banks, especially some of the more "political" ones, faced the prospects of being eliminated through mergers. In some respects, the Egyptian banking system, though healthier than Algeria's, seemed weaker than Tunisia's. The first infitah had led to an orgy of political lending that, however helpful to elite factions, tended to support a dependent form of capitalism. Few of Egypt's third-sector banks displayed healthy balance sheets, and their market shares were tiny. The largest of the healthy ones, Nile Bank, had less than 1 percent of the market. Under competitive pressures from the leading institutional joint ventures and the foreign branches, some of the third-sector banks might compete for loans to good customers, but they would no longer be able to finance dubious projects and expect easy rescues from the public sector. They would have to diversify their portfolios rather than build up networks of friends and followers. Structural adjustment of the financial sector would diminish any structural power accumulated by the commercial banking system's third sector.

The experience of infitah under Sadat and Mubarak further confirmed the Tunisian lesson that greater concentrations of finance capital in banking oligopolies and business groups would be needed to lay the economic groundwork for substantive political change. Financial pluralism and fragmented finance capital had not built up business constituencies that might press for political pluralism, much less a transition to democracy. However, Egypt's financial system briefly appeared in the mid-1980s to be accumulating finance capital that augured substantive political change. The privately owned banks of the Islamic sector had concentrated significant segments of Egyptian finance capital. In conjunction with other Islamic financial institutions, they appeared to be building a capital base that could support a more pluralistic politics. Their rise and decline are the subject of the following chapter.

Chapter 8

Islamic Capital and Islamist Politics in Egypt

> The struggle over the future of the ["Islamic"] money management companies was not simply a struggle over the future of the financial system and the means of mobilizing and investing remittances but a struggle over the very future of [Egypt's] political and economic system.
>
> (Abd al-Fadil 1989: 66)

The rise of Islamic banking in Egypt held out the possibility that financial pluralism—as practiced in a relatively autonomous and competitive commercial banking system—could generate powerful business coalitions in support of political change. Indeed, it may well have been the specter of Islamic economic power that drove the government to curtail, contain, and eventually, in 1988, to liquidate substantial segments of the Islamic business community. The hypothesis that political and financial competition could be mutually reinforcing, discussed in chapter 1, was not to be subjected to a fair test in Egypt. On the one hand, much of the ostensibly "Islamic" capital accumulated by Islamic financial institutions was never incorporated into the formal banking system, and most "Islamic" business groups did not have time to develop strong foundations. On the other hand, the political competition between Islamist and other political forces degenerated into armed confrontations in the 1990s. This form of political competition obviously did not offer bankers and businesses incentives to exchange reliable information and thereby alleviate Islamic banking's competitive disadvantage.

Egypt's Islamic Banking Legacy

Before the government crackdown, however, Islamic finance displayed remarkable vitality in Egypt. As early as the 1960s, in fact, President Nasser had demonstrated how Islamic banks might serve the political strategies of authorities as well as Islamist oppositions. He encouraged the founding of the Muslim world's first known prototype of an Islamic bank, preceded only by a short-lived initiative of Pakistani landlords in a rural area in the late 1950s to exchange interest-free loans without collecting deposits (or "investments") from the public (Wilson 1983: 75). In 1963 Nasser permitted Dr. Ahmad Al-Najjar to set up a bank in Mit El Kom, Dakahlia, based upon the German credit cooperatives, the Sparkassen, which he had encountered as a student. Perhaps Nasser had intended to neutralize the appeal of the Muslim Brotherhood, four leaders of which he had executed in 1955. Nasser released a number of Muslim Brothers from prison in 1964, and as late as 1966, after he had cracked down a second time against the Muslim Brotherhood, Najjar recalls still enjoying official support and favorable publicity when he opened a branch of his bank in Heliopolis, Cairo (Interview 6 July 1988). Najjar's experiment in interest-free banking apparently failed for economic reasons rather than because the government was "hostile to private initiative and suspicious of religion" (Kuran 1993: 313). Some of the bank's interest-free loans were not repaid, and the bank lost much of its capital (Parigi 1989: 170).

Sadat in 1971 sponsored the establishment of the Nasser Social Bank along similar Islamic lines. Just as Nasser had promoted his own political agenda by supporting Najjar's efforts, so Sadat also harbored political designs (courting Islamist opinion against the apparatchiks of Nasser's Arab Socialist Union). Sadat's designs converged with those of some of the conservative Gulf states, which as early as 1970 had promoted a resolution at the Second Conference of Islamic Foreign Ministers recommending a feasibility study for an Islamic bank. The Islamic Development Bank was duly set up in 1975 as a consortium of 44 members of the Conference of Islamic States, but it would be overshadowed by a more dynamic private sector of multinational Islamic banking networks. In 1975 the Dubai Islamic Bank became the first privately owned institution established on Islamic principles, and by the end of 1991 at least 68 Islamic banks had spread across the Muslim world from Senegal, Mauritania, and Algeria to Bangladesh. More would emerge in Muslim parts of the former Soviet Union.

In the 1980s Egypt was one of the most fertile fields in the Muslim world for viewing the potential synergies between private Islamic capital and political pluralism. Roughly one-quarter of Egypt's privately owned banking capital had gravitated to Islamic institutions, and the banking system operated in a political system that displayed a multiplicity of Islamist as well as other tendencies. In Figure 8–1 the deposit base acquired by Egypt's Islamic banking sector in the 1980s is compared with those of other Arab countries and Turkey. Only in Jordan, Kuwait, and the Sudan, where Islamist political movements contended for power, had Islamic banks made greater in-

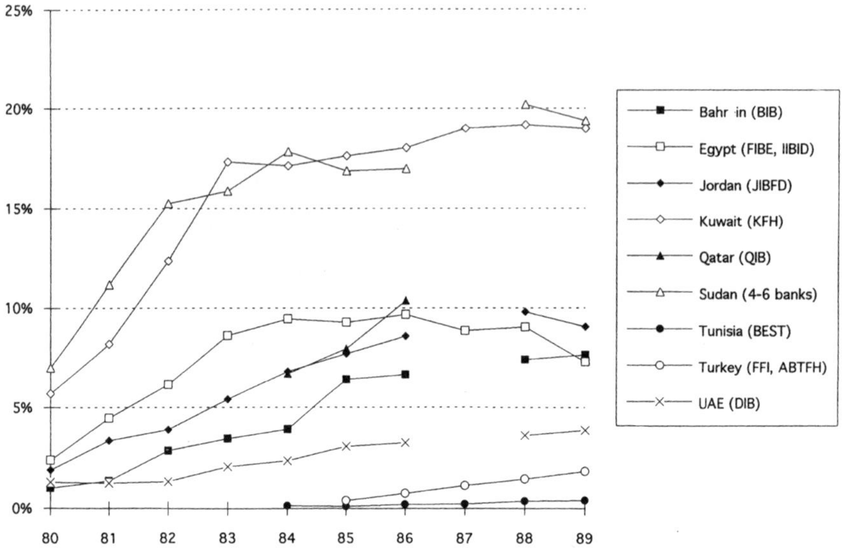

Fig. 8.1. Islamic banks' deposits as percentage of total commercial banking deposits, 1980–89. *Sources:* Metwally 1988, 1991; author's database of commercial banks.

roads than in Egypt. The Islamic share of Turkey's commercial bank deposits was barely 2 percent at the end of the decade, compared with Egypt's 7 to 8 percent.

The political environment was less favorable to synergies between bankers and Islamist moderates in Egypt than in Turkey in at least two respects, however. Competitive politics in Egypt was far less institutionalized. Mubarak's regime allowed political Islamists token representation (under other party labels or as independents) in the parliaments elected in 1984, 1987, and 1990, but the electoral process inspired widespread apathy and cynicism, and the outcomes were not perceived to represent the full weight of Islamist opinion. Egyptian elections, unlike Turkey's, did not offer even an imperfect way of gauging the weight of Islamist opinion. Egypt's regime remained authoritarian, its political opening too tentative and controlled to inspire much credibility. Moreover, the regime was "decaying" (Springborg 1989: 9) as it desperately attempted to delay controversial economic reforms in the 1980s, only in the end to embrace them in the 1990s. Islamists confronted a state already dissipated by years of crony capitalism. The contrast of Özal's strong state, buttressed by oligopolistic concentrations of finance capital, could not be starker.

The weak Egyptian regime lost control of capital accumulation. Infitah, an appeal for foreign capital to invest in Egypt, became an open door for capital flight. We have seen in chapter 2 how the informal money-changers sabotaged the state's last-gasp effort in 1985 to control foreign exchange markets. By then the money-changers were developing informal financial empires by converting their sidewalk customers into depositors and investors. In Egypt, unlike Turkey, a vast informal Islamic finance sector escaped all government regulation: the *sharīqāt tawẓīf al-amwāl* ("companies for placing funds"; translated by Sadowski [1991: 229] as money management companies). This group would compete with and outperform the official Islamic banking sector, with serious political as well as economic consequences. Much of the informal sector, which appealed for funds in the name of Islam, was not subjected like the official sector either to Central Bank controls or to supervision by religious authorities. However, the explosive growth of the money management companies tended not only to reduce the market share of official Islamic banks but politically to undermine the liberal vocation of Islamic capital and to strengthen the forces of unconditional Islamist opposition by politicizing their confrontations with the state's financial regulators. The story of Islamic capital in Egypt is one of lost opportunities for synergies with political liberalization.

Raw Capital in the Service of Islam

By 1982, when most of the money management companies began their operations, Islam was already proving to be a major vehicle in Egypt for attracting private finance or banking capital. Islam generated confidence, eliciting the trust of wide sectors of the population. Small investors flocked to Islamic banks, not conventional ones, while the bigger investors, examined in the previous chapter, also tended to minimize their exposure to the infitah banks. The Islamic sector accounted for 15 percent of the Egyptian commercial banking system's total capital in 1989 (against deposits and loans amounting to 6.8 percent and 8.9 percent of the respective totals), and the weight of the Islamic sector in privately owned Egyptian bank capital was substantially greater (table 7–1). Private shareholders had invested about LE 66 million in conventional infitah banks by the end of 1982. By this time, the equity accumulated by Faisal Islamic Bank of Egypt (FIBE) amounted to $34 million (LE 28.3 million), and that of the International Islamic Development and Investment Bank (IIBID) to about LE 5 million. Half of the former and all of the latter belonged to private Egyptian shareholders. In other words, the official Islamic sector already deployed one-quarter of Egypt's private bank capital by 1982. If the capital structure of banks reflected that of the economy at large, Islamic businesses had already established a substantial economic presence.

Islam's presence in the private sector was also visibly reflected in these banks' growing shares of deposits (fig. 8–2). FIBE was Egypt's largest private sector bank, and it attracted roughly one-quarter of the total amounts deposited in Egypt's joint venture and private sector commercial banks. The bank proudly reported, "The number of bank accounts rose from 5,464 accounts in 1979 to nearly 485 thousand . . . in 1989. These figures show that the Islamic investment pools . . . were met with an unprecedented acceptance by customers in Egypt and in the Islamic world" (FIBE 1990: 21). Indeed, investment pools were so popular that Banque Misr and a number of infitah banks rushed to exploit these new market opportunities. They established 58 special Islamic branches in the early and mid-1980s. By 1991 Banque Misr claimed 24 (out of 342) branches, attracting LE 2.8 billion, over 12 percent of the bank's total deposits and slightly over half those of FIBE (Galloux 1993: 245, 263). The Principal Bank for Development and Agricultural Credit (PBDAC), which manages some 800 village banks, carried deposits in 1991 of LE 102 million (about 2 percent of FIBE's) in an unspecified number of Islamic banks. In addition, the National Bank of Development had 17 Islamic branches (out of 50), distributed in many provinces where FIBE had not received permits to open branches. The Suez Canal Bank, the Arab Investment Bank, Mohandes Bank, Egypt Gulf Bank, Nile Bank, Al Watany Bank of Egypt, Bank of Commerce and Development (Al Tegariyoon), and the Bank of Cairo and the Far East had all established Islamic branches, mainly in Cairo. The collective deposit base of Egypt's Islamic branches in 1991, including Banque Misr's, amounted to LE 3.2 billion, compared with FIBE's total base of LE 5.5 billion (Galloux 1993: 263). Although it was not a commercial bank, Nasser Social Bank, which Sadat had established in 1971, also deserves mention. It collected *zakat* (Muslim alms tax) on behalf of the government and distributed interest-free loans to its clients through 26 branches. Deposits amounted to LE 185 million in 1989 (table 7–1), and the government increased its capital that year from LE 28 to LE 140 million (Directory 1991: 88).

Islamist entrepreneurship became a driving force behind an awakened civil society. Much of Egypt's new private capital, accumulating in the form of remittances from professionals, entrepreneurs, and laborers working in the Gulf states, might have been siphoned into Egypt's official banking system, intensifying commercial competition and strengthening a broad spectrum of infitah banks. Much of it fled instead to the aggressive new informal sector, while successive governments under Sadat and Mubarak delayed

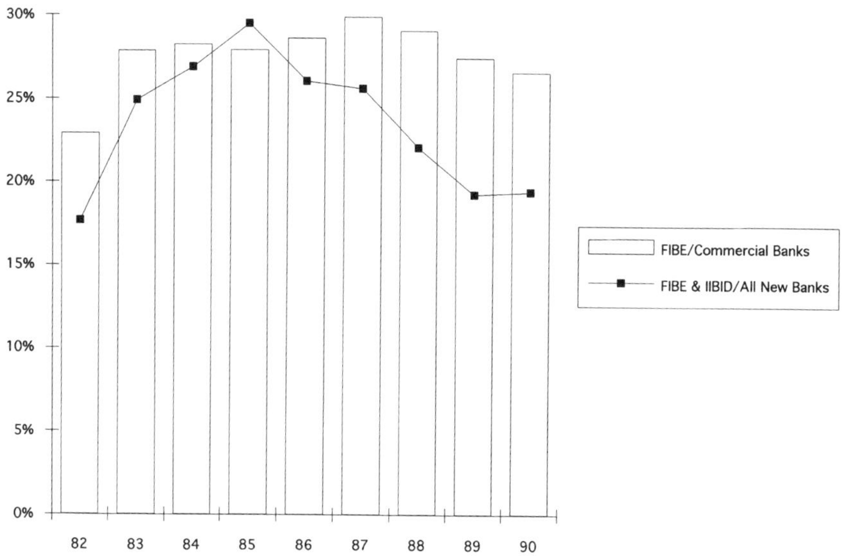

Fig. 8.2. Islamic banks' shares of Egyptian private sector bank deposits, 1982–90. *Sources:* Central Bank of Egypt; author's database of commercial banks.

liberalizing exchange rates and other reforms that would have obviated an informal sector. Some fifty Islamic money management companies, founded after 1981, gained the lion's share of Egyptian overseas deposits, mainly from migrant workers and cadres in Saudi Arabia. The leading companies, Al-Rayan and Saad, were run by foreign exchange dealers who had acquired their first financial experience working on the black market dominated by Sami Ali Hassan. They were among the 55 most prominent black market foreign exchange dealers targeted by Dr. Mustafa Said, minister of the economy from 1983 to 1985 (Abd al-Fadil 1989: 161–63). Despite the efforts of successive governments to enforce official exchange rates, the "parallel" or "free" market flourished, enjoying a certain legitimacy among bankers, Western governments, and Egyptian workers alike.

People like Saad and the three Abd al-Fattah brothers who ran Al-Rayan merely exploited market inefficiencies. Their money management companies transferred "free" spot market transactions into unregulated savings accounts, bypassing the Egyptian banking system. As Egyptian Central Bank governor Ali Negm pointed out in a press interview, there was nothing inherently Islamic about the companies. By the mid-1980s, their vigorous campaigns against "usurious interest" had mobilized hundreds of thousands of small depositors into the new profit-sharing institutions. Negm argued, however, that "if the motive were uniquely religious, founded on the fear of [being accused of] usury, [their] capital would have gone to the Islamic banks; but in fact what most motivates these individuals are the high revenues promised to them—otherwise none would get involved with these companies" (Rycx 1988: 195). As Sadowski has observed, however, "Many Egyptians began to think that the parallel economy offered solutions to the country's problems that the official economy could not. They viewed the businessmen in this sector not as criminals or barter-bound primitives, but as the best entrepreneurial talent in the country. They thought the parallel sector illustrated how successful the economy could be if the government deregulated and permitted Egyptian capitalists to work on their own. . . . Its expansion, while official economic institutions contracted, seemed almost miraculous, almost as if its Islamic allegiance had earned it God's favor" (1991: 233–34).

The black marketeers cannibalized the markets of the traditional Islamic banks, for the latter no longer enjoyed any official advantages over other commercial banks. By 1985 FIBE was considered sufficiently profitable to lose its special tax exemptions. It was obliged to respect the standard deposit requirements of the Central Bank and would come under pressure in 1988 to reduce its equity investments to conform with new capital structure ratios. Assisted by its Saudi partners, FIBE held on to its share of the official market, as figure 8–2 shows, but it could not tap into the new cash flows. FIBE was hard pressed to pay out enough "profits" on its investment accounts to keep up with the fixed interest conventional banks paid on deposits. In 1985 FIBE could not afford to pay an average on its dollar and pound accounts of more than 8 percent, and certainly less in 1986 and 1987, when conventional banks were paying 9 percent or more on Egyptian pound accounts. Egypt's other large Islamic bank, IIBID, was in more serious difficulties in 1985. After its manager had incurred heavy losses speculating in U.S. commodities markets, the bank fell temporarily under the management of the Central Bank. The "Islamic" branches of the conventional banks were equally uncompetitive. They could do no better than their conventional parent banks.

By this time the money management companies were paying their depositors more than twice the prevailing interest rates on Egyptian pounds (and enabling savers to keep up with inflation). The newspaper *Al-Ahali*, representing the Nasserite Left, the most vigorous adversary of the money management companies, leaked a confidential Central Bank report alleging that up to LE 8.1 billion worth of accounts in the official banking system were transferred into the money management companies between mid-1983 and mid-1986 (Rycx 1988: 204). Mahmud Abd al-Fadil estimates that the companies had accumulated between LE 3.4 billion and 8 billion by 1988, held by approximately half a million depositors (Abd al-Fadil 1989: 16, 17; cf. Aly 1992: 54). Subsequently the government claimed that thirty-three of the companies, holding 95 percent of the "Islamic" investments, had acquired 435,000 accounts containing $1.47 billion (or LE 3.8 billion; *MEED* 7 July 1989: 20), but some funds might have escaped the official audit. The total pool of household deposits in the official banking system amounted in mid-1988 to about LE 27.2 billion (Central Bank of Egypt, *Economic Review* no. 1 (1991/92): 114, 122). Of this, FIBE alone, comparable to the money management companies in number of depositors, had LE 3.5 billion, and Banque Misr almost LE 1 billion (Galloux 1993: 245). Including the informal money managers, the Islamic sector had captured 30 to 40 percent of the market for household deposits and informal investments, and the informal "Islamic" sector was rivaling and possibly surpassing the formal sector of Islamic banks and bank branches.

Few of the new money managers had much education, in either business or Islamic studies. Ahmed Tawfiq Abd al-Fattah was the best educated of the three brothers in charge of Al-Rayan, the leading money management company, had studied veterinary science but had not completed his college degree. He helped his older brother Fathy start up the company. Fathy claims to have saved LE 1 million while working in Libya and then to have entered the egg distribution business, riding his bicycle door to door, on returning to Egypt (Al-Sharqawi 1988). His name appeared on Dr. Mustafa Said's list of black marketeers, associated with that of another self-made multimillionaire, Sami Ali Hassan (*MEED,* 14 October 1988: 44–46). The Abd al-Fattah brothers had little formal education but they acquired substantial marketing skills. They selectively developed support among politicians, officials, professionals, and military officers; sometimes investments generated enormous profits: the money of certain influential clients simply had *baraka,* or God's blessings. In fact, one of their publicity slogans was "Al-baraka wara' al-najāh" ("the blessings behind success," *Al-Ahram Al-Iqtisadi,* 18 July 1988: 28). One secret of their success was that they could use their vast reserves of foreign currency to corner import markets for commodities and control prices. In domestic markets, too, their power became visible: Saad, a car dealer before entering the money management business, became the largest distributor of domestically made Fiats and he set their price.

Islamic Money and Political Islam

Islam was more than a marketing device for the minority of the money management companies that allegedly supported "a certain political tendency" in the 1984 parliamentary elections (Hilāl 1988: 17). One of the largest and most respectable of them—backed by industrial and other assets estimated to be worth LE 600 million, plus $6.5 million in hard currency (Al-Sharqawi 1988: 100–106; Abd al-Fadil 1989: 62)—was run by Abd al-Latif al-Sharif, reputed to be a staunch Muslim Brother. Like most banks, however, the vast majority of the money management companies shied away from any overt identification with partisan political forces. By definition, the official Islamic banking sector worked with host governments, through their respective central banks, whereas the informal sector escaped regulation, but it would be too facile to argue that the informal sector financed radical Islamist oppositions while the formal banks supported tame Islamist or governmental parties. Very little material on the financing of Islamist movements has come to light, and none of it points to any special division of labor whereby the official sector, plus Sharif, financed the Muslim Brotherhood, and the informal sector financed more radical associations or candidates in parliamentary elections. Banks and investment holdings, Islamic or not, rarely exposed themselves openly to political relationships. Egyptian Muslim Brothers founded a single Islamic bank, Al-Taqwa ("Piety"), but its overt political identification was unacceptable to Egypt's financial authorities, and Al-Taqwa, registered in the Bahamas, did not receive permission in 1988 to operate as a commercial bank in Egypt. It published its balance sheets in *Al-Sha'ab,* the official organ of the Progressive Labor Party, allied with the Muslim Brotherhood, and its Islamic supervisory committee was headed by Dr. Yussef Al-Qardawi, an Egyptian champion of Islamic banking (Galloux 1993:148–49). The bank may have attracted some offshore deposits but its total balance sheet was only 6 percent of FIBE's in 1990 (Ray 1995: 176, 178). The more successful money management companies, by contrast, avoided any overt political identification. But whether they were "truly Islamic," whatever that might mean economically or politically, was not at issue. "What is at issue . . . is that . . . [they] became a part of the Islamic phenomenon in Egypt," as an Egyptian journalist astutely observed (Aly 1992: 54), and that they alarmed the government (53).

Egyptian governments, battling politicized Islam on other fronts, also had to tread carefully. In October 1985, Central Bank governor Ali Negm was informed of speculative movements into gold and foreign currencies of huge volumes of private Egyptian deposits in American banks. But the best the government could do was to issue official warnings to depositors and to enact Law 89, which regulated new money management companies but left existing ones untouched. The companies enjoyed key support in parliament (Abd al-Fadil 1989: 84). A showdown between the government and the companies finally occurred in November 1986, after *Middle East Money* reported that Al-Rayan had lost nearly $100 million speculating in gold. The November issue of this glossy British magazine was widely circulated in Egypt's financial community. When a Cairo daily reported that the authorities had prohibited one of Al-Rayan's owners from leaving the country, it provoked a run on the company on November 9. The company, in turn, placed ads in Egyptian publications lambasting the government for plotting against it. "Islam will in the end impose itself as an economic power with which others will have to reckon. This system is quite capable of presenting new solutions to economic problems in countries which apply it integrally in a coherent manner" (Parigi and Malowany 1987). Or so Mohammed Tewfik Abd al-Fattah, the director general of Al-Rayan claimed, as if the Egyptian government were responsible for the company's losses. With help from local banks and possibly from Saudi banks, Rayan withstood the panic, paid off queues of depositors, and then proclaimed victory when the Central Bank governor was replaced within days.

Ali Negm categorically denied to me, however, that his removal from the Central Bank was related to the Al-Rayan panic (interview 11 July 1988). Money management companies were under the formal jurisdiction of the Capital Markets Board, not the Central Bank. Negm claimed that the principal reason for his resignation was his frustration over negotiations with the IMF. Mubarak had undercut him and, as another source also explained to me, a ministerial reshuffle had been planned before the financial panic erupted. Negm moved over to the private sector, becoming chairman of the giant UBAF consortium bank in Paris. He was also elected to the board of Mustafa Khalil's Arab consortium, Arab International Bank, in Cairo.

Despite Negm's removal from the Central Bank, relations between the money management companies and the government deteriorated in 1987 amid rumors of new regulations. The companies bought up local enterprises and partially restructured themselves to appear more in comformity with Law 89 of 1986. Al-Rayan, Saad, Badr, and Al-Huda came to resemble Al-Sharif, a holding company with considerable tangible assets in Egypt, although their publicity claims could not be verified. Al-Rayan, for instance, presented an income statement showing a 32 percent return on investments of LE 1.5 billion, half of them Egyptian assets (industry: LE 150 million; agriculture and livestock: LE 100 million; real estate and housing: LE 200 million; cultural, religious, and educational: LE 100 million; internal trade and services: LE 100 million), but the numbers seemed too neat to be plausible and did not add up properly (Al-Sharqawy 1988: 58).

The elections of April 1987 pitted the Muslim Brotherhood and other Islamic revivalists against government candidates. There was press "speculation that the IMMCs [Islamic money management companies] had made a $6 million contribution to the Muslim Brothers' war chest . . . [as well as having] contacts with more radical, underground Islamist movements" (Sadowski 1991: 238). However, the manager of Al-Rayan categorically denied charges to this effect by *Al-Ahali,* the organ of the Nasserite Left (cited by Springborg 1989: 49). Ahmed Tawfik Abd al-Fattah insisted, that "The business of working with money requires stability, not continous change or surprises, and certainly not getting into dangerous political games. How could we be supporting independents or parties in the elections, or terrorist operations for that matter, when we are under a microscope?" (Al-Sharqawi 1988: 44). The only discernible link between Al-Rayan and political Islamists was that Ahmed had served as "the amir (prince) of an Islamic fundamentalist society during his university years" (Aly 1992: 53). Another suspect, Abd al-Latif al-Sharif reputed once to have been a staunch Muslim Brother, insisted, "I am an ordinary Muslim. I refuse political action and I do not belong to any group or party" (Al-Sharqawi 1988: 84, cited by Rousillon 1988: 89). Subsequently Tariq al-Bishri observed that "the money management institutions were not formally part of the Islamic political movement, nor were the individuals involved" (1988: 23). Bishri, one of Egypt's leading Islamist liberals (Binder 1988: 243–93), argued that the confusions between intellectual, political, and economic Islamists were ultimately detrimental to culture, polity, and economy even though many secularists as well as many Islamists entertained or played upon them. Indeed, the money managers' publicity campaigns exaggerated and tried to appropriate the power of political Islam, thereby contributing to polarization of the political climate. The reputation of political Islam would also suffer by identification with the money dealers, once their financial empires collapsed. But in the mid-1980s the government and the companies alike played to a public opinion that did not distinguish between financial and political forces.

Strategies of Legitimation

The government and the money management companies made a temporary truce during the winter and spring of 1987. Advertisements in both the government and opposition press displayed President Mubarak smiling and consorting with the managers of Al-Rayan and Al-Sharif. "The unmistakable message was that the government . . . was now trying to woo [the investment companies]. . . . The implied trade-off was that the political appeal that these companies possessed would be placed at the disposal of the President and his ruling party" (Springborg 1989: 57). Some of the money management companies also tried in other ways to gain respectability and admission into the formal banking system on favorable terms. Al-Sharif purchased a controlling interest in the troubled International Islamic Bank for Investment and Development, and Al-Rayan hired Sadat's former economics minister, Dr. Abd al-Razaq Abd al-Maguid, to acquire Bank of America's shares in the Misr American International Bank (MAIB). His efforts did not succeed, but Al-Rayan had meanwhile embarked on another strategy to gain respectability. It tried to gain entry into the International Association of Islamic Banks (IAIB), founded by Prince Mohammed with headquarters in Heliopolis. The association served as a forum in which information about distinctively Islamic practices could be exchanged. All of the banks affiliated with the prince's Dār al-Māl al-Islāmi (Islamic Finance House) were members. Other Islamic banks including the Kuwait Finance House and the Dubai Islamic Bank were also members, although banks of the Al-Baraka Group, with one exception, stayed away from Prince Mohammed's association. Rather than paying their membership dues, they attended seminars within their own group for exchanges of ideas between religious authorities and professional bankers. The other major holdout was the giant Al-Rajhi Company for Currency Exchange and Commerce, a Saudi bank more than triple the size of the Faisal Islamic Bank of Egypt.

In an effort to gain admission for Al-Rayan into the International Association of Islamic Banks, Fathy Tawfiq Abd al-Fattah, the founder and chief executive of the money management company, visited Cyprus in 1985 and offered to buy the entire Faisal Islamic Bank of Cyprus (FIBC). He was eventually permitted to buy 18 percent of its shares for $220,000 (*Al-Sharq al-Awsat,* 9 January 1989: 7), and "Sheikh" Muhiydeen Hilāl, founder of another, smaller Egyptian money management company, similarly acquired shares supposedly worth $340,000 (Tayi' 1989: 14–16). The little Cyprus bank had an interesting history. Dr. Ahmad Al-Najjar, who had pioneered the concept of Islamic banking in rural Egypt in Nasser's day, had founded the bank to "revitalize and bring to work the philosophy of 'private development banking' in a rural setting" (Nienhaus 1986: 10). Dr. Al-Najjar also served as general secretary of the IAIB. In conjunction with Prince Mohammed al-Faisal's efforts to promote Islamic banking through the IAIB, the little bank was to be an Islamic bank training center, financed by the prince. However, the training ceased by 1984, two years after it opened, for lack of participants. Dr. Al-Najjar apparently encouraged the Islamic money managers to invest in the bank, which continued to work under the umbrella of the IAIB. Fathy and Hilāl presumably hoped in this way to achieve admission into the association and a respectable Islamic status for their respective companies. Al-Rayan subsequently applied for membership in the IAIB but was turned down shortly after the run on the company that resulted from the Central Bank's disclosure of its losses on the gold market.

Although the little Cyprus bank did not claim any net profits for the year 1984, it reported a paid-up capital of $6.1 million and total assets of $21 million, only $7.6 million of which were lent out (Metwally 1986: 52–55). It seems, however, that the reports either misrepresented the bank's assets or confounded them with training institute funds. Two years later, on 31 December 1986, a new audit indicated that the total assets had dwindled to $1.6 million, including only $400,000 of paid-in capital (Metwally 1988). Prince Mohammed coincidentally sold off his shares just one month after the new report became available, in the spring of 1988. The Bahraini buyer paid $5.25 per share, or $3.45 more than their book value ('Amir 1989:16). It seems, too, that the bank's creative accountants then engineered a two-for-one stock split, increasing the bank's marketable capital to over $2 million. The "market" value of the shares had almost tripled, for reasons of which the prince could hardly have approved. Instead of channeling Islamic banking technologies among Turkish, Egyptian, and other Islamic bank managers, the little bank was becoming a major source of embarrassment for the official Islamic financial institutions of the prince's Dār al-Māl al-Islāmi. Understandably, Prince Mohammed might not want to be associated with the Egyptian money managers.

Indeed, the IAIB rejected the membership applications not only of Rayan but also of Sharif's money management company. In other words, these companies failed to obtain any independent certification of their "Islamic" practices that might have helped them gain credibility and be integrated into Egypt's formal Islamic financial sector. To be sure, a number of them had gained accolades from respected religious authorities, and their rosters of religious consultants included former ministers, religious orators, and a prominent Islamist member of parliament, Salah Abu Ismai'l (Aly 1992: 53). Their emergence no doubt contributed to a "new role for ulama" (Galloux 1993: 52), namely, to legitimate the practices of Islamic banks. To demonstrate their Islamic character, most of the banks designated special advisory boards of religious scholars. "What is important is your name and your shari'a board's reputation," the chief executive officer of a new Islamic financial institution observed (*MEED*, 25 September 1992: xv). On occasion a religious supervisory board has significantly redefined a bank's strategy. Faisal Islamic Bank of Egypt, for instance, was obliged in 1987 to terminate forward contracts in foreign exchange markets (Issawi 1987: 29). No similar religious controls constrained the financial behavior of the money management companies.

The Crisis of the Money Management Companies

Egypt had meanwhile reached agreement with the IMF in May 1987, after laborious negotiations. Egypt's official exchange rates were finally brought more closely in line with the parallel market, so that the money management companies could no longer speculate with assurance against the Egyptian pound. They needed other means of generating income to keep up the high payments their investors had come to expect. They continued to grow despite government warnings to depositors.

In January 1988, "Sheikh" Muhiydeen Hilāl fled the country with $9 million of his depositors' funds. Apparently his company's financial condition was so bad that Al-Rayan had to abandon efforts to rescue it (Walker 1988). The issue of regulation was once more on the government's agenda. In March Mohammed Tawfiq Abd al-Fattah, the youngest of the brothers in Al-Rayan, was convicted of illegally selling on the open market substandard beans that he had originally imported for the army. Then, in early May, Al-Rayan and Saad astonished the business world by proclaiming a merger of their operations and the formation of a new mega–holding company. The Capital Markets Board immediately declared the merger to be illegal, and Al-Rayan backed down a few days later.

Ominously for depositors, dissension surfaced within Al-Rayan. The police had first got wind of it in April, when two of the Al-Rayan owners had ganged up against their older brother Fathy and kidnapped one of his advisers, a former professor and business program director at the American

University in Cairo, which had let him go because of alleged financial irregularities. The professor claimed that the two Al-Rayan owners had threatened him with "an AIDS injection" unless he signed bad checks they could use as blackmail against him (Hammam 1988: 7–8). Fathy himself, rumored to be a drug addict but probably just exhausted, was hospitalized, then bizarrely kidnapped by his two brothers to sign over management of the company. The root of the fraternal disagreements seems to have been Fathy's decision to merge with Saad. The bad publicity provoked a run on Al-Rayan as well as Saad. Together with Al-Huda Misr, shortly after the end of Ramadan (17 May), they announced a freeze until early June on all payments and blamed the government for spreading false rumors. On 4 June, Al-Rayan extended the freeze for three months, again blaming the government.

The government finally felt obliged to act. On 5 June top officials quickly finalized Law 146, only slightly moderating earlier drafts (*Middle East Economic Survey,* 13 June 1988), and rammed it through the People's Assembly on 10 June. "Not since the socialist decrees of April 1961 has an economic law stirred up so much struggle" (Hilāl 1988:18; cf. Rousillon 1988). Virtually the entire opposition, except the Nasserite Left, which was not represented in parliament, opposed the new law. It required the money management companies to reconstitute themselves as joint stock companies, to repatriate their funds to Egypt, and to submit to supervision by the Capital Markets Board and to independent audits. Naturally the Islamic Alliance opposed the new legislation, reckoning it to be "the government's plan to destroy the money management companies. . . . This law serves Israel, Zionism, and America, for the money management companies are fighting in the name of Islam" (Hilāl 1988: 18–19). The New Wafd's line of argument was more interesting. In support of a strong and autonomous private sector, Dr. Ahmed Abou Ismail wrote: "Egypt has not accumulated such large amounts of capital . . . mainly from the people, since the times of Talaat Harb and Ahmad 'Abbud. This law has restricted these companies and will affect the private sector." He urged that the companies oppose the law and return the funds, so that the people could be in the position of confronting the government, not the companies (Hilāl 1988: 19). In fact, depending on how the law was implemented, it might adversely affect foreign investment as well.

Rayan responded to the new law in a full-page advertisement in the New Wafd's newspaper on June 16. "If it is said that the aim [of the law] is to protect the owners of the funds, then I say that the biggest danger threatening their safety is *riba* [interest]" (Abd al-Fadil 1989: 96). The companies, however, called off a demonstration against the government and prudently bided their time, possibly negotiating the terms of the law's implementing decree behind the scenes. Promised for late June, the decree was not published until 9 August, and within days the major money management companies promised to comply with it. The government pledged that it would not interfere with their investment choices or strategies, and it also hinted at some flexibility on the critical issue of deadlines for repatriating foreign capital. In effect, the new legislation was obliging the companies to engage in equity financing compatible with Islam inside Egypt, rather than to speculate in international foreign exchange and bullion markets. Al-Rayan failed to comply with the new regulations, but many of the other companies, including Al-Saad as well as Al-Sharif, received permission to remain in business (*MEED,* 25 August 1989: 16).

In the end, however, none of the companies survived. The government relentlessly applied the letter of the law. Suffering a liquidity squeeze, Al-Sharif, the strongest of the conglomerates, was unable to pay off its depositors, much less share any profits. Nor did the government permit it to convert existing deposits into equity, a suggestion welcomed by many of the potential shareholders. Hundreds of thousands of Egyptians were deprived of their savings as well as their expected incomes, and many of them blamed the government more than the companies for their financial misfortune. In early 1992 President Mubarak finally stepped in to urge that the companies be liquidated and the depositors reimbursed as quickly as possible. Assets of the money management companies were then gradually auctioned off for tens of millions of Egyptian pounds, but the depositors were missing billions. Al-Sharif tried to raise his LE 600 million of depositors' claims in 1993 by selling off 95 percent of his industrial assets to Sheikh Salah Kamel, the Saudi founder of Al-Baraka's international network of Islamic banks. The nine factories included some of Egypt's largest plants producing plastics. Although agreements were signed and reported in the international press, they were not consummated (*MEED,* 21 May 1993: 23; 16 July 1993: 18). The investors in the money management companies were bound to be disappointed with any eventual partial compensation for their losses.

These investors could hardly have ignored the government's decision to reimburse in full, to the tune of $400 million, the far wealthier depositors—alleged to include a central bank vice-governor—of the BCCI's defunct Egyptian joint venture, the BCCM. The government lent Banque Misr LE 1 billion, repayable in 10 years, to acquire the BCCM, complete with the depositors' liabilities. In addition to BCCM's choice branch locations, Banque Misr acquired its lucrative Visa Card operations. Misr's management estimated that it would keep most of BCCM's depositors, at an effective cost of about LE 200 million, the prevailing value of the loan repayment (Interview with Dr. Bahaa El Din Helmy, 6 January 1993). Legal differences between registered commercial banks and informal money management companies perhaps explained the government's greater responsiveness to wealthy depositors than to the misguided masses, but Islamists could point to yet another instance of injustice and corruption.

The government had been caught in a no-win situation, and so, too, had Islamist and other Egyptian liberals. Economic liberals like Ahmad Abou Ismail had hoped for an infusion of expatriate funds to strengthen the private sector. Had the companies been financially viable, they could have mobilized much of the private sector's venture capital. They might then have marshaled the resources to buy out the public sector enterprises that the international financial community was obliging Egypt to sell off in the early 1990s as a condition for substantial debt relief. Many Egyptian liberals—Wafdists as well as Islamists—believe that the government clamped down on the companies because it feared their independence and financial clout. If they were so badly mismanaged, why did top government officials, including President Mubarak himself, consort with their chief executive officers in public, implicitly giving them the stamp of approval?

Yet if, as reliable sources such as Mahmud Abd al-Fadil and former Central Bank governor Ali Negm indicate, most of the companies were in fact swindling the public in classic Ponzi schemes—paying high dividends out of a growing deposit base—what else could the government have done? Decisive regulatory action in 1985 might have limited the damage to the public, but a righteous Islamist public perceived any government regulation to be intimidation. Mubarak's subtle strategy at the time, co-opting moderate Islamists so as to isolate the extremists, played into the hands of the companies, which marketed themselves as part of an Islamist mainstream. The fact, too, that the companies could buy off so many prominent officials (Abd al-Fadil 1989: 65–67) suggested that the government was as mismanaged and corrupt as it alleged the companies to be. Intentionally or not, the companies had served the political purposes of Islamist insurrectionists, not the mainstream. The confrontation between the companies and the government may also have "contributed to slowing down the privatization of the Egyptian economy" (Aly 1992: 54).

One final irony was that Dr. Najjar, who had founded Egypt's first Islamic bank in 1963, lost control of his little bank in Cyprus to other Arab shareholders. The Egyptian valiantly tried to defend against the hostile take-over by devising golden parachutes for himself and his clerks in Cyprus—end-of-service indemnities totaling $400,000, the book value of the bank. But two

Bahraini brothers, laying claim to the Al-Rayan shares in addition to the 25 percent of the shares they had acquired amicably, literally locked him out of the bank. Dr. Al-Najjar then sued them in Cyprus and in Cairo for having acquired the Al-Rayan shares illegally. He also mounted a press campaign in Cairo. Since hundreds of thousands of swindled depositors were avid for news of Al-Rayan assets, Dr. Al-Najjar had no trouble getting press coverage. He argued not only that Al-Rayan's shares had been acquired through an irregular power of attorney (for Fathy had died and his brother was in jail) but also that they were in fact worth much more than the price paid by the Bahrainis. In the words of a critical journalist, Najjar "revealed that this bank, which has branches all over the world [i.e., the Dār al-Māl al-Islāmi group, with finance companies in Bahrain, Egypt, Guinea, Jersey, Luxembourg, Niger, Pakistan, Qatar, Saudi Arabia, Senegal, the Sudan, Switzerland, Turkey, the United Arab Emirates, and the United Kingdom] and has this base in an unrecognized country, could have a great potential in the smuggling . . . and laundering of arms and drug money" ('Amir 1989b: 24). Al-Najjar even offered to raise $10 million from the bank's other shareholders to reimburse the Egyptian authorities in charge of liquidating Al-Rayan's assets, in return for al-Rayan's FIBC shares and control of the bank. Meanwhile Prince Mohammed, who had cut all ties with Dr. Al-Najjar's "social experiment," appointed a new general secretary to administer the International Association of Islamic Banks. The Bahrainis kept up the IAIB membership of Faisal Islamic Bank of Kibris, Ltd., and promoted Dr. Najjar's former student, a certain Prince Amro bin Mohammed Al-Faisal, to the board of directors, but the annual report of 1989 no longer listed branches or correspondent banks outside the unrecognized state of Northern Cyprus. The report also indicated that the bank needed to triple its meager capital by the end of 1991 to meet the requirements of the banking law in [Northern] Cyprus.

The Official Islamic Banking Sector

Egypt's official Islamic banking sector survived the crisis of the money management companies and offered a channel for reconciling the Islamist mainstream to Egypt's political economy. Islamic financial institutions had played a major role in earlier economic and political transitions. Supported as early as 1974 by Dr. Abd al-Aziz Higazy, the liberal prime minister who was infitah's chief proponent, the Faisal Islamic Bank had opened in 1979 and helped to legitimate Sadat's policy of infitah by giving conservative Islamist opinion some stake in it. Subsequently Islam's other multinational financial enterprise, the Al-Baraka Group, helped to rectify one of infitah's excesses. In 1988, after lengthy negotiations with the Central Bank, Sheikh Salah Kamel acquired a controlling interest in the ailing Al Ahram Bank and converted it into Egypt's third official Islamic bank, the Egyptian Saudi Finance Bank. Al Ahram had fallen into government receivership after engaging in illegal transactions with Sami Ali Hassan, the leading black market money-changer, in 1983. While the bank was being reorganized, the Egyptian government recapitalized the Islamic International Bank for Investment and Development.

Led by FIBE, the Islamic banks and branches established by 11 conventional banks collectively extended their financial innovations across a full spectrum of Egyptian society. The National Bank of Development and PBDAC were reaching new rural constituencies of the sort Dr. Najjar had tried to penetrate in the 1960s. FIBE, though limited by the Central Bank to branches in Greater Cairo, Alexandria, Suez, and six provincial capitals (Damanhur, Benha, Tanta, Mansura, Assiut, and Sohag), also made efforts to attract small depositors by setting the minimum for an investment account at $200 or its equivalent in Egyptian pounds. "This attracted investors which the traditional banks failed to attract," FIBE claimed (1990: 22). Banque Misr, too, was substantially extending Egypt's Islamic investment base with its 24 Islamic branches, many of them in places FIBE could not reach. In addition to Greater Cairo and Alexandria, Banque Misr had founded Islamic branches in Damanhur, Desouk (Kafr al-Shaikh), Tanta, Mahalla, Mansura, Shebin El Kom, Zagazig, Zefta, Toukh, Ismailia, Port Said, El Arish, El Fayoum, Beni Sweif, El Menya, Mallawi, Luxor, Aswan, and Tanta.

On the eve of Egypt's second infitah, the Islamic banks still enjoyed a substantial share of the private sector's business, reflecting the political regime's traditional tactic of accommodating moderate Islamist opinion. Islamic banks and the Islamic branches of conventional banks held about 18 percent of Egypt's LE 50.4 billion of household and private business sector deposits in 1990 (Galloux 1993: 262; Central Bank of Egypt, *Economic Review* 31:4 (1990/91): 134, 142). The Islamic economy was apparently becoming institutionalized despite the unhappy legacy of the "Islamic" money managers. But it faced new challenges as the government accelerated economic reform in the wake of Desert Storm.

The major challenge was political: in late 1992 the Mubarak regime's strategy toward political Islam underwent a sea change. As a result of attacks on tourists, the Ministry of the Interior bore down not only on extremist groups but also on moderate elements in the Muslim Brotherhood.

The minister presumably reflected Mubarak's new strategy when he argued against making distinctions between the moderates and the extremists: "These groups have the same objectives. There can be no distinction between those who claim to be reasonable, that is, the (Muslim) Brotherhood, and the others" (*Al-Ahram Weekly*, 7–13 January 1993: 1). He was dismissed from office in May 1993 when he attempted to reach political understandings with elements of the Islamist opposition. Mubarak's new strategy no longer appeared to be one of encouraging political pluralism incrementally and co-opting moderate Islamist forces. The regime bore down, for instance, on professional syndicates that had been taken over by elements of the Muslim Brotherhood committed to working within the system. Any potential synergies between Islamic banking and Islamist oppositions were now at risk, as Egypt veered toward a head-on collision with a probable majority of its politicized population. Egypt was already coordinating its campaign against political Islam with the bunker states of Algeria and Tunisia.

The other major challenge was economic. After the passage of the Banking Law of June 1992, the infitah banks faced a major shake-out and series of mergers, as well as new competition from foreign banks once the law's executive regulations were modifed to favor them. Islam's flagship bank faced major difficulties. As noted in the previous chapter, the Faisal Islamic Bank of Egypt had lost at least $338 million in 1991, when BCCI was closed down, leaving FIBE, as one of its managers delicately explained, with "a forward contract on its sale of goods" that BCCI could no longer honor. Prince Mohammed's holding company, Dār al-Māl al-Islāmi (DMI), was reported to have lost more than $400 million in the BCCI debacle. In 1991 FIBE rushed to reclaim $400 million of the $500 million it had deposited with the Central Bank, but it had to raise more capital as well as a loan of $150 million from sister banks of the DMI.[1] Whatever Prince Mohammed's success in raising more money, FIBE appeared to be seriously crippled by the loss. Figure 8–3 illustrates aspects of its financial performance from 1980 to 1991. Even before its big loss, the bank had needed more capital; though its capital, almost 6 percent of total assets in 1991, was only slightly below the Egyptian norm, the bank's investments in other companies consumed over 60 percent of it. FIBE's profitability had been mediocre over the years; after strong performances in the early 1980s, its return on assets slipped to less than 0.5 percent in 1991. Spreads diminished as a percentage of total assets, squeezing profits. FIBE did not seem to have higher costs of funds than other banks, but it had some difficulties on the revenue side, to be discussed later.

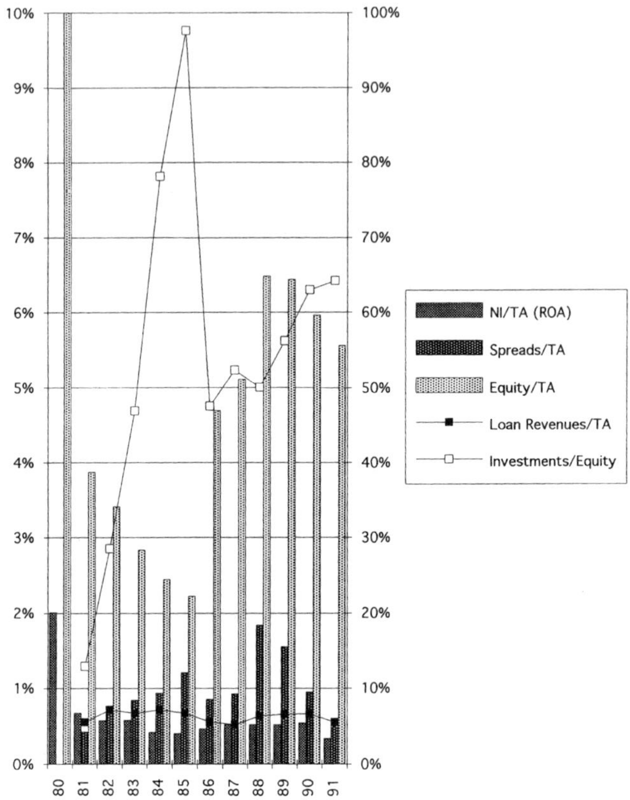

Fig. 8.3. Faisal Islamic Bank of Egypt: financial indicators, 1980–91. *Sources:* annual reports of Faisal Islamic Bank of Egypt.

Egypt's other seasoned Islamic bank had also experienced serious trouble. Plagued by shareholder disagreements, IIBID had twice been put into government receivership. Sharif, the respected informal financier, had bought into the bank in 1988, but his investment company then suffered liquidity problems and suspended payments. In 1989 IIBID lost over half its deposits, though it recovered some of them in 1990. Reinjected with public sector capital, it displayed a relatively healthy balance sheet in 1990. Its capital base seemed comfortable (11.3 percent of total assets) although it was still incurring losses from nonperforming loans. From having just over half FIBE's deposit base in 1985, IIBID had fallen to less than one-tenth, and it risked being surpassed in the early 1990s by Al-Baraka's new bank. Fortunately, IIBID's investment in a housing project in the Muqattem hills overlooking Cairo proved its worth by surviving the earthquake of 1992.

The Egyptian Saudi Finance Bank, Egypt's third Islamic bank, was saddled with debts from its defunct predecessor, Al Ahram Bank. In 1990 the balance sheet still featured loans (almost half of which were irrecoverable) amounting to twice its deposits. However, the bank was quite small and well capitalized, and Sheikh Salah already had a substantial group of businesses in Egypt to which he had planned to add Al-Sharif's substantial industrial assets in 1993. Salah had a nucleus of reliable borrowers, and his bank appeared well positioned to weather the second wave of infitah.

Assuming that Prince Mohammed could raise the necessary funds to offset FIBE's losses to the BCCI, the Islamic banks were in no worse shape than many other infitah banks, and the sheer size of FIBE probably guaranteed it continued support from the Central Bank. In FIBE's favor, too, Prince Mohammed had recruited Ahmad Zendo to fill the position of governor, the bank's chief management position, after one of Egypt's top professional bankers had turned down an offer to replace the previous governor, who in 1987 had presided over losses of at least $50 million on international bullion markets. Zendo was a former minister and Central Bank governor who had served under both Nasser and Sadat and was highly respected in official financial circles. FIBE was able to make special arrangements with the Central Bank in 1988 to bolster its sagging revenues. A full third of its depositors' "investments" were placed with the Central Bank, which, acting as a *mudarub,* or Islamic entrepreneur, imported basic foods and returned a prearranged share of the profits to FIBE. Whereas the money management companies had tried to corner these commodity markets on their own account, FIBE worked with the government. With its help, FIBE's performance was viable until 1991. It was in no worse shape than Egypt's other large banks, the Big Four of the public sector, and it kept up with at least two large private sector banks.

The principal challenge of the Islamic banks, discussed in chapter 1, was to generate enough earnings equivalent to other banks' interest revenues to pay competitive rates to depositors. As long as they were unable to engage in much mudaraba or musharaka, their revenues were bound to suffer. FIBE claimed in its *Annual Report* for 1990 to have placed 80 percent of its domestic "investments" (i.e., loans, not shareholding in other companies) in medium- or long-term operations, but its annual reports do not break down the distribution by the type of lending instrument. Islamic banks that provide such information generally lend over 90 percent in the form of short-term *murabaha* (trade financing). The loss in 1991 to BCCI was symptomatic; FIBE had apparently been unable to place its funds elsewhere for a good return.

The critical test of FIBE's financial performance was the amount of revenue, including the "profits" accorded it by the Central Bank, it could generate. Figure 8–4 compares FIBE's revenues from lending with the interest revenues of Egypt's seven other large commercial banks, presented in the order of their size. FIBE, with over 6 percent of the deposits and 7 percent of the loans of the commercial banking system, ranks just after the four big public sector banks. It appeared to be outperforming all of them after 1988, when it made its special arrangement with the Central Bank. Although the Islamic bank could not keep up with Egypt's big joint ventures, which served multinational corporations, it was also faring better than the Suez Canal Bank. With respect to the spreads between profits earned and those distributed to its depositors, however, FIBE's performance was marginal (see fig. 7–4).[2]

After deregulation in early 1991, rising interest rates on deposits squeezed FIBE's spreads as well as those of other banks. FIBE's quarterly payments on local currency deposits in the winter of 1992 were calculated to be about 16 percent on an annual basis, more or less the prevailing rate. Fortunately for the bank, however, less than one-quarter of FIBE's "investment" deposits were denominated in local currency.[3] Since international market rates on dollars had drastically fallen, FIBE's cost of funds in fact declined by more than 1 percent during the year 1990–91, when depositors received an average of only 6.3 percent on their investment accounts. FIBE was being squeezed, but probably no more so than other banks, including such top performers as the Export Development Bank of Egypt, obliged in 1992 to adapt to new Egyptian preferences for high returns on local currency over the safety of much lower rates on foreign currencies. FIBE suffered from the same lack of productive investment outlets in Egypt that afflicted many conventional Egyptian banks. The Central Bank, however, was paying high rates of interest on treasury bills. If FIBE could raise funds to cover its losses to BCCI, the Central Bank was probably ready to renew its special arrangements rather than let FIBE fail. Despite earlier failures of Islamic investment companies, Islam's largest commercial bank in Egypt had developed solid institutional roots and might further tap potential constituencies in the Gulf and elsewhere in the Muslim world.

In 1992 a prominent Kuwaiti Islamic banker claimed that "deposits with Islamic banks do not exceed a market share in the Gulf of 10 percent, but

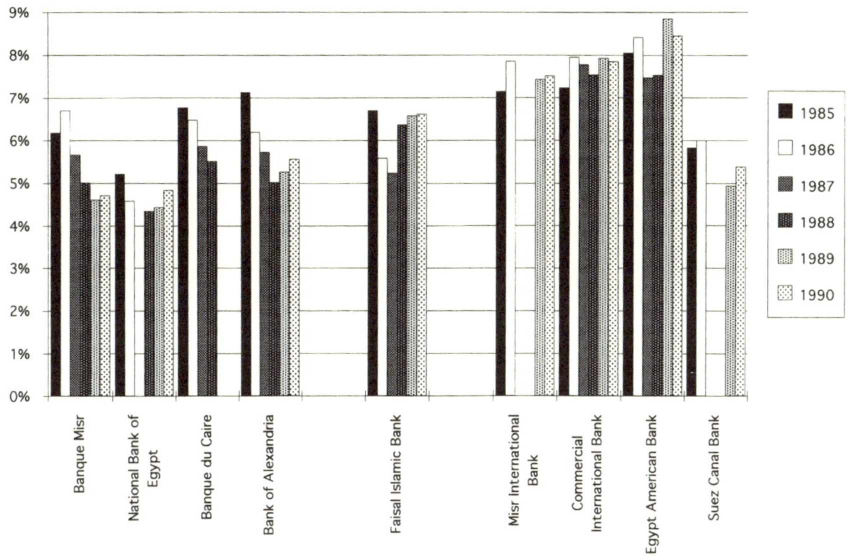

Fig. 8.4. Interest revenues/"profits" as a percentage of total assets of Egypt's eight largest commercial banks, 1985–90. *Source:* author's database of commercial banks.

its true potential is nearer 50–70 percent" (*MEED,* 25 September 1992: viii). Kuwaiti and Saudi investors were establishing a new transnational investment company in Kuwait, the International Investor, to complement the Islamic commercial banking system. Refinanced, FIBE might find better out lets for its dollars and other foreign currencies than the defunct BCCI.

Meanwhile, the private Islamic banking sector competed and cooperated with the Islamic branches of other public and private sector banks as well as with Egyptian banks. Within the Banks' Association of Egypt, they shared an interest with other commercial banks, including some in the large public sector as well as infitah banks, in greater autonomy for their respective institutions. While promoting Islamic financial practices, their principal drawback as political and cultural intermediaries might be that they appeared too transparently liberal and submissive to authority to be plausible rallying points for radicals bent on recreating an Islamic society. Yet in the political sphere other Islamists were still working gradually to make positive law conform with the shari'a, much as the Islamic bankers worked toward a more dominant role in the banking system and its eventual transformation. Further progress along both tracks might be a modest price to pay for functional pluralism and political stability. Egypt in 1992 was already so Islamic in many respects that eventual rule in the name of an Islamist majority might make little difference to bankers, businesspeople, politicians, or citizens at large, including the various minorities.

The root of the problem was political. Were Egypt to weather its political crisis and return, either under Mubarak or a successor, to a political strategy of incremental change, the Islamic banks would still be in position to play a constructive role. In the last analysis, their chances of reinforcing civil society depended on the willingness of the regime to entertain more political pluralism. In Egypt, as in Tunisia and Algeria, the political transition to an effective multiparty system ground to a halt in 1992, signaling an impending crisis. Gentle commerce, including Islamic banking, seemed unlikely to strengthen civil society and reinforce constraints on the arbitrary exercise of power until the politicians found new ways of accommodating political Islam rather than indiscriminately repressing it. In the early 1990s, however, regional tensions were discouraging political accommodations.

Chapter 9

The Debt Crescent in Comparative Perspective

> Not violence, but credit may be a rather ultimate seat of control within modern societies.
>
> (C. Wright Mills, cited by Zeitlin and Ratliff 1988: 108)

This book focuses on possible relationships between financial structural readjustment and political change, but the new world order has temporarily marginalized tendencies in North Africa toward greater political pluralism and democracy. No study of bankers and politics along the Mediterranean Debt Crescent, especially one written by an American, could ignore America's new aerial diplomacy in the region, even though it bore no apparent relation to the IMF's technical recipes for structural adjustment. The principal American concerns were not structural adjustment or democracy but assured access to oil at a reasonable price and security for Israel through containment of its enemies. The crisis precipitated by Iraq's invasion of Kuwait on 2 August 1990 exposed the Saudi-American underpinnings of the international oil regime that had emerged in the mid-1970s after the collapse of the multinationals' cartel (Gillespie and Henry 1995: 11–13). Reactions to Desert Shield, exacerbated by Desert Storm, polarized most Muslim communities, including Saudi Arabia. While many of the official Muslim leaders followed "Saudi-America," much of the rank and file viewed the Western intrusion into Islam's heartland as sacrilege. Across the Maghrib, from Morocco to Tunisia, the masses were virtually unanimous in condemning American imperialism as a greater evil than Iraqi aggression. While public opinion in Egypt and Turkey was more divided, polarization enhanced political Islam's mobilizing capacities in these countries, too, and contributed to weakening their respective regimes, which supported the American-led coalition against Iraq.

The Clinton administration's policy of dual containment of Iran and Iraq, while helping Israel, further isolated the ruling families of the Gulf Cooperation Council from much of the rest of the Arab-Islamic world and increased their dependence on the United States. The American presence was no longer "over the horizon," as embarrassed local protégés would have preferred, and continued aerial exercises further enraged most Islamists and other citizens of the region, putting more pressure on pro-American regimes. Islamists and Arab nationalists of the crescent countries, incensed by the United States and its British and French allies' bombing of Iraq, also perceived further manifestations of imperialism when Israel hit Lebanon by land, sea, and air and even raided Tunisia with impunity, while America stood by. Indeed, gunboats were back in action in 1993 and 1994 off the coast of Lebanon, though they were Israeli this time, not European. European gunboats no longer patrolled the southern and eastern shores of the Mediterranean in the service of the great powers' imperial strategies or bondholders' interests, but the United States threatened "terrorist states" like Iraq, Libya, and possibly Iran with overwhelming naval and air power. Aircraft and "smart" missiles had supplemented the gunboats, perfecting the arts of imperialism. They served American strategic interests in the region, although they did not fly in direct support of IMF prescriptions. International economic intervention, at least in the debt crescent, relied instead on the governments' fear of capital flight. The international experts of the IMF, the World Bank, and various donor countries were a century removed from the aggressive finance capital of Europe's imperial states and the crusading impulses of their racist publics. But perceptions of imperialism endured in the region.

One consequence of the Gulf War was a diminished flow to the debt crescent of petrodollars, already reduced by lower oil prices in the late 1980s. Egypt received some debt relief but withdrew its troops from the Gulf War in May 1991 for lack of adequate funding. Relatively impoverished by their U.S. security umbrella, Saudi Arabia and Kuwait perhaps also felt less need to buy goodwill from their northern neighbors. Two years after its "liberation," Kuwait could not forgive the Tunisian government for its tilt toward Iraq during the war, and Tunisia's foreign minister cut short a stormy courtesy visit to return home empty-handed (*Middle East International,* 25, June 1993: 9; cf. *MEED,* 2 July 1993: 37). Another legacy of the war was the international sanctions against Iraq: they were still costing Turkey billions of dollars worth of trade and transit fees in 1995. The Gulf War also had a destabilizing impact upon domestic political order in the crescent countries. Despite American lip service to human rights and democracy, American connections further complicated any efforts of governments in the region to make the necessary accommodations with their respective political oppositions. Repressing the opposition, however, intensified domestic strife and strengthened the more radical Islamist elements. Played up by the international media, violence in Egypt reinforced the tendency of the American public to perceive Arab Muslims as fanatics and terrorists. These perceptions, though devoid of a sense of cultural mission or imperial responsibility, were reminiscent of the racism that had once buttressed European imperialisms.

As long as the debt crescent's regimes remained incapable of accommodating their Islamist political oppositions, the entire mechanism of financial controls was at risk. Algeria's reform program, tacitly supported by the Front of Islamic Salvation in 1990, stalled when the regime declared war on the movement in 1992. Algeria amplified the crescent's tensions, just as it had in the past. Just as its colonization had been the most violent and intensive, its war of national liberation the most protracted and bitter, and its industrial development the most determinedly utopian, in the 1990s it experienced the greatest polarization between political Islamists and regime elites. Algeria's military rulers exaggerated the crescent's bunker mentality in the face of political and economic change. But however exaggerated, the Algerian example was contagious, and the Egyptian and Tunisian authorities, too, intensified their repression of Islamist oppositions. The bunker mentality seemed symptomatic of a broader conflict between Western and Arab-Islamic civilizations.

Political Islam rekindled nationalist memories of struggles against colonialism and imperialism and redefined them, like Samuel P. Huntington on the other side of the barricades, in terms of clashing civilizations (Huntington 1993). The new Islamic moment of the colonial dialectic projected the bunker regimes as outposts of Western imperialism, and the latter reacted in North Africa much like their colonial predecessors. The Western powers, while paying lip service to human rights activists, naturally tried to reinforce the bunkers, thereby lending additional credibility and impetus to a continuing colonial dialectic. As the confrontation deepened, the international bankers and their local partners, including Islamic banks, became ever more closely associated with the bunkers. Islamist radicals, like Huntington (1993: 39), perceived them as accomplices of Western civilization.

The shared Islamist and Western ideological discourse about a "clash of civilizations" perhaps reflected not only the end of the Cold War but also a disenchantment with modernization theory. The new dialectic might have been dismissed as a "postmodern" exercise in cultural narcissism, lacking in political content, had not political Islam twice, in June 1990 and December 1991, mobilized the majority of Algerians in free elections and frightened neighboring regimes. Islamist movements also constituted the only viable oppositions in Tunisia and Egypt, where the people might have voted their respective regimes out of office if given the chance. Political Islam had become the popular vehicle to power in the former single-party states, whereas the Turkish and Moroccan multiparty systems still offered alternative channels of electoral opposition in the early 1990s.

In the face of these confrontations, bankers could not—at least not in the short run—be the pivots of economic and political transitions in their respective societies. The optimistic hypothesis that had guided my inquiry into banking was that more autonomous financial systems would reinforce tendencies in the region toward greater political pluralism and competition, but the new confrontations with political Islam discouraged incremental political change. Algeria's commanders cast aside interrelated political and economic reforms in 1992. Ben Ali and Mubarak, too, waged war almost indiscriminately on their respective Islamist oppositions. Turkey's war against its Kurds reached new levels of violence in 1993, while its international credit ratings plummeted under the impact of increasing government deficits. Although Turkey and Morocco enabled bankers to exercise their arts of credit allocation, their structural power, discussed in chapters 4 and 5, only reinforced existing regimes.

The new discourse cast an especially dark shadow over the debt crescent because its states lay along the cultural fault line dividing the Western and Islamic heartlands. Each state seemed besieged by issues of cultural identity. But these were not weak states, although their patrimonial regimes were being contested. The states of the debt crescent remained relatively strong by Third World standards, at least in their ability to extract taxes to pay for law and order and modest levels of social welfare. Whoever governed—incumbent authoritarians, Islamist radicals, or more flexible coalitions of incumbent and aspiring elites—each state was bound to be further integrated into the world economy, for commercial activity flourished across the cultural fault lines of the Mediterranean. Either the expanding populations of Europe's Mexico would import more Western products or the countries would export more of their people north and westwards. Montesquieu's theory of capital flight was acquiring new human as well as electronic dimensions. And finance capital seemed bound to become more concentrated as structural adjustment proceeded, propelling banks to the commanding heights of the crescent economies. Although constellations of private business interests were crystallizing very slowly, financial reforms still seemed to be eroding the patronage networks of authoritarian states and enhancing the structural power of the commercial banks. Setbacks in the early 1990s were transitory and explicable, at least in part, by the intensified polarization between regimes and Islamist oppositions resulting from America's destruction of Iraq. The bankers' work in progress still deserved to be reviewed along the lines originally suggested in this book.

Capital Movements

All of the crescent countries were becoming more dependent upon the outside world, principally Europe, for capital, goods, and services. The most revealing indicator of their growing dependence was the steady and apparently irreversible increase in their imports relative to GNP. Tunisia increased its imports from 32 to 55 percent of GNP from 1970 to 1990, and Egypt followed closely behind. Despite belt tightening in the late 1980s, Morocco, too, was importing substantially more in 1990, proportionate to GNP, than two decades earlier. Imports as percentages of GNP peaked in 1981 for Egypt, Tunisia, and Morocco but were again rising in the late 1980s. Turkey, unlike the others, was self-sufficient in food, but it, too, showed steady increases resulting from the major reforms launched in 1980. Algeria was the apparent exception, but it had cut its imports to the bone by 1987. While it no longer imported capital goods with the abandon permitted by oil booms, it still had to feed its people, and official data did not include many of the "informal" imports associated with trabendo. The new discipline of the debtor states encouraged by the IMF entailed increasing exports, not cutting imports.

However poignant the cultural polarizations along the Mediterranean fault line, they could not obscure the secular trend toward greater trade. As the traffic increased, so too did the financial flows. The direct effect was more trade financing, but trade also facilitated capital transfers. Governments experienced ever more difficulties controlling capital movements. Rude administrative techniques like suddenly withdrawing large bills from circulation (tried by Russia, too, in July 1993) or clamping down on suitcase merchants at airports no longer worked. As the Tunisian authorities had so clearly understood, the business environment had to be altered in ways that might attract capital rather than repel it. Specters of capital flight were driving reform all along the debt crescent, as Montesquieu had predicted. Commercial banks had to strengthen their balance sheets to keep up with new international standards, lest their European correspondent banks cut off their credits.

Capital, indeed, had become far more mobile than in Montesquieu's day. Whether speeded by faxes and electronic mail, hidden in false invoices, or contracted informally between friends and cousins, capital transfer no longer even depended upon a piece of paper like the fabled lettre de change.

The acid test of the effects of gentle commerce hypothesized by Montesquieu was Algeria, because its regime was the rudest, the least financially experienced, and the most disdainful of bankers. It also wielded the most powerful club against European statesmen and their bankers. Offsetting the specters of capital flight were the hordes of potential migrants, educated elites as well as the unemployed, who might join their cousins in France.

In the short run the threat of population flight could temper northern threats to reduce trade financing and debt relief for southern neighbors. France was reported to have encouraged the Algerian officers to cut short Chadly's free elections when an Islamist victory appeared inevitable, for fear that a flood of Algerian refugees would seek asylum in France, compounding existing tensions associated with Muslim immigrants. Montesquieu never argued, however, that threats of capital flight would immediately open bunker doors. It is not so much the threat to withdraw capital as the expectation of future flows that offers the incentive for authoritarian rulers to improve their business climates. Even Algeria, the most refractory of the crescent regimes, actively encouraged foreign investment, especially in the petroleum sector, while backtracking on Chadly's political and financial reforms. It also opened its commercial banking sector, the exclusive preserve of state banks until 1991, to joint ventures and private Algerian banks. Though Algeria's opening to foreign banks and private capital was far more cautious than Egypt's original infitah, it appeared to be part of an irreversible process of economic liberalization. As long as the Saudi-American oil regime kept prices relatively low for Algerian oil and gas exports, the country had no other choice than to proceed with reforms designed to attract foreign capital. By the end of 1993 it had reduced its ratio of domestic credit to GDP by about one-third, to 68 percent, since the high point of 1988 (fig. 2–1). Cash in circulation also diminished substantially relative to the supply of money, from 39.4 percent in 1990 (fig. 6–3) to 29.7 percent at the end of 1994 (IMF, April 1995: 80–81, 111). In these respects, at least, Algeria seemed to be on the way to financial normalcy despite its civil war.

Algeria also proceeded in 1991 to raise its stake in the Union des Banques Arabes et Françaises (UBAF), a leading consortium bank based in Paris. Working closely with the Bank Al-Maghrib (Morocco's central bank), the Crédit Populaire d'Algérie subscribed to a capital increase that enabled France's Crédit Lyonnais to wrest control of the bank from an Arab consortium dominated by Egypt and to reorient the bank's strategy toward financing trade and joint projects in ways that took advantage of UBAF's global reach. Increased profits for UBAF France in 1992, for instance, came largely from financing trade between the Gulf Cooperation Council countries and the Far East (*MEED,* 30 July 1993: 7) as well as between France and the North African countries. A similar restructuring of UBAF Arab American, UBAF's New York affiliate, further signaled increasing interdependence in the banking sector between France and Algeria. The Crédit Populaire d'Algérie increased its stake in UBAF Arab American to 35 percent, in the fall of 1991, whereas Libyan and Syrian shareholders did not participate in the capital increase (*MEED,* 20 September 1991: 6).

Physical proximity and specters of mass migration also strengthened commercial ties between the European Community and Morocco, Tunisia, and Turkey. As a French institutional investor proposed in 1993, "Morocco must become for Europe what Mexico is for the United States" (*MEED,* 6 August 1993: 27). French banks retained important presences in the former French protectorates, as discussed in chapters 5 and 6. They also seemed willing to participate in most of the capital increases that the Moroccan and Tunisian authorities were requiring of their commercial banks. The only major exception was Crédit Lyonnais's refusal to invest more funds in Tunisia's Union Internationale des Banques. In addition to reorienting UBAF toward the Maghrib, however, Crédit Lyonnais also remained active in Morocco and had returned to Algeria. Spain, too, was reinforcing its presence in Morocco, and Moroccan banks were expanding their presences in France and developing operations in Spain.

Turkey had also reopened its commercial banking system to Europe. While a number of leading Turkish banks established branches in Europe to attract remittances from the guest workers, Istanbul became host to branches of leading German and French as well as American banks. Joint ventures were established with Turkey's major conglomerates—while Akbank, Turkey's leading private sector bank, consolidated its presence in the European Community with a branch in London. European investment in Turkish commercial banks, including the venerable Osmanli Bankası, remained modest compared with investments in Morocco, but they facilitated increasing flows of goods and capital. With the breakup of the Soviet Union, moreover, Turkey was acquiring new strategic importance as Europe's principal gateway to the Central Asian republics. Central Asian oil and gas might stimulate further interdependence between Turkey and Europe, just as Algerian gas exports would soon bring Morocco as well as Algeria and Tunisia into distribution systems for Europe.

Egypt still seemed—as in the nineteenth century—to be the most open of the crescent debtors to foreign banks. As chapter 7 concluded, the foreign branches were poised in 1993 to take over substantial shares of business in domestic currency, further eroding the shares of the public sector banks as well as those of some of the weaker infitah banks. The financial reforms of 1991 had at least temporarily reversed the trend toward the "dollarization" of the Egyptian banking system, as deposits denominated in foreign currencies declined from 54 to 33 percent of total commercial, business, and investment bank deposits (CBE, *Economic Review* 33:3 (1992/93): 108,116). Despite its much larger population, Egypt imported almost as much relative to its GNP as Tunisia and was in chronic need of debt relief, aid, and foreign investment. While its migrant workers and educated elites could not move in large numbers to Europe, Egypt depended more than the other crescent countries upon large numbers of tourists moving the other way. Egypt still had to attract people as well as capital. While the killing of a tourist in October 1992 had prompted the government to crack down on the Islamists, the economy could not long survive violent confrontations. It simply could not afford Algeria's civil war. Indeed, Egypt seemed to be the most fertile terrain for the therapeutic values of commerce hypothesized by Montesquieu. With respect to tourists, foreign officials, academics, and businesspeople, at least, Egypt had returned, at least for the time being, to the nineteenth century: "With its large number of European residents and swarms of foreign tourists, [Egypt] lives, so to speak, constantly under the eye of civilized mankind" (Milner 1899: 21).

Egypt was also favored by the oil rentier regimes and private investors of the Arabian Peninsula. Private Gulf investment flows had never ceased, despite the official break in diplomatic and financial relationships with most Arab countries after Egypt and Israel signed their peace treaty in 1979. Egypt's official isolation, accompanied by declines in oil revenues in the 1980s, dashed earlier Egyptian hopes of a new Arab order based on Gulf Arab capital, Western technology, and Egyptian labor and management. However, the Gulf states resumed modest public assistance to Egypt in 1986. In 1989 alone, all official Arab assistance and Egyptian labor remittances totaled $4.3 billion, 15.4 percent of Egypt's GNP (van den Boogaerde 1991: 76, 87). By siding with the coalition against Iraq, Egypt gained substantial debt relief from the Gulf states as well as Western creditors. Private Gulf investors were also active, and a number of them seemed prepared in 1993 to join in some of the capital increases that Egypt's new banking law was requiring of all commercial banks by 1996. Saudi investors, for instance, apparently agreed to pump tens of millions of pounds into Mohandes Bank, one of the most troubled of the infitah banks. The bank's chief executive officer claimed the Saudi investors were ready to take 30 percent of the bank, to be capitalized immediately at LE 100 million, and that they would also lend the Engineers' Syndicate much of its 30 percent share of capital (Interview with Dr. Naim Abou Taleb, 7 January 1993).

Though oriented more toward Europe, Morocco and Turkey also gained from their official positions against the Iraqi invasion of Kuwait. And though Kuwait cut some of its development commitments in Tunisia, the Gulf states still had significant presences in its banking system as well as in other industries, notably tourism. Gulf participation in capital increases for the Banque Internationale Arabe de Tunisie (BIAT), for instance, contributed to Tunisia's economic liberalization, even though Tunisia's great expectations of Arab capital had dwindled as its joint venture development banks ran out of investment funds.

Economic forces associated with gentle commerce still worked upon the debt crescent, but heightened perceptions of renewed imperialism and the "clash of civilizations" did not presage any easy transitions. If, as Algeria had been last to discover, a command economy was unsustainable, efforts to restructure it required political will and ways of implementation as well as technical blueprints and legislation. Financial and commercial interdependence set the stage for change but did not offer a script. Not so much the amounts as the *structure* of the capital seemed to be the key. By focusing on commercial banking, it was possible to gain comparative insight into capital structure because the commercial banks deployed the bulk of each country's finance capital. The management of credit allocation did not always, as Egyptian banking made abundantly clear, reflect the views or interests of the principal shareholders, but comparisons underline the critical role of capital structure in shaping economic and political transitions.

Concentrations of Capital

This book has focused on the local structure of finance capital rather than on the sources, levels of supply, or types of control exercised by various public and private foreign investors or donors, which may critically condition the control of capital in postcolonial systems (Winters 1994: 447–49). The recipient structures were all subjected to broadly similar stimuli of financial structural adjustment, and the central questions raised at the outset of this study were whether such adjustment enhanced the structural power of a commercial banking system and whether greater power might in turn encourage business coalitions to promote political transitions. "Structural power," however, is an inherently elusive concept because it assumes anticipated reactions rather than measuring certain types of responses to clearcut demands. In banking, it is not sufficient to review formal concentrations of market structure and then simply assume that a highly concentrated system exercises structural power. Nor is ownership particularly revealing if the private sector is heavily dependent on public favors. In fact, it was necessary to analyze income statements and balance sheets of the commercial banks of the Mediterranean Debt Crescent to discern the "good" oligopolists capable of promoting structural power. Whether they were public or private sector was less important than the health of their balance sheets, but it turned out, as expected, that the public sector banks were not in financial shape to be good oligopolists.

Reflecting their respective colonial legacies, Morocco and Turkey were alone among the crescent countries in accumulating the concentrations of finance capital characteristic of Hilferding's Imperial Germany. They also marched furthest in implementing the structural reforms promoted by the IMF and the World Bank in the financial sector. And as the analyses in chapters 2 and 3 of their economic and political strategies revealed, the respective concentrations of capital had faciliated the structural changes. While the World Bank did not consciously advocate oligopoly, its prescriptions of financial autonomy reinforced the existing oligopolies. Financial deregulation enhanced the structural power of "good" oligopolists.

The state banking systems of Algeria and Egypt during Nasser's time were sectoral monopolies, but they lacked autonomy. Reduced to cash registers, they passively implemented credit allocations decided by higher authorities and had little impact upon the amounts of credit or interest rates. To have an impact, an oligopoly presupposes a set of relatively autonomous actors capable of making independent decisions in pursuit of their economic interests. The strongest players in the crescent—"good" oligopolists who resolved their dilemmas of common interest—were financed by private capital. Though Turkey and Morocco included large public sector banks in their banking oligopolies, the driving force was the private sector. In the years following Turkey's transition to multiparty politics, private capital had become ever more concentrated into industrial conglomerates, which were in turn reflected in the commercial banking system. In Morocco, too, the king acquired and preserved France's principal conglomerate while encouraging others to emulate it by forming other groups in the shadow of the makhzan.

The striking financial resemblance of Turkey and Morocco to Imperial Germany pointed to similar power relationships. A small number of bankers could effectively articulate the interests of a relatively concentrated group of property holders in industrial and other economic sectors. They also commanded a much larger surface of finance capital than their formal share holdings, because their bank loans—in the form of evergreen facilities rolled over periodically—were the principal source of business enterprises' working capital. Given the scarcity of capital in the debt crescent's highly leveraged economies (and in Imperial Germany, too, for that matter), their finance capital became a major source of power. Turkish and Moroccan commercial banks were acquiring the structural power to command the heights of their respective economies, in the tradition of their German ancestors as described by Hilferding and Lenin.

The other crescent banking systems simply did not measure up to Hilferding's heirs in this respect. Though the public sector banks in Egypt and Tunisia no longer controlled market shares substantially larger than those of the Turkish and Moroccan public sectors, their commercial banking systems still lacked the necessary autonomy. It was all very well for their governments to proclaim autonomy. In Algeria, where the banks continued to be cash registers, the Money and Credit Law of 1990 had made the Banque d'Algérie as powerful on paper as the German Bundesbank. But the banking systems could not acquire significant structural power. On the one hand, the public sector banks in both Egypt and Tunisia were virtually insolvent, overrun by nonperforming loans, for the most part to public enterprises. Consequently they could not become aggressive oligopolists, relatively independent of their respective public sector authorities. On the other hand, the private sector banks remained weak and fragmented.

Analysis of the Egyptian banks' market shares and financial statements indicated that the four largest private sector banks, Faisal Islamic Bank, Misr International Bank, Commercial International Bank, and the Suez Canal Bank, collectively held only 16 percent of the deposits (table 7–1). At least two of them, Faisal and Suez, teetered on the brink of insolvency. Closer study of the capital structure of Egypt's banking system revealed very low degrees of concentration, reflecting the fragmented nature of the business sector. Wealthy private investors preferred investing small amounts of capital in a number of banks to taking control over one of them. Most of the private sector banks, moreover, were largely if not exclusively financed by public sector institutions. The only exceptions were the Islamic banks and one small family holding, the Nile Bank. Evidently the Egyptian infitah had not yet, after two decades, given rise to groups or conglomerates. Though some businesspeople of the pre-Nasser era joined the new elite, they did not reconstitute the old groups. The most famous of them, headed by Banque Misr, had dissolved into Egypt's vast public sector. One new combine, UNIMEG, shared a significant minority position in the Hong Kong

Egyptian Bank, but the group's principal common interest, exporting to the former Soviet Union, was dissipating. As discussed in chapter 7, infitah's major beneficiary, Osman Ahmed Osman, had apparently invested relatively little of his wealth in Egypt.

Private capital seemed less dispersed in Tunisia than in Egypt. Two private banks showed some dynamism, and one of them, BIAT, had become a leading member of Tunisia's commercial banking oligopoly. But the public sector banks still dominated the system and seemed even less experienced and less prepared than their Egyptian counterparts to implement the formal autonomy enunciated in Tunisia's financial reform program. Banking oligopolies commanded by the public sector seemed incapable of reaching the commanding heights of either the Tunisian or the Egyptian economy. Both regimes, moreover, took preventive measures against private sector institutions that threatened to acquire structural power and business constituencies. The Tunisian authorities could not tolerate independent control of its smallest commercial bank, the Banque Franco-Tunisienne, much less allow BIAT to acquire structural power that might support an independent center of political power. The Egyptian authorities' treatment of the Islamic banks and money management companies demonstrated a similar fear that the structural power of finance capital might be turned against the regime. The actions of these patrimonial regimes reinforced the view developed in chapter 1 that greater concentrations of private capital would be needed to generate sufficient structural power to render governments accountable to their respective business communities.

Constellations of Interest

As was noted in chapter 1, Max Weber had suggested that "domination by virtue of constellation of interests" might be gradually converted into "domination by authority." One of his examples was that of a bank acquiring seats on the board of directors of an enterprise beholden to the bank for credit. Market power over credit allocation is thereby translated into administrative authority over the enterprise. More generally, the market power of a banking oligopoly could be converted, as in Hilferding's example of the Berlin banks, into command over other industries. Seats on boards of directors might not even be necessary in highly indebted economies characterized by capital scarcity and highly leveraged enterprises. Banking oligopolies were achieving significant structural power in Turkey and Morocco even though financial structural adjustment required commercial banks to limit their investments in other business enterprises. These financial oligopolies supported regimes that exhibited greater degrees of political pluralism than those of the other crescent countries. Turkey and Morocco recognized opposition parties and periodically conducted elections that oppositions had some chance of winning. It was suggested that increases in the structural power of the other countries' commercial banking systems might promote greater political pluralism.

The argument concerned processes of change, not correlations between financial and political structures at any given point in time. Financial concentration was needed for bankers to acquire sufficient structural power to constrain patrimonial regimes. Once a banking system had acquired structural power, there was no particular reason to expect the degree of political pluralism to be correlated with the degree of concentration of commercial banking system. Indeed, Turkey's banking system was becoming slightly less oligopolistic, as new private sector actors took greater shares of the market. Increasing commercial competition seemed to be associated with a consolidation of democracy. Islam's "special finance houses" were seen in chapter 4 to be facilitating the secular elite's political accommodations with Islamist elements. Financial and political pluralism could be mutually reinforcing, once political competition was institutionalized and the banking system had become relatively autonomous.

In the patrimonial regimes of North Africa, however, financial pluralism seemed simply to serve the incumbent rulers. As Max Weber might have predicted, greater competition could undermine administrative authority. Going back to his original example of a bank's market power, the enterprise could get rid of its bank board member and stop any other meddling of the bank in its affairs if it could safely turn to other banks for loans in a competitive market without fear of reprisals. To generalize, increasing competition among banks might erode a state's centralized patronage networks that permeated private as well as public sector business enterprises. Egyptian infitah beautifully illustrated the hypothesis, for Sadat deliberately multiplied centers of power and let the new banks serve his political purposes. Elite factionalism, which Nasser had never quite suppressed (Beattie 1994: 171–74), extended its roots into economic enterprises and eroded the command economy. But elite factionalism and fragmentation, however much it diminishes a state's capacity to implement difficult choices (such as controlling foreign exchange dealers), is not tantamount to political pluralism. The evidence from the debt crescent suggests that competition among banks could not promote political pluralism unless they had already acquired structural power.

The problem was that unregulated competition merely weakened the commercial banking system rather than enhancing its structural power. Only oligopolies, as Max Weber had indicated, could convert their market power into real command over credit allocation. The Central Bank of Egypt lost control over the infitah banks in the late 1970s and 1980s, but they did not thereby gain autonomy. Rather, they became leaky vessels of public as well as private capital—leveraging it into loans for the private owners and their cronies. Egypt's major political opposition of Islamists might have coalesced with the managers of Egyptian remittances and achieved real market power had the money managers been integrated into Egypt's banking system. But neither the financial nor the political system could absorb the shock.

Financial reform and political transitions toward greater pluralism faced similar dilemmas in Egypt and Tunisia. Real autonomy of their banking systems presupposed a critical nucleus of healthy, competitive banks that could dominate their respective oligopolies. Banks collectively had to reach the commanding heights before they could engage in meaningful competition; otherwise, the state would continue to dominate credit allocation through its central bank and leading public sector banks. Yet significant competition also seemed essential if the banks were to develop their clienteles of depositors and borrowers. Islamic banking had offered an interesting potential shortcut toward simultaneous economic and political transitions because Islamic capital, supplemented by the Saudis, might have offered the respective banking systems sufficient autonomy as well as competition. Had the "Islamic" money management companies been integrated into the official Islamic sector, a critical nucleus of finance capital could have constituted a "constellation of interests" for collective action. That may be one reason why these companies had to fail. Their distinctive economic clienteles might have facilitated the integration of the Islamists into a more truly competitive political system. Analogous developments were never allowed to happen in Tunisia.

Officially recognized Islamic banks and moderate Islamist oppositions might still support gradual, simultaneous financial and political transitions were the incumbent regimes to change their tactics. But the regimes, not the bankers, continued to control the finance capital, and private capital remained dispersed and fragmented. If the regimes insisted on excluding the Islamists, they could not permit substantive political liberalization. As long as they remained responsive to advice from international financial institutions to develop their respective private sectors, however, greater concentrations of capital could be expected.

In this respect Algeria, Egypt, and Tunisia might well follow the path of the region's other former one-party state. It had taken several decades for major business conglomerates to emerge in Republican Turkey. Though neither Nasser nor Bourguiba had eliminated their business elites in the manner of the Turks after World War I (or the Algerians at independence for that matter), another decade or two were perhaps required for comparable conglomerates to emerge in any of these North African countries. As private capital became more concentrated, the bankers would acquire more meaningful autonomy and structural power. In this respect Morocco was well ahead of the rest of North Africa.

Structural Power and Political Change

Of the patrimonial regimes discussed in this book, Morocco's seemed best positioned to effect a transition to constitutional democracy. Morocco met most of the conditions that were suggested to be most conducive to a democratic transition. Although per capita income, $1,030 in 1991, was well below Huntington's suggested threshold for democratization, the structure of business enterprises compensated for their low total volume of activity. Organized into conglomerates, they were capable of collective action, and the banks, indeed, were acquiring significant structural power in the face of heavily indebted enterprises. The astute monarch offered good circumstantial evidence that structural power could transform a patrimonial regime. He protected himself from this possibility and reinforced his rule instead, by having his personal staff acquire a critical nucleus of these banks, including Morocco's top performer, before proceeding with financial liberalization. The Omnium Nord Africain (ONA), which had acquired controlling interests in several banks, remained the makhzan's preferred investment vehicle. A capital increase in May 1994 gave it a more popular image, for the Moroccan public was permitted to acquire 20 percent of the new equity, but these shares amounted to less than 3 percent of the conglomerate's total capital (*MEED*, 29 April 1994: 6, 35). Corporate ownership enabled the makhzan to preserve its control over patronage and to simplify the patron's task by reducing critical political players to a manageable number. Impersonal market forces could keep the business enterprises of Morocco's new capitalist class dependent on royal favor. Political order seemed further intertwined with business order in 1994, when the king appointed as prime minister the father of his ONA director (who, it will be recalled, was the king's son-in-law). The prime minister, in turn, appointed one of ONA's senior executives to be the new finance minister (*MEED*, 29 July 1994: 12).

Elsewhere in North Africa the patrimonial rulers did not enjoy King Hassan's plenitude of economic and political power. Dependent capitalism would eventually give rise to conglomerates, but it did not seem likely that incumbent rulers or their successors could brake any emerging structural power of finance capital by personally acquiring it. Nor could they expropriate it without incurring unacceptable losses of international confidence. Even so, Sylvia Maxfield's (1990) study of banking and politics in Mexico showed that the nationalization of its banks in 1982 paradoxically reinforced Mexico's "bankers' alliance."

Her study explained variations in the strength of the alliance as a function of the scarcity of international capital in different time periods, whereas this book focuses on contemporary variations in the structure of the banking industry in different countries. From her cursory description of industry structure, it can be surmised that Mexico's "financial-industrial-commercial conglomerates" reflected the "German" pattern of financial development. In Brazil, by contrast, the industry was slightly more concentrated but apparently displayed considerably less structural power because the state planners controlled credit allocation, coordinated through one large bank that was owned predominantly by the government (Maxfield 1990: 180). To answer one reviewer's question (Winters 1994: 428) speculatively from this book's perspective, state leaders probably did not nationalize the Brazilian private banking sector because it was not perceived to be worth the trouble. Mexico's banks, by contrast, were a highly visible scapegoat, even though nationalization could not break their political alliance with proponents of financial orthodoxy inside the government. The new managers appointed by the state to run the banks would respect conventional financial practices; in fact, credit allocation became further concentrated under their management in the mid-1980s, while the former owners developed new forms of financing for the corporate elite through private nonbank institutions (Maxfield 1990:154, 157).

The case of Mexico in fact sheds further light on the debt crescent countries, which constitute Europe's Mexico. In Mexico a financial oligopoly promoted an institutionalized form of pluralism within a single-party system. Owners of capital learned to coexist with populist forces and, conversely, the populists tempered their economic radicalism. Mexico's financial and business communities had sufficient resources, and the freedom to deploy them, to support a ruling party hungry for patronage as well as a token opposition party. In Turkey, despite a formal multiparty system, the outcome was not dissimilar. Big business supported an array of contending parties, and elections usually produced Center-Right governing coalitions.

Along the rest of the debt crescent, by contrast, business communities have not yet acquired their share of power.

Current structural adjustment will enhance the business communities' respective chances. The structural power of the respective commercial banking systems may be a more useful predictor of business power than other alleged economic preconditions of democracy, such as per capita income or the relative strength of the private sector versus the public sector economy. In the very limited sample of the debt crescent countries, structural power seems quite unrelated to per capita income. Structural power is visible in the financial statements of commercial banks and indicates a system's potential for collective action. A relatively concentrated system of financially healthy banks can be assumed to wield structural power unless other public authorities dictate credit allocation. Morocco's banking system, though subject to some external influence, seems more powerful along these dimensions than do the other North African systems. Despite having a lower per capita income than Algeria or Tunisia, Morocco may be better positioned, economically, for a transition to democracy.

Algeria, with nominally twice Morocco's per capita income and more than triple Egypt's, seems to be in the worst position. Its six banks remain incapable of allocating credit autonomously. A business community more capable of collective action might have lent support to Chadly's simultaneous economic and political reforms. Its weakness, reflected in the financial statements of the Algerian banks, also helps to explain the failure to consolidate democracy.

Tunisia, with a per capita income of $1,500 in 1991, was well ahead of Morocco and Egypt and only slightly behind Turkey and Algeria. Its commercial banking system has clearly acquired more structural power than Algeria's, but less than Turkey's or Morocco's. Despite a relatively unfavorable colonial legacy, its structural power also exceeds Egypt's. Tunisia's leading private sector banks seem in better financial shape than their Egyptian counterparts, and the system is more concentrated. However, the Tunisian authorities have seemed determined to limit the power and market shares of the private sector, just as the Egyptians had curtailed the development of Islamic financial institutions. Their preemptive actions underlined the potential political significance of structural power in patrimonial political systems.

As one of the most internally indebted regions of the Third World, the crescent was an ideal site from which to view the workings of structural power. But whatever their domestic indebtedness, external debt pressures are reinforcing processes of financial liberalization in most Third World countries, enhancing the structural power of commercial banking systems. These systems deploy most of the finance capital of all but the most highly advanced capitalist systems. In much of Africa and parts of Asia, they still face patrimonial authoritarian states. One clue to the political development of these states, like those of the Mediterranean Debt Crescent, may be the emerging structural power of their banking systems. Neither structural power nor a certain level of per capita income can be viewed as a necessary or sufficient condition for a transition to democracy, but structural power lays a groundwork for collective action that may integrate political change with capitalist development.

Notes

Chapter 1. Financial Reform and Political Change

1. The extractive capability, which Snider calls "relative political capacity," is the ratio of actual tax revenues to those predicted by an econometric model developed by fiscal economists. Expected revenues will be proportional to the value of mineral production and the value of exports expressed as percentages of GDP, and inversely proportional to agriculture's share of GDP. For details, see Snider 1990: 1268–71 and his references.

2. Hilferding acquired German citizenship after World War I, in which he had served as a physician in the Austrian army. He was elected to the Reichstag in 1924 and again in 1928 but fled Germany in 1933. The French handed him over to the Gestapo in 1941, and he was tortured to death.

Chapter 2. External Debts and Economics of Adjustment

1. The ratio of total domestic credit to GDP averaged .774 for the five countries of the debt crescent in 1987, compared with an average of .727 for nine other Middle Eastern countries and .417 for 34 other lower-middle-income countries. An analysis of variance indicated that the differences between the Middle Eastern and the other countries were significant at the .004 level. The calculations are based on IMF data.

2. Figure 2–2 does not include short-term debt because the World Bank's *World Debt Tables* do not include data before 1977. Short-term debt reached 19 percent of the total Turkish external debt in 1987 and 16 percent of Egypt's in 1986, but it rarely exceeded 10 percent in the other North African countries.

3. Figure 2–3 may slightly exaggerate the increase in 1977 of Turkey's debt service ratio because service on short-term debt is not included for previous years. Turkey's short-term debt increased from $229 million in 1974 to $1,388 million in 1975 and $3,342 million in 1976. But the additional debt service for these years was probably negligible. Turkey postponed repayment, accumulating arrears of $1,580 million in interest payments on the short-term debt. The arrears is included in the total debt service requirements for 1977. See Hewin et al. 1988: 109.

4. The Egyptian government promised to cut the budget deficit, to curb imports, to float the pound, and to reduce subsidies on semi-luxury goods, but Waterbury

(1983: 410), citing the local press, reports that subsidies were not to be cut on basic staple products. Hilāl (1987: 102) insists, however, that subsidies for bread and other basics were to be cut, and he lists the full range of products for which subsidies were to be reduced or eliminated (219–30).

5. The factor analysis used balance of trade data from the *World Debt Tables* but did not include the IMF *International Financial Statistics* measure of the trade balance or government finance surplus/deficits. The correlation coefficients of these measures with factor 2 were, respectively, .41 and .39.

6. The twin deficits and per capita income explained 46.3 percent of the variation in factor 2. A dummy variable dichotomizing the crescent and other countries in the sample, which was added to the model, explained an additional 7.4 percent of the variation. All of the independent variables were significant at the .05 level or better.

7. The distribution of shares was as follows: Libyan Arab Commerce Bank 40 percent, the Kuwait Investment Bank 20 percent, and the Turkish banks İş and Anadolu (amalgamated with Emlak into Konutbank in 1988), 20 percent each. See Öztin Akgüç 1987: 57–58.

8. One simple measure of concentration of market shares in any industry is the Herfindahl-Hirschmann Index (HHI). HHI is defined as the sum of the squares of the market shares of all enterprises in the industry (Rose 1987: 181). Thus the HHI of a perfect monopoly would be 1, while an industry consisting of only two firms, each enjoying half of the market, would score $(.5)^2 + (.5)^2 = .5$, or 50 percent, and an industry consisting of 10 firms, each with one-tenth of the market, would score .1, or 10 percent. The lower the score, the less the concentration of market shares; the greater the dispersion (toward an ideal of perfect competition), the closer HHI approaches 0.

Chapter 3. Political Strategies of Reform

1. Ismail Khelil became a member of the RCD's Political Bureau in 1988. He was governor of the Central Bank from 1987 to 1990 and then, after briefly serving as foreign minister, was named ambassador to the United States in 1991.

2. The government proposed majority list voting and reduced the number of inhabitants required to sponsor candidates on a list from 200 to 100 at the request of the opposition parties. All of the opposition parties to take a stand opposed the electoral law's majority-winner-take-all approach in favor of proportional representation. They also disliked the provision for sponsorship because local authorities had intimidated sponsors of opposition lists in previous elections.

3. Of 13,260,000 eligible voters, 7,820,000 went to polls, but 900,000 spoiled their ballots (*MEED* 10 January 1992: 10). FIS received 3,260,222 votes, the FLN 1,612,947, the FFS 510,661, and Hamas (another Islamist party) 368,697, followed by the RCD and PRA with less than 200,000 votes each and a host of weaker parties (*Algérie Actualité* 9 January 1992: 7).

Chapter 4. Turkey: The Financial Levers of Power

1. The special finance houses collectively earned a 2.2 percent return on assets in 1990 and 1.4 percent in 1991. The collective balance sheets and income statements are presented in Central Bank of the Republic of Turkey, *Quarterly Bulletin* 1991: I, and 1992: I.

2. Since the Islamic banks book as loans ("investments") the amounts due, including expected "profits," this estimate of their share of lending may be slightly inflated.

Chapter 5. Finance Capital in Morocco

1. Zola's novel portrays a financial speculator operating in Paris at the end of the Second Empire. The editors of the Pléiade edition of Zola's work relate the stunning rise and crash of his fictitious Banque Universelle to the real trajectory of the Union Générale, which operated along parts of the debt crescent in the subsequent decade. After retiring from Egypt in 1868, Edouard Dervieu, David Landes's principal figure in *Bankers and Pashas,* played a minor role in this bank (1958: 312). Hilferding would view all of these characters as shortsighted speculators, to be sharply contrasted with rational finance capitalists having long-term strategies. Zola shows them living in the Parc Monceau, a charming little residential retreat for the *nouveaux riches* of the Second Empire, not far from from the Arc de Triomphe honoring the first of Napoleon's victories (Zola 1967 [1891]: 13, 49). In real life, Dervieu retired to the Parc (Landes 1958: 311), as did many of the wealthy Galata bankers, typically Christian or Jewish minorities, from Istanbul (Blaisdell 1929: 39).

Chapter 6. Algeria and Tunisia: In Search of Financial Power

1. International Monetary Fund, *International Financial Statistics* 45:5 (May 1992), pp. 84–85, dividing the banks' demand and time deposits (lines 24 and 25) by the banks' claims on the government and "private sector"—that is, mainly state enterprises (lines 22a and d).

2. For the rebuttal by Abdesselam's chief villain, the minister of energy and petrochemical industries from 1979 to 1988, see Belkacem Nabi 1991.

3. Under new management, the STB finally recognized 269 million TD of "Other Credits to the Clientele" in its balance sheets for the year ending 31 December 1989. Under the accounting rules supported by the Central Bank since 1987, this rubric consists mainly of nonperforming loans. As an outsider not privy to Tunisia's banking secrets, I have tried in table 6–3 to take advantage of the new glimmers of accounting *glasnost.* Problem loans are estimated by weighting the banks' respective declarations of "other credits" so as to add up to the totals officially published in *Statistiques Financière* by the BCT. Capital, total assets, and provisions for nonper-

forming loans are similarly estimated. The numbers given by the individual banks and published in the annual reports of the APBT are reconciled with the BCT's statistics.

4. Cash flow is a better indication of a bank's basic health than the bottom line of net income after taxes, because banks have a tendency to massage those ultimate indicators of profitability: net income to total assets and to equity (Ben Othmane and Souissi, 1987b: 69).

5. If the annual values for total assets had been converted to annual averages, the annual ratios and totals would be slightly higher.

6. The last account of the judicial struggles is Mechri 1988: 18–19. A more independent French language weekly, *Le Grand Maghreb,* was financially pressured to cease reporting the story before itself being forced out of business. The account that follows in the text is based on interviews conducted with Abdelmajid Bouden in 1989 and 1990 and with the Tunisian lawyers who served as arbitrators in the Paris International Chamber of Commerce Court of Arbitration proceedings between the BFT and the Arab Business Consortium International Finance and Investment Company (ABCI). Bouden kindly provided a copy of the ICC Court of Arbitration's award sentence (affair no. 59535/JJA, 10 August 1987). He also provided copies of the minutes of the BFT's general assemblies of 31 March 1988 and 9 May 1988, together with supporting documents.

7. Figure 6–4 is based on data provided by each commercial bank to the Association Professionelle des Banques de Tunisie. It may underestimate the market shares of banks that do not practice "window dressing" by inflating their deposit bases at the end of the calendar year for cosmetic accounting purposes. BIAT claims in its annual report of 1985, for instance, to have captured almost 13 percent of the deposits, whereas the writer's data base indicates 11.6 percent. Slight differences may be due to different denominators. Figure 6–4 uses the totals of the deposits indicated in the banks' annual reports for December 31 of each year, whereas BIAT used Central Bank data. Boubaker Mabrouk, president of the board of the Banque de Tunisie, claimed that the writer's data underestimated his bank's share of deposits by about one percentage point (Interview June 6, 1989). He showed the writer his bank's monthly data and argued that other banks did window dressing, which can be detected from monthly data series provided in Banque Centrale de Tunisie, *Statistiques Financières.*

8. Banque Centrale de Tunisie, annual reports, 1989, p. 221, and 1990, p. 169. Possibly the BCT redefined the private sector in 1990, because the 1990 report claims that private sector enterprises had received 82.6 percent, not 69.1 percent, of the credits in 1989.

9. Association Professionnelle des Banques de Tunisie 1990, p. 77, listed a total of 606 branches by 1990, not including the 29 branches of the specialized Housing Bank, which was then formally part of the commercial banking system. Geographical breakdowns were not published.

Chapter 7. Egypt's Fragmented Finance Capital

1. By international convention, banks were supposed to increase their core capital to cover 8 percent of their total risk assets—not only loans but other items off the balance sheet, duly weighted to reflect their risk. Data are not available to calculate the total risk assets of each bank, but the National Bank of Egypt, for instance, had additional off–balance sheet exposure totaling LE 9 billion in 1989, some of which may have required some capital cover.

2. In 1989 the Central Bank estimated that the government sector and public sector companies received, respectively, LE 5,240 million and 8,964 million of credit and in turn deposited LE 5,033 million and 7,417 million back into the system (Central Bank of Egypt, *Annual Report* 1989/90: 117). By subtracting these sums from the totals of the Big Four and from the grand total of deposits and loans recorded in 1989, the distributions by banking sector of loans to the private sector could be calculated.

3. Spreads, of course, are only one source of income. Despite other sources, such as letters of credit, foreign exchange dealing, and other treasury operations, spread rates nevertheless explained more than half of the variation in returns on total assets within our sample of Egyptian banks.

4. Return on total assets (ROA) for any given year is the bank's net income divided by the total assets listed on the balance sheet. It was a better indicator of profitability than return on equity because the banks varied greatly in their degree of leverage of capital to total assets. It should be borne in mind, however, that ROA tends to bias results slightly in favor of the more highly capitalized banks because, all else equal, they will borrow less and have a lower cost of funds (Vittas 1991: 5). Net income could still be manipulated by managers by way of the amount of revenues they allocated to provisions for loan or investment losses. But cash flow provisions and other expenses added back to net income could not be used as a measure of profitability because a standard practice until June 1991 was to declare interest on nonperforming loans as income and then to deduct provisions from the income. It should also be noted that this book compares annual ROAs rather than the technically more correct return on average annual assets, which would have required two consecutive years of data. Averaging ROAs over recent years squeezed more out of a limited data set but also slightly, albeit consistently, biased the results downward. The same considerations applied to lending rates, but the spread rates, being differences between lending rates and costs of funds, were less biased.

5. Average spreads of interest rates were computed by subtracting the interest received by a bank, divided by its loans and deposits with other banks, from the interest paid, divided by deposits of clients and other banks, and averaging the results over the years of available data.

6. For lack of extensive data, Dakahlia Development Bank was not included in

figure 7.6. Spread rates were −3.8 percent and −3.6 percent, respectively, in 1989 and 1990.

Chapter 8. Islamic Capital and Islamist Politics in Egypt

1. The $500 million "invested" with the Central Bank was still on FIBE's 1991 balance sheet, but the closing date of the statement was 12 July 1991, too soon after the collapse of BCCI for the cash to have been transferred. The loan and plans for a capital increase were reported in the bank's annual report for 1991.

2. Encouraged to use my data base of Egyptian commercial banks, Nicholas Ray drew similar conclusions from comparing some of FIBE's ratios, including interest revenues or "profits" to total assets, with those of eight other banks for the years 1979–90 (1995: 125–62).

3. By comparing the dollar value of FIBE's investment deposits given in its 1990 annual report with the corrected value, under a different rate of exchange, in the 1991 annual report, the writer calculated that local currency constituted 23.2 percent of FIBE's pool of investment deposits at the end of the 1990 accounting year. The annual report for 1990 stated (p. 14) that 75 percent of the bank's total assets were denominated in foreign currencies.

Bibliography

Abd al-Fadil, Mahmud. 1989. *The Biggest Financial Swindle: The Economy and Politics of the Money Management Companies* (in Arabic). Cairo: Dar al-Mustaqbal al-Arabi.

Abdesselam, Belaid. 1990. *Le gaz Algérien: Stratégies et enjeux*. Algiers: Bouchene.

Addi, Lahouari. 1991. "Les réformes économiques et leurs limites," *Les Cahiers de l'Orient.* 23 (3d trimester): 115–22.

Ajami, Fouad. 1981. *The Arab Predicament.* Cambridge: Cambridge University Press.

Akgüç, Öztin. 1987. *100 Questions about Turkish Banking* (in Turkish). Istanbul: Gerçek Yayinevi.

Al-Ahnaf, M., Bernard Botiveau, and Franck Frégosi. 1991. *L'Algérie par ses islamistes.* Paris: Karthala.

Al-Baraka Turkish Finance House. 1987. "Regulations and Communiqués Related to Special Finance Houses" (March). Ankara and Istanbul: Al-Baraka Turkish Finance House.

———. Various years. *Annual Reports.* Ankara.

Al-Bawab, Sayyid. 1985. "The Banks of Infitah: How Can We Clean Up Their Management" (in Arabic). *Al-Ahram al-Iqtisad* 841 (24 February): 59.

Ayata, Sencer. 1993. "The Rise of Islamic Fundamentalism and Its Institutional Framework." In Enalp et al. 1993, 51–68.

Al-Bishri, Tariq. 1988. "Methods of the Struggle for the Investment of Capital" (in Arabic). *Al Ahram Al-Iqtisadi* 1018 (18 July): 23.

Ali, Abdel-Fatah Diab. 1986. "Toward an Islamic Managerial Alternative: An Analysis of Faisal Islamic Bank of Egypt." Ph.D. dissertation, Claremont Graduate School.

Al-Sharqawi, Jammal. 1988. *The Truth about the Circumstances of the Money Management Companies* (in Arabic). Cairo: Al Fajr al-Taba'a.

Aly, Abdel Monem Said. 1992. "Privatization in Egypt: The Regional Dimensions." In Harik and Sullivan, 46–59.

Amin, Samir. 1982. "Y a t-il une économie politique du fondamentalisme islamique?" *Peuples Méditerranéens* 21, cited by Ghasan Salamé, " 'Strong' and 'Weak' States." In Luciani 1990, 56.

'Amir, Nabil. 1989a. "The Retrieval of al-Rayan's Money from Abroad" (in Arabic). *Rose al-Yusuf* (6 March).

———. 1989b. "Al-Najjar and Al-Kawhaji Disagreed, and so Al-Rayan's Money Surfaced in Cyprus" (in Arabic). *Rose al-Yusuf* (20 March).

Anderson, Lisa. 1986. *The State and Social Transformation in Tunisia and Libya, 1830–1980*. Princeton: Princeton University Press.

Arendt, Hannah. 1958 [1951]. *The Origins of Totalitarianism*. New York: Meridian.

Arıcanlı, Tosun. 1990. "Exogenous Factors in Turkey's External Debt." In Arıcanlı and Rodrik, 230–53.

Arıcanlı, Tosun, and Dani Rodrik, eds. 1990. *The Political Economy of Turkey: Debt, Adjustment and Sustainability*. New York: St. Martin's Press.

Association Professionnelle des Banques de Tunisie. Various years. *Rapport*. Tunis.

Axelrod, Robert. 1984. *The Evolution of Cooperation*. New York: Basic Books.

Bagehot, Walter. 1978 [1915]. *Lombard Street*. New York: Arno Press.

Bakri, Midhat. 1991. "Reform of the Banking Apparatus: A Condition for the Success of Economic Reform" (in Arabic). *Al-Ahram al-Iqtisadi* 1180 (26 August): 20–23.

Banks Association of Turkey. 1960–91. *Annual Reports*. Ankara.

Banque Centrale de Tunisie. Various years. *Rapport Annuel*. Tunis.

———. Various years. *Statistiques Financières*. Tunis.

Banque Internationale Arabe de Tunisie (BIAT). 1986. *Dix Ans*. 1976–86. Tunis.

Barbulesco, Luc. 1989. "L'économie islamique dans ses rapports avec l'économie globale et en particulier avec le mouvement de liberalisation." *Les Cahiers du C.E.R.P.* Tunis: Faculté de Droit.

Barker, James M., et al. 1951. *The Economy of Turkey: Report of a Mission Sponsored by IBRD in Collaboration with the Government of Turkey*. Washington: Johns Hopkins Press.

Başgöz, Aslı, Peter Finlay, and John Provine. 1988. "Foreign Investment Regulation and Incentives." In Hewin, Brien, and Finlay, 138–53.

Beattie, Kirk J. 1994. *Egypt during the Nasser Years: Ideology, Politics and Civil Society*. Boulder, Colo.: Westview Press.

Beaty, Jonathan, and S. C. Gwynne. 1993. *The Outlaw Bank: A Wild Ride into the Secret Heart of BCCI*. New York: Random House.

Bechir, Tahsin. 1992. "I Support You But Do Not Legitimate You" (in Arabic). *Wafd*, 3 September.

Bechri, Mohamed Z. 1989. "The Political Economy of Interest Rate Determination in Tunisia." In Mustafa K. Nabli and Jeffrey B. Nugent, eds., *The New Institutional Economics and Development Theory: Theory and Tunisian Case Studies*. Amsterdam: North Holland.

Belassa, Bela, and F. Desmond McCarthy. 1984. *Adjustment Policies in Developing Countries, 1979–83: An Update*. World Bank Staff Working Papers, no. 675. Washington: World Bank.

Benissad, Hocine. 1991. *La réforme économique en Algérie.* 2d ed. Algiers: Office des Publications Universitaires.
Bennoune, Mahfoud, and Ali El-Kenz, eds. 1990. *Le Hasard et l'Histoire: Entretiens avec Belaid Abdesselam.* 2 vols. Algiers: Entreprise nationale des arts graphiques.
Benothmane, Mohamed Larbi. 1985. *La profession bancaire au Maroc.* Rabat: Editions La Porte.
Ben Othmane, Mongi, and Mohtar Souissi. 1987. "Rentabilité et performances des banques commerciales tunisiennes." *Finances et Développement au Maghreb* 1(January), 45–49, and 2(December), 66–70.
Bernard, Stéphane. 1963. *Le Conflit Franco-Marocain 1943–1956* (in French). 3 vols. Brussels: Institute of Sociology of the Free University.
Berrada, Mohamed. 1986. In O. Akalay et al., *Les Relations Banques-Entreprises au Maroc,* 185–203. Casablanca: Editions Toubkal.
Bianchi, Robert. 1989. *Unruly Corporatism: Associational Life in Twentieth-Century Egypt.* Oxford: Oxford University Press.
Binder, Leonard. 1978. *In a Moment of Enthusiasm: Political Power and the Second Stratum in Egypt.* Chicago: University of Chicago Press.
———. 1988. *Islamic Liberalism.* Chicago: University of Chicago Press.
Bistolfi, Robert. 1967. *Structure économique et indépendance monétaire.* Paris: Editions Cujas.
Black, Antony. 1984. *Guilds and Civil Society in European Political Thought from the Twelfth Century to the Present.* London: Methuen.
Blaisdell, Donald C. 1929. *European Financial Control in the Ottoman Empire.* New York: Columbia University Press.
Blunt, Wilfred Scawen. 1907. *Secret History of the English Occupation of Egypt.* London: Unwin.
Bouvier, Jean. 1960. "Les intérêts financiers et la question d'Egypte (1875–1876)." *Revue Historique* 124:75–104.
Bouvier, Jean, René Girault, and Jacques Thobie. 1982. *La France Impériale, 1880–1914.* Paris: Editions Mégrelis.
Brahimi, Abdelhamid. 1991. *L'Economie algérienne: Défis et enjeux.* 2d ed. Algiers: Editions Dahlab.
Braudel, Fernand. 1981. *Civilization and Capitalism.* Vol. I. London: Collins.
———. 1984. *Civilization and Capitalism.* Vol. III. London: Collins.
Bretton, Henry. 1980. *The Power of Money.* Albany: SUNY Press.
Brown, L. Carl. 1974. *The Tunisia of Ahmad Bey, 1937–1955.* Princeton: Princeton University Press.
———. 1984. *International Politics and the Middle East: Old Rules, Dangerous Game.* Princeton: Princeton University Press.
Bryant, Ralph C. 1987. *International Financial Intermediation.* Washington: Brookings Institution.
Burgat, François. 1988a. "L'Algérie: de la laïcité islamique à l'islamisme." *Maghreb-Machrek* 121 (July): 43–59.

———. 1988b. *L'Islamisme au Maghreb: La voix du Sud.* Paris: Karthala.

———. 1993. *The Islamic Movement in North Africa.* Austin: University of Texas Press.

Cameron, Rondo, et al. 1967. *Banking in the Early Stages of Industrialization.* New York: Oxford University Press.

Cameron, Rondo, ed. 1972. *Banking and Economic Development: Some Lessons of History.* New York: Oxford University Press.

Campbell, Tim S. 1979. "Optimal Investment Financing Decisions and the Value of Confidentiality." *Journal of Financial and Quantitative Analysis* 14: 913–24.

Carnevale, Francesca. 1991. *Algeria.* London: Euromoney Publications.

Caselli, Clara. 1982. *L'internationalisation bancaire en Egypte.* Milan: Giuffrè Editore.

Central Bank of the Republic of Turkey. Various years. *Annual Report.* Ankara.

———. Various years. *Quarterly Bulletin.* Ankara.

Charlot, Jean, and Charlot, Monica. 1985. "L'interaction des groupes politiques. In Madelaine Grawitz and Jean Leca, eds., *Traité de Science Politique* 3: 497–536. Paris: Presses Universitaires de France.

Chater, Khelifa. 1984. *Dépendance et mutations précoloniales: La Régence de Tunis de 1815 à 1857.* Tunis: Université de Tunis.

Çizakça, Murat. 1987. "Rise of Islamic Banks and the Potential for Venture Capital in the Middle East." In Erol Manisali, ed., *The Middle East and Eastern Mediterranean,* 74–90. Istanbul: International Girne Conferences.

Claisse, Alain. 1987. "Makhzen Traditions and Administrative Channels." In Zartman, ed., 1987, 34–58.

Collier, David, and James E. Mahon, Jr. 1993. "Conceptual 'Stretching' Revisited: Adapting Categories in Comparative Analysis." *American Political Science Review* 87, 4 (July): 560–94.

Corm, George. 1982. "L'endettement des pays en voie de développement: origine et mécanismes." In J. C. Sanchez Arnau, ed., *Dette et Développment.* Paris: Publisud.

Coşan, Fatih M., and Hasan Ersel. 1987. "The Turkish Financial System: Its Evolution and Performance, 1980–1986." *Inflation and Capital Markets.* Capital Market Board Publications, no. 7. Ankara.

Cromer, Earl of (Evelyn Baring). 1908. *Modern Egypt.* Vol. I. London: Macmillan.

Crouchley, Arthur E. 1938. *The Economic Development of Modern Egypt.* London: Longmans, Green.

———. 1977 [1936]. *The Investment of Foreign Capital in Egyptian Companies and Public Debt.* New York: Arno Press.

Davis, Eric. 1983. *Challenging Colonialism: Bank Misr and Egyptian Industrialization, 1920–1941.* Princeton: Princeton University Press.

Davison, Roderic H. 1990. *Essays in Ottoman and Turkish History, 1774–1923.* Austin: University of Texas Press.

Dawisha, Adeed. 1986. *The Arab Radicals*. New York: Council on Foreign Relations.

Deutsch, Karl. 1952. *Nationalism and Social Communication*. New York: Wiley.

Diouri, Mooumen. 1992. *A qui appartient le Maroc?* 3d ed. Paris: Harmattan.

Directory Egypt's Banks 1990–1991. 1991. Cairo: Dār al-Sharūq.

Djeghloul, A. 1990. "Le multipartisme à l'algérienne." *Maghreb-Machrek* 127 (January–February), 194–210.

Doumou, Abdelali. 1987. *Etat et capitalisme au Maroc*. Rabat: Edino.

Drake, P. J. 1980. *Money, Finance and Development*. Oxford: Martin Robertson.

Edwards, Sebastian. 1987. "Sequencing Economic Liberalization in Developing Countries." *Finance and Development* 9–12 (December).

Egyptian Businessmen's Association. 1992. List of EBA Members. Cairo.

Eickelman, Dale F. 1987. "Religion in Polity and Society." In Zartman, ed., 1987, 84–97.

El Hassani, Mohammed. 1988. *Les groupes de sociétés au Maroc*. Casablanca: Editions Toukbal.

El Kenz, Ali. 1987. *Le complexe sidérurgique d'El Hadjar*. Paris: Centre National de la Recherche Scientifique.

Entelis, John P. 1986. *Algeria: The Revolution Institutionalized*. Boulder, Colo.: Westview Press.

Entelis, John, and Lisa J. Arone. 1992. "Algeria in Turmoil." *Middle East Policy* 1, no. 2: 23–35.

Enalp, Atila, Tünay Muharrem, and Binol Yeşilada. *The Political and Socioeconomic Transformation of Turkey*. Westport, Conn.: Praeger.

Ersel, Hasan, and Güven Sak. 1988. "Public Borrowing and the Development of Financial Markets in Turkey." Central Bank of the Republic of Turkey, mimeographed. January.

Faisal Islamic Bank of Egypt (FIBE). *Ten Years of Giving*. Cairo, 1990.

Feis, Herbert. 1930. *Europe, the World's Banker, 1870–1914*. New Haven: Yale University Press.

Fieldhouse, D.K. 1973. *Economics and Empire, 1830–1914*. London: Weidenfeld and Nicolson.

Fischer, Jeff, and Clement Henry. 1994. "Pre-Election Technical Assessment: Tunisia." Typescript. Washington: International Foundation for Electoral Systems.

Frieden, Jeffry A. 1991. *Debt, Development and Democracy: Modern Political Economy and Latin America, 1965–1985*. Princeton: Princeton University Press.

Galbraith, John Kenneth. 1983. *Money: Whence It Came, Where It Went*. Harmondsworth, U.K.: Penguin.

Galloux, Michel. 1993. "Finance Islamique et Contrôle de l'Etat: Le Cas Egyptien, 1960–1992." Ph.D. dissertation, Paris. Institut d'Etudes Politiques.

Ganiage, Jean. 1959. *Les Origines du Protectorate Français en Tunisie, 1861–1881*. Paris: Presses Universitaires de France.

Gellner, Ernest. 1983. *Muslim Society*. London: Cambridge University Press.

Ghoneim, Ahmad. 1991. *Al-Ahram al-Iqtisadi* 1185 (30 September): 24–28.

Gillespie, Kate. 1984. *The Tripartite Relationship: Government, Foreign Investors, and Local Investors during Egypt's Economic Opening.* New York: Praeger.

Gillespie, Kate, and Clement M. Henry, eds. 1995. *Oil in the New World Order.* Gainesville: University Press of Florida.

Gilpin, Robert. 1987. *The Political Economy of International Relations.* Princeton: Princeton University Press.

Goldsmith, Raymond W. 1969. *Financial Structure and Development.* New Haven: Yale University Press.

———. 1975. "The Quantitative International Comparison of Financial Structure and Development." *Journal of Economic History* 35:216–37.

Groupement Professionnel des Banques du Maroc. 1991. *Annuaire des Banques du Maroc, 1991–1992.* Casablanca: Imprimerie Najah el Jadida.

Guillen, Pierre. 1967. *L'Allemagne et le Maroc de 1870 à 1905.* Paris: Presses Universitaires de France.

———. 1971. *Les emprunts marocains, 1902–1904.* Paris: Editions Richelieu.

———. 1984. *L'expansion, 1881–1898.* Paris: Imprimerie Nationale.

Gürsel, Nadim. 1986. "Yacher Kemal, Romancier d'une période de transition." In Altan Gokalp, ed., *La Turquie en transition—disparités, identités,* 97–124. Paris: Editions Maisonneuve Larose.

Haggard, Stephan. 1990. "The Political Economy of the Philippine Debt Crisis." In Nelson, ed., 215–55.

Haggard, Stephan, and Robert R. Kaufman, eds. 1992. *The Politics of Economic Adjustment.* Princeton: Princeton University Press.

Haggard, Stephan, Chung H. Lee, and Sylvia Maxfield, eds. 1993. *The Politics of Finance in Developing Countries.* Ithaca: Cornell University Press.

Hale, J. R. 1977. *Florence and the Medici: The Pattern of Control.* London: Thames and Hudson.

Hammam, Talaat. 1988. "The Financial Investment Companies: Egyptian Studies" (in Arabic). Cairo: Dar Rabia' Al-Tabaa'a.

Hanna, Milad. 1992. *Le logement en Egypte: Essai critique.* Cairo: CEDEJ.

Harik, Iliya, and Denis J. Sullivan, eds. 1992. *Privatization and Liberalization in the Middle East.* Bloomington: Indiana University Press.

Haseeb, Khair el-Din, and Samir Makdisi, eds. n.d. *Arab Monetary Integration.* London: Croom Helm.

Havrylyshyn, Oli, et al. 1990. *Maroc 2000.* UNDP, World Bank.

Hegel's Philosophy of Right. 1953 [1821]. Translated by T. M. Knox. Oxford: Clarendon Press.

Henni, Ahmed. 1991. *Essai sur l'économie parallèle: cas de l'Algérie.* Algiers: ENAG Editions.

Hershlag, Zvi Yehuda. 1968. *Turkey: The Challenge of Growth.* 2d ed. Leiden: Brill.

———. 1988. *The Contemporary Turkish Economy.* London: Routledge.

Hewin, Sarah, Richard O. Brien, and Peter Finlay. 1988. *Turkey's International Role.* London: Euromoney.

Hilāl, Rida. 1987. *The Construction of Dependency* (in Arabic). Cairo: Dār Al-Mustaqbal Al-'Arabi.

———. 1988. "The Political Struggle and the Future of Financial Investment" (in Arabic). *Al-Ahram al-Iqtisadi.* 1018 (18 July 1988).

Hilferding, Rudolf. 1981 [1910]. *Finance Capital: A Study of the Latest Phase of Capitalist Development.* London: Routledge.

Hinnebusch, Raymond. 1985. *Egyptian Politics under Sadat.* Cambridge: Cambridge University Press.

Hirschman, Albert O. 1977. *The Passions and the Interests.* Princeton: Princeton University Press.

Hobson, John A. 1938 [1902]. *Imperialism: A Study.* London: Allen and Unwin.

Horton, Brendan. 1990. *Morocco: Analysis and Reform of Economic Policy.* Washington: World Bank, Economic Development Institute.

Hughes, Stephen. 1985. "Steady Pace in the Maghreb." *The Banker* (December): 117–24.

Huntington, Samuel P. 1984. "Will More Countries Become Democratic?" *Political Science Quarterly* 99:2 (Summer): 193–218.

———. 1991. *The Third Wave: Democratization in the late Twentieth Century.* Norman: University of Oklahoma Press.

———. 1993. "The Clash of Civilizations?" *Foreign Affairs* 72:3 (Summer): 22–49.

Hutchcroft, Paul D. 1993. "Selective Squander: The Politics of Preferential Credit Allocation in the Philippines." In Haggard, Lee, and Maxfield, eds.

Ibn Khaldun. 1967. *The Muqaddimah, An Introduction to History.* Translation by Franz Rosenthal. 3 vols. Princeton: Princeton University Press.

Imām, Sāmia Sa'īd. 1986. *Who Owns Egypt?* (in Arabic). Cairo: Dār al-Mustaqbal al-'Arabi.

International Monetary Fund (IMF). Various years. *International Financial Statistics.* Washington: International Monetary Fund.

İş Bankası. 1974. *50 İş 1924–1974.* Ankara: Doğuş Ltd.

Islamic Development Bank. 1988. *Thirteenth Annual Report 1408 AH (1987 88).* Jidda, Saudi Arabia.

Issawi, Charles. 1980. *The Economic History of Turkey, 1800–1914.* Chicago: University of Chicago Press.

———. 1981. *The Arab World's Legacy.* Princeton: Darwin.

Issawi, Rawiya. 1987. "Fireworks at the Faisal Bank Board Meeting" (in Arabic). *Al-Ahram Al-Iqtisadi,* 3 March.

Julien, Charles-André. 1964. *Histoire de l'Algérie Contemporaine: La Conquête et les Débuts de la Colonisation (1827–1971).* Paris: Presses Universitaires de France.

Kandiller, Riza. 1986. *Banka Hukuku ve Bankalar Kanunumuzun Başlıca Hükümleri.* Ankara.

Kapil, Arun. 1990. "Algeria's Elections Show Islamist Strength." *Middle East Report* 166 (September–October): 31–36.

———. 1990. "Chiffres-clés pour une analyse." *Les Cahiers de l'Orient* 23 (3d trimester).

Kapstein, Ethan B. 1989. "International Coordination of Banking Regulations." *International Organization* 43:2 (Spring): 323–34.

Karm, Ahmed El. 1989. "La stratégie de libéralisation financière externe en Tunisie." Mimeo. Banque Centrale de Tunisia (May).

Karpat, Kemal H. 1959. *Turkey's Politics: The Transition to a Multi-Party System.* Princeton: Princeton University Press.

Kaufman, Robert R. 1986. "Democratic and Authoritarian Responses to the Debt Issue: Argentina, Brazil, Mexico." In Miles Kahler, ed., *The Politics of International Debt.* Ithaca: Cornell University Press.

Keyder, Çağlar. 1981. *The Definition of a Peripheral Economy: Turkey, 1923–1929.* Cambridge: Cambridge University Press.

———. 1987. *State and Class in Turkey.* New York: Verso.

Khadr, Ali, and James Parks. 1991. "Algeria: Inflation in the Transition." World Bank, Internal Discussion Paper, Report No. IDP-0084. February.

Khelil, Ismail. 1988. "La stratégie de la réforme du système financier tunisien." Banque Centrale de Tunisie (May 23 speech).

———. 1989. "Les nouveaux impératifs de la gestion bancaire." Banque Centrale de Tunisie (May 11 speech).

———. Other speeches (by date). Banque Centrale de Tunisie.

Kindleberger, Charles P. 1970. *Power and Money.* New York: Basic Books.

Kiray, Emine. 1990. In Arıcanlı and Rodrik, eds.

Koç, Vehbi. 1977. *My Life Story.* Istanbul: Vehbi Koç Foundation.

Kuran, Timur. 1986. "The Economic System in Contemporary Islamic Thought: Interpretation and Assessment." *International Journal of Middle East Studies* 18:2 (May): 135–64.

———. 1989. "Economic Justice in Contemporary Islamic Thought." *International Journal of Middle East Studies* 21:2 (May): 171–91.

———. 1993. "The Economic Impact of Islamic Fundamentalism." In Martin Marty and R. Scott Appleby, eds., *Fundamentalisms and the State: Remaking Polities, Economies, and Militance,* 302–41. Chicago: University of Chicago Press.

Landes, David. 1958. *Bankers and Pashas: International Finance and Economic Imperialism in Egypt.* Cambridge: Harvard University Press.

Layachi, A., and A. Haireche. 1992. "National Development and Political Protest: Islamists in the Maghreb Countries." *Arab Studies Quarterly* 1:4 (Spring–Summer): 69–92.

Leca, Jean. 1990. "Social Structure and Political Stability." In Luciani, ed., 150–88.

Leca, Jean, and J. C. Vatin. 1979. "Le système politique algérien (1976–1978)." In J. Leca et al., *Développements politiques au Maghreb,* 15–80. Paris: Centre National de la Recherche Scientifique.

Leff, Nathaniel H. 1979a. "Entrepreneurship and Economic Development: The Problem Revisited." *Journal of Economic Literature* 17 (March): 46–64.

———. 1979b. "'Monopoly Capitalism and Public Policy in Developing Countries." *International Review for Social Sciences* 32, 4:718–38.
Lenin, V.I. 1939 [1917]. *Imperialism: The Highest Stage of Capitalism.* New York: International Publishers.
Lerner, Daniel. 1958. *The Passing of Traditional Society.* Glencoe, Ill.: Free Press.
Leveau, Rémy. 1985. *Le fellah marocain défenseur du trône* (in French). 2d ed. Paris: Fondation Nationale des Sciences Politiques.
———. 1987. "Stabilité du pouvoir monarchique et financement de la dette" (in French). *Maghreb-Machrek* 118 (October–December): 5–19.
———. 1993. *Le sabre et le turban: l'avenir du Maghreb.* Paris: François Burin.
Lindblom, Charles E. 1977. *Politics and Markets: The World's Political Economies.* New York: Basic Books.
Lipson, Charles. 1985. "Bankers' Dilemmas: Private Cooperation in Rescheduling Sovereign Debts." *World Politics* 38:200–225.
Lofgren, Hans. 1993. "Economic Policy in Egypt: A Breakdown of Reform Resistance." *International Journal of Middle East Studies* 25:3 (August): 407–21.
Luciani, Giacomo, ed. 1990. *The Arab State.* Berkeley: University of California Press.
Mabro, Robert. 1974. *The Egyptian Economy, 1952–1972.* Oxford: Clarendon Press.
Machiavelli, Niccolo. n.d. *The History of Florence and The Prince.* London: Bohn's Standard Library.
McKinnon, Ronald I. 1973. *Money and Capital in Economic Development.* Washington: Brookings Institution.
McKinnon, Ronald I., and Donald J. Mathieson. 1981. *How to Manage a Repressed Economy.* Essays in International Finance, no. 145. Princeton University, Department of Economics.
Mahjoub, Azzam. 1983. *Industrie et accumulation du capital en Tunisie: Première partie: De la fin du XVIIIe siècle jusqu'à la seconde guerre mondiale.* Tunis: Imprimerie officielle.
Mamou, Yves. 1988. *Une machine de pouvoir: La Direction du Trésor* (in French). Paris: Editions La Découverte.
Markham, James M. 1989. "Tunisia Is Pulling a Democratic Rabbit out of a Dictator's Hat." *New York Times,* 10 April.
Marlowe, John. 1975. *Spoiling the Egyptians.* New York: St. Martin's Press.
Marx, Karl. 1977 [1867]. *Capital: A Critique of Political Economy.* Vol. 1. New York: Vintage Books.
Mattione, Richard P. 1985. *OPEC Investments and the International Financial System.* Washington: Brookings Institution.
Maxfield, Sylvia. 1990. *Governing Capital: International Finance and Mexican Politics.* Ithaca: Cornell University Press.
Mechri, Hedi. 1988. "Majid Bouden: L'intelligence sans artifice." *Réalités* 153 (16 July): 8–19.

Metwally, Samir Mostefa. 1986. "Analysis of the Combined Balance Sheet of Islamic Banks and Financial Institutions" (in Arabic). *Al-Ahram Al-Iqtisadi* 930 (10 November): 52–55.

———. 1988. "The Aggregate Balance Sheet of Member Banks of the International Association of Islamic Banks (IAIB) as at 30/12/86." Manuscript. Cairo: IAIB, March.

———. 1991. "The Aggregate Balance Sheet and Results of Transactions and Financial Indicators for Islamic Banks and Financial Institutions Members of the International Association of Islamic Banks for the Year 1409H/1989." Manuscript. Cairo: IAIB, February.

Mezoughi, Abdelaziz. 1988a. "Les enjeux du Congrès du Salut." *Le Maghreb* III (29 July):4–8.

———. 1988b. "Congrès du Salut: Positif, malgné tout. . . ." *Le Mahreb* 112 (5 August):6–9.

Middle East Economic Digest (MEED). Various dates. London.

Miège, Jean-Louis. 1961. *Le Maroc et l'Europe (1830–1894)* (in French). 4 vols. Paris: Presses Universitaires de France.

Migdal, Joel S. 1988. *Strong Societies and Weak States.* Princeton: Princeton University Press.

Milner, Sir Alfred (Lord). 1899. *England in Egypt.* London: Edward Arnold.

Misr Iran Development Bank (MIDB). 1990. *Annual Report.* Cairo.

Mitchell, Timothy. 1988. *Colonizing Egypt.* Cambridge: Cambridge University Press.

———. 1991. "The Limits of the State: Beyond Statist Approaches and Their Critics." *American Political Science Review* 85:1 (March): 77–96.

Montesquieu, Charles-Louis de Secondat. 1964. *Oeuvres complètes* (in French). Paris: Seuil.

Moore, Clement Henry. 1970. *Politics in North Africa.* Boston: Little, Brown.

———. 1986. "Money and Power: The Dilemma of the Egyptian Infitah." *Middle East Journal* 40:4 (Autumn): 634–50.

———. 1987. "Prisoners' Financial Dilemmas: A Consociational Future for Lebanon?" *American Political Science Review* 81 (March): 201–18.

———. 1988. "La Tunisie après vingt ans de crise de succession." *Maghreb-Machrek* 120 (April): 5–22.

———. 1990. "Islamic Banks and Competitive Politics in the Arab World and Turkey." *Middle East Journal* 44:2 (Spring).

———. 1993 "Political Parties." In I. William Zartman and William Mark Habeeb, eds., *Polity and Society in Contemporary North Africa,* 42–67. Boulder, Colo.: Westview.

———. 1994. *Images of Development: Egyptian Engineers in Search of Industry.* 2d ed. Cairo: American University in Cairo Press.

Moran, Theodore H. 1987. "Managing an Oligopoly of Would-Be Sovereigns: The Dynamics of Joint Control and Self-Control in the International Oil Industry Past, Present, and Future." *International Organization* 41 (Autumn): 575–607.

Mumcu, Uğur. 1988. *Tarikat Siyasat Ticaret*. Istanbul: Tekin.
Mzali, Mohamed. 1987. *Lettre ouverte à Habib Bourguiba*. Paris: Alain Moreau.
National Bank of Egypt. Various years. *Economic Bulletin*. Cairo.
Nelson, Joan M., ed. 1990. *Economic Crisis and Policy Choice: The Politics of Adjustment in the Third World*. Princeton: Princeton University Press.
Nicholas, Peter. 1988. *The World Bank's Lending for Adjustment*. Washington: World Bank.
Nienhaus, Volker. 1983. "Profitability of Islamic PLS Banks Competing with Interest Banks: Problems and Prospects." *Journal of Research in Islamic Economics* 1:1: 37–47.
———. 1986. "Notes on the Background, Achievements and Problems of Islamic Banks." United Nations Industrial Development Organization, Workshop on Industrial Financing Activities of Islamic Banks, Vienna, 16–20 June.
North, Douglass C. 1981. *Structure and Change in Economic History*. New York: Norton.
Nugent, Jeffrey B. 1989. "Collective Action in Tunisia's Producer Organizations: Some Variations on the Olsonian Theme." In M. T. Nabli and J. B. Nugent, eds., *The New Institutional Economics and Development and Tunisian Case Studies*. Amsterdam: North Holland.
O'Donnell, Guillermo A. 1979a. *Modernization and Bureaucratic-Authoritarianism*. Berkeley: Institute of International Studies.
———. 1979b. "Tensions in the Bureaucratic-Authoritarian State and the Question of Democracy." In David Collier, ed., *The New Authoritarianism in Latin America*. Princeton: Princeton University Press.
Öncü, Ayşe. 1989. "The Interaction of Politics, Religion and Finance: Islamic Banking in Turkey." Berlin Institute for Comparative Social Research, Symposium on Muslims, Migrants, and Metropolis (June): 13–18.
Onis, Ziya, and James Riedel. 1993. *Economic Crises and Long-term Growth in Turkey*. Washington: World Bank.
Owen, Roger. 1972. "Egypt and Europe: From French Expedition to British Occupation." in E.R.G. Owen, and R. B. Sutcliffe, eds., *Studies in the Theory of Imperialism*. London: Longman.
———. 1981. *The Middle East in the World Economy, 1800–1914*. London: Methuen.
Parigi, Stéphanie. 1989. *Des banques islamiques: argent et religion*. Paris: Editions Ramsay.
Parigi, Stéphanie, and Isabel Malowany. 1987. "Une solution islamique pour l'économie égyptienne?" (in French). *Médias France Intercontinents*. 65 (18 March).
Perrault, Giles. 1990. *Notre Ami le Roi*. Paris: Gallimard.
Poindexter, Roy Mark. 1991. "Subscription Television in the Third World: The Moroccan Experience." *Journal of Communications* (Summer): 26–39.
Przeworski, Adam, and Michael Wallerstein. 1988. "Structural Dependence of the State on Capital." *American Political Science Review* 82: 11–30.

Quataert, Donald. 1983. *Social Disintegration and Popular Resistance in the Ottoman Empire, 1881–1908: Reactions to European Economic Penetration.* New York: New York University Press.

Ray, Nicholas Dylan. 1995. *Arab Islamic Banking and the Renewal of Islamic Law.* London and Boston: Graham and Trotman.

République tunisienne, Ministère du Plan et des Finances. 1987. "Memorandum sur la situation et les perspectives de développement de l'économie tunisienne."

Richards, Alan. 1993. "Economic Imperatives and Political Systems." *Middle East Journal* 47:2 (Spring): 217–27.

Richards, Alan, and John Waterbury. 1990. *A Political Economy of the Middle East.* Boulder, Colo.: Westview Press.

Robins, Philip. 1991. *Turkey and the Middle East.* New York: Council on Foreign Relations.

Roe, Alan, and Paul A. Popiel. 1988. *Managing Financial Adjustment in Middle-Income Countries.* World Bank: EDI Policy Seminar Report no. 11.

Roe, Alan, et al. 1989. *Economic Adjustment in Algeria, Egypt, Jordan, Morocco, Pakistan, Tunisia, and Turkey.* Washington: World Bank.

Roover, Raymond de. 1966. *The Rise and Decline of the Medici Bank, 1397–1494.* New York: Norton.

Rose, Peter S. 1987. *The Changing Structure of American Banking.* New York: Columbia University Press.

Roussillon, Alain. 1988. *Sociétés islamiques de placement de fonds et "ouverture économique."* Dossiers du CEDEJ 3. Cairo: Le CEDEJ.

Rueschemeyer, Dietrich, E. H. Stephens, and John D. Stephens. 1992. *Capitalist Development and Democracy.* Chicago: University of Chicago Press.

Rustow, Dankwart A. 1987. *Turkey: America's Forgotten Ally.* New York: Council on Foreign Relations.

Rycx, Jean François. 1988. *Islam et déregulation financière.* Cairo: CEDEJ.

Saâdi, Mohamed Saïd. 1989. *Les groupes financiers au Maroc* (in French). Casablanca: Okad.

Saâdi, Mohamed Saïd, and Abdelkader Berrada. 1992. "Le Grand Capital Privé Marocain." In Jean-Claude Santucci, ed., *Le Maroc actuel,* 325–93. Paris: Centre National de la Recherche Scientifique.

Sabancı, Sakip. 1988. *This Is My Life.* Avon, U.K.: Bath Press.

Sadat, Mohamed Anwar El. 1974. *The October Working Paper, April, 1974.* Cairo: Ministry of Information.

Sadowski, Yahya M. 1991. *Political Vegetables? Businessman and Bureaucrat in the Development of Egyptian Agriculture.* Washington: Brookings Institution.

Safra, Mongi. 1987. "Note sur le plan de redressement tunisien de 1986." *Finances et développement au Maghreb* (1 January).

Sagou, M'hamed. 1987. *Repertoire Permanent de Groupes de Sociétés.* Casablanca: Idguel Editions.

Sahli, Mohamed Chérif. 1986. *Décoloniser l'histoire: l'Algérie accuse le complot contre les peuples africains.* Algiers: Entreprise Algérienne de Presse.

Saidane, Ezzedine. 1988. "Réflexion sur la dynamisation du marché monétaire." *Finances et développement au Maghreb* (4 December).

Salim, 'Ali, Muhammad. 1982. *The Rescue of Bank Misr under Law No. 40 of 1941* (in Arabic). Cairo: Egyptian General Book Authority.

Sammut, Carmel. 1983. *L'impérialisme capitaliste français et le nationalisme tunisien (1881–1914).* Paris: Publisud.

Saulniers, Alfred H. Forthcoming. "Privatization in Morocco: Recent Developments and Perspectives." In Rodney Lord, ed., *Privatization Yearbook 1992.*

Schumpeter, Joseph. 1955. *Social Classes and Imperialism.* New York: Meridian Books.

Sebag, Paul. 1951. *La Tunisie: essai de monographie* (in French). Paris: Editions Sociales.

Sehimi, Mustapha. 1985. "Les élections legislatives au Maroc." *Maghreb-Machrek* 107: 23–51.

———, ed. 1986. *La grande encyclopédie du Maroc: Les institutions politiques.* Rabat: GEM, 21 Zankat Assafi.

Shafe'i. 1991. *Al-Ahram al-Iqtisadi.* 1094 (December): 30–32.

Shaw, Edward S. 1973. *Financial Deepening in Economic Development.* New York: Oxford University Press.

Shepard, William E. 1987. "Islam and Ideology." *International Journal of Middle East Studies* 19: 307–36.

Shoman, Abdelmajeed. 1984. *The Indomitable Arab: The Life and Times of Abdulhameed Shoman (1890–1974).* London: Third World Centre.

Signoles, Pierre. 1985. *L'Espace tunisien: Capitale et Etat-Région.* Tours: Fascicule de Recherches no. 14 (2 vols.).

"Sisters in the Wood: A Survey of the IMF and the World Bank." 1991. *The Economist* 12–18 October 1991, after p. 56.

Skocpol, Theda. 1979. *States and Social Revolutions.* Cambridge: Cambridge University Press.

Snider, Lewis. 1990. "The Political Performance of Third World Governments and the Debt Crisis." *American Political Science Review* 84:4 (December): 1263–80.

Soudan, François. 1988a. "Le jour où Chadly a voulu démissionner." *Jeune Afrique* 1451 (26 October).

——— 1988b. "Point final ou point de départ en Algérie?" *Jeune Afrique* 1453 (9 November).

Springborg, Robert. 1989. *Mubarak's Egypt.* Boulder, Colo.: Westview Press.

Stern, Fritz. 1979. *Gold and Iron: Bismarck, Bleichröder, and the Building of the German Empire.* New York: Random House.

Stigler, George J. 1984. "The Politics of Regulation." In T. Ferugson and J. Rogers, eds., *The Political Economy.* Armonk, N.Y.: Sharpe.

Tangeaoui, Saïd. 1993. *Les Entrepreneurs marocains* Paris: Karthala.

Tayi', Jamal. 1989. "Rose al-Yusuf Finds an Owner in Hiding of a Money Management Company" (in Arabic). *Rose al-Yusuf* (13 March): 14–16.

Thobie, Jacques. 1983. "Conjoncture et stratégie: le groupe financier de l'*Ottomane* en 1914." In Jean-Louis Bacqué-Grammont and Paul Dumont, eds., *Economie et Sociétés dans l'Empire Ottoman (Fin du XVIIIe–Début du XXe siècle,* 471–83. Paris: Editions du Centre National de la Recherche Scientifique.

Tignor, Robert L. 1966. *Modernization and British Colonial Rule in Egypt, 1882–1914.* Princeton: Princeton University Press.

———. 1984. *State, Private Enterprise, and Economic Change in Egypt, 1918–1952.* Princeton: Princeton University Press.

———. 1989. *Egyptian Textiles and British Capital, 1930–1956.* Cairo: American University in Cairo Press.

Tilly, Charles. 1985. "War Making and State Making as Organized Crime." In Peter V. Evans et al., *Bringing the State Back In.* New York: Cambridge University Press.

Turan, Ilter. 1992. "The Politics of the 24 January 1980 Economic Stabilization Program." Manuscript prepared for Anne O. Krueger and Ilter Turan. In Robert H. Bates and Anne O. Krueger, eds., *Political and Economic Interactions in Economic Policy Reform.* Cambridge: Blackwell, 1993.

TÜSİAD (Turkish Industrialists' and Businessmen's Association). 1988 and various other years. *The Turkish Economy '88* [and various years]. Istanbul.

Udovitch, Abraham L. 1970. *Partnership and Profit in Medieval Islam.* Princeton: Princeton University Press.

U.S. Department of State. *Country Reports on Human Rights Practices for 1991.* Washington: Government Printing Office, 1992.

van den Boogaerde, Pierre. 1991. *Financial Assistance from Arab Countries and Arab Regional Institutions.* Washington: IMF.

Vitalis, Robert J. 1995. *When Worlds Collide: Business Conflict and the End of Empire in Egypt.* Berkeley: University of California Press.

———. 1990. "On the Theory and Practice of Compradors: The Role of 'Abbud Pasha in the Egyptian Political Economy." *International Journal of Middle East Studies* 22: 291–315.

Vittas, Dimitri. 1991. "Measuring Commercial Bank Efficiency: Use and Misuse of Bank Operating Ratios." World Bank: Country Economics Department, Policy Research Working Papers, November.

Walker, Tony. 1988. "El Helal Investment Company Collapses." *Financial Times,* 20 January.

Wålstedt, Bertil. 1980. *State Manufacturing Enterprise in a Mixed Economy: The Turkish Case.* Baltimore: Johns Hopkins University Press.

Ware, Lewis B. 1984. "The Role of the Tunisian Military in the Post-Bourguiba Era." *Middle East Journal* 39 (Winter): 27–47.

Waterbury, John. 1970. *The Commander of the Faithful.* London: Weidenfeld and Nicolson.

———. 1976. "Corruption, Political Stability and Development." *Government and Opposition* 11: 426–45.
———. 1978. *Egypt: Burden of the Past, Options for the Future*. Bloomington: Indiana University Press.
———. 1983. *The Egypt of Nasser and Sadat*. Princeton: Princeton University Press.
Weber, Max. 1978 [1922]. *Economy and Society*, edited by Guenther Roth and Claus Wittich. 2 vols. Berkeley: University of California Press.
Wilczynski, Joseph. 1978. *Comparative Monetary Economics*. London: Macmillan.
Williamson, John. 1994. *The Political Economy of Policy Reform*. Washington: Institute for International Economics.
Wilson, Rodney. 1983. *Banking and Finance in the Arab Middle East*. New York: St. Martin's Press.
Winters, Jeffrey A. 1994. "Power and the Control of Capital." *World Politics* 46:3 (April): 419–52.
World Bank. 1988, 1989, and various other years. *World Development Report*. New York: Oxford University Press.
———. 1990. *Turkey: A Strategy for Managing Debt, Borrowings, and Transfers under Macroeconomic Adjustment*. Washington: World Bank.
Yeşilada, Birol. 1988. "Islamic Movements in Turkey and the Saudi Connection" (in Turkish). *Bilim vs Sanat* no. 91 (July): 24–26.
———. 1989. "Islamic Fundamentalism in Turkey and the Saudi Connection." Field Staff Reports, University Field Staff International, Africa/Middle East No. 18.
———. 1993. "Turkish Foreign Policy toward the Middle East." In Eralp, 169–92.
Zartman, I. William. 1988. "The Opposition as a Support of the State." In A. Dawisha and I. W. Zartman, eds., *Beyond Coercion: The Durability of the Arab State*, 61–87. London: Croom Helm.
———, et al. 1982. *Political Elites in North Africa*. New York: Longman.
Zartman, I. William, ed. 1987. *The Political Economy of Morocco*. New York: Praeger.
———. 1991. *Tunisia: The Political Economy of Reform*. Boulder: Lynne Rienner
Zeitlin, Maurice, and Richard E. Ratcliff, *Landlords and Capitalists: The Dominant Class of Chile*. 1988. Princeton: Princeton University Press.
Ziady, Hassan. 1989. "Maroc: Le rapprochement ONA/BCM irrite le monde des affairs." *Jeune Afrique Economie* 115/116 (January–February): 52.
Zola, Émile. 1967 [1891]. *L'Argent, in Les Rougon-Macquart: histoire naturelle et sociale d'une famille sous le Second Empire*. Paris: Pléiade.
Zysman, John. 1983. *Governments, Markets, and Growth: Financial Systems and the Politics of Industrial Change*. Ithaca: Cornell University Press.

Index